HIGH COURT CASE SUMMARIES

COMMERCIAL LAW

Keyed to Whaley's Casebook on
Commercial Law,
9th Edition

WEST.
A Thomson Reuters business

Thomson Reuters created this publication to provide you with accurate and authoritative information concerning the subject matter covered. However, this publication was not necessarily prepared by persons licensed to practice law in a particular jurisdiction. Thomson Reuters does not render legal or other professional advice, and this publication is not a substitute for the advice of an attorney. If you require legal or other expert advice, you should seek the services of a competent attorney or other professional.

High Court Case Summaries and Thomson Reuters are registered trademarks used under license.
All rights reserved. Do not duplicate.

© West, a Thomson business, 2003, 2006
© 2009 Thomson Reuters
    610 Opperman Drive
    St. Paul, MN 55123
    1-800-313-9378
Printed in the United States of America

ISBN: 978-0-314-90529-1

Table of Contents

	Page
CHAPTER ONE. Basic Concepts	**1**
Milau Associates, Inc. v. North Avenue Development Corp.	3
Analysts Intern. Corp. v. Recycled Paper Products, Inc.	5
Anthony Pools v. Sheehan	7
Siemen v. Alden	9
CHAPTER TWO. Contract Formation	**11**
St. Ansgar Mills, Inc. v. Streit	13
Columbia Nitrogen Corp. v. Royster Co.	17
Diamond Fruit Growers, Inc. v. Krack Corp.	21
Bayway Refining Co. v. Oxygenated Marketing and Trading A.G.	23
Leonard Pevar Co. v. Evans Products Co.	25
Klocek v. Gateway, Inc.	27
CHAPTER THREE. Warranties	**31**
Moore v. Pro Team Corvette Sales, Inc.	35
Shaffer v. Victoria Station, Inc.	37
Daniell v. Ford Motor Company	39
Webster v. Blue Ship Tea Room, Inc.	41
Bell Sports, Inc. v. Yarusso	43
Cate v. Dover Corp.	45
Bowdoin v. Showell Growers, Inc.	49
Rinaldi v. Iomega Corp.	51
Wilson Trading Corp. v. David Ferguson, Ltd.	53
Pierce v. Catalina Yachts, Inc.	55
Fitl v. Strek	57
Reed v. City of Chicago	59
East River Steamship Corp. v. Transamerica Delaval, Inc.	61
Ventura v. Ford Motor Corp.	63
Colonial Pacific Leasing Corp. v. McNatt, Datronic Rental Corp.	67
CHAPTER FOUR. Terms of the Contract	**71**
Landrum v. Devenport	73
Cook Specialty Co. v. Schrlock	75
Rheinberg-Kellerei GMBH v. Vineyard Wine Co.	77
CHAPTER FIVE. Performance of the Contract	**79**
Cherwell-Ralli, Inc. v. Rytman Grain Co.	81
Wilson v. Scampoli	83
Ramirez v. Autosport	85
Plateq Corp. of North Haven v. Machlett Laboratories, Inc.	87
Waddell v. L.V. R.V.	89
Jakowski v. Carole Chevrolet, Inc.	91
Arabian Score v. Lasma Arabian Ltd.	93
Louisiana Power & Light Co. v. Allegheny Ludlum Industries, Inc.	95
CHAPTER SIX. Remedies	**99**
Teradyne, Inc. v. Teledyne Industries, Inc.	101
Hughes Communications Galaxy, Inc. v. United States	103
Tongish v. Thomas	105
Poli v. DaimlerChrylser Corp.	107
CHAPTER SEVEN. Negotiability	**109**
Triffin v. Dillabough	111
Woodworth v. The Richmond Indiana Venture	115
CHAPTER NINE. Holders in Due Course	**117**
Falls Church Bank v. Wesley Heights Realty, Inc.	119
General Investment Corp. v. Angelini	121

TABLE OF CONTENTS

	Page
Any Kind Checks Cashed, Inc. v. Talcott	123
Winter & Hirsch, Inc. v. Passarelli	127
Jones v. Approved Bancredit Corp.	129
Sullivan v. United Dealers Corp.	131
Triffin v. Somerset Valley Bank	133
Federal Deposit Insurance Corp. v. Culver	135
Sea Air Support, Inc. v. Herrmann	137
Kedzie & 103rd Currency Exchange, Inc. v. Hodge	139
Virginia National Bank v. Holt	141
Herzog Contracting Corp. v. McGowen Corp.	143

CHAPTER TEN. The Nature of Liability — 145

Ward v. Federal Kemper Insurance Co.	147
Floor v. Melvin	149
Chemical Bank v. PIC Motors Corp.	151
London Leasing Corp. v. Interfina, Inc.	153
Messing v. Bank of America, N.A.	155
Makel Textiles, Inc. v. Dolly Originals, Inc.	157
Norton v. Knapp	159
Galyen Petroleum Co. v. Hixson	161
Mundaca Investment Corp. v. Febba	163
Nichols v. Seale	165

CHAPTER ELEVEN. Banks and Their Customers — 167

Twin City Bank v. Isaacs	169
Walter v. National City Bank of Cleveland	171
Parr v. Security National Bank	173
Canty v. Vermont National Bank	175
Patriot Bank v. Navy Federal Credit Union	177
Rock Island Auction Sales, Inc. v. Empire Packing Co.	179
First National Bank of Chicago v. Standard Bank & Trust	181
Valley Bank of Ronan v. Hughes	183

CHAPTER TWELVE. Wrongdoing and Error — 185

Leeds v. Chase Manhattan Bank, N.A.	187
Price v. Neal	189
Decibel Credit Union v. Pueblo Bank & Trust Co.	191
Wachovia Bank, N.A. v. Foster Bancshares, Inc.	193
Hutzler v. Hertz Corp.	195
The Bank/First Citizens Bank v. Citizens and Associates	197
Travelers Cas. & Sur. Co. of America v. Wells Fargo Bank N.A.	199
Falk v. Northern Trust Co.	201

CHAPTER THIRTEEN. Electronic Banking — 205

Grain Traders, Inc. v. Citibank, N.A.	207
Corfan Banco Asuncion Paraguay v. Ocean Bank	209
Bank of America N.T.S.A. v. Sanati	211

CHAPTER FOURTEEN. Investment Securities — 213

First American National Bank v. Christian Foundation Life Insurance Company	215
Jennie Clarkson Home for Children v. Missouri, Kansas and Texas Railway	217
Powers v. American Express Financial Advisors, Inc.	221

CHAPTER FIFTEEN. Documents of Title — 225

Procter & Gamble Distributing Co. v. Lawrence American Field Warehousing Corp.	227
Dunfee v. Blue Rock Van & Storage, Inc.	229
G.A.C. Commercial Corp. v. Wilson	231
Cleveland v. McNabb	233
Agricredit Acceptance, L.L.C. v. Hendrix	235
Rheinberg Kellerei GmbH v. Brooksfield National Bank of Commerce	239

CHAPTER SIXTEEN. Letters of Credit — 241

Voest–Alpine Trading Co. v. Bank of China	243
Sztejn v. Henry Schroder Bank Corp.	247
Intrinsic Values Corp. v. Superintendencia De Administracion Tributaria	249

TABLE OF CONTENTS

	Page
CHAPTER SEVENTEEN. Introduction to Secured Transactions	**251**
Benedict v. Ratner	253
CHAPTER EIGHTEEN. The Scope of Article 9	**257**
In re Fabers, Inc.	259
In re Architectural Millwork of Virginia, Inc.	261
Philko Aviation, Inc. v. Shacket	265
CHAPTER NINETEEN. The Creation of a Security Interest	**267**
In re Troupe	269
Morgan County Feeders, Inc. v. McCormick	271
In re Grabowski	273
Border State Bank of Greenbush v. Bagley Livestock Exchange, Inc.	275
In re Howell Enterprises, Inc.	279
CHAPTER TWENTY. Perfection of the Security Interest	**281**
In re Short	283
General Electric Capital Commercial Automotive Finance, Inc. v. Spartan Motors, Ltd.	285
In re Wood	287
CHAPTER TWENTY–ONE. Multistate Transactions	**289**
Metzger v. Americredit Financial Services, Inc.	291
CHAPTER TWENTY–TWO. Priority	**293**
In re Wollin	295
Galleon Industries, Inc. v. Lewyn Machinery Co.	299
Kunkel v. Sprague National Bank	301
International Harvester Co. v. Glendenning	303
First National Bank and Trust Co. of El Dorado v. Ford Motor Credit Co.	305
Clovis National Bank v. Thomas	307
Farm Credit Bank of St. Paul v. F & A Dairy	309
In re Arlco, Inc.	311
George v. Commercial Credit Corp.	315
Lewiston Bottled Gas Co. v. Key Bank of Maine	317
Maplewood Bank & Trust v. Sears, Roebuck & Co.	319
United States v. Estate of Romani	321
Plymouth Savings Bank v. U.S. I.R.S.	323
CHAPTER TWENTY–THREE. Bankruptcy and Article 9	**327**
In re Smith's Home Furnishings, Inc.	329
CHAPTER TWENTY–FOUR. Proceeds	**333**
Farmers Cooperative Elevator Co. v. Union State Bank	335
HCC Credit Corp. v. Springs Valley Bank & Trust Co.	337
CHAPTER TWENTY–FIVE. Default	**339**
State Bank of Piper City v. A-Way, Inc.	341
Klingbiel v. Commercial Credit Corp.	345
Williamson v. Fowler Toyota, Inc.	347
Hilliman v. Cobado	349
R & J of Tennessee, Inc. v. Blankenship–Melton Real Estate, Inc.	351
Coxall v. Clover Commercial Corp.	355
Reeves v. Foutz & Tanner, Inc.	359

*

Alphabetical Table of Cases

Agricredit Acceptance, LLC v. Hendrix, 82 F.Supp.2d 1379 (S.D.Ga.2000), 235
Analysts Intern. Corp. v. Recycled Paper Products, Inc., 45 UCC Rep.Serv.2d 747 (N.D.Ill.1987), 5
Anthony Pools, a Div. of Anthony Industries, Inc. v. Sheehan, 295 Md. 285, 455 A.2d 434 (Md.1983), 7
Any Kind Checks Cashed, Inc. v. Talcott, 830 So.2d 160 (Fla.App. 4 Dist.2002), 123
Arabian Score v. Lasma Arabian Ltd., 814 F.2d 529 (8th Cir.1987), 93
Architectural Millwork of Virginia, Inc., In re, 226 B.R. 551 (Bkrtcy.W.D.Va.1998), 261
Arlco, Inc., In re, 239 B.R. 261 (Bkrtcy.S.D.N.Y.1999), 311

Bank of America v. Sanati, 14 Cal.Rptr.2d 615 (Cal.App. 2 Dist.1992), 211
Bayway Refining Co. v. Oxygenated Marketing and Trading A.G., 215 F.3d 219 (2nd Cir.2000), 23
Bell Sports, Inc. v. Yarusso, 759 A.2d 582 (Del.Supr.2000), 43
Benedict v. Ratner, 268 U.S. 353, 45 S.Ct. 566, 69 L.Ed. 991 (1925), 253
Border State Bank of Greenbush v. Bagley Livestock Exchange, Inc., 690 N.W.2d 326 (Minn.App.2004), 275
Bowdoin v. Showell Growers, Inc., 817 F.2d 1543 (11th Cir. 1987), 49

Canty v. Vermont Nat. Bank, 25 UCC Rep.Serv.2d 1184 (Vt.Super.1994), 175
Cate v. Dover Corp., 790 S.W.2d 559 (Tex.1990), 45
Chemical Bank v. PIC Motors Corp., 87 A.D.2d 447, 452 N.Y.S.2d 41 (N.Y.A.D. 1 Dept.1982), 151
Cherwell–Ralli, Inc. v. Rytman Grain Co., Inc., 180 Conn. 714, 433 A.2d 984 (Conn.1980), 81
Cleveland v. McNabb, 312 F.Supp. 155 (W.D.Tenn.1970), 233
Clovis Nat. Bank v. Thomas, 77 N.M. 554, 425 P.2d 726 (N.M.1967), 307
Colonial Pacific Leasing Corp. v. McNatt, 268 Ga. 265, 486 S.E.2d 804 (Ga.1997), 67
Columbia Nitrogen Corp. v. Royster Co., 451 F.2d 3 (4th Cir.1971), 17
Cook Specialty Co. v. Schrock, 772 F.Supp. 1532 (E.D.Pa. 1991), 75
Corfan Banco Asuncion Paraguay v. Ocean Bank, 715 So.2d 967 (Fla.App. 3 Dist.1998), 209
Coxall v. Clover Commercial Corp., 4 Misc.3d 654, 781 N.Y.S.2d 567 (N.Y.City Civ.Ct.2004), 355

Daniell v. Ford Motor Co., Inc., 581 F.Supp. 728 (D.N.M. 1984), 39
Decibel Credit Union v. Pueblo Bank & Trust Co., 996 P.2d 784 (Colo.App.2000), 191
Diamond Fruit Growers, Inc. v. Krack Corp., 794 F.2d 1440 (9th Cir.1986), 21
Dunfee v. Blue Rock Van & Storage, Inc., 266 A.2d 187 (Del.Super.1970), 229

East River S.S. Corp. v. Transamerica Delaval, Inc., 476 U.S. 858, 106 S.Ct. 2295, 90 L.Ed.2d 865 (1986), 61
Estate of (see name of party)

Fabers, Inc., In re, 12 UCC Rep.Serv. 126 (Bkrtcy.D.Conn. 1972), 259
Falk v. Northern Trust Co., 327 Ill.App.3d 101, 261 Ill.Dec. 410, 763 N.E.2d 380 (Ill.App. 1 Dist.2001), 201

Falls Church Bank v. Wesley Heights Realty, Inc., 256 A.2d 915 (D.C.App.1969), 119
Farm Credit Bank of St. Paul v. F & A Dairy, 165 Wis.2d 360, 477 N.W.2d 357 (Wis.App.1991), 309
Farmers Co-op. Elevator Co. v. Union State Bank, 409 N.W.2d 178 (Iowa 1987), 335
Federal Deposit Ins. Corp. v. Culver, 640 F.Supp. 725 (D.Kan. 1986), 135
First Am. Nat. Bank v. Christian Foundation Life Ins. Co., 242 Ark. 678, 420 S.W.2d 912 (Ark.1967), 215
First Nat. Bank and Trust Co. of El Dorado v. Ford Motor Credit Co., 231 Kan. 431, 646 P.2d 1057 (Kan.1982), 305
First Nat. Bank of Chicago v. Standard Bank & Trust, 172 F.3d 472 (7th Cir.1999), 181
Fitl v. Strek, 269 Neb. 51, 690 N.W.2d 605 (Neb.2005), 57
Floor v. Melvin, 5 Ill.App.3d 463, 283 N.E.2d 303 (Ill.App. 3 Dist.1972), 149

G. A. C. Commercial Corp. v. Wilson, 271 F.Supp. 242 (S.D.N.Y.1967), 231
Galleon Industries, Inc. v. Lewyn Machinery Co., Inc., 50 Ala.App. 334, 279 So.2d 137 (Ala.Civ.App.1973), 299
Galyen Petroleum Co. v. Hixson, 213 Neb. 683, 331 N.W.2d 1 (Neb.1983), 161
General Elec. Capital Commercial Automotive Finance, Inc. v. Spartan Motors, Ltd., 246 A.D.2d 41, 675 N.Y.S.2d 626 (N.Y.A.D. 2 Dept.1998), 285
General Inv. Corp. v. Angelini, 58 N.J. 396, 278 A.2d 193 (N.J.1971), 121
George v. Commercial Credit Corp., 440 F.2d 551 (7th Cir. 1971), 315
Grabowski, In re, 277 B.R. 388 (Bkrtcy.S.D.Ill.2002), 273
Grain Traders, Inc. v. Citibank, N.A., 960 F.Supp. 784 (S.D.N.Y.1997), 207

HCC Credit Corp. v. Springs Valley Bank & Trust Co., 669 N.E.2d 1001 (Ind.App.1996), 337
Herzog Contracting Corp. v. McGowen Corp., 976 F.2d 1062 (7th Cir.1992), 143
Hilliman v. Cobado, 131 Misc.2d 206, 499 N.Y.S.2d 610 (N.Y.Sup.1986), 349
Howell Enterprises, Inc., In re, 934 F.2d 969 (8th Cir.1991), 279
Hughes Communications Galaxy, Inc. v. United States, 271 F.3d 1060 (Fed.Cir.2001), 103
Hutzler v. Hertz Corp., 39 N.Y.2d 209, 383 N.Y.S.2d 266, 347 N.E.2d 627 (N.Y.1976), 195

In re (see name of party)
International Harvester Co. v. Glendenning, 505 S.W.2d 320 (Tex.Civ.App.-Dallas 1974), 303
Intrinsic Values Corp. v. Superintendencia De Administracion Tributaria, 806 So.2d 616 (Fla.App. 3 Dist.2002), 249

Jakowski v. Carole Chevrolet, Inc., 180 N.J.Super. 122, 433 A.2d 841 (N.J.Super.L.1981), 91
Jennie Clarkson Home for Children v. Missouri, K. & T. Ry. Co., 182 N.Y. 47, 74 N.E. 571 (N.Y.1905), 217
Jones v. Approved Bancredit Corp., 256 A.2d 739 (Del. Supr.1969), 129

Kedzie and 103rd Currency Exchange, Inc. v. Hodge, 156 Ill.2d 112, 189 Ill.Dec. 31, 619 N.E.2d 732 (Ill.1993), 139
Klingbiel v. Commercial Credit Corp., 439 F.2d 1303 (10th Cir.1971), 345
Klocek v. Gateway, Inc., 104 F.Supp.2d 1332 (D.Kan.2000), 27

ALPHABETICAL TABLE OF CASES

Kunkel v. Sprague Nat. Bank, 128 F.3d 636 (8th Cir.1997), 301

Landrum v. Devenport, 616 S.W.2d 359 (Tex.Civ.App.-Texarkana 1981), 73
Leeds v. Chase Manhattan Bank, N.A., 331 N.J.Super. 416, 752 A.2d 332 (N.J.Super.A.D.2000), 187
Leonard Pevar Co. v. Evans Products Co., 524 F.Supp. 546 (D.Del.1981), 25
Lewiston Bottled Gas Co. v. Key Bank of Maine, 601 A.2d 91 (Me.1992), 317
London Leasing Corp. v. Interfina, Inc., 53 Misc.2d 657, 279 N.Y.S.2d 209 (N.Y.Sup.1967), 153
Louisiana Power & Light Co. v. Allegheny Ludlum Industries, Inc., 517 F.Supp. 1319 (E.D.La.1981), 95

Makel Textiles, Inc. v. Dolly Originals, Inc., 4 UCC Rep.Serv. 95 (N.Y.Sup.1967), 157
Maplewood Bank and Trust v. Sears, Roebuck and Co., 265 N.J.Super. 25, 625 A.2d 537 (N.J.Super.A.D.1993), 319
Messing v. Bank of America, N.A., 143 Md.App. 1, 792 A.2d 312 (Md.App.2002), 155
Metzger v. Americredit Financial Services, Inc., 273 Ga.App. 453, 615 S.E.2d 120 (Ga.App.2005), 291
Milau Associates v. North Ave. Development Corp., 42 N.Y.2d 482, 398 N.Y.S.2d 882, 368 N.E.2d 1247 (N.Y.1977), 3
Moore v. Pro Team Corvette Sales, Inc., 152 Ohio App.3d 71, 786 N.E.2d 903 (Ohio App. 3 Dist.2002), 35
Morgan County Feeders, Inc. v. McCormick, 836 P.2d 1051 (Colo.App.1992), 271
Mundaca Inv. Corp. v. Febba, 143 N.H. 499, 727 A.2d 990 (N.H.1999), 163

Nichols v. Seale, 493 S.W.2d 589 (Tex.Civ.App.-Dallas 1973), 165
Norton v. Knapp, 64 Iowa 112, 19 N.W. 867 (Iowa 1884), 159

Parr v. Security Nat. Bank, 680 P.2d 648 (Okla.App. Div. 1 1984), 173
Patriot Bank, N.A. v. Navy Federal Credit Union, 58 Va. Cir. 251 (Va.Cir.Ct.2002), 177
Philko Aviation, Inc. v. Shacket, 462 U.S. 406, 103 S.Ct. 2476, 76 L.Ed.2d 678 (1983), 265
Pierce v. Catalina Yachts, Inc., 2 P.3d 618 (Alaska 2000), 55
Plateq Corp. of North Haven v. Machlett Laboratories, Inc., 189 Conn. 433, 456 A.2d 786 (Conn.1983), 87
Plymouth Savings Bank v. United States I.R.S., 187 F.3d 203 (1st Cir.1999), 323
Poli v. DaimlerChrysler Corp., 349 N.J.Super. 169, 793 A.2d 104 (N.J.Super.A.D.2002), 107
Powers v. American Express Fin. Advisors, Inc., 238 F.3d 414 (4th Cir.2000), 221
Price v. Neal, 3 Burr. 1354, 97 Eng. Rep. 871 (1762), 189
Procter & Gamble Distributing Co. v. Lawrence Am. Field Warehousing Corp., 16 N.Y.2d 344, 266 N.Y.S.2d 785, 213 N.E.2d 873 (N.Y.1965), 227

Ramirez v. Autosport, 88 N.J. 277, 440 A.2d 1345 (N.J.1982), 85
Reed v. City of Chicago, 263 F.Supp.2d 1123 (N.D.Ill.2003), 59
Reeves v. Foutz and Tanner, Inc., 94 N.M. 760, 617 P.2d 149 (N.M.1980), 359
Rheinberg Kellerei GmbH v. Brooksfield Nat. Bank of Commerce Bank, 901 F.2d 481 (5th Cir.1990), 239
Rheinberg-Kellerei GMBH v. Vineyard Wine Co., Inc., 53 N.C.App. 560, 281 S.E.2d 425 (N.C.App.1981), 77
Rinaldi v. Iomega Corp., 41 UCC Rep.Serv.2d 1143 (Del.Super.1999), 51
R & J of Tennessee, Inc. v. Blankenship–Melton Real Estate, Inc., 166 S.W.3d 195 (Tenn.Ct.App.2004), 351
Rock Island Auction Sales, Inc. v. Empire Packing Co., 32 Ill.2d 269, 204 N.E.2d 721 (Ill.1965), 179

Romani, Estate of, United States v., 523 U.S. 517, 1998-49 I.R.B. 6, 118 S.Ct. 1478, 140 L.Ed.2d 710 (1998), 321

Sea Air Support, Inc. v. Herrmann, 96 Nev. 574, 613 P.2d 413 (Nev.1980), 137
Shaffer v. Victoria Station, Inc., 91 Wash.2d 295, 588 P.2d 233 (Wash.1978), 37
Short, In re, 170 B.R. 128 (Bkrtcy.S.D.Ill.1994), 283
Siemen v. Alden, 34 Ill.App.3d 961, 341 N.E.2d 713 (Ill.App. 2 Dist.1975), 9
Smith's Home Furnishings, Inc., In re, 265 F.3d 959 (9th Cir.2001), 329
St. Ansgar Mills, Inc. v. Streit, 613 N.W.2d 289 (Iowa 2000), 13
State Bank of Piper City v. A–Way, Inc., 115 Ill.2d 401, 105 Ill.Dec. 452, 504 N.E.2d 737 (Ill.1987), 341
Sullivan v. United Dealers Corp., 486 S.W.2d 699 (Ky.1972), 131
Sztejn v. J. Henry Schroder Banking Corp., 177 Misc. 719, 31 N.Y.S.2d 631 (N.Y.Sup.1941), 247

Teradyne, Inc. v. Teledyne Industries, Inc., 676 F.2d 865 (1st Cir.1982), 101
The Bank/First Citizens Bank v. Citizens and Associates, 44 UCC Rep.Serv.2d 1072 (Tenn.Ct.App.2001), 197
Tongish v. Thomas, 16 Kan.App.2d 809, 829 P.2d 916 (Kan. App.1992), 105
Travelers Cas. and Sur. Co. of America v. Wells Fargo Bank N.A., 374 F.3d 521 (7th Cir.2004), 199
Triffin v. Dillabough, 552 Pa. 550, 716 A.2d 605 (Pa.1998), 111
Triffin v. Somerset Valley Bank, 343 N.J.Super. 73, 777 A.2d 993 (N.J.Super.A.D.2001), 133
Troupe, In re, 340 B.R. 86 (Bkrtcy.W.D.Okla.2006), 269
Twin City Bank v. Isaacs, 283 Ark. 127, 672 S.W.2d 651 (Ark.1984), 169

United States v. _____ (see opposing party)

Valley Bank of Ronan v. Hughes, 334 Mont. 335, 147 P.3d 185 (Mont.2006), 183
Ventura v. Ford Motor Corp., 180 N.J.Super. 45, 433 A.2d 801 (N.J.Super.A.D.1981), 63
Virginia Nat. Bank v. Holt, 216 Va. 500, 219 S.E.2d 881 (Va.1975), 141
Voest–Alpine Trading Co. v. Bank of China, 167 F.Supp.2d 940 (S.D.Tex.2000), 243

Wachovia Bank, N.A. v. Foster Bancshares, Inc., 457 F.3d 619 (7th Cir.2006), 193
Waddell v. L.V.R.V. Inc., 122 Nev. 15, 125 P.3d 1160 (Nev. 2006), 89
Walter v. National City Bank of Cleveland, 42 Ohio St.2d 524, 330 N.E.2d 425 (Ohio 1975), 171
Ward v. Federal Kemper Ins. Co., 62 Md.App. 351, 489 A.2d 91 (Md.App.1985), 147
Webster v. Blue Ship Tea Room, Inc., 347 Mass. 421, 198 N.E.2d 309 (Mass.1964), 41
Williamson v. Fowler Toyota, Inc., 956 P.2d 858 (Okla.1998), 347
Wilson v. Scampoli, 228 A.2d 848 (D.C.App.1967), 83
Wilson Trading Corp. v. David Ferguson, Limited, 23 N.Y.2d 398, 297 N.Y.S.2d 108, 244 N.E.2d 685 (N.Y.1968), 53
Winter & Hirsch, Inc. v. Passarelli, 122 Ill.App.2d 372, 259 N.E.2d 312 (Ill.App. 1 Dist.1970), 127
Wollin, In re, 249 B.R. 555 (Bkrtcy.D.Or.2000), 295
Wood, In re, 67 B.R. 321 (W.D.N.Y.1986), 287
Woodworth v. Richmond Indiana Venture, 13 UCC Rep. Serv.2d 1149 (Ohio Com.Pl.1990), 115

CHAPTER ONE

Basic Concepts

Milau Associates, Inc. v. North Avenue Development Corp.

Instant Facts: Higgins (D) installed pipes which burst damaging North Avenue's (D) property.

Black Letter Rule: When service predominates, and the transfer of personal property is an incidental feature of the transaction, the implied warranty standards of the UCC will not apply.

Analysts Intern. Corp. v. Recycled Paper Products, Inc.

Instant Facts: When a retailer refused to pay for defective customized merchandising software, the designer claimed UCC implied warranties were inapplicable because custom software is more "service" than "good".

Black Letter Rule: Under Illinois law, standard software is regulated as a "good," but custom software may be either "good" or "service," depending on the contract's "dominant purpose."

Anthony Pools v. Sheehan

Instant Facts: Sheehan (P) fell off a diving board and sought to hold the pool company responsible under an implied warranty theory.

Black Letter Rule: Even in a predominantly service transaction, if consumer goods are sold which retain their character as consumer goods, and the loss or injury resulted from a defect in the goods, the UCC implied warranties will apply to the goods.

Siemen v. Alden

Instant Facts: Siemen (P) purchased a saw from Korleski (D) which exploded and injured Siemen (P).

Black Letter Rule: Under UCC Article 2 a merchant is a person who deals in goods of the kind or otherwise holds himself out as having knowledge or skill peculiar to the goods involved. A person making an isolated sale of goods is not a "merchant."

Milau Associates, Inc. v. North Avenue Development Corp.

(*General Contractor*) v. (*Tenant*)
42 N.Y.2d 482, 368 N.E.2d 1247, 398 N.Y.S.2d 882 (1977)

THE IMPLIED WARRANTY STANDARDS OF THE UCC WILL NOT APPLY TO A TRANSACTION WHERE THE SERVICE ASPECT PREDOMINATES, AND THE TRANSFER OF GOODS IS AN INCIDENTAL FEATURE OF THE TRANSACTION

■ **INSTANT FACTS** Higgins (D) installed pipes which burst damaging North Avenue's (P) property.

■ **BLACK LETTER RULE** When service predominates, and the transfer of personal property is an incidental feature of the transaction, the implied warranty standards of the UCC will not apply.

■ **PROCEDURAL BASIS**

Appeal from the trial court's denial of North Avenue's (P) request to submit their implied warranty case to the jury.

■ **FACTS**

North Avenue Development Corp. (P) were tenants in a warehouse built by Milau Associates (D), the general contractor, and Higgins Fire Protection, Inc. (D), the subcontractor which designed and installed the sprinkler system. An underground section of pipe burst, causing water damage to bolts of textiles owned by North Avenue (P) and stored in the warehouse. Evidence at trial showed that the break was caused by a "water hammer." This occurs when an interruption in the flow from the city water main is followed by extreme pressure when the flow is released. North Avenue (P) produced experts alleging that a V-shaped notch discovered at the end of the conduit fractured. The notch was alleged to have been produced by a dull tooth on the hydraulic squeeze cutter used by Higgins (D) to cut the pipe. North Avenue (P) alleged that a few months of operation had caused enough rusting at the base of the notch to affect the entire system. Milau (D) and Higgins (D) produced testimony that the pipe was neither defective nor improperly installed. The trial court submitted the case to the jury on the question of negligent installation. The jury found no negligence on the part of Higgins (D) as installer or Milau (D) as the supervisor. North Avenue (P) appealed, arguing the V-shaped notch in the ruptured section of the pipe was a defect in the "goods" furnished under the hybrid sales-service contract, and that they were entitled to have the jury decide whether there was a breach of an implied warranty under § 2–315 of the Uniform Commercial Code.

■ **ISSUE**

Should the UCC implied warranties apply to a predominantly service contract?

■ **DECISION AND RATIONALE**

(Wachtler, J.) No. When a service predominates, and the transfer of personal property is an incidental feature of the transaction, the exacting warranty standards for imposing liability without fault under the Uniform Commercial Code will not apply. Those who hire experts for the predominant purpose of rendering services cannot expect infallibility. Unless the parties have contractually bound themselves to a higher standard of performance, an injured party can only expect reasonable care and competence

Milau Associates, Inc. v. North Avenue Development Corp. (Continued)

from practitioners in the particular trade or profession. The parties here were free to adopt a higher standard of performance. In the subcontract, Higgins (D) was obligated to furnish and install the sprinkler system in accordance with the New York Fire Insurance Rating Organization. Additionally, by affixing its corporate signature to the subcontract, Higgins (D) expressly warranted that all materials would be new and all work would be of good quality, free from faults and defects, and in conformity with the contract documents. Here, North Avenue (P) had the opportunity to test the construction of the written warranty in the work subcontract at the trial level. They instead opted to attempt to prove fault; when that failed, they now seek enforcement of a warranty imposed by law for the sale of goods unfit for their intended purpose. They have failed to show that the subcontract was anything more than a series of performance undertakings, plans, and specifications for the installation of the sprinkler system. It was a predominantly labor-intensive endeavor. The parties contemplated a workmanlike performance of a service. The fact that something went wrong six months after the performance does not change the underlying nature of the agreement. This was a predominately service-oriented transaction, and neither the Uniform Commercial Code nor the common law grants relief for the non-negligent performance of Higgins (D) or Milau (D). Other courts that have examined service contracts have imposed no more than a warranty that the performer would not act negligently and would perform in a workmanlike manner. Higgins's (D) and Milau's (D) performance was tested under this standard and found to have been acceptable. Sound public policy dictates that strict tort liability without fault be imposed on manufacturers of defective and dangerous products. Sellers of goods encourage mass public reliance on the safety and fitness of their products through advertising and packaging. This is reflected in the fact that the Code's warranties attaching to the sale of goods are based on an assumption of reasonable reliance by the buyer. In the service arena, however, the standards of performance are usually set contractually. In this case, there is no reason in policy or law to read a warranty of perfect results into the contractual relationship defined by the parties in this action. Affirmed.

Analysis:
Section 2–315 of the UCC implies a warranty of fitness for a particular purpose that arises "[w]here the seller at the time of contracting has reason to know any particular purpose for which the goods are required and that the buyer is relying on the seller's skill or judgment to select or furnish suitable goods." North Avenue (P) sought to use this section to impose liability on Higgins (D). However, UCC Article 2 applies only to "goods" and the court concluded this was predominantly a service contract. This contract could also be described as a hybrid. It contained both "service" and "goods" aspects. Should the UCC warranties apply to the "goods" portion of the contract? Why must it be all or nothing? Other cases fashion a more flexible rule for hybrid transactions.

Analysts Intern. Corp. v. Recycled Paper Products, Inc.

(*Software Designer*) v. (*Software Buyer*)
1987 WL 12917, 45 UCC Rep.Serv.2d 747 (N.D.Ill.1987)

STANDARD SOFTWARE IS A "GOOD," BUT CUSTOMIZED SOFTWARE MAY BE "SERVICE"

■ **INSTANT FACTS** When a retailer refused to pay for defective customized merchandising software, the designer claimed *UCC* implied warranties were inapplicable because custom software is more "service" than "good."

■ **BLACK LETTER RULE** Under Illinois law, standard software is regulated as a "good," but custom software may be either "good" or "service," depending on the contract's "dominant purpose."

■ **PROCEDURAL BASIS**

In contract suit, plaintiff's motion for summary judgment against defendant's counterclaims.

■ **FACTS**

Retail firm Recycled Paper Products ("RPP") (D) hired software designer Analysts International Corp. ("AIC") (P) to design a computer-assisted merchandising program ("CAMP") to automate order shipping. RPP (D) and AIC (P) contracted for designing CAMP. The agreement was part oral, part written, and its terms are disputed. RPP (D) claims that AIC (P) specified a fixed price. AIC (P) claims its written price was only an estimate, and that it was to be paid per hour. AIC (P) finished CAMP late, and CAMP did not work, creating many errors and disruptions. AIC (P) tried to repair CAMP, charging AIC (P) an additional $928,000. Finally, outside experts concluded CAMP was unrepairable. RPP (D) refused to pay AIC's (P) latest $330,000 in invoices. AIC (P) sued for breach of contract, etc. RPP (D) countersued, alleging (i) breach of contract and (ii) breach of the UCC's implied warranties of (A) merchantability and (B) fitness for a particular purpose, etc. AIC (P) moved for summary judgment against the warranty claims, claiming these warranties were not implied by law because the contract was predominantly for services (programming), so that the *UCC*'s implied warranties are inapplicable. RPP (D) defended, claiming it primarily purchased a good (a complete software program).

■ **ISSUE**

Are the *UCC*'s implied warranties of merchantability and fitness for a particular purpose applicable to customized software?

■ **DECISION AND RATIONALE**

(Grady) Yes. Under Illinois law, standard software is regulated as a "good," but custom software may be either "good" or "service," depending on the contract's "dominant purpose." The issue is whether the *UCC* applies to purchases of custom computerized programs, which turns on whether their sale is a "transaction in goods" under the *UCC*. Some prior cases held that sales of custom software are not "goods" transactions, because programming contracts involve primarily the programmers' skill rather than the physical disks on which programs are stored. However, these cases' reasoning is not persuasive. Software necessarily has both tangible and intangible elements; the programmer's knowledge is important, but only insofar as it allows him to produce the software ordered. Other past cases also held that contracts for unique, custom-made products involve primarily creative services.

Analysts Intern. Corp. v. Recycled Paper Products, Inc. (Continued)

However, the cases cited are distinguishable or unpersuasive. Under Illinois law, if an agreement involves both goods and services, we classify it under a "dominant purpose" test; the court must inquire whether the "essence or dominant factor" in forming the contract was providing goods. Here, RPP (D) provided uncontroverted evidence that this contract was essentially for a computer program; the service aspect was incidental. Custom software is not necessarily classified a "service," because any custom item's manufacturer must necessarily perform the work required to create it. However, standard, off-the-shelf software would be a "good." AIC's (P) motion for summary judgment denied.

Analysis:

The classification of contracts involving both finished products and installation/creative services is unsettled. Some courts apply the "predominant factor" test, thus necessarily classifying the end result as either goods or services. Some courts apply the more forgiving "gravamen" test, which tends to extend the UCC's greater implied protections to consumer items, even if a large part of the contract was their installation rather than manufacture. This case illustrates the controversial sub-issue of computer software, Which tends to be analyzed separately under its own rule. Most courts deem *standard* (non-custom) software to be "goods" but they *may* make exceptions for *custom*-designed software, as this case does. Note that this case represents the *minority* rule.

■ CASE VOCABULARY

FITNESS FOR A PARTICULAR PURPOSE: Warranty implied by the *UCC* in special circumstances. Basically, when the buyer of goods (i) knows nothing about the goods' quality, (ii) explains to the seller that he needs the good for a specified purpose, and (iii) relies reasonably on the seller's assurance that the product is fit for that purpose, then the product must actually be usable for that purpose, or the seller is liable. Thus, it protects buyers who rely on the seller's recommendation.

MERCHANTABILITY: Warranty implied by the *UCC*, requiring that a product sold be salable "as a product of that kind," meaning it must fulfill the ordinary functions generally expected of products of that kind. E.g., a product sold as a "chair" must be capable of doing the basic tasks people would expect of a chair. Basically, this means the item must not be defective, and cannot be marketed as something that it is not.

WARRANTY: Promise (explicit or implicit) made by a product's seller about the product's quality. If the product does not meet the quality promised by the warranty, the seller is liable for damages.

Anthony Pools v. Sheehan
(Pool Company) v. *(Injured Consumer)*
295 Md. 285, 455 A.2d 434 (Ct. App. 1983)

UCC IMPLIED WARRANTIES APPLY TO CONSUMER GOODS, EVEN IN A PREDOMINATELY SERVICE TRANSACTION, IF THE CONSUMER GOODS RETAIN THEIR CHARACTER AS CONSUMER GOODS, AND THE INJURY OR LOSS RESULTED FROM A DEFECT IN THE GOODS

■ **INSTANT FACTS** Sheehan (P) fell off a diving board and sought to hold the pool company responsible under an implied warranty theory.

■ **BLACK LETTER RULE** Even in a predominantly service transaction, if consumer goods are sold which retain their character as consumer goods, and the loss or injury resulted from a defect in the goods, the UCC implied warranties will apply to the goods.

■ **PROCEDURAL BASIS**

Appeal from an appellate court's ruling reversing the trial court's directed verdict in favor of Anthony (D) on an implied warranty issue.

■ **FACTS**

Mr. Sheehan (P) was injured when he fell from the side of a diving board of his new backyard swimming pool designed and built by Anthony Pools (D). Anthony (D) also manufactured and installed the diving board as part of the transaction. The pool was "Grecian" in style, meaning that it had two curved alcoves on each side. The diving board bisects the alcove on the deep end of the pool. Sheehan (P) slipped from the right end of the diving board and struck the side of the pool. Sheehan (P) argued that the implied warranty of merchantability was breached, in that the skid resistant material on the top of the diving board did not extend to the very edge of the board. Sheehan (P) also tried to prove the board was defective, in that its position in the alcove made it unreasonably dangerous. The trial court directed a verdict for Anthony (D) on the warranty issue because the written contract between the parties provided that the express warranties it contained were in lieu of any other warranties, either express or implied. The case went to the jury on a strict liability tort theory, which returned a verdict in favor of Anthony (D).

■ **ISSUE**

Does the UCC apply to the goods in a predominantly service transaction, if the goods retain their character as consumer goods, and the loss or injury resulted from a defect in the goods?

■ **DECISION AND RATIONALE**

(Rodowsky, J.) Yes. The warranty issue involves the implied warranty of merchantability under § 2–314. Anthony (D) contends that the swimming pool is not "goods" within the meaning of the Maryland Uniform Commercial Code and that the exclusion of implied warranties is allowed. We disagree. The Maryland UCC applies to transactions in goods. The Code provides that "goods" means all things that "are movable at the time of identification to the contract for sale." The Code further provides that a warranty of merchantability is implied in a contract for their sale if the seller is a merchant with respect to goods of that kind. Maryland UCC § 2–316.1(2) provides that any language attempting to exclude or

Anthony Pools v. Sheehan (Continued)

modify any implied warranties in contracts for the sale of consumer goods is unenforceable. Consumer goods are defined as those used or bought primarily for personal, family, or household purposes. The contract at issue here described the work to be performed and the specific items to be installed. The reverse side of the contract contains the implied warranty exclusion. This contract is a hybrid transaction which is in part a contract for services and in part a contract for the sale of goods. In determining whether the UCC applies to such hybrid transactions, a majority of courts use the predominant purpose test. This test asks whether the predominant factor, the thrust, or the purpose of a contract is a transaction of sale with labor involved, or vice versa. Under this approach, if the service aspect predominates, no warranties of quality are imposed in the transaction, even if the defect relates to the goods that were involved rather than to the services. The few reported cases involving whether Article 2 of the UCC applies to swimming pool installations are not uniform. In the present case, Anthony (D) undertook the construction and installation of a swimming pool. The predominant factor of the contract was the furnishing of labor by Anthony (D), and the sale of the diving board was incidental to the construction of the pool. If the predominant factor test is mechanically applied to this case, there would be no warranty of merchantability implied. However, here the contract expressly states that Anthony (D) agrees to construct the swimming pool and to sell the related equipment selected by Sheehan (P). The board was an optional accessory, as were the other options such as a pool ladder or a sliding board. The diving board is movable and detachable from its support. The diving board is a "good," and had it been purchased separately, there would have been an implied warranty of merchantability. Many commentators have advocated a more policy-oriented approach to determine whether warranties of quality are implied to goods sold as part of a hybrid transaction in which service predominates. The support for this position emphasizes loss shifting, risk distribution, and consumer reliance. Dean Hawkland has suggested a "gravamen" test which focuses on whether the action arises from the goods or the services. For example, if gas escaped from a pipe and caused an explosion because of a defective fitting or connector, the case could be characterized as one involving the sale of goods. If the gas escaped because of poor work, the case might be characterized as one involving services. In this state, § 2–316.1 (1) and (2) provide that the warranty of merchantability may not be excluded for "consumer goods ... services, or both." Therefore, the legislature implicitly recognized the type of hybrid transaction involved in this case. To mechanically apply the predominant purpose test and find that the implied warranties do not apply to the diving board would be contrary to the legislative policy implicit in these sections. We hold that where, as part of a commercial transaction, consumer goods are sold which retain their character as consumer goods after completion of the performance, and where the injury or loss resulted from a defect in the consumer goods, the warranties of merchantability implied by the Maryland UCC apply to the goods, even if the transaction is predominantly for consumer services. Thus, the board sold to Sheehan (P) carried an implied warranty of merchantability and the contractual disclaimer was ineffective. The appellate court was correct in finding that the trial court erred in directing a verdict for Anthony (D). Affirmed.

Analysis:

The court here rejected the "predominant factor" test in favor of a more flexible "gravamen" test. If the injury or loss occurred because of a defect in the goods, the warranty of merchantability will apply even in a predominantly service-oriented transaction. Maryland UCC § 2–316.1 provided that any "language used by a seller of consumer goods and services, which attempts to exclude or modify any implied warranties ... is unenforceable." Compare this with Uniform Commercial Code § 2–316, which allows the exclusion or modification of implied warranties. There is no such limitation on sellers of consumer goods and services.

■ CASE VOCABULARY

GRAVAMEN: The material part of a cause of action or complaint; the specific injury complained of.

Siemen v. Alden
(Injured Consumer) v. *(Manufacturer)*
34 Ill.App.3d 961, 341 N.E.2d 713 (1975)

UNDER THE UCC, A PERSON MAKING AN ISOLATED SALE IS NOT A "MERCHANT"

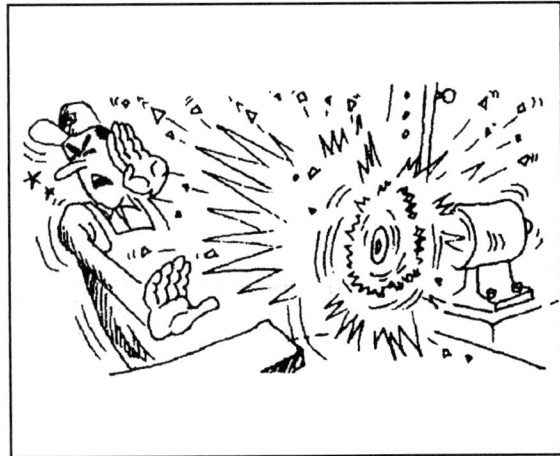

■ **INSTANT FACTS** Siemen (P) purchased a saw from Korleski (D) which exploded and injured Siemen (P).

■ **BLACK LETTER RULE** Under UCC Article 2 a merchant is a person who deals in goods of the kind or otherwise holds himself out as having knowledge or skill peculiar to the goods involved. A person making an isolated sale of goods is not a "merchant."

■ PROCEDURAL BASIS
Appeal from the grant of summary judgment in favor of Korleski (D).

■ FACTS
Siemen (P) was injured while operating an automated multi-rip saw manufactured by Lloyd G. Alden (D) and purchased from Ed Korleski (D). Siemen (P) originally contacted Alden (D) about purchasing a rip saw to increase his production of decking pallets. Alden (D) told Siemen (P) that a new saw could not be delivered in less than six months and suggested that Siemen (P) call Korleski (D), who owned two Alden saws. Korleski (D) informed Siemen (P) that he owned an older saw that was not working, which he would be willing to sell. Korleski (D) demonstrated the use of a newer saw which operated in the same manner as the older saw. Siemen's (P) son accompanied Siemen to examine the saw which needed new blades and other parts to be restored to working order. The parties agreed on a purchase price of $2,900, and Siemen (P) was thereafter injured when a piece of wood exploded while being fed through the saw. Siemen (P) proceeded on appeal only against defendant Korleski (D).

■ ISSUE
Can the sale of a single item by someone who does not normally deal in goods of that kind make the seller a "merchant" for purposes of UCC Section 2?

■ DECISION AND RATIONALE
(Moran, J.) No. Siemen (P) argues the summary judgment in favor of Korleski (D) should be reversed because Korleski (D) should be held strictly liable for the sale of the defective product and because Korleski (D) is liable under the UCC § 2–314 and § 2–315 for implied warranties. Section 402A of the Restatement of the Law of Torts, 2d, provides that a seller of a defective product in an unreasonably dangerous condition is liable to the consumer if the seller is engaged in the business of selling such a product, and the product reaches the consumer without a substantial change in its condition. The rule applies even though the seller exercised all possible care, and the consumer has no contractual relationship with the seller. The comment accompanying this rule provides that an occasional seller is explicitly excluded. Siemen (P) has failed to meet the requirement of the rule that the seller be engaged in the business of selling the particular product. It is uncontested that this was Korleski's (D) only sale of a saw or sawmill equipment. Siemen (P) next contends that under the UCC a genuine issue of fact exists as to Korleski's (D) liability arising from his saw-related knowledge and skill and

Siemen v. Alden (Continued)

Siemen's (P) reliance on this knowledge. Section 2-314 provides that a warranty of merchantability is implied in a contract for the sale of goods if the seller is a merchant with respect to goods of that kind. Section 2-104(1) defines a merchant as "a person who deals in goods of the kind or otherwise by his occupation holds himself out as having knowledge or skill particular to the practices or goods involved . . ." Siemen (P) argues that Korleski (D) is a merchant because he holds himself out as "having knowledge or skill." However, this is not the test for determining who is a merchant under the Code. The UCC's Comments make it clear that the warranty of merchantability applies only to a person, who in a professional capacity, sells the particular kind of goods at issue. The Comments specifically provide that a person making an isolated sale of goods is not a "merchant." It is clear that Korleski (D) is in the sawmill business, and the sale here was an isolated transaction. Siemen (P) further claims that UCC § 2-315 applies here. This provision states that where the seller has reason to know any particular purpose for which the goods are to be used and that the buyer is relying on the seller's skill and judgment to select or furnish the goods, there is an implied warranty that the goods will be fit for that purpose. Here, Korleski (D) knew Sieman (P) wanted the saw to make pallets. However, Siemen (P) did not rely on Korleski's (D) judgment or skill in selecting the saw. The record shows that Sieman (P) had already decided to purchase an Alden saw before he contacted Korleski (D). Furthermore, Siemen (P) brought his son to view the saw to help determine if it was what they needed. This suggests that Seimen (P) relied on his son's judgment, not Korleski's (D). The trial court properly granted Korleski's (D) motion for summary judgment. Affirmed.

Analysis:

Note the similarity between § 402A of the Restatement (Second) of Torts and UCC § 2-104(1). Both require the seller to be engaged in the business of selling such products or be a person who "deals in goods of the kind." The rationale is to provide special and clear rules for transactions involving professionals that should not apply to the casual or inexperienced seller. A law student selling her used car to a fellow student would clearly not be a "merchant" under the UCC, but what about a farmer who sells produce once a year to a wholesaler? The cases are split as to whether farmers selling produce are merchants under the Code. Some hold that it would stretch the imagination to conclude that farming operations worth millions of dollars are exempt from coverage, but one case held that a man who owned some cows and made occasional sales of corn was not a merchant.

CHAPTER TWO

Contract Formation

St. Ansgar Mills, Inc. v. Streit

Instant Facts: A corn buyer refused delivery of an oral contract on the ground the written confirmation was sent too late, even though he routinely ignored or delayed past confirmations.

Black Letter Rule: Whether a written confirmation sent to satisfy the statute of frauds has arrived in "reasonable" time is usually a question of fact for the jury.

Columbia Nitrogen Corp. v. Royster Co.

Instant Facts: Columbia (D) refused to accept phosphate shipments it had contracted to buy from Royster (P).

Black Letter Rule: Evidence of course of dealing and usage of trade is admissible to explain and supplement an agreement if such evidence is consistent with the express terms of the agreement.

Diamond Fruit Growers, Inc. v. Krack Corp.

Instant Facts: Krack (D) manufactured a cooling unit which contained Metal–Matic (D) tubing which broke damaging Diamond's (P) fruit.

Black Letter Rule: When an acceptance of an offer expressly conditions its acceptance on assent to the additional terms contained therein, the additional terms become part of the contract only if the other party gives specific and unequivocal assent to the additional terms.

Bayway Refining Co. v. Oxygenated Marketing and Trading, A.G.

Instant Facts: When an oil seller's acceptance incorporated, by reference, a document requiring the buyer to pay excise taxes, the buyer refused.

Black Letter Rule: When an acceptance adds a term to the offer, the party challenging the addition must prove the alteration is "material."

Leonard Pevar Co. v. Evans Products Co.

Instant Facts: Pevar (P) purchased defective plywood from Evans (D) which tried to limit its liability and disclaim most warranties.

Black Letter Rule: A buyer accepting and paying for goods does not constitute assent to additional terms proposed in a seller's counteroffer.

Klocek v. Gateway, Inc.

Instant Facts: A computer buyer sued the seller in court, even though the seller included with his purchase a contract requiring arbitration if he kept the computer.

Black Letter Rule: [In some states] an arbitration clause included with a shipped product is not binding merely because the buyer keeps the product.

St. Ansgar Mills, Inc. v. Streit

(Corn Seller) v. (Corn Buyer)
613 N.W.2d 289 (Iowa 2000)

STATUTE OF FRAUDS REQUIRES SOME CONTRACTS BE IN WRITING

■ **INSTANT FACTS** A corn buyer refused delivery of an oral contract on the ground the written confirmation was sent too late, even though he routinely ignored or delayed past confirmations.

■ **BLACK LETTER RULE** Whether a written confirmation sent to satisfy the statute of frauds has arrived in "reasonable" time is usually a question of fact for the jury.

■ **PROCEDURAL BASIS**

In contract action, following summary judgement for Streit (D), appeal.

■ **FACTS**

Corn dealer St. Ansgar Mills, Inc. (P) regularly sold corn to hog breeder Streit (D). St. Ansgar Mills' (P) price for each shipment depended on then-current futures prices; whenever buyers orally accepted a shipment at current prices, St. Ansgar Mills (P) would hedge by committing itself to buy at that price. Duane Streit (D) was a long-time customer of St. Ansgar Mills (P), and their prior transactions were informal. Usually, Streit's (D) son/agent John would stop by St. Ansgar Mills' (P) office monthly to pay, so St. Ansgar Mills (P) would type the acceptance and give it when he arrived. At other times, St. Ansgar Mills (P) mailed Streit (D) the acceptance; often, Streit (D) returned it late, or failed to return it, but always accepted delivery and paid. In the disputed transaction, Streit (D) ordered corn at the then-current price. St. Ansgar Mills (P) wrote out the confirmation, and set it aside for Streit's (D) agent, who was expected to come in that week. Streit's (D) agent did not come for 40 days. St. Ansgar Mills (P) asked his friend to tell him to come in. When Streit's (D) agent arrived, St. Ansgar Mills (P) gave him the confirmation. St. Ansgar Mills (P) admitted it should have sent the confirmation sooner, and had no excuse for delay. Meanwhile, corn prices had plummeted [so Streit (D) found it advantageous to buy his corn on the market, at current low prices]. Streit (D) refused delivery. St. Ansgar Mills (P) sued Streit (D) for breach of contract. Streit (D) moved for summary judgement, claiming the confirmation was invalid because it did not satisfy the statute of frauds, since (i) Streit (D) was not a "merchant," and (ii) the confirmation was not received within a reasonable time after the oral agreement. At trial, the District Court granted summary judgement for Streit (D), finding (i) the issue of whether Streit (D) is a "merchant" is a question of fact for the jury, but (ii) St. Ansgar Mills (P) confirmation did not occur within reasonable time, as a matter of law. St. Ansgar Mills' (P) appeals.

■ **ISSUE**

Is a confirmation sent 40 days after an oral contract invalid as "unreasonably" late under the statute of frauds?

■ **DECISION AND RATIONALE**

(Cady) No. Whether a written confirmation sent to satisfy the statute of frauds has arrived in "reasonable" time is usually a question of fact for the jury. The statute of frauds is a famous, venerable contract rule, requiring certain types of contracts to be in writing to be enforceable. It originated

St. Ansgar Mills, Inc. v. Streit (Continued)

historically in 17th Century England, where court rules forbade contractual parties from testifying as witnesses, so that oral contracts could be proven only by testimony from third parties. Under this scheme, if witnesses could be persuaded to give false testimony, this gave one party an advantage. To prevent perjury used to claim oral contracts, Parliament enacted the statute of frauds, requiring written proof for contracts which were either especially susceptible to fraud (e.g., contracts with now-dead people), or risked especially serious consequences (e.g., land deeds). American law adopted the statute of frauds concept, which was finally codified in the UCC. Some states, including ours, apply the UCC statute of frauds only to transactions over $500. Although the statute of frauds is deeply ingrained, many policy reasons for it have now changed, so some of its rigid requirements were modified. One such modification is the statute of frauds's application to "merchants," per UCC § 2201(2). Previously, parties who received written confirmation of an oral agreement could hold the other party liable, but were not themselves bound. Now, as to merchants, the statute of frauds is satisfied if a written confirmation is sent within a reasonable time and the merchant receiving it has reason to know of its contents, unless written objection is given within 10 days after receipt. Thus, writing is still required, but it need not be signed. This change puts professional buyers and sellers on equal footing, and encourages the prudent practice of sending memos to confirm oral agreements. What constitutes "reasonable" time to send a confirmation is decided under flexible standards, which must specifically consider "the nature, purpose and circumstances." UCC § 1–204. Also, generally, the UCC is intended to permit individualized commercial practices through the parties custom and practice, UCC § 1–102 cmt. 2, so "reasonableness" should include course of dealings, trade usage, and/or course of performance. Thus, "reasonableness" should consider all relevant circumstances. Generally, "reasonableness" is a question of fact for the jury. Summary judgment is appropriate only in rare cases where the evidence is one-sided. Other jurisdictions' cases often consider what constitutes reasonable time, often finding delays of several months reasonable. However, these are necessarily case-by-case decisions. Here, the District Court found the delay unreasonable based on the sale's large quantity, volatile market conditions, and lack of explanation for the delay. These are valid considerations, but not the only ones. Other relevant factors include these parties' custom/practice of delaying confirmation, long-standing business relationship, and prior similar transactions. That there is no particular explanation does not automatically make conduct unreasonable. Also relevant is Streit's (D) agent's failure to follow his customary practice of coming monthly. These factors reveal a genuine factual dispute, which is a question of fact for the jury. Summary judgment for Streit (D) reversed.

Analysis:

This case explains the basic statute of frauds concept, as well as the historical and policy reasons behind it. The original policy reasons are still somewhat valid: when there is no written record of a contract, any lawsuit tends to involve one party's word against the other's, so there is a high probability of jury error. However, the rule is both over- and under-inclusive, since it can invalidate an actual, provable oral contract, just because one party knew the law and avoided writing anything down. Practically speaking, anyone involved in an agreement should get it in writing to will avoid any later statute of frauds issues and the expense, aggravation, and wasted time of litigating.

■ CASE VOCABULARY

FUTURE [POSITION]: Financial instrument whose value is based on the difference in the price of a commodity today, and in the future. Such instruments are used to hedge (protect) against price swings for needed raw materials, or for speculation. Ex. Say you make corn meal from raw corn, and know you will need 100 tons of corn 6 months from now, for Anna Nicole Smith's birthday breakfast. However, you are afraid that corn prices may rise by that date, making performance expensive. If you bought a future, it would amount to the *right* to buy 100 tons of corn *at today's price* (for a fee). If the price rose, the counterparty on your future would pay you the price difference.

HEDGE: Practice of protecting against price changes in a product which a person is contractually obligated to deliver later. Here, St. Ansgar Mills (P) took corn orders now at fixed prices, but was required to deliver the corn later, when prices might have risen. To hedge (insure), St. Ansgar Mills (P) would buy a "futures position" for that amount of corn at today's price. Thus, if the price rose, the future position would pay St. Ansgar Mills (P) the price difference.

MERCHANT: A professional dealer in a specific good or service. Under the UCC, merchants are often held to stricter standards than amateurs engaged in a rare, unfamiliar business transaction.

STATUTE OF FRAUDS: Rule requiring certain contracts to be in writing to be enforceable, to prevent error and perjury. This rule is now codified in the UCC.

Columbia Nitrogen Corp. v. Royster Co.
(Buyer) v. (Seller)
451 F.2d 3 (4th Cir. 1971)

COURSE OF DEALING AND USAGE OF TRADE ARE ADMISSIBLE TO SUPPLEMENT OR EXPLAIN A CONTRACT IF SUCH EVIDENCE IS CONSISTENT WITH THE EXPRESS TERMS OF THE CONTRACT

■ **INSTANT FACTS** Columbia (D) refused to accept phosphate shipments it had contracted to buy from Royster (P).

■ **BLACK LETTER RULE** Evidence of course of dealing and usage of trade is admissible to explain and supplement an agreement if such evidence is consistent with the express terms of the agreement.

■ **PROCEDURAL BASIS**
Appeal from judgment entered against Columbia (D) on breach of contract action.

■ **FACTS**
Royster (P) is a maker of fertilizers. Columbia (D) is a large producer of nitrogen. For years, Royster (P) had been a major purchaser of Columbia's (D) products, but Columbia (D) had never been a significant customer of Royster (P). However, in 1966 Royster (P) had extra phosphate available that it agreed to sell to Columbia (D). Royster (P) was to sell a minimum of 31,000 tons of phosphate each year for three years to Columbia (D), with an option to extend the term. The price per ton was stated subject to escalation dependent on production costs. When phosphate prices plunged, Columbia (D) ordered only part of the scheduled tonnage. Royster (P) lowered its price for some of the phosphate, but specified that subsequent shipments would be at the original contract price. Columbia (D) ordered less than a tenth of what Royster (P) was to ship the first contract year. Royster (P) eventually sold the product Columbia (D) would not accept at a price substantially below the contract price.

■ **ISSUE**
Can evidence of course of dealing and usage of trade be admitted to supplement or explain a contract if such evidence can be construed as consistent with the contract?

■ **DECISION AND RATIONALE**
(Butzner, J.) Yes. Columbia (D) argues that the district court erred in excluding all evidence on usage of trade and course of dealing between the parties. It offered testimony at trial that because of uncertain weather and other conditions, the price and quantity terms in contracts in the fertilizer industry are mere projections subject to adjustment. Columbia (D) also offered testimony of its past dealings with Royster (P). Royster (P) was generally the buyer in these transactions rather than the seller, and evidence was offered to show that there was often substantial deviation from the contract terms. Columbia (D) asserted that the total variance was more than $500,000 in reduced sales, and that these past experiences were the basis on which the contract was negotiated. The trial court excluded the evidence finding that course of dealing is not admissible to contradict the plain language of a valid contract. Virginia case law provides that extrinsic evidence cannot be used to explain or supplement a written contract absent ambiguity. However, this rule has been changed by the Uniform Commercial Code adopted by Virginia. Section 2–202 authorizes usage of trade and course of dealing between the

Columbia Nitrogen Corp. v. Royster Co. (Continued)

parties to be used to explain or supplement a contract. The official comment states that this section rejects the old rule that such evidence can only be introduced when the contract is ambiguous. We hold that a finding of ambiguity is not required for the admission of extrinsic evidence about usage of trade or course of dealing. Royster (P) claims that the evidence should nevertheless be excluded because it is inconsistent with the express terms of the agreement. The Uniform Commercial Code follows the well established rule that usage of trade and course of dealing should be excluded when it is inconsistent with the terms of the contract. Royster (P) contends that because the contract contains price terms, minimum tonnage, and delivery schedules, it is complete on its face and extrinsic evidence should be excluded. However, § 2-202 expressly allows such evidence to explain or supplement terms intended by the parties as a final expression of the agreement. Section 2-202 along with § 1-205(4) make clear that the test for admissibility is not whether the contract is complete, but whether evidence of course of dealing and usage of trade can be construed as consistent with the express terms of the agreement. The testimony showing that price, quantity, and delivery terms fluctuate to reflect market conditions can be construed as consistent with the express terms of the contract. The contract does not expressly state that course of dealing and usage of trade cannot be used. The contract neither permits nor prohibits adjustment of price and quantity to reflect market conditions. Tonnages and quantities are expressed as "Products Supplied Under Contract" not "Products Purchased Under Contract." The default clause refers only to the failure of the buyer to pay for delivered phosphate. The contract fails to state any consequences of Columbia's (D) refusal to take delivery. Royster (P) asks us to fill in this gap by applying general contract law which permits recovery of damages when a buyer refuses delivery under a contract. This is not what the UCC prescribes. Before damages are allowed, there must first be a default. This must be determined by reference to trade usage and course of dealing. Columbia (D) is seeking only to show a practice of mutual adjustment so prevalent in the industry and in dealings between the parties that it formed a part of the agreement. A clause of the contract states that "[n]o verbal understanding will be recognized by either party..." Royster (P) contends that the testimony should be excluded under this clause. However, § 2-202 draws a distinction between supplementing a contract by consistent additional terms and supplementing it by course of dealing and usage of trade. Evidence of additional terms is excluded when a court finds the writing was intended to be an exclusive statement of the terms of the agreement. No similar exclusion applies to course of dealing or usage of trade. The official comment notes that course of dealing and usage of trade are admissible to supplement the terms of any writing, and that contracts should be read in light of commercial practices and the surrounding circumstances. The judgment against Columbia (D) is set aside.

Analysis:

Course of dealing evidence is allowed, to supplement or explain the language in a writing. Such evidence shows how the parties themselves interpreted their own deal. In this case, the dealings between the parties supposedly showed a history of deviation from the terms of the contract. Royster (P) was the buyer in these transactions rather than the seller. Even though the status of the parties was reversed in these past transactions, they were still admissible and relevant to show what the parties intended in the contract at issue. Columbia (D) also sought to introduce evidence of usage of trade. Generally, a party relying on usage of trade must show that the behavior has such regularity as to justify an expectation that it will be observed in the transaction in question. Unless the contract expressly negates it, there is a presumption that the parties intended to incorporate widespread practices in the trade.

■ CASE VOCABULARY

COURSE OF DEALING: Previous conduct between the parties to a particular transaction which can be regarded as establishing a common basis of understanding for interpreting their expressions and other conduct. See UCC § 1-205(1).

EXTRINSIC EVIDENCE: Facts or evidence outside the face of the document, such as oral statements.

Columbia Nitrogen Corp. v. Royster Co. (Continued)

USAGE OF TRADE: Any practice or method of dealing having such regularity in a vocation or trade as to justify an expectation that it will be observed with respect to the transaction in question. *See* UCC § 1–205(2).

Diamond Fruit Growers, Inc. v. Krack Corp.
(Purchaser) v. (Manufacturer)
794 F.2d 1440 (9th Cir. 1986)

THE ADDITIONAL TERMS CONTAINED IN AN ACCEPTANCE CONDITIONED ON ASSENT TO THE ADDITIONAL TERMS WILL BECOME PART OF THE CONTRACT ONLY IF THE OTHER PARTY GIVES SPECIFIC AND UNEQUIVOCAL ASSENT TO THEM

■ **INSTANT FACTS** Krack (D) manufactured a cooling unit which contained Metal-Matic (D) tubing which broke, damaging Diamond's (P) fruit.

■ **BLACK LETTER RULE** When an acceptance of an offer expressly conditions its acceptance on assent to the additional terms contained therein, the additional terms become part of the contract only if the other party gives specific and unequivocal assent to the additional terms.

■ **PROCEDURAL BASIS**

Appeal from the denial of Metal-Matic's (D) motion for a judgment n.o.v. after a verdict in favor of Diamond (P).

■ **FACTS**

Krack (D) manufactures cooling units that contain steel tubing purchased from Metal-Matic (D) and other suppliers. Krack (D) would send a blanket purchase order to Metal-Matic (D) at the beginning of each year stating how much tubing it would need for the year. Throughout the year when Krack (D) needed tubing, it would send release purchase orders requesting that the tubing be shipped. Metal-Matic (D) would respond with an acknowledgment form and then ship the tubing. Metal-Matic's (D) acknowledgment form disclaimed all liability for consequential damages and limited its liability for defects to a refund of the purchase price or replacement of the tubing. Allen Zver, Krack's (D) purchasing manager, discussed the disclaimer with Robert Van Krevelen, Executive Vice President of Metal-Matic (D). Zver objected to the terms and wanted them changed. Van Krevelen refused to make the changes, and Krack (D) continued to order and pay for tubing. In 1981, Krack (D) sold a cooling unit to Diamond Fruit Growers (P). In 1982, the unit began leaking ammonia from a coil made of steel tubing. Diamond's (P) engineer, Joseph Smith, traced the leak to a small pinhole in the cooling coil. Diamond (P) sued Krack (D) to recover the loss in value of fruit it was forced to move from the storage unit because of the leak. Krack (D) then brought a third-party complaint against Metal-Matic (D) and Van Huffel Tube Corporation (D), another of its tubing suppliers. The jury returned a verdict in favor of Diamond (P) and against Krack (D). It also found that Krack (D) was entitled to thirty percent contribution from Metal-Matic (D).

■ **ISSUE**

Does continued acceptance of and payment for a product amount to assent to additional terms inserted in an acceptance which is conditioned on the other party's assent to the additional terms?

■ **DECISION AND RATIONALE**

(Wiggins, J.) No. Metal-Matic (D) argues that it is not liable to indemnify Krack (D) for part of Diamond's (P) damages because it disclaimed all liability in its contract. Krack (D) claims that under

Diamond Fruit Growers, Inc. v. Krack Corp. (Continued)

UCC § 2–207 the disclaimer did not become part of the contract. The parties here exchanged purchase orders and acknowledgment forms that contained different or additional terms. Section 2–207 provides rules of contract formation in such a situation. It changes the common law's mirror-image rule, where an acceptance that varies the terms of the offer is a counteroffer and operates as a rejection of the original offer. Under § 2–207(1) if the responding form contains a definite expression of acceptance, it is an acceptance. The terms of the responding form that correspond to the offer constitute the contract. Between merchants the additional terms become part of the contract, unless the offer is specifically limited to its terms, the offeror objects to the additional terms, or the additional terms materially alter the terms of the offer. However, if the expression of acceptance expressly conditions acceptance on the offeror's assent to the additional terms, the additional terms do not become part of the contract unless the offeror assents to those terms. If the offeror does not assent and the parties proceed as if they have a contract, the terms of the contract are those on which the parties' forms agree, plus any terms supplied by the UCC. Here, Metal-Matic (D) expressly conditioned its acceptance on Krack's (D) assent to the additional terms contained in its acknowledgment form. Therefore, we must determine whether Krack (D) assented to Metal-Matic's (D) limitation of liability term. Even though a representative of Krack (D) orally objected to the limitations on liability, the parties continued to do business. We must determine what constitutes assent to additional terms for purposes of § 2–207(1). One of the principles underlying this section is neutrality. Neither party should gain an advantage simply because it happened to send the first or last form. The "last shot" rule of the common law has been eliminated. All of the terms on which the parties' forms do not agree drop out, and the UCC supplies the missing terms. This result is fair because the parties could have negotiated a contract and agreed on its terms but failed to do so. Therefore, neither party should get its terms. If we were to accept Metal-Matic's (D) argument that Krack (D) assented to the disclaimer by continuing to accept and pay for tubing, we would be reinstating the common law's last shot rule. For example, assume the parties sent the same forms but in reverse order, and Krack's (D) form stated that Metal-Matic (D) is liable for all consequential damages. If Metal-Matic (D) objected to these terms but continued to ship tubing, Krack's (D) term would become part of the contract. Thus, the result would turn on which party sent the last form. This result is inconsistent with § 2–207 which does away with the last shot rule. In a case like this, the seller is most responsible for introducing ambiguity into the contract. If Metal-Matic (D) truly wanted its additional terms to become part of the contract, it must obtain a specific and unequivocal expression of assent to the additional terms from the buyer. Metal-Matic (D) could have protected itself by not shipping additional tubing until it obtained that assent from Krack (D). Affirmed.

Analysis:

This case demonstrates a classic "battle of the forms" where each side is using its own form contracts. The seller's forms are written to give the seller an advantage, and the buyer's forms are drafted to give the buyer an advantage. The forms naturally diverge. Here, Metal-Matic (D) conditioned its acceptance of Krack's (D) offer on Krack's (D) assent to the additional terms, the disclaimer of liability. Krack (D) never specifically assented to the additional terms, and the parties acted as if there was a contract and continued doing business. Therefore, § 2–207(3) kicks in and provides that the contract consists of the terms on which the writings agree, together with any supplementary terms supplied by the UCC. The forms did not agree on the limitation of liability so that term did not become a part of the contract. However, § 2–207(3) acts as a gap filler to supply additional terms. Could an implied warranty enter the contract through this provision even though the parties did not expressly agree to one? In some cases, the UCC may provide a term nearly identical to one of those rejected. The bottom line seems to be that if a party must have a term, it should bargain with the other party for that term. If a seller such as Metal-Matic (D) needs a term to reduce its liability and it cannot get the other side to agree to it, it will have to buy insurance, raise its prices, or not make the sale.

Bayway Refining Co. v. Oxygenated Marketing and Trading A.G.

(Oil Seller) v. (Oil Buyer)
215 F.3d 219 (2d Cir. 2000)

IN "BATTLE OF THE FORMS," PARTY OPPOSING ADDED TERM MUST PROVE IT INVALID

■ **INSTANT FACTS** When an oil seller's acceptance incorporated, by reference, a document requiring the buyer to pay excise taxes, the buyer refused.

■ **BLACK LETTER RULE** When an acceptance adds a term to the offer, the party challenging the addition must prove the alteration is "material."

■ **PROCEDURAL BASIS**

In contract action, appeal from summary judgment for Bayway (P).

■ **FACTS**

Bayway Refining Co. (P) contracted to sell MTBE-type gasoline to Oxygenated Marketing and Trading, A.G. ("OMT") (D). In the transaction, OMT (D) faxed Bayway (P) an offer letter, saying the letter constituted the entire agreement, and that any objections must be made within 2 days. The next day, Bayway (P) faxed OMT (D) an acceptance, saying the acceptance supersedes any prior negotiations, and saying the offer would incorporate (by reference) Bayway's (P) General Terms document. Bayway's (P) General Terms included a "Tax Clause," providing that the buyer is liable for oil excise taxes. (Federal tax law imposes the tax on the *seller*, by default, but apparently the buyer can avoid liability for the tax by registering with the I.R.S.) Bayway (P) did not send its General Terms with the acceptance. OMT (D) did not read the General Terms, and did not object. When OMT (D) did not pay the excise tax, Bayway (P) paid it ($464K). Bayway (P) then demanded repayment. OMT (D) refused. Bayway (P) sued, claiming OMT (D) was bound by the Tax Clause. OMT (D) defended, claiming it never assumed tax liability. At trial in District Court (on diversity jurisdiction), Bayway (P) moved for summary judgment. The court held for Bayway (P), finding (i) Bayway's (P) failure to include the General Terms with its acceptance was immaterial, because OMT (D) could have asked for it, and (ii) under UCC § 2–207(2) ("battle of the forms" framework), OMT (D) failed to prove that Bayway's (P) Tax Clause altered the contract materially, (iii) partly because "custom and practice" evidence shows gasoline sellers routinely shift the tax liability to buyers. OMT (D) appeals, claiming (i) the Tax Clause was a material alteration, and (ii) the court should not have considered "custom and practice" evidence.

■ **ISSUE**

When an acceptance incorporates, by reference, terms shifting tax liability, does the addition become part of the contract?

■ **DECISION AND RATIONALE**

(Jacobs) Yes. When an acceptance adds a term to the offer, the party challenging the addition must prove the alteration "material." A. This case must be decided under New York law, because Bayway's (P) General Terms' choice of law provision chose it, and OMT (D) agreed. The relevant provision is

Bayway Refining Co. v. Oxygenated Marketing and Trading, A.G. (Continued)

UCC § 2–207. It is undisputed that Bayway's (P) fax is effective as an acceptance, even though it stated additional terms (including the Tax Clause), because it was not made expressly conditional on OMT's (D) assent to the additions. UCC § 207(2). Therefore, under § 2–207(2), any additional terms (i.e., the Tax Clause) is deemed a proposal for an addition to the contract. The parties are both "merchants." Thus, additional proposed terms are presumed to become part of the contract, unless one of the three exceptions in § 2–207(2) applies. 1) Burden of Proof: Here, OMT (D) invokes the exception of "material alteration." § 2–207(2)(b). For this exception, the burden of proof is apportioned by state law. We hold that the party opposing inclusion of additional terms bears the burden of proving the alteration's materiality. This is in line with the general rule of presumptions, and almost all other jurisdictions agree. 2) Materiality: Alterations are "material" if they would "result in "surprise" or "hardship" if incorporated without express awareness by the other party." § 2–207 cmt. 4. Certain alterations are automatically deemed material, as a matter of law. These include: arbitration clauses, waivers of warranties of merchantability or fitness for a particular purpose, and clauses letting sellers cancel upon the buyer's failure to pay any invoice. We find the Tax Clause here is not serious enough to be material per se, because the liability is fixed and discrete, and no protected rights are waived. 3) Surprise: Next, "surprise" has both subjective and objective elements. To prove surprise, parties must prove that it cannot be presumed that a reasonable merchant would have consented to the added term under the circumstances. OMT (D) proved the Tax Clause subjectively surprised its executives. However, OMT (D) offered no evidence to show objectively that a reasonable oil merchant would be surprised; such evidence would usually include prior dealings, prior written confirmations, industry custom, and/or the term's conspicuousness. In fact, Bayway (P) introduced "industry custom" evidence showing such tax clauses are common, and we find this evidence compelling. Further, public policy dictates the excise tax should fall on buyers, because they can best avoid it by registering with the I.R.S. Thus, there was no reasonable surprise here. 4) Hardship: "Hardship" is technically independent of "surprise," but is judged under a high standard, such as "impossibility" or another related excuse doctrine. Courts have usually found hardship when a term creates an prolonged, open-ended liability. OMT's (D) defense—the common complaint that a small business cannot afford a lower profit—is insufficient here. Judgment for Bayway (P) affirmed.

Analysis:

This case presents a well-organized roadmap for how to analyze "battle of the forms" problems on an exam, under UCC § 2–207. Its of reasoning is straightforward. The major addition of this case is allocating the burden of proof to the party challenging the term, which is the majority rule. Note the first prong of § 2–207(1). If the so-called "proviso clause"—"unless acceptance is expressly made conditional on assent to the ... different terms"—is included, then the parties are steered to § 2–207(2). If it is not included, the parties must refer to § 2–207(3). Thus, parties never have to deal with *both* subsection (2) *and* (3).

■ CASE VOCABULARY

"BATTLE OF THE FORMS": Situation where the offer does not match the acceptance perfectly, because each party sends its own form offer and acceptance letter, which have conflicting terms favorable to them. This situation is resolved under the rule of UCC § 2–207(2).

EXCISE TAX: Tax on sale of goods.

INCORPORATION BY REFERENCE: Practice of saying that another, specified document is made a part of the contract, even if the document is not included with the contract.

Leonard Pevar Co. v. Evans Products Co.
(*Buyer*) v. (*Seller*)
524 F.Supp. 546 (D.Del. 1981)

A BUYER DOES NOT ASSENT TO ADDITIONAL OR DIFFERENT TERMS IN A SELLER'S COUNTEROFFER BY SIMPLY ACCEPTING AND PAYING FOR THE GOODS

■ **INSTANT FACTS** Pevar (P) purchased defective plywood from Evans (D) which tried to limit its liability and disclaim most warranties.

■ **BLACK LETTER RULE** A buyer accepting and paying for goods does not constitute assent to additional terms proposed in a seller's counteroffer.

■ **PROCEDURAL BASIS**
Memorandum opinion denying both parties' motions for summary judgment.

■ **FACTS**
Leonard Pevar Co. (P) obtained several price quotations for medium density plywood for its use in constructing buildings. On October 12, 1977 Marc Pevar, Pevar's (P) contract administrator, had a telephone conversation with Kenneth Kruger of Evans (D) to obtain a price quote. Pevar (P) claims that it again called Evans (D) on October 14, ordered plywood, and entered into an oral contract of sale. Pevar (P) then sent a written purchase order for the plywood. In the order, Pevar (P) made no mention of warranties or remedies. A few days later, Evans (D) sent an acknowledgment to Pevar (P) which contained boilerplate language on the reverse side, providing that the contract of sale would be expressly contingent upon Pevar's (P) acceptance of all the terms contained in the document. One of the terms disclaimed warranties and another limited the buyer's remedy by limiting liability if the plywood was defective.

■ **ISSUE**
Does a buyer assent to the additional and different terms in a seller's counteroffer by accepting and paying for the goods?

■ **DECISION AND RATIONALE**
(Latchum, J.) No. Evans (D) argues that if Pevar (P) entered into an oral contract it would be unenforceable because it did not comply with the statute of frauds. Section 2–201(2) of the UCC provides that if there is written confirmation sent to the receiving party without objection within 10 days, then the contract is enforceable. Evan's (D) acknowledgment fails to provide any objection to Pevar's (P) confirmation. The statute of frauds will not bar Pevar (P) from proving the existence of a contract. Section 2–201 applies only when the statute of frauds should bar the existence of a contract. This is no longer at issue here, rather this action involves § 2–207. Section 2–207 eliminates the common law's "mirror image" rule requiring an acceptance or confirmation to be identical to the terms of the original offer. Section 2–207 recognizes that a buyer and seller can enter into a contract by three different methods. First, § 2–207(1) applies where an oral agreement has been reached and then followed by one or more formal memoranda. If the confirmatory writing contains additional terms they are treated as proposals under § 2–207(2) and will become part of the agreement unless they materially alter it. Here, the disclaimer of warranty and limitation of liability terms in Evan's (D) acknowledgment are generally found to materially alter a contract. However, the issue of material alteration depends on the

Leonard Pevar Co. v. Evans Products Co. (Continued)

facts of each case. If the additional terms are found to materially alter the contract, they will not be included in the agreement. If they do not materially alter the contract, the terms will be incorporated into the contract. If the facts show no oral agreement was entered, § 2–207(1) may still apply but in a different manner. The second situation where § 2–207(1) may apply is where there is no oral agreement, but the parties exchange writings that differ in their terms. In such a case, Pevar's (P) purchase order constitutes an offer to purchase. Evan's (D) form contained a proviso stating that its terms would become part of the agreement unless acceptance was made conditional on assent to the additional or different terms. Evans (D) argues that by inserting this proviso its acknowledgment effectively rejected Pevar's (P) offer and became a counteroffer which Pevar (P) accepted by receiving and paying for the goods. Thus, Evans (D) argues, its disclaimer of warranties and limitation of liability are part of the contract. Evans (D) relies on *Roto-Lith v. F.P. Bartlett & Co.* for the proposition that a buyer accepts the terms of the seller's counteroffer by receiving and paying for the goods. *Roto-Lith* reflects the orthodox common law reasoning which the Code and this court reject. The Code disfavors any attempt by one party to impose conditions that would create a surprise or hardship on the other party. Thus, before a counteroffer such as this one is accepted, the counter offeree must expressly assent to the new terms. Accepting and paying for the goods is not express assent, and no contract was created pursuant to § 2–207(1). Section 2–207(3) is the third method by which parties may enter into a contract. This applies when there is no oral or written contract, but the parties act as if there is one. In such a case, the terms of the contact consist of those terms on which the writings agree, together with any supplementary terms incorporated by the UCC. Here, the parties' conduct shows that they recognized the existence of a contract. If this court finds after trial that Pevar (P) and Evans (D) failed to enter an oral agreement, § 2–207(3) will apply. The terms of the contract will be those on which the purchase order and acknowledgment agree, together with the "gap filler" provisions of Article 2. Whether Pevar (P) and Evans (D) entered into an oral contract is an issue of material fact that precludes summary judgment. Both parties' motions for summary judgment are denied.

Analysis:

This case provides a nice summary of the different types of situations that can develop in a § 2–207 "battle of the forms" context. First, there may be an oral contract followed by one or more confirmatory writings. Additional terms in the confirmations are treated as proposals between merchants and become part of the contract unless they materially alter it, or one of the other exceptions in § 2–207(2) applies. When the parties exchange writings with different terms, the additional or different terms in a counteroffer must be expressly assented to by the counter offeree. Acceptance of and payment for the goods is not sufficient. Finally, if there is no written or oral contract, but the parties conduct themselves as if there is, the contact consists of the terms on which the writings agree, together with the "gap filler" provisions of the Code. Finally, note that while § 2–207 addresses contract formation, parties most often ask courts to use § 2–207 to decide the terms of their contract after a dispute arises.

Klocek v. Gateway, Inc.
(*Computer Buyer*) v. (*Seller*)
104 F.Supp.2d 1332 (D.Kan. 2000)

IN SOME STATES, FORMS ENCLOSED WITH PRE-PURCHASED PRODUCTS ARE NOT BINDING

■ **INSTANT FACTS** A computer buyer sued the seller in court, even though the seller included with his purchase a contract requiring arbitration if he kept the computer.

■ **BLACK LETTER RULE** [In some states] an arbitration clause included with a shipped product is not binding merely because the buyer keeps the product.

■ **PROCEDURAL BASIS**
In individual/class contract/warranty action, Gateway's (D) motion to dismiss, in favor of arbitration.

■ **FACTS**
Mr. Klocek (P) mail-ordered a computer from dealer Gateway, Inc. (D). Gateway (D) shipped the computer with a copy of its Standard Terms and Conditions. It came with a (prominent) notice, telling customers, "By keeping your ... computer ... beyond ... 5 ... days after ... delivery, you accept these Terms ...." Among the Terms is an arbitration clause, requiring all disputes to be settled by arbitration, not litigation. Eventually, Klocek (P) sued Gateway (D) (and others, not relevant here), apparently because his computer proved incompatible with his scanner, and Gateway's (D) technical support refused to help. Klocek (P) filed suit for breach of contract and warranty (that the computer is compatible with standard peripherals and internet service), and a class action alleging Gateway (D) induced consumers to buy with false promises of technical support. Klocek (P) filed his suit *in District Court*. Gateway (D) moved to dismiss, claiming the dispute must be resolved through arbitration, because the arbitration clause is binding, and because the Federal Arbitration Act and case law favor enforcement of arbitration agreements. Klocek (P) opposed, apparently claiming the arbitration agreement was unenforceable because Klocek (P) did not assent to its inclusion into the contract, especially since he received the Terms after purchase. (The other motions filed are irrelevant.)

■ **ISSUE**
If a buyer receives an arbitration clause with his product and keeps the product, is he bound to arbitrate?

■ **DECISION AND RATIONALE**
(Vrath) No. Under the relevant states' laws, an arbitration clause included with a shipped product is not binding merely because the buyer keeps the product. If Klocek's (P) claims are subject to arbitration, then dismissal (in favor of arbitration) is appropriate, because the Federal Arbitration Act requires it. The burden of proving arbitrability is on Gateway (D), much like the proof burden for summary judgment; Gateway (D) must present evidence sufficient to demonstrate an enforceable arbitration agreement. If defendant does, then the burden shifts to plaintiff to submit evidence demonstrating genuine issues requiring trial. Before staying or dismissing cases pending arbitration, courts must determine whether parties have a valid, written agreement to arbitrate. In deciding this, courts apply ordinary state law governing contracts' formation; arbitration becomes effective by contractual agree-

Klocek v. Gateway, Inc. (Continued)

ment. If the parties dispute having agreed to arbitrate, then jury trial on such agreement's existence is appropriate if the record reveals genuine issues of material fact regarding the agreement. Here, both states involved [likely the home states of Klocek (P) and Gateway (D)] adopted the UCC, which governs contract formation for goods sales, like this one. The issue is whether the contract should include Gateway's (D) Standard Terms. This is an issue of first impression in Kansas and Missouri courts, which have not decided whether terms received *with* a product become part of the parties' agreement. Other courts' precedent is split. Such cases often turn on whether the parties are deemed to form their contract *before* or *after* the vendor communicated the added terms to the purchaser. Gateway (D) urges us to ignore UCC § 2–207, and instead follow cases holding that, since payment often precedes detailed communications, additional terms included with the product operate as a proposal, which the buyer is deemed to accept by using/keeping the product after having sufficient time to read the terms. We are not persuaded that this approach is the one which state courts should follow. UCC § 2–207 ["battle of forms"] is usually applied in a conflict between *two* forms, but its language does not preclude applying it to only *one* disputed form. ["(1) A definite and seasonable expression of acceptance or a written confirmation ... sent within a reasonable time operates as an acceptance even [if] it states [additional or different terms], unless acceptance is expressly made conditional on assent to the additional ... terms. (2) The additional terms are ... construed as proposals for addition to the contract [if either party is a non-merchant]."]. Literally, § 2–207 applies to any acceptance or confirmation; it does not require two forms. Similarly, its comments provide that it applies "where an agreement has been reached orally ... and is followed by one or both ... parties sending ... memoranda." UCC § 2–207, cmt. 1. Since the relevant state's courts followed this analysis previously, we conclude they would apply it here. While Gateway (D) urges us to follow cases holding the vendor is the offeror and thus controls the offer, this reasoning is unpersuasive. In typical consumer transactions, the purchaser is the offeror, because he orders the product in person or via catalog. Also, here, Gateway (D) offered no evidence proving it the offeror. Thus, under § 2–207, we assume that the Standard Terms constitute either an acceptance or written confirmation. As an acceptance, Gateway's (D) Standard Terms constitute a counter-offer only if Gateway (D) expressly made its acceptance conditional on Klocek's (P) assent to the Standard Terms. Gateway (D) offered no evidence that, at the time of transaction, it told Klocek (P) that the sale was conditional on his assent. Mere delivery by Gateway (D) with the Terms attached was insufficient to communicate to Klocek (P) Gateway's (D) unwillingness to proceed without his assent to the Standard Terms. Since Klocek (P) is not a merchant, additional terms are not binding on him unless he expressly agreed to them. We find Klocek's (P) mere silence, or keeping the goods over 5 days, is insufficient to demonstrate his express agreement to the addition. Gateway's (D) motion to dismiss denied.

Analysis:

This case involves a circuit split, so its holding is not necessarily the law in all states. UCC § 2–207, while usually reserved for a "battle of forms," can also be applied in cases where vendors foist additional terms on unsuspecting buyers, knowing that no buyer has the time or inclination to read them. As adhesion contracts go, arbitration is not particularly onerous for either side, since it is much faster than litigation, and often cheaper. However, big companies favor it because there is no jury, and the arbitrator "judge" is not likely to award punitive damages, so egregious corporate crooks can spare themselves the risk of an outraged jury by sneaking in an arbitration clause.

■ CASE VOCABULARY

ARBITRATION CLAUSE: Contractual terms requiring disputes be sent to arbitration, rather than litigated in court. Arbitration is often lower-cost, because formalities are reduced, especially costly discovery. It is also faster, because arbitration panels do not have crowded dockets.

CLASS ACTION: Lawsuit filed by a single individual on behalf of the entire class (group) of people in similar circumstances. It can be used to get a large verdict where a company wrongs many people, but not seriously enough for any one to go to the trouble and expense of suing.

STAY: Court order freezing litigation, usually to await the final outcome of some trial. Here, staying the case would amount to dismissing it, since it would be sent to arbitration, and decided there.

CHAPTER THREE

Warranties

Moore v. Pro Team Corvette Sales, Inc.
Instant Facts: Pro Team (D) disclaimed all warranties on a car it sold to Moore (P), and Moore (P) later learned that the car had been stolen.

Black Letter Rule: In order to be effective, a disclaimer of the warranty of title must state what title, if any, the seller is transferring, instead of just saying how the seller's liability will be limited.

Shaffer v. Victoria Station, Inc.
Instant Facts: A restaurant patron who had a glass of wine shatter in his hand is suing the restaurant for breach of the implied warranty of merchantability and strict liability.

Black Letter Rule: The implied warranty of merchantability requires that, in order to be merchantable, a good must be adequately contained, packaged, and labeled.

Daniell v. Ford Motor Company
Instant Facts: An automobile purchaser who intentionally locked herself in the trunk of her car sued the manufacturer for breach of implied warranty of merchantability and breach of implied warranty for a particular purpose because the trunk did not have an inside latch.

Black Letter Rule: The Implied Warranty of Merchantability means only that goods will be fit for the purpose for which they are ordinarily used.

Webster v. Blue Ship Tea Room, Inc.
Instant Facts: A woman who choked on a fishbone contained in a bowl of fish chowder served to her in a restaurant, sued the restaurant for breach of implied warranty of merchantability.

Black Letter Rule: The implied warranty of merchantability is not an assurance that a product will be free of defects which may be inherent to certain products.

Bell Sports, Inc. v. Yarusso
Instant Facts: When a motorcyclist fell and was not protected from paralysis by his helmet, he sued the manufacturer for breach of warranty, claiming that the warranty implied greater neck protection.

Black Letter Rule: A product manual's factual affirmations about the product may create an express warranty, which cannot be disclaimed.

Cate v. Dover Corp.
Instant Facts: A transmission repair company which had purchased hydraulic lifts for its shop sued the manufacturer of the lifts for breach of implied warranty of merchantability when the lifts failed to work properly.

Black Letter Rule: There is an implied warranty of merchantability for all contracts for the sale of goods unless there is a statement to the contrary which would be conspicuous to a reasonable person.

Bowdoin v. Showell Growers, Inc.
Instant Facts: A chicken farmer injured by a spray rig sued the manufacturer for breach of the implied warranties of merchantability and fitness for a particular purpose although the manufacturer had disclaimed all such warranties in a manual delivered after the sale of the spray rig.

Black Letter Rule: A post-sale disclaimer of warranties is ineffective as a matter of law.

Rinaldi v. Iomega Corp.

Instant Facts: A disk drive buyer instituted a class action against the manufacturer when the drive erased and destroyed itself, arguing the disclaimer of the implied warranty of merchantability was ineffective because it came inside the packaging (i.e., after the sale).

Black Letter Rule: In Delaware, a disclaimer of the implied warranty of merchantability may be "conspicuous" under UCC § 2–316(2), even if it is located inside the packaging and not readable until after purchase.

Wilson Trading Corp. v. Davis Ferguson, Ltd.

Instant Facts: A seller of yarn, although acknowledging the yarn sold to be defective, nevertheless sued the buyer for payment on the grounds that the buyer had waited too long to complain of the defect.

Black Letter Rule: A freely negotiated term of a contract is nonetheless not enforceable if it serves to deprive the contract of its essential purpose.

Pierce v. Catalina Yachts, Inc.

Instant Facts: A couple bought a defective boat under a limited warranty. When the seller refused to repair the boat for 6 months, the buyers sued for consequential damages.

Black Letter Rule: In some jurisdictions, a limited warranty's bar of consequential damages is unenforceable if (i) the warranty "fails of its essential purpose," and (ii) under the circumstances, enforcing the warranty would be "unconscionable."

Fitl v. Strek

Instant Facts: Fitl (P) purchased a baseball card from Strek (D) in 1995, and in 1997 Fitl (P) learned that the card had been altered and was valueless.

Black Letter Rule: The determination of whether a seller received notification of a defect in goods is a factual question and depends upon whether the policies behind the notice requirement—allowing the seller to correct the defect, prepare for negotiation and litigation, and protect against stale claims—were unfairly prejudiced.

Reed v. City of Chicago

Instant Facts: Reed's (P) son hanged himself with a paper gown issued to him by the Chicago (D) jail, and she claimed a breach of warranty, based on the gown's failure to tear.

Black Letter Rule: An action for breach of warranty may be brought a person who is the intended beneficiary of the warranty, regardless of whether that person is in privity with the maker of the warranty.

East River Steamship Corp. v. Transamerica Deleval, Inc.

Instant Facts: The owner of a supertanker is suing the manufacturer of the supertanker's turbine under a products liability theory for damages caused to the turbine when a ring in the turbine failed.

Black Letter Rule: When a product fails and causes only economic damage or damage to the product itself, the proper remedy is under warranty law, not products liability law.

Ventura v. Ford Motor Corp.

Instant Facts: An automobile purchaser was allowed to sue the dealer and manufacturer for breach of the implied warranty of merchantability even though the dealer had disclaimed any implied warranties and he did not have a direct contract with the manufacturer.

Black Letter Rule: A buyer is not required to buy directly from a manufacturer in order to have privity of contract with the manufacturer.

Colonial Pacific Leasing Corp. v. McNatt Datronic Rental Corp.

Instant Facts: A lessee is attempting to sue the lessor of equipment for breach of the implied warranties of merchantability and fitness for a particular purpose. The lessor has filed countersuit against the lessee seeking payment on the lease.

Black Letter Rule: A supplier's agent may be held liable for breach of the implied warranties of merchantability and fitness for a particular purpose.

Moore v. Pro Team Corvette Sales, Inc.

(*Car Buyer*) v. (*Dealer*)
152 Ohio App.3d 71, 786 N.E.2d 903, 48 UCC Rep. Serv. 2d 528 (2002)

DISCLAIMERS OF THE WARRANTY OF TITLE MUST BE EXPLICIT

■ **INSTANT FACTS** Pro Team (D) disclaimed all warranties on a car it sold to Moore (P), and Moore (P) later learned that the car had been stolen.

■ **BLACK LETTER RULE** In order to be effective, a disclaimer of the warranty of title must state what title, if any, the seller is transferring, instead of just saying how the seller's liability will be limited.

■ **PROCEDURAL BASIS**

Appeal from an order dismissing Moore's (P) claims for breach of warranty.

■ **FACTS**

Moore (P) purchased a 1974 Corvette from Pro Team Corvette Sales (D). The sales agreement provided that the car was being sold "as is," and that all warranties, including the warranty of title, were disclaimed. When Moore (P) attempted to register the car, he learned that it had been reported stolen in Texas, and could not be registered. The car was confiscated and returned to Texas.

Moore (P) brought suit against Pro Team (D), claiming that the warranty disclaimer in the agreement was not sufficient to disclaim the warranty of title. Moore (P) also alleged unjust enrichment, negligence, and violations of the Consumer Sales Protection Act. He moved for summary judgment, claiming that Pro Team's (D) disclaimer was legally insufficient to disclaim the warranty of title, but his motion was denied. Moore (P) voluntarily dismissed all his claims, except for the breach of warranty claim. The trial court dismissed the warranty claims, holding that the language in the sales agreement was sufficiently specific to exclude the warranty of title.

■ **ISSUE**

Was the general disclaimer sufficient to exclude the warranty of title?

■ **DECISION AND RATIONALE**

(Walters, J.) No. In order to be effective, a disclaimer of the warranty of title must state what title, if any, the seller is transferring, instead of just saying how the seller's liability will be limited. While a warranty of title may be excluded, the language that excludes the warranty must give the buyer reason to know that the seller is only selling such title as the seller may possess. The buyer must be told that the disclaimer relates to title to the goods, not just their quality. A disclaimer that only says that the seller's liability will be limited is ineffective. An example of an effective disclaimer would be one that says explicitly that the seller makes no warranty as to title, and that the buyer assumes all risk that the seller does not own the goods. The language of Pro Team's (D) disclaimer is insufficiently specific to disclaim the implied warranty of title. Reversed and remanded.

Moore v. Pro Team Corvette Sales, Inc. (Continued)

Analysis:
The court mentions, briefly, that most buyers would expect a disclaimer of warranty to relate only to warranties of quality, not title. A car buyer—especially a buyer like Moore (P), who probably was buying the Corvette more as a collectible, rather than for transportation—might not think anything of a disclaimer of a warranty of quality. Such disclaimers are routine. On the other hand, a potential buyer may very well pause if a seller tells him or her that there are no promises that the seller has legal title to the goods. This is especially true when the sale is of an item, like a car, whose ownership must be registered and recorded, but that is still frequently stolen and resold.

■ CASE VOCABULARY

SUMMARY JUDGMENT: A judgment granted on a claim about which there is no genuine issue of material fact and upon which the movant is entitled to judgment as a matter of law. This procedural device allows the speedy disposition of a controversy without the need for trial.

UNJUST ENRICHMENT. The retention of a benefit conferred by another, without offering compensation, in circumstances where compensation is reasonably expected; a benefit obtained from another, not intended as a gift and not legally justifiable, for which the beneficiary must make restitution or recompense; the area of law dealing with unjustifiable benefits of this kind.

Shaffer v. Victoria Station, Inc.
(Diner) v. (Restaurant)
91 Wash.2d 295, 588 P.2d 233 (1978)

THE IMPLIED WARRANTY OF MERCHANTABILITY REQUIRES THAT A GOOD BE ADEQUATELY CONTAINED, PACKAGED, AND LABELED

■ **INSTANT FACTS** A restaurant patron who had a glass of wine shatter in his hand is suing the restaurant for breach of the implied warranty of merchantability and strict liability.

■ **BLACK LETTER RULE** The implied warranty of merchantability requires that, in order to be merchantable, a good must be adequately contained, packaged, and labeled.

■ **CASE VOCABULARY**

IMPLIED WARRANTY OF MERCHANTABILITY: Section 2–314 of the UCC provides that, whenever a merchant sells a product, there is an implied warranty that the product will be fit for the ordinary purpose for which such goods are used.

■ **PROCEDURAL BASIS**

Appeal to Washington Supreme Court from Washington Court of Appeals' decision to affirm trial court's decision to grant defendant's motion to dismiss.

■ **FACTS**

Mr. Shaffer (P) ordered a glass of wine at the Victoria Station, a restaurant operated by Victoria Station, Inc. (D) (Victoria) and was injured when the wine glass shattered in his hand. Mr. Shaffer (P) filed suit against Victoria (D) under theories of negligence, breach of implied warranty under the Uniform Commercial Code (UCC), and strict liability under section 402A of the Restatement of Torts. Prior to trial, Mr. Shaffer (P) dropped his claim of negligence for lack of proof but still requested that the trial judge submit his claims of breach of implied warranty and strict liability to the jury. Victoria (D) argued that it could not be held liable under either a theory of breach of implied warranty or strict liability because it was not a merchant with respect to wine glasses and, furthermore, it had not sold a wine glass to Mr. Shaffer (P). The trial court agreed and, accordingly, dismissed the case. On appeal, the Court of Appeals affirmed the trial court's ruling and Mr. Shaffer (P) appealed to the Washington Supreme Court.

■ **ISSUE**

Does the implied warranty of merchantability apply to the packaging in which goods sold are contained as well as the actual goods themselves?

■ **DECISION AND RATIONALE**

(Dolliver, J.) Yes. Section 2–314 of the UCC states, in part, that "a warranty that goods shall be merchantable is implied in a contract for their sale if the seller is a merchant with respect to goods of that kind. Under this section the serving for value of food or drink to be consumed on the premises or elsewhere is a sale." From this section, it is clear that there was an implied warranty of merchantability for the wine Victoria (D) sold to Mr. Shaffer (P). Victoria (D) argues that even if the wine itself is covered

Shaffer v. Victoria Station, Inc. (Continued)

by the UCC, Victoria (D) did not extend an implied warranty of merchantability to the wine glass because it is not a merchant with respect to wine glasses. This argument, however, misses the point because Section 2-312 further states that, in order to be merchantable, goods must be "adequately contained, packaged, and labeled as the agreement may require." Victoria (D) does not need to be a merchant of wine glasses in order for the UCC to apply. The implied warranty of merchantability extends to the glass because the wine necessarily had to be served in a glass or some other container. Under Section 2-312 of the UCC, the container, or glass in this case, must be *adequate*. Of additional help in resolving this issue is Section 1-103 of the UCC which provides that, unless displaced by a particular provision of the UCC, principles of law and equity shall be used to supplement the code and to resolve any questions of law. Turning to case law then, we find situations where plaintiffs have subscribed to services which deliver milk or mineral water and have then been injured when the bottles containing these products failed. Although the plaintiffs had purchased only the product in the bottles and not the bottles themselves, courts in those cases held that an implied warranty of merchantability extended to not only goods actually bought under a contract but also to goods *supplied* under a contract of sale. In this instance, Victoria (D) supplied the wine glass under a contract for sale of wine. It is clear to us then that, both under the plain language of Section 2-312 and under principles of case law, Mr. Shaffer (P) has stated a cause of action under a theory of breach of an implied warranty. We also hold that Mr. Shaffer (P) stated a cause of action under a theory of strict liability. Businesses engaged in the selling of a product may be held strictly liable (liable without a showing of negligence) when that product fails and causes injury. Strict liability extends beyond the core product and applies to all integral aspects of a sale including packaging so that when the packaging itself is dangerous, the product will be considered to have been sold in a dangerous condition. In this case, Mr. Shaffer (P) has stated a cause of action under a theory of strict liability because he alleges that the glass was defective. This cause will be remanded for trial. The Court of Appeals is reversed.

Analysis:

In this case, the Washington Supreme Court applies UCC § 2-314 as well as case law to directly refute Victoria's (D) argument that there was no implied warranty of merchantability for the wine glass. Looking at the UCC, it is rather difficult to imagine how the lower court found otherwise. Section 2-314, which covers implied warranties, clearly states that it applies to restaurants and that, in order to be merchantable, a good must be adequately packaged. In dismissing Mr. Shaffer's (P) suit for failure to state a claim under the UCC, it seems that the lower court overlooked because it was concerned with the potential of opening a floodgate of litigation should it rule in Mr. Shaffer's (P) favor. The supreme court rejected the lower court's concerns, stating that it would deal with future litigation as it came. Under the facts of this case, the court correctly found that Mr. Shaffer (P) had effectively stated a cause of action under both a theory of breach of implied warranty of merchantability and strict liability.

■ CASE VOCABULARY

SUMMARY JUDGMENT: A court's decision to dismiss a case due to there being no material facts in dispute and the facts, as alleged, do not establish a prima facie cause of action.

Daniell v. Ford Motor Company.
(*Auto Purchaser*) v. (*Auto Seller*)
581 F.Supp 728, 38 UCC Rep. Serv. 464 (D.N.M. 1984)

AN IMPLIED WARRANTY OF MERCHANTABILITY DOES NOT EXTEND BEYOND THE ORDINARY PURPOSE FOR WHICH A GOOD IS USED

■ **INSTANT FACTS** An automobile purchaser who intentionally locked herself in the trunk of her car sued the manufacturer for breach of implied warranty of merchantability and breach of implied warranty for a particular purpose because the trunk did not have an inside latch.

■ **BLACK LETTER RULE** The implied warranty of merchantability means only that goods will be fit for the purpose for which they are ordinarily used.

■ **PROCEDURAL BASIS**
Ford filed a motion for summary judgment directly to the United States District Court for New Mexico.

■ **FACTS**
Ms. Daniell (P) decided to commit suicide by locking herself in the trunk of her 1973 Ford LTD. After she had locked herself in the trunk, she decided that she no longer wanted to die. When she tried to release herself however, she found that the car did not have a mechanism which would allow her to open the trunk from within. She remained in the car's trunk for nine days before someone let her out and as a result she suffered considerable psychological and physical injury. Ms. Daniell (P) sued Ford Motor Company (D) (Ford) under theories of strict liability, negligence, and breach of express warranty and implied warranties of merchantability and fitness for a particular purpose. Ford (D) filed a motion for summary judgment under all three theories which was granted by the United States District Court of Appeals for New Mexico.

■ **ISSUE**
Is there an implied warranty of merchantability and implied warranty of fitness for a particular purpose when a buyer uses the product for something other than its ordinary purpose.

■ **DECISION AND RATIONALE**
(Baldock, J.) No. Section 2–314 of the Uniform Commercial Code (UCC) states, in part, that a merchant of goods issues an implied warranty that goods sold are "fit for the ordinary purpose for which goods are used." The usual and ordinary purpose of an automobile trunk is to transport and store goods. Ms. Daniell (P) did not sufficiently state a claim that Ford (D) breached the implied warranty of merchantability because her use of the trunk was not ordinary but, rather, highly extraordinary. Furthermore, Ms. Daniell (P) has offered no evidence that the trunk was not fit for the ordinary purpose for which it was intended which is, as noted, the transport and storage of goods. Similarly, Ms. Daniell's (P) claim that Ford (D) breached an implied warranty of fitness for a particular purpose also fails. Section 2–315 of the UCC states that when a seller knows that the buyer intends to use a product for a particular purpose and the buyer is relying on the seller's skill or judgment, the seller implicitly warranties that the product will be fit for such purpose. Here, Ford (D) had no reason to expect that Ms. Daniell (P) would climb into the car's trunk and it therefore could not have, implicitly or

Daniell v. Ford Motor Company. (Continued)

otherwise, issued a warranty that the car would be fit for that purpose. Ms. Daniell (P) herself acknowledged in her deposition that, at the time she purchased the car, she did not contemplate crawling into the car's trunk. She could not under the circumstances have relied on any implied warranty of fitness for a purpose she herself did not anticipate the car would be used. Simply put, a buyer cannot intentionally misuse a product as Ms. Daniell (P) did here, and then expect the seller to be held liable for her misconduct. Because there has been no allegation that the vehicle was not fit for the ordinary purpose for which it was sold, Ford's (D) motion for summary judgment on the claim of breach of implied warranty is granted. Likewise, because Ms. Daniell (P) does not claim that she relied on any promise from Ford (D), implied or otherwise, that the car would be fit for the purpose for which she eventually used it, she has failed to state a claim for breach of implied warranty of fitness for a particular purpose and Ford (D) is accordingly granted summary judgment under that theory as well. Defendant's motion for summary judgment is granted.

Analysis:

The Court in this case seems to put a great deal of emphasis on the fact that Ms. Daniell (P) intentionally misused Ford's (D) product and that she should therefore not be allowed to recover. The court finds that Ford (D) did not breach the implied warranty of merchantability when it failed to put a latch inside the car's trunk because, when used for ordinary purposes, a car's trunk does not require an inside latch. Similarly, the court finds that Ford (D) did not breach an implied warranty of fitness for a particular purpose because Ford (D) could not have expected that Ms. Daniell (P) would use the car's trunk as she did. At first glance, the court's rationale seems perfectly reasonable, as does the result; denying relief to a person who intentionally misuses a product as Ms. Daniell (P) did in this case seems perfectly proper. The court's rationale does not appear to be quite as sensible however when one considers that it would also serve to deny relief to a three-year-old child accidentally locked in the car's trunk. Clearly, a person who buys a car relies upon the seller's implied assurance that the car is safe.

■ **CASE VOCABULARY**

SUMMARY JUDGMENT: A court's decision to dismiss a case due to there being no material facts in dispute and the facts, as alleged, do not establish a prima facie cause of action.

Webster v. Blue Ship Tea Room, Inc.

(*Customer*) v. (*Restaurant*)
347 Mass. 421, 198 N.E.2d 309 (Sup.Judicial Ct. 1964)

IMPERFECTIONS WHICH ARE INHERENT IN A PRODUCT WILL NOT RENDER THE PRODUCT UNMERCHANTABLE OR UNFIT FOR A PARTICULAR PURPOSE

■ **INSTANT FACTS** A woman who choked on a fishbone contained in a bowl of fish chowder served to her in a restaurant sued the restaurant for breach of implied warranty of merchantability.

■ **BLACK LETTER RULE** The implied warranty of merchantability is not an assurance that a product will be free of defects which may be inherent to certain products.

■ **PROCEDURAL BASIS**

Appeal from trial court's refusal to direct a verdict in favor of the defendant.

■ **FACTS**

Ms. Webster (P), a native New Englander, ordered a bowl of fish chowder at the Blue Ship Tearoom, a quaint Boston restaurant owned by Blue Ship Tearoom, Inc. (D) (Blue Ship). Blue Ship (D) promptly served Ms. Webster (P) a hot and hearty bowl of chunky fish chowder. Ms. Webster (P) stirred the fish chowder a bit to cool it down and then proceeded to eat. No sooner had she taken four spoonfuls, however, when she began to choke on a fishbone which had lodged in her throat. Ms. Webster (P) was quickly transported to Massachusetts General where doctors had to perform two esophagoscopies in order to remove the bone. Ms. Webster (P) sued Blue Tea (D) for damages, alleging that Blue Tea (D) had breached an implied warranty of merchantability when it served her fish chowder with bones in it. The case was first submitted to an auditor who found for Ms. Webster (P). The case was then tried before a judge and jury, and the jury also returned a verdict in Ms. Webster's (P) favor. Blue Tea (D) appealed the jury verdict, claiming that the trial court had erred in three ways: (1) by refusing to strike certain portions of the auditor's report, (2) by refusing to direct a verdict in Blue Tea's (D) favor, and (3) by denying Blue Tea's (D) motion for a verdict in its favor under leave reserved.

■ **ISSUE**

Is the implied warranty of merchantability meant to assure the consumer that a product will be free of all imperfections?

■ **DECISION AND RATIONALE**

(Reardon, J.) No. Certain hazards or imperfections, such as fish bones in a chunky fish chowder, are inherent in some products. The implied warranties of merchantability and fitness of the Uniform Commercial Code (UCC) are not meant to assure a consumer that a product will be free of hazards or imperfections which the consumer should reasonably anticipate. Here, Ms. Webster (P) is a native New Englander who is presumably accustomed to eating fish chowder and, specifically, the hearty variety of this region. It is well known that New England chowders are not thin, watered-down broths of the sort served to hospital convalescents. Rather, our chowders are thick and chunky and full of natural ingredients which have not been rendered into insipid simulacrums of their former selves through factory processing. A New England restaurant patron who orders genuine New England fish chowder

Webster v. Blue Ship Tea Room, Inc. (Continued)

in a quaint Boston restaurant, as Ms. Webster (P) did here, should be prepared to cope with the hazards of fish bones, the occasional presence of which in chowders is, it seems to us, to be anticipated. This case is clearly distinguishable from a case where a restaurant has served an unwholesome dish, such as one containing spoiled fish, or one containing a foreign substance. A person who sits down to consume a good New England fish chowder embarks on a gustatory adventure which may entail the removal of some fish bones from his bowl as he proceeds. The UCC provisions which address implied warranties and which we do not need to cite here [easy for the court to say] are not meant to render products perfect. Blue Tea (D) served a fish chowder which conformed to the recipes and traditions of this region and Ms. Webster (P) should well have anticipated finding a fish bone in such a fish chowder. This court will not interpret the UCC to deprive citizens of one of the joys of life in New England: the ready availability of fresh fish chowder. Judgment for Blue Tea (D).

Analysis:

UCC § 2–314 focuses on the quality of the product itself where UCC § 2–315 places greater emphasis on the knowledge and expectations of the buyer and the seller. It seems in this case that the court concluded that Blue Tea (D) did not breach the implied warranty of merchantability under UCC § 2–314 because the chowder it served, bone and all, conformed with historical standards for fish chowder. The court seems to further conclude that Blue Tea (D) did not breach the implied warranty of fitness for a particular purpose under UCC § 2–315 because, as a New England Native, Ms. Webster (P) could not have reasonably relied on any implied assertion from Blue Tea (D) that the chowder would be bone-free. It seems possible then, following the court's logic, that if Blue Tea (D) had served the same bowl of perfectly merchantable chowder to a person not from New England, it may well have breached the implied warranty of fitness for a particular purpose.

■ CASE VOCABULARY

IMPLIED WARRANTY OF FITNESS FOR A PARTICULAR PURPOSE: Section 2–315 of the Uniform Commercial Code provides that when a seller knows that a buyer plans to use a product for a particular purpose and also knows that the buyer is relying on the seller's judgment to furnish a product suitable for the buyer's needs, there is an implied warranty that the product sold will be fit for the buyer's purpose.

Bell Sports, Inc. v. Yarusso
(Helmet Manufacturer) v. (Helmet Buyer)
759 A.2d 582 (Del. 2000)

PRODUCT DESCRIPTIONS OR MANUALS MAY CREATE AN EXPRESS WARRANTY

■ **INSTANT FACTS** When a motorcyclist fell and was not protected from paralysis by his helmet, he sued the manufacturer for breach of warranty, claiming that the warranty implied greater neck protection.

■ **BLACK LETTER RULE** A product manual's factual affirmations about the product may create an express warranty, which cannot be disclaimed.

■ **PROCEDURAL BASIS**

In action for negligent product design/construction and breach of warranty (merchantability and fitness for particular purpose), following verdict for Yarusso (P), appeal.

■ **FACTS**

Motorcyclist Yarusso (P) was paralyzed when his off-road cycle hit a dirt mogul (bump) and he fell headfirst, crushing a vertebra. At the time, Yarusso (P) wore a special helmet, the Bell Moto-5, made by Bell Sports, Inc. (D). Bell's (D) helmet was designed for off-road use, met federal safety standards, and was certified safe by a leading lab. Bell's (D) helmet includes a plastic liner designed to crush on impact, thus reducing the impact passed on to the head and neck. Bell (D) included a manual with its helmet, which said, "Any Bell helmet found . . . to be defective in materials or workmanship within five years . . . will be repaired or replaced . . . . This warranty is expressly in lieu of all other warranties, and any implied warranties of merchantability or fitness for a particular purpose . . . are limited in duration to [5 years]. . . . Introduction: Your new . . . helmet is another in the long line of innovative off-road helmets . . . [T]he primary function of a helmet is to reduce the harmful effect of a blow to the head. However, . . . recognize . . . that . . . wearing . . . a helmet is not an assurance of absolute protection. NO HELMET CAN PROTECT THE WEARER AGAINST ALL FORESEEABLE IMPACTS. Helmet Performance: The Moto-5 is designed to absorb the force of a blow first by spreading it over as wide an area . . . as possible, and second by the crushing of the inner liner." Yarusso's (P) complaint alleged, alternately, that (A) the helmet was negligently designed and constructed, because it did not crumple enough to reduce impact to the spine, (B) breach of express warranty, because he purchased the helmet based on the manual's specific assertions that it would "reduce the harmful effects of a blow to the head," [Not likely, unless he read the manual before buying.], and/or (C) breach of implied warranty of warrantability, because the helmet was sold as "off-road" (i.e., designed for impact on dirt) but was actually more suited to on-road use (i.e., impact on pavement). A pivotal issue was whether the helmet crushed properly. Yarusso's (P) expert witnesses testified that the lining was too dense and did not compact itself enough to avoid transferring excess force to Yarusso's (P) spine. [When one of Yarusso's (P) witnesses altered his testimony slightly, Bell (D) moved for mistrial, and apparently challenged his qualifications. The judge denied Bell's (D) motion, allowing the testimony to proceed through cross-examination.] Bell's (D) experts testified that the helmet was designed properly by being reasonably compatible with all terrain types, and worked properly, but that no helmet can offer much neck protection. After discovery, Bell (D) moved for summary judgement. The court granted Bell (D) summary judgement on the claim of suitability for particular purpose, but not the rest, which were

Bell Sports, Inc. v. Yarusso (Continued)

charged to the jury. [During deliberations, one juror was dismissed for doing outside research. Due to this, Bell (D) moved for mistrial, unsuccessfully.] Finally, the jury found that Bell (D) was not negligent in designing or manufacturing the helmet, but that it had breached some express *and/or* implied warranty, and awarded Yarusso (P) $1.8M. Bell (D) appeals, demanding summary judgement or retrial, contending (i) the jury's verdict—non-negligent but in breach of warranty—was inconsistent, and (ii) there was no warranty.

■ ISSUE

Can a warranty be created by statements in a product manual?

■ DECISION AND RATIONALE

(Walsh) Yes. A product manual's factual affirmations about the product may create an express warranty, which cannot be disclaimed. III. Preliminarily, the jury is permitted to find liability under alternative forms of breach of warranty—express and/or implied, without differentiating them, because Bell (D) never objected to charging the jury thus. IIIA. When an express warranty is breached in a sale of goods, damages are allowed, under [UCC § 2-313]. The UCC's commentary reveals its drafters intended its warranty protections to be applied liberally to protect buyers. See UCC § 2-313 cmt. 1, 3, 4. Analogously, this policy is applicable to state versions of the UCC. Warranties can be created without formal wording, or even the seller's specific intention. Other jurisdictions hold that express warranties can arise from owners' manuals and similar textual representations, even where not specifically labeled as such. Here, Bell's (D) manual created a warranty, because it contained textual representations constituting affirmations of fact, upon which buyers are entitled to rely ("[T]he primary function of a helmet is to reduce the harmful effect of a blow to the head...." and "the [helmet] is designed to absorb the force of a blow by spreading it over as wide an area of the outer shell as possible ...."). Bell (D) may not disclaim this express warranty nor limit it to 5 years, as a matter of law under UCC § 2-316(1). While the manual contains disclaimers that helmets cannot prevent all injuries, other representations assure buyers that the helmet's liner was designed to reduce impact; those representations constituted essential elements of an express warranty, which cannot be disclaimed. Bell (D) argues this warranty was not breached, because the manual promised to protect only the head, not the neck, and the helmet did so. However, we find the jury's finding of breach had a factual predicate, since the jury could have logically concluded the warranties include protecting both the head and neck. IIIB. Our decision in Part IIIA makes it unnecessary to consider Bell's (D) claims on implied warranty (that Yarusso (P), to prove his implied warranty claim, was obligated to present evidence of a safer alternative design, as a matter of law.) We note that Yarusso's (P) experts presented evidence that helmets could be designed with a softer lining, which theoretically would reduce impact, so this was sufficient factual predicate for submitting the implied warranty claim to the jury. IV. Next, Bell (D) argues the jury's finding—that Bell (D) was not negligent, but breached express and/or implied warranties—is inconsistent, because its helmet was not defective. Claims for breach of warranty, express or implied, are conceptually distinct from negligence claims; negligence focuses on the manufacturer's conduct, while breach of warranty evaluates the product itself. Thus, the jury's verdict was not inconsistent. Judgement affirmed.

Analysis:

Once express warranties are made, they are almost impossible to disclaim, by operation of UCC § 2-316(1). This rule is obvious from the statute. More interesting legally is how easy it is to unintentionally created a warranty based on any writing, especially a product description in an owner's manual. Here, the manual passages which the court found to create a warranty are actually rather unspecific, saying basically that helmets in general are designed to prevent head injuries, and that this one crumples to reduce impact (which it did, though maybe not enough). When drafting a manual, it may be best to keep representations to a minimum, especially since the manual does not induce buyers to buy.

Cate v. Dover Corp.

(Mechanic) v. *(Manufacturer)*
790 S.W.2d 559 (Tex. 1990)

AN IMPLIED WARRANTY OF MERCHANTABILITY APPLIES TO ALL CONTRACTS FOR THE SALE OF GOODS UNLESS THERE IS A STATEMENT TO THE CONTRARY WHICH WOULD BE CONSPICUOUS TO A REASONABLE PERSON

■ **INSTANT FACTS** A transmission repair company which had purchased hydraulic lifts for its shop sued the manufacturer of the lifts for breach of implied warranty of merchantability when the lifts failed to work properly.

■ **BLACK LETTER RULE** There is an implied warranty of merchantability for all contracts for the sale of goods unless there is a statement to the contrary which would be conspicuous to a reasonable person.

■ **PROCEDURAL BASIS**
Appeal to the Texas Supreme Court from trial court's summary judgment in favor of Dover Corp. (D).

■ **FACTS**
Edward Cate (Cate) (P), the owner of Cate's Transmission Service, bought three lifts from Beech Tire Mart. The lifts were manufactured by Dover Corp. (Dover) (D) and were to be used in Cate's (P) shop for the purpose of elevating vehicles brought in for repair. In spite of several efforts at repair made by Beech and Dover (D), however, the lifts never functioned properly. Cate (P) sued Dover (D) for breach of implied warranty of merchantability. Dover filed a motion for summary judgement claiming that it had expressly disclaimed all implied warranties of merchantability in writing contained in an express warranty it had provided to Cate (P). Dover (D) further claimed that, in addition to written notice, there was no implied warranty of merchantability for the lifts and Cate (P) had actual knowledge that there was no implied warranty of merchantability. The trial court granted Dover's (D) motion for summary judgement, and Cate (P) appealed to the Texas Supreme Court.

■ **ISSUE**
Does an implied warranty of merchantability arise in a contract for the sale of goods unless such warranty is expressly excluded by conspicuous language?

■ **DECISION AND RATIONALE**
(Dogget, J.) Yes. Section 2–314 of the Uniform Commercial Code (UCC) as adopted by Texas states that there arises in all contracts for the sale of goods an implied warranty of merchantability. Section 2–316 of the UCC provides that the implied warranty of merchantability may only be disclaimed by conspicuous language. The only instance when the requirement of conspicuous disclaimer language may be overlooked is when it can be shown that the seller brought otherwise inconspicuous language to the buyer's attention or that the buyer had actual knowledge that the implied warranty of merchantability would not apply to the sale. In the case at bar, Dover (D) claims that the trial court properly granted its motion to dismiss because Dover (D) expressly disclaimed all implied warranties of merchantability in conspicuous language contained in a warranty agreement provided to Cate (P). Dover (D) further claims that the disclaimer language in the warranty agreement was particularly

Cate v. Dover Corp. (Continued)

conspicuous as applied to Cate (P), because Cate (P) is a merchant who regularly makes transactions of the type seen in this case. In any event, Dover (D) claims that the issue of conspicuousness is moot as applied to this case, because Cate (P) had actual knowledge of the disclaimer of the implied warranty of merchantability. None of these arguments persuade us that a summary judgment was proper in this case. First, addressing the issue of conspicuousness, we look to the warranty agreement which Dover (D) provided Cate (P) in this case. The warranty prominently extols its virtues in large bold-faced type at the top of the agreement. Further down the agreement, in smaller type which is in no way distinguished from any other part of the agreement, Dover (D) inserted language which disclaimed any implied warranties of merchantability. This disclaimer language was, by definition, not conspicuous because there is nothing to distinguish it from any other language in the agreement. We further find that Dover's (D) claim that a lesser standard of conspicuousness should apply in this case because Cate (P) is a merchant is without merit. The commentary to the UCC as adopted in Texas clearly contemplates that an objective standard is to be applied to the question of conspicuousness; the fact that Cate (P) is a merchant is therefore irrelevant. Finally, we reject Dover's (D) argument that summary judgment was properly granted because Cate (P) had actual knowledge of the disclaimer. While the UCC seems to recognize that actual knowledge of a disclaimer overrides the question of conspicuousness, it remains that the issue of knowledge is a question of material fact to be determined by a jury. Summary judgment is only proper when no material issues of fact are in dispute and the facts, as alleged, do not establish a legal claim. In this case it is clear that the material issues of conspicuousness and knowledge are both in dispute. Reversed and remanded.

■ CONCURRENCE

(Spears, J.) While I concur with the majority's opinion and its reasoning, I write to encourage the legislature to repeal UCC 2–316 and thereby prohibit all disclaimers of the implied warranty of merchantability. The rationale for permitting disclaimers of the implied warranty of merchantability is the belief that parties to a contract should be allowed to bargain for and set terms of a contract as they see fit. This position however rests on the premise that contractual disclaimers are generally freely bargained for elements of a contract; this premise simply does not comport with the realities of the modern market place. The truth is that the majority of contracts entered into in the modern market place are form contracts, the terms of which are not subject to negotiation. It is indeed very difficult to imagine a situation where parties would freely negotiate a contractual term which expressly disclaims the merchantability of a product. In addition to protecting the consumer, implied warranties of merchantability serve to promote the production of higher quality products and to place responsibility for faulty products on those who profit from their sale. To allow merchants to undermine the policy considerations underlying the implied warranty of merchantability by simply placing conspicuous disclaimer language in a form contract is unconscionable. Accordingly, UCC 2–316 should be repealed and disclaimers of the implied warranty of merchantability should be declared void as against public policy.

■ DISSENT

(Ray, J.) I concur with the portion of the majority's opinion which concludes that, in order to be effective, a disclaimer of the implied warranty of merchantability must be conspicuous to a reasonable person. I take exception, however, with the majority's conclusion that a showing of actual knowledge of a disclaimer may override the need for a conspicuous disclaimer. There is no language in the UCC which would support such a conclusion and I would hold that the extent of a buyer's knowledge of a disclaimer is irrelevant to a determination of its enforceability under the UCC. An absolute rule that an inconspicuous disclaimer is invalid, regardless of a buyer's actual knowledge, will encourage sellers to make their disclaimers conspicuous and will also save our courts from the burden of having to determine the issue of whether a buyer had actual knowledge. The majority's decision condemns our court to a parade of such cases.

Analysis:

The court states here, that knowledge that the implied warranty of merchantability has been disclaimed may result from a buyer's prior dealings with a seller or by a seller specifically bringing an inconspicuous waiver to a buyer's attention. The UCC does not specifically require a written waiver; an oral disclaimer may be effective under some circumstances. Seemingly, then, a seller could effectively disclaim the implied warranty of merchantability by simply declaring orally to a buyer that the warranty does not apply. But, such a rule, would be contrary to the UCC as well as to general principles of contract law. A more reasonable interpretation of the court's decision as well as the UCC would require a seller to, at minimum, put all disclaimers in writing. The question would still remain however, at what point, if any, a disclaimer of the implied warranty of merchantability becomes so inconspicuous that the disclaimer will be considered ineffective, even if it can be shown that a buyer had actual knowledge.

■ CASE VOCABULARY

DISCLAIMER: Denial of a right of another; denial or disavowal of legal claim; Section 2-316 of the Uniform Commercial Code provides that unless there are reasons to believe that a buyer was aware that no implied warranty attached to a product, a merchant must may effectively disclaim an implied warranty only through a conspicuous, written disclaimer.

Bowdoin v. Showell Growers, Inc.

(Chicken Farmer) v. (Manufacturer)
817 F.2d 1543 (11th Cir. 1987)

A DISCLAIMER OF THE IMPLIED WARRANTIES OF MERCHANTABILITY AND FITNESS FOR A PARTICULAR PURPOSE WHICH IS NOT MADE UNTIL AFTER A SALE IS COMPLETE IS INEFFECTIVE AS A MATTER OF LAW

■ **INSTANT FACTS** A chicken farmer injured by a spray rig sued the manufacturer for breach of the implied warranties of merchantability and fitness for a particular purpose although the manufacturer had disclaimed all such warranties in a manual delivered after the sale of the spray rig.

■ **BLACK LETTER RULE** A post-sale disclaimer of warranties is ineffective as a matter of law.

■ **PROCEDURAL BASIS**

Appeal to United States Court of Appeal for the Eleventh Circuit of District Court's decision to grant summary judgment in favor of FMC (D).

■ **FACTS**

Mrs. Bowdoin (P), an Alabama chicken farmer, was severely injured when she was sucked into the intake shaft of a high pressure spray rig which had been supplied to her by her employer, Showell Grower's Inc (Showell) (D), for the purpose of cleaning her chicken house. Showell (D) had purchased the spray rig from its manufacturer, FMC Corporation (FMC) (D) and the safety shield and drive shaft components of the spray rig which had most directly contributed to Mrs. Bowdoin's (P) injuries were supplied to FMC (D) by NEAPCO, Inc. (D). Mrs. Bowdoin (P) filed suit against Showell (D), FMC (D) and NEAPCO (D) alleging, among other things, that FMC (D) and NEAPCO (D) had breached the implied warranties of merchantability and fitness for a particular purpose. The U.S. District Court dismissed Mrs. Bowdoin's (P) implied warranties claims finding that FMC (D) and NEAPCO (D) had effectively disclaimed all implied warranties for the spray rig. When it delivered the spray rig to Showell (D), FMC (D) had also provided Showell (D) with a manual which contained a written disclaimer of all implied warranties. The U.S. Court of Appeals reversed finding that the disclaimer in the manual was not effective because FMC (D) had not provided it to Showell (D) at the time of the sale but rather, two weeks after the sale when it delivered the spray rig. The court concluded that a disclaimer made after a deal has been struck is not part of the basis for a bargain and is consequently ineffective.

■ **ISSUE**

Can a post-sale disclaimer effectively disclaim or modify the implied warranties of merchantability or fitness for a particular purpose?

■ **DECISION AND RATIONALE**

(Wisdom, J.) No. In order to be effective, a disclaimer of the implied warranties of merchantability and fitness must be part of the basis of any bargain struck. In this case, FMC (D) did not provide a written disclaimer of the implied warranties of merchantability and fitness until actually delivering the spray rig. The problem is that FMC (D) did not deliver the spray rig to Showell (D) until two weeks after the two had struck the bargain for the sale of the rig. (Note: Although Showell is styled as the defendant in this

Bowdoin v. Showell Growers, Inc. (Continued)

case, the opinion treats Showell as if it is standing in the place of Mrs. Bowdoin, the plaintiff. FMC (D) is a defendant) The fact that FMC (D) did not provide Showell (D) with the disclaimer until two weeks after the sale renders the disclaimer ineffective as a matter of law. By definition, a disclaimer that appears for the first time after a sale has been consummated is not a part of the basis of the bargain and is consequently not binding on the buyer. Thus, Showell (D) is not bound by a disclaimer to which it had never agreed at the time of the sale and of which it learned for the first time when it received FMC's (D) manual. FMC (D) argues that the post-sale disclaimer is effective as applied to Showell (D) because Showell (D) is a sophisticated commercial enterprise which the court should regard in a different light than it would an individual consumer. Case law and, indeed common sense, however, indicate that whether a buyer is an individual or a corporation is a distinction without a difference; a post-sale disclaimer is ineffective against any party. Furthermore, we are not persuaded by FMC's (D) assertion that the post-sale disclaimer was effective because it was conspicuous. The fact is that no reasonable person against whom the disclaimer was to operate could have noticed the disclaimer before the consummation of the transaction for the simple reason that FMC (D) did not disclose the disclaimer until after the transaction took place. Finally, FMC (D) argues that its prior dealings with Showell (D) put Showell (D) on notice that FMC's (D) practice was to disclaim implied warranties with respect to high pressure spray rigs. The fact that Showell (D) had previously purchased a spray rig and received a disclaimer from FMC (D), however, is immaterial. We repeat: A disclaimer must be conspicuous before the sale in order to be effective, for only then will the law presume that the disclaimer was part of the bargain. The fact that Showell (D) had received earlier disclaimers on other spray rigs is therefore without significance. The decision of the district court is therefore reversed.

Analysis:

UCC § 2–316 provides that, in order to modify or disclaim the implied warranties of fitness, a disclaimer must be conspicuous. Applying the rule of UCC § 2–316 to the facts before it, the court here found that FMC (D) had not effectively disclaimed any implied warranties on the spray rig. As the court stated, a post-sale disclaimer is by definition not conspicuous because the disclaimer does not exist at the time of sale. The court rightly rejected FMC's (D) argument that the sophisticatoin of the buyer makes a difference. Whether the buyer is an individual or a sophisticated corporate dealer makes no difference on the issue of conspicuousness—no buyer could be aware of a disclaimer that is not disclosed until a sale takes place. But consider the possible scenario in which a disclaimer is not provided until after a sale, yet by virtue of the parties' course of dealing, the court is able to find that the implied warranties of merchantability and fitness had nonetheless been disclaimed.

Rinaldi v. Iomega Corp.
(*Computer Hardware Buyer, as Class*) v. (*Seller*)
41 UCC Rep. Serv. 2d 1143 (Del.Superior Ct. 1999)

IN SOME JURISDICTIONS, DISCLAIMERS INSERTED INTO PACKAGING ARE VALID

■ **INSTANT FACTS** A disk drive buyer instituted a class action against the manufacturer when the drive erased and destroyed itself, arguing the disclaimer of the implied warranty of merchantability was ineffective because it came inside the packaging (i.e., after the sale).

■ **BLACK LETTER RULE** In Delaware, a disclaimer of the implied warranty of merchantability may be "conspicuous" under UCC § 2–316(2), even if it is located inside the packaging and not readable until after purchase.

■ **PROCEDURAL BASIS**

In class action, Iomega's (D) motion to dismiss claim for breach of implied warranty of merchantability.

■ **FACTS**

Iomega Corp. (D) manufactures computer Zip drives (high-capacity floppy disks). In sales, Iomega (D) disclaims the implied warranty of merchantability through a document included *inside the packaging* [i.e., which buyers could not read until after purchase]. The disclaimer is otherwise conspicuous, appearing in ALL CAPITALS as part of a document marked "IOMEGA LIMITED WARRANTY." Iomega's (D) drives apparently contain a catastrophic glitch (known as the "Click of Death"), which damages the drive, erases all data, and infects other Zip drives when users insert damaged disks into them. [Other than that, it works great!] Buyers, including Rinaldi (P), filed a class action on behalf of all Zip buyers against Iomega (D), stating several claims, including Count I: Iomega (D) breached its implied warranty of merchantability by manufacturing a product unfit for its ordinary purpose, and its disclaimer was not sufficiently "conspicuous," as required by UCC § 2–316(2), as a matter of law, *because buyers could not see it until after purchase.* [Rinaldi's (P) other counts are irrelevant.] Iomega (D) moved to dismiss Count I for failure to state a claim, citing case law holding that terms included inside the packaging are valid.

■ **ISSUE**

Is a disclaimer of the implied warranty of merchantability not "conspicuous," as a matter of law under UCC § 2–316(2), just because it is located inside the packaging?

■ **DECISION AND RATIONALE**

(Cooch) No. In Delaware, a disclaimer of the implied warranty of merchantability may be "conspicuous" under UCC § 2–316(2), even if it is located inside the packaging and not readable until after purchase. The sole issue is whether Count 1 (breach of merchantability) should be dismissed because it was not "conspicuous," under UCC § 2–316, because the disclaimer was contained inside the packaging, and thus not "discovered" by buyers before purchase. UCC § 2–316(2) provides, ". . . to exclude or modify the implied warranty of merchantability . . . the language must mention merchantability and [any written disclaimer] must be conspicuous . . . ." Usually, "conspicuousness" claims

Rinaldi v. Iomega Corp. (Continued)

complain that, e.g., the type size was too small, the disclaimer was hidden inside the warranty's text, or the disclaimer was improperly worded. Here, Rinaldi (P) instead claims Iomega's (D) warranty was not "conspicuous" as a matter of law, solely because disclaimers located inside the packaging would not be called to buyers' attention until after the sale is consummated. This is an issue of first impression, because it involves disclaimers of merchantability; however, other contractual terms (e.g., shrinkwrap licenses, arbitration clauses, license agreements) located inside packaging have been considered. In deciding whether "conspicuousness" is implicated here, we must look to UCC § 2-316(2)'s purpose, which is to "protect a buyer from unexpected and unbargained for ... disclaimer." Other courts upheld contractual terms shipped with the packaging, often because they found this was an efficient way of getting contractual terms to buyers. *ProCD, Inc. v. Zeidenberg* [shrinkwrap license sent inside packaging is enforceable, because pay-before-inspect transactions are common, requiring terms to be printed on the box is impractical, and holding otherwise would not allow most disclaimers to be enforced]; *Hill v. Gateway 2000, Inc.* [arbitration clause inside packaging is enforceable for practical considerations; approve-or-return is more efficient than costly, useless telephone recitations]; *M.A. Mortenson Co. v. Timberline Software Corp.* [licensing agreement valid, because use of software manifested assent]; *Step-Saver Data Systems, Inc. v. Wyse Technology* [disclaimer of merchantability inside packaging should consider notice's "location" and "conspicuousness" separately]. This Court also addressed UCC § 2–316(2) "conspicuousness" in *Lecates v. Hertrick Pontiac Buick Co.* [disclaimer of merchantability located in sales invoice was "conspicuous"], noting (in dicta) that disclaimers are ineffective "if it appeared that the documents in which such clauses appeared were given to the buyer after the sale [was] consummated." However, *Lecates* is distinguishable; it addressed which terms/conditions became part of the original contract, while Iomega's (D) disclaimer operates as an additional term. Also, we find Iomega's (D) "sale" was not consummated until after Rinaldi (P) had the opportunity to inspect the product and additional terms, and accept or reject them. This holding is mandated by the commercial practicalities; it is reasonable to allow sellers to place any disclaimers inside the packaging, since this lets buyers inspect and reject them later, and is more efficient than any alternative way of communicating the terms to buyers (e.g., printing them on the box's outside in microscopic print, reciting them by phone). Thus, Iomega's (D) disclaimer of merchantability was "conspicuous" under UCC § 2–316(2), and thus effective. Iomega's (D) motion to dismiss Count I (breach of merchantability) granted.

Analysis:

Rinaldi shows that some jurisdictions do accept disclaimers made after the money changed hands, especially for computer hardware/software purchases. The most efficient way to communicate extensive warranty information to purchasers is to ship it with the packaging. However, the more fundamental question is whether manufacturers should be able to disclaim merchantability at all. The better policy may be to ban disclaimers of merchantability completely, unless the buyer is fully aware that this means *the manufacturer is admitting that its product simply does not work*, assents expressly, and receives a discounted price. But, UCC § 2–316 does permit waiver, thus allowing sellers to sell known defective products to unsuspecting buyers without remedy.

Wilson Trading Corp. v. David Ferguson, Ltd.

(Yarn Seller) v. (Yarn Purchaser)
23 N.Y.2d 398, 244 N.E.2d 685, 297 N.Y.S.2d 108 (1968)

PARTIES MAY NOT NEGOTIATE TERMS OF A CONTRACT WHICH WOULD DEPRIVE THE CONTRACT OF ITS ABILITY TO BE ENFORCED

■ **INSTANT FACTS** A seller of yarn, although acknowledging the yarn sold to be defective, nevertheless sued the buyer for payment on the grounds that the buyer had waited too long to complain of the defect.

■ **BLACK LETTER RULE** A freely negotiated term of a contract is nonetheless not enforceable if it serves to deprive the contract of its essential purpose.

■ PROCEDURAL BASIS

Appeal to New York Court of Appeals from Appellate Court's decision to affirm trial court's summary judgment for Wilson (P).

■ FACTS

Wilson Trading Company (Wilson) (P) sued David Ferguson, Ltd. (Ferguson) (D) for the contract price of a quantity of yarn. Ferguson (D) had refused to pay for the yarn claiming that it was defective because it had "shaded" when Ferguson (D) washed it. Consequently, Ferguson (D) filed a counter-suit against Wilson (P) claiming that Wilson (P) had breached the sales contract by failing to provide workmanlike goods. The sales contract between Wilson (P) and Ferguson (D) provided specifically that no claims relating to shading could be made either more than ten days after the receipt of a shipment or after a shipment had been processed. Applying the language of the sales contract, the trial court granted Wilson (P) a summary judgment for the contract price of the yarn and simultaneously dismissed Ferguson's (D) counter-claim on the grounds that Ferguson (D) had not complained of the shading within the timeframe set forth in the sales contract. The Appellate Court affirmed the trial court without opinion. The Court of Appeals for New York reversed, finding that the time limitation clause of the sales contract could not have effect, because it is the essence of a sales contract to allow at least minimal adequate remedies for its breach, and the ten-day time limitation effectively deprived Ferguson (D) of any remedy. Consequently, the court reversed the summary judgment and remanded the case to the trial court to answer the question of whether Ferguson (D) gave Wilson (P) notice of the shading defect within a reasonable time of its discovery.

■ ISSUE

Are there limitations on the extent parties to a contract may modify or exclude warranties or limit remedies for breach of warranty?

■ DECISION AND RATIONALE

(Jasen, J.) Yes. The Uniform Commercial Code (UCC) allows the parties to a contract, within the limits established by the Code, to modify or exclude warranties and to limit remedies for breach of warranty. Parties may not however modify a contract to such an extent that the contract is rendered a nullity. The Official Comments to § 2–719 of the UCC makes clear that it is the very essence of a sale contract that

Wilson Trading Corp. v. David Ferguson, Ltd. (Continued)

at least minimal adequate remedies be available for its breach. Under the circumstances of the case at bar, the requirement that Ferguson (D) notify Wilson (P) of any defects in the yarn before processing essentially deprived Ferguson (D) of any remedy for breach of warranty; the fact is, Ferguson (D) could not have been aware of any defect in the yarn until after processing. The Official Comment to UCC 2-719 states that when an apparently fair and reasonable clause, because of circumstances, operates to deprive either party of the substantial value of its bargain, it must give way to the general remedy provisions of the UCC. The requirement that Ferguson (D) notify Wilson (P) of any defects in the yarn before processing clearly served to deprive Ferguson (D) of its ability to seek a remedy in the event of a breach of contract. A contract which does not provide for a remedy in the event of a breach fails of its essential purpose. Because we find that the clause requiring Ferguson (D) to complain of the defect in the yarn before Ferguson (D) could have possibly discovered the defect caused the contract to fail of its essential purpose, we find that the clause must be struck. We replace the time limitation clause of the contract with the general provisions of the UCC that a buyer has a reasonable time to notify the seller of a breach of contract after he discovers or should have discovered a defect. While it is true that parties may by agreement set limits on the time in which a party may complain of a breach, such time limitations must nevertheless be reasonable. Because, under the circumstances of this case, the time limitation imposed on Ferguson (D) was not reasonable, it must be struck. We remand this case to the trial court to answer the question of whether Ferguson (D) notified Wilson (P) of the breach of implied warranty within a reasonable time of its discovery. Reversed.

■ CONCURRENCE

(Fuld, C.J.) I agree that the Appellate Court's decision to uphold summary judgment should be reversed but for reasons much simpler than those supplied by the majority. In my view, the question before the court is simply whether the clause limiting the time in which to make a claim is "manifestly unreasonable." The question of whether the clause was manifestly unreasonable is a question of fact which should be submitted to a jury.

Analysis:

While the court seems to have arrived at a reasonable and legal solution to the problem raised by the facts of this case, the question nevertheless remains: how free are parties to bargain for terms and conditions of a contract? The answer seems to be that parties are free to bargain for terms of a contract as long as the terms bargained for do not deprive the contract of its essential purpose. In this case, the court found that a contract that has no remedy for breach is a contract that has been deprived of its essential purpose. Consequently, the court turned to the UCC and supplied the contract with its own remedy for breach. While the court's solution appears to be fair, it is also paternalistic. As noted, Wilson (P) and Ferguson (D) were equally sophisticated parties who were equally capable of bargaining for terms of a contract that they felt to be in their interests. If the court is going to step in to rescue a party from the consequences of a poor bargain as it did in this case, is it really in a party's interest to negotiate for advantageous contractual terms?

Pierce v. Catalina Yachts, Inc.
(Boat Buyers) v. (Seller)
2 P.3d 618 (Alaska 2000)

COURTS SPLIT ON WHEN TO ENFORCE LIMITED WARRANTIES

■ **INSTANT FACTS** A couple bought a defective boat under a limited warranty. When the seller refused to repair the boat for 6 months, the buyers sued for consequential damages.

■ **BLACK LETTER RULE** In some jurisdictions, a limited warranty's bar of consequential damages is unenforceable if (i) the warranty "fails of its essential purpose," and (ii) under the circumstances, enforcing the warranty would be "unconscionable."

■ **PROCEDURAL BASIS**

In action for contract, tort, and fraud, following partial verdict for Pierce (P), appeal by Pierce (P), seeking consequential damages.

■ **FACTS**

Mr. and Mrs. Pierce (P) contracted to buy a boat from manufacturer Catalina Yachts, Inc. (D). Catalina's (D) contract included a limited warranty, promising that if the boat's smooth hull resin blistered, Catalina (D) would repair it, or pay for repair. Catalina's (D) contract disclaimed consequential damages. When Pierce (P) discovered blistering, he submitted a repair estimate ($10K) to Catalina (D). Catalina (D) refused the estimate, insisting only minor patching was required, and stalled for 6 months. Pierce (P) sued Catalina (D) in contract, tort, and unfair trade practices. Before trial, the court ruled the warranty's provision barring consequential damages was not unconscionable, and thus enforceable. At trial, the jury found Pierce (P) gave timely notice, Catalina (D) breached its warranty and acted in bad faith in ignoring its warranty obligations, and Pierce (P) could not have avoided the damages, awarding Pierce (P) $12K for reasonable repair costs. Pierce (P) appeals, claiming [among other counts, irrelevant here] the court erred in enforcing the limited warranty, which was unconscionable.

■ **ISSUE**

If a limited warranty fails in its purpose, should a separate limitation on consequential damages be enforced?

■ **DECISION AND RATIONALE**

(Bryner) Yes. A limited warranty's bar of consequential damages is unenforceable if (i) the warranty "fails of its essential purpose," and (ii) under the circumstances, enforcing the warranty would be "unconscionable." This is an issue of first impression: if a limited warranty fails, should its bar on consequential damages survive? This is governed by [UCC § 2–719]. Paragraph 1 authorizes limited warranties, letting parties "limit or alter the ... damages recoverable ... as by limiting the buyer's remedies to ... repair and replacement," and to agree that the limited remedy is the "exclusive, ... sole remedy." But when a limited remedy fails, Paragraph 2 nullifies the warranty's limitation ("if circumstances cause an exclusive or limited remedy to fail of its essential purpose, remedy may be had as provided in the [UCC]"). Courts agree that a limited warranty to repair "fails of its essential

Pierce v. Catalina Yachts, Inc. (Continued)

purpose" when either (A) the seller is unable or unwilling to conform the goods to the contract, regardless of good or bad faith, or (B) there is unreasonable delay in repairing or replacing. However, the UCC's next Paragraph 3 separately provides that consequential damages may be limited "unless the limitation or exclusion is unconscionable." This creates an inconsistency, because this *could* be read to mean either (A) the limited warranty's failure means that all remedies are available, or (B) consequential damages are still limited, unless the limitation would be "unconscionable." Courts are split. Some hold the 2 sections are dependent, so that when a warranty fails, all remedies are restored. Others apply a case-by-case analysis. Most jurisdictions view Paragraphs 2 and 3 as independent, so that when a warranty fails, any separate provision barring consequential damages will survive, unless unconscionable. We follow this majority approach, because it is the best public policy, letting sellers contract around consequential damages while protecting buyers from unconscionable results. In deciding whether enforcing the limitation would be unconscionable, courts consider the totality of circumstances, including why the warranty failed, how the contract was formed/signed, and whether the parties could not competently allocate risk. Factors suggesting unconscionability include: non-merchants, disparate bargaining power, and/or pre-printed form contracts. Factors suggesting enforceability include freely-negotiated terms between sophisticated parties, especially 2 merchants. Also, courts can examine, from hindsight, whether the type of damage which actually occurred was within the realm of expectable losses, to see whether the warranty assigned so much/varied risk to the buyer that the warranty essentially fails in its purpose. In deciding why a limited warranty failed its essential purpose, courts consider it significant if the seller acted unreasonably or in bad faith. Here, enforcing Catalina's (D) limited warranty would be unconscionable to Pierce (P). Their bargaining power was unequal, since Pierce (P) is not a merchant, and Catalina (D) drafted the warranty in a unilateral form contract. Further, the high cost of repair suggests that Catalina's (D) breach deprived Pierce (P) of significant protection expected under their bargain. The decisive factor is Catalina's (D) conscious, bad faith breach. Letting Catalina (D) hide behind one warranty provision while repudiating another would conflict with the UCC's policy of encouraging good faith and enforcing parties' expected agreements. Thus, the trial court erred in enforcing the warranty's bar on consequential damages. Judgment vacated and remanded for retrial on consequential damages.

Analysis:

Generally, a warranty can disclaim consequential damages. However, as here, sometimes those disclaimers will be found unconscionable, and thus voided. Note, though, that courts can follow any of the three rules described here, and remain sharply divided. Also, if both parties are merchants, then courts are much more likely to uphold limited warranties, even if they seem to fail in their essential purpose. With consumer form contracts (and, similarly, with merchants who lack bargaining power against the counter-party), strictly enforcing the limited warranty would work an injustice where one party refuses to honor its repair duties promptly, thus multiplying consequential damages for the other through sheer delay.

■ **CASE VOCABULARY**

CONSEQUENTIAL DAMAGES: Indirect damages from an act, usually including the monetary cost of the delay, or the cost of buying an emergency replacement for the contracted-for item. For example, here, Pierce's (P) consequential damages could have included the cost of renting a replacement boat, the time and cost lost in securing a replacement, etc. Note that consequential damages can be very large, often more than the cost of *the item*.

CROSS-APPEAL: Appeal by the party which nominally won a motion/trial, usually because it is dissatisfied with the amount it won, or with some aspect of the decision.

LIMITED WARRANTY: Warranty which limits certain damages, especially consequential damages, usually by limiting the seller's obligations to repairing or replacing the item (or, as here, paying for outside repair).

VACATE: Nullify [a *judgment*].

Fitl v. Strek

(Baseball Card Purchaser) v. *(Card Seller)*
269 Neb. 51, 690 N.W.2d 605 (2005)

REASONABLE TIME FOR NOTIFICATION OF DEFECTS DEPENDS ON THE CIRCUMSTANCES OF THE CASE

■ **INSTANT FACTS** Fitl (P) purchased a baseball card from Strek (D) in 1995, and in 1997 Fitl (P) learned that the card had been altered and was valueless.

■ **BLACK LETTER RULE:** The determination of whether a seller received notification of a defect in goods is a factual question and depends upon whether the policies behind the notice requirement—allowing the seller to correct the defect, prepare for negotiation and litigation, and protect against stale claims—were unfairly prejudiced.

■ **PROCEDURAL BASIS:**

Appeal from a judgment for Fitl (P) entered after a bench trial.

■ **FACTS:**

Fitl (P) purchased a 1952 Mickey Mantle Topps baseball card from Strek (D) at a sports card show in 1995. According to Fitl (P), Strek (D) stated that the card was in near mint condition. The price of the card was $17,750.

In 1997, Fitl (P) sent the card to a grading service for sports cards. The service told him that the card was ungradable because it had been discolored and doctored. Fitl (P) wrote to Strek (D) to tell him that he planned to pursue "legal methods." Strek (D) replied that Fitl (P) should have returned the card sooner so that Strek (D) could have confronted his source and remedied the situation.

At trial, Fitl (P) offered expert testimony on the issue of grading sports cards. The expert testified that an altered card was not gradable because alteration would make the card valueless. The expert opined that any touchup or trimming of a card would make it valueless, and that an altered card was worth no more than the paper on which it was printed. The expert examined the card Fitl (P) purchased and said that it had no value. According to the expert, the standard for sports memorabilia was a lifetime guarantee, and reputable dealers would refund the purchase price if an item they sold was fake, or if it had been altered.

Strek (D) offered no evidence at trial. Judgment was entered against him for $17,750. The court disagreed with Strek's (D) argument that Fitl (P) should have determined the authenticity of the card immediately after he purchased it.

■ **ISSUE:**

Was the notification of the card's defects made in a reasonable time?

■ **DECISION AND RATIONALE:**

(Wright, J.) Yes. The determination of whether a seller received notification of a defect in goods is a factual question and depends upon whether the policies behind the notice requirement—allowing the

Fitl v. Strek (Continued)

seller to correct the defect, prepare for negotiation and litigation, and protect against stale claims—were unfairly prejudiced. In this case, even if Fitl (P) had notified Strek (D) immediately that the card was worthless, there was no evidence that Strek (D) could have done anything to correct the defect or minimize liability. There is also no evidence that earlier notification of the defect would have allowed Strek (D) to pursue the party who provided him with the defective card. In addition, any issues Strek (D) could raise with the source of the card were separate from his transaction with Fitl (P).

In order for Fitl (P) to have determined that the card was worthless, he would have had to conduct an investigation. There is no requirement that a buyer do so. A buyer is justified in relying on a positive statement of fact if an investigation would be required to determine that the statement was false. Affirmed.

Analysis:

The length of time between the sale and the notice of the defect may have prejudiced Strek's (D) efforts to recover from the supplier of the card, but that has nothing to do with Fitl (P). Fitl (P) was sold a worthless card, and he is entitled to a full refund from Strek (D), the party with whom he had dealings. Fitl's (P) recovery does not depend on when or how Strek (D) came into possession of the card. Strek (D) must address that issue with his supplier.

Reed v. City of Chicago

(Mother of Detainee) v. (Jail Operator)
263 F.Supp.2d 1123, 50 UCC Rep. Serv. 2d 146 (N.D. Ill. 2003)

PRIVITY IS NOT NECESSARY IN BREACH OF WARRANTY ACTIONS

■ **INSTANT FACTS** Reed's (P) son hanged himself with a paper gown issued to him by the Chicago (D) jail, and she claimed a breach of warranty, based on the gown's failure to tear.

■ **BLACK LETTER RULE** An action for breach of warranty may be brought a person who is the intended beneficiary of the warranty, regardless of whether that person is in privity with the maker of the warranty.

■ PROCEDURAL BASIS

Decision on a motion to dismiss for failure to state a claim upon which relief can be granted.

■ FACTS

Reed's (P) son was arrested and placed in a detention cell by Chicago (D) police officers. Reed (P) alleged that the officers (D) knew her son was mentally unstable and suicidal, and that they failed to monitor his cell. Reed's (P) son was given a paper isolation gown designed and manufactured by Edwards (D), Cypress (D), and Medline (D). Reed (P) alleged that her son used this gown to hang himself. Reed (P) alleged that Edwards (D), Cypress (D), and Medline (D) breached implied and express warranties when the gown failed to tear away. Cypress (D) moved to dismiss the breach of warranty claim, for failure to state a claim upon which relief can be granted.

■ ISSUE

May a non-purchaser recover from the manufacturer and designer of a product for breach of warranty?

■ DECISION AND RATIONALE

(Moran, J.) Yes. The former requirement that the plaintiff in a breach of warranty action be in privity with the manufacturer has been eliminated in Illinois. An action for breach of warranty may be brought a person who is the intended beneficiary of the warranty, regardless of whether that person is in privity with the maker of the warranty. The UCC lists specific exceptions to the privity requirement, but those listed exceptions are not intended to be exclusive. Privity is no longer required for buyers who claim a breach of warranty against a remote manufacturer, or in food and drug cases.

More recently, the privity requirement has been abolished in cases in which the person claiming a breach of warranty is an employee of the ultimate purchaser of a product. The courts have held that an employee is essentially a third-party beneficiary to the sale, and that the employee's safety is either explicitly or implicitly part of the basis of the bargain when the employer purchased the product. Similarly, in this case, Reed's (P) son was the intended beneficiary of any warranty made by the designer and manufacturer of the gown. Cypress (D) contemplated that the gown would be used by jail detainees, and the safety of those detainees was a part of the bargain between Cypress (D) and Chicago (D). If protection is not provided to users like Reed's (P) son, any warranty on the gown would have little, if any effect. Motion to dismiss denied.

Analysis:

Elimination of privity requirements acknowledges that warranties are not like other contracts. A warranty is more than a promise that a product will perform; it is a promise that it will perform safely. That promise means nothing to a purchaser who does not use the product. Rather than hold that the warranty in this case was, in effect, meaningless, the court extended its protections to users (or, in this case, those who misuse the product).

■ CASE VOCABULARY

HORIZONTAL PRIVITY: The legal relationship between a party and a nonparty who is related to the party (such as a buyer and a member of the buyer's family).

VERTICAL PRIVITY: The legal relationship between parties in a product's chain of distribution (such as a manufacturer and a seller).

East River Steamship Corp. v. Transamerica Delaval, Inc.
(Charterer) v. (Engine Manufacturer)
476 U.S. 858, 106 S.Ct. 2295 (1986)

A MANUFACTURER CANNOT BE HELD LIABLE UNDER A PRODUCTS LIABLITY THEORY IF A DEFECT IN ITS PRODUCT RESULTS ONLY IN ECONOMIC DAMAGE OR IN DAMAGE TO THE PRODUCT ITSELF

■ **INSTANT FACTS** The owner of a supertanker is suing the manufacturer of the supertanker's turbine under a products liability theory for damages caused to the turbine when a ring in the turbine failed.

■ **BLACK LETTER RULE** When a product fails and causes only economic damage or damage to the product itself, the proper remedy is under warranty law, not products liability law.

■ **PROCEDURAL BASIS**

Appeal to United States Supreme Court from the Third Circuit's decision to affirm District Court's decision to grant summary judgment to Delaval (D).

■ **FACTS**

Transamerica Delaval, Inc. (D) (Delaval) built four giant turbine engines which were installed in four supertankers. Four different companies chartered the supertankers and each company took full responsibility for the repair and maintenance of each ship. Soon after the ships entered service, it became apparent that there were problems with the turbines manufactured by Delaval (D). Specifically, an improperly designed ring in the turbines failed and caused damage to other parts of the turbines. Three of the ships suffered varying degrees of trouble as a result of the turbine defects and each had to have its turbines repaired. A fourth ship which was equipped with a properly manufactured turbine, nevertheless suffered problems because Delaval installed the turbine incorrectly. None of the ships suffered damage beyond damage to the turbines themselves. The charterers, one of whom was East River Steamship Corp. (P) (East River) filed suit in the United States District Court for New Jersey. The law suit sought damages from Delaval (D) for repair to the ships as well as income lost while the ships were out of service due to the failure of the turbines. Four counts of the lawsuit alleged that Delaval (D) was strictly liable for the design defects in the turbines, the fifth and remaining count alleged that Delaval (D) was negligent when it failed to properly install the fourth ship's turbine. The U.S. District Court granted summary judgment in favor of Delaval (D) and the U.S. Court of Appeals for the Third Circuit affirmed. The Third Circuit held that there can be no tortious liability for a product defect which does not pose a risk to persons and which causes no harm to property. Disappointments over the quality of a product, held the court, should be addressed under warranty law, not under the laws of negligence and strict liability. East River (P) and the other charterers appealed the Third Circuit's decision to the United States Supreme Court.

■ **ISSUE**

Is there a cause of action in either negligence or strict liability when a defect in a commercial product causes injury to nothing but the product itself?

East River Steamship Corp. v. Transamerica Delaval, Inc. (Continued)

■ DECISION AND RATIONALE

(Blackmun, J.) No. A commercial manufacturer has no liability either under a negligence or a strict products liability theory if its product malfunctions and causes no damage beyond economic damage or damage to the product itself. East River's (P) remedy in this case, if any, lay in warranty law, not in the law of negligence or strict liability. The reason that East River (P) may have a cause of action in warranty but not in negligence or strict liability is simply one of public policy. The law of products liability grew out of a public policy judgment that people need more protection from dangerous products than is afforded by the law of warranty. Over the years, the law has expanded a manufacturer's tort liability to include not just injuries to persons but also injuries to property. The law has not yet expanded so far, though, that it will hold a manufacturer liable in tort when a product defect causes no injury beyond economic injury or injury to the product itself. In this case, there is no allegation that the defects in the turbines caused any injury beyond economic injury to East River (P) and injury to the turbines themselves. In essence, East River (P) is claiming that the turbines failed to function properly, and that as a result, it suffered economic injury. A claim that a product did not function properly and thereby caused economic damages is the essence of a warranty action. To allow a party to sue under a theory of tort when a product's failure causes harm to no more than the product itself would be to erase the distinction between tort law and warranty law. The court will not find tort liability unless a product defect results in injury to a person or to property other than the product itself. When a person or property is injured, the loss of time, money or health may be an overwhelming misfortune which would justify the public cost of holding a manufacturer liable under a products liability theory. When a product failure results in no more than a dissatisfied customer, however, warranty law is the proper recourse. Customer dissatisfaction is simply not a harm which would justify exposing a manufacturer to the indefinite liability a tort action could bring. East River (P) and the other charterers have adequate recourse under a warranty theory. Recovery under a warranty theory would give the plaintiffs their repair costs and lost profits and would place them in the position they would have been in had the turbines functioned properly. Accordingly, the summary judgment of the products liability claim in favor of Delaval (D) is affirmed.

Analysis:

As Justice Blackmun acknowledges, products liability law grew out of a public policy judgment that people needed more protection from dangerous products than was afforded by warranty law. Nevertheless, the Court cautioned, we must maintain limits on how far products liabilty law will be allowed to expand. If we were to allow a manufacturer to be held liable under a products liability theory every time a product failed, as Justice Blackmun put it, contract law would drown in a sea of tort. The Court's mission in this case then was to attempt to draw the line between where warranty liability ends and products liability begins. But as long as there are lawyers to argue facts, it will be very difficult to draw a bright line distinction between products liability and warranty liability. How exactly do we determine whether a product's failure has caused damage to something other than the product itself? There is also the problem of distinguishing between economic damages and property damages. The Court clearly stated that where a product's failure results in no more than economic damages, a warranty action is the only proper remedy. But when will the connection between economic loss and other injury become too tenuous to support a products liability action? These cases will continue to be litigated on a case by case basis.

Ventura v. Ford Motor Corp.

(Buyer) v. (Manufacturer)
180 N.J.Super. 454, 33 A.2d 801 (App.Div. 1981)

A BUYER MAY SUE A MANUFACTURER FOR BREACH OF THE IMPLIED WARRANTIES OF MERCHANTABILITY AND FITNESS FOR A PARTICULAR PURPOSE EVEN IF THE BUYER DID NOT BUY DIRECTLY FROM THE MANUFACTURER

■ **INSTANT FACTS** An automobile purchaser was allowed to sue the dealer and manufacturer for breach of the implied warranty of merchantability even though the dealer had disclaimed any implied warranties and he did not have a direct contract with the manufacturer.

■ **BLACK LETTER RULE** A buyer is not required to buy directly from a manufacturer in order to have privity of contract with the manufacturer.

■ **PROCEDURAL BASIS**

Appeal to New Jersey Superior Court from trial court's award of damages resulting from a breach of contract.

■ **FACTS**

Mr. Ventura (P) bought a new Ford from a dealership, Marino Auto Sales (Marino) (D). At the time he bought the car, Marino (D) supplied Mr. Ventura (P) with a copy of Ford's (D) express warranty for the car. At the same time, while Marino (D) agreed that it would perform all conditions of the owner's service policy, it specifically disclaimed all express and implied warranties for the car. Mr. Ventura (P) began to experience problems with the car soon after taking delivery. When Marino (D) failed to adequately address his complaints, Mr. Ventura (P) returned the car and sued for rescission of the purchase contract. Marino (D), in turn, filed suit seeking indemnification from Ford (D). Ford (D) argued, first, that Mr. Ventura (P) could not make a claim against Marino (D) because Marino (D) had effectively disclaimed all express and implied warranties. Secondly, Ford (D) claimed that, even if the court granted rescission of the contract, Marino (D) could not seek indemnification because, under the Magnuson-Moss Warranty Act (Magnuson), rescission of a contract is not an appropriate remedy for the breach of the type of limited warranty Ford had extended to Mr. Ventura (P). The trial court held Mr. Ventura (P) could rescind the purchase contract with Marino (D) and that Marino (D) could, in turn, seek indemnification from Ford (D) for its damages. Ford (D) appealed.

■ **ISSUE**

May a buyer sue a manufacturer for breach of an implied warranty even if the buyer did not buy directly from the manufacturer?

■ **DECISION AND RATIONALE**

(Botter, J.) Yes. A buyer may sue a manufacture for breach of an implied warranty under both the Magnuson-Moss Warranty Act (Magnuson Act) and under the Uniform Commercial Code (UCC). In the case at bar, the first issue to be decided by the court is whether Marino's (D) disclaimer of all express and implied warranties with respect to the automobile was effective. We find that it was not. Marino (D) supplied Mr. Ventura (P) with a written warranty at the time of sale whereby it agreed to fulfill

Ventura v. Ford Motor Corp. (Continued)

obligations and guarantees made in Ford's (D) written warranty. Having furnished a written warranty to the consumer, Marino (D), as a dealer and supplier, could not disclaim or modify any implied warranties connected with the sale of the automobile. The Magnuson Act specifically prohibits a supplier who has provided a written warranty to a consumer from disclaiming or modifying any other implied warranties made to the consumer. Because Marino (D) had not effectively disclaimed the implied warranties of merchantability and fitness, Mr. Ventura (P) properly sought rescission of the contract with Marino (D) as a remedy for breach of those warranties. The question then becomes whether Marino (D) could have properly sought indemnification from Ford (D) for damages it incurred as a result of the rescission. Ford (D) argues that the Magnuson Act specifically precludes rescission as a remedy for breach of a limited warranty. We find that Ford (D) is correct that the Magnuson Act provides for rescission of a contract only in cases where there is a breach of a full warranty and we find, furthermore, that Ford (D) extended only a limited warranty to Mr. Ventura (P). Nevertheless, we believe that rescission was appropriate in this case. The effect of the Magnuson Act is to eliminate the requirement of privity of contract between a consumer and a warrantor. Under the Magnuson Act, a consumer has a direct remedy against the manufacturer and warrantor of a product, in this case Ford (D), even if the consumer does not have a direct contract with the warrantor. As noted, we agree that the Magnuson Act does not provide for rescission of a contract where there is breach only of a limited warranty of the type seen in this case. However, it is our opinion that Mr. Ventura (P) had rights against Ford (D) without regard to the Act and that rescission was still therefore an appropriate remedy. The UCC permits a buyer to rescind a contract against a seller in privity when the buyer discovers that there are substantial defects in the product which is the subject of the contract. Under the facts of this case, it would be intellectually dishonest for this court to find that there was no privity of contract between Mr. Ventura (P) and Ford (D). Ford (D), in this case, extended a warranty for the purpose of inducing a sale and that warranty created a direct contractual obligation to the buyer. A direct contractual relationship is the essence of privity. Although Ford (D) may have intended to limit any remedy under the warranty to the repair and replacement of defective parts, its failure to see that the remedy was fulfilled justifies rescission of the contract against Ford (D) in this case. Affirmed.

Analysis:

This opinion stands for the simple premise that a buyer does not always need to have direct privity of contract with a seller before a court will enforce a remedy for breach of the implied warranties of merchantability and fitness. The court first discusses the Magnuson-Moss Warranty Act, which statutorily enhances a consumer's position in warranty disputes by removing the requirement of direct privity of contract before a buyer can enforce rights against a seller for breach of the implied warranties of merchantability and fitness. Under the Magnuson Act, a buyer has rights against all warrantors, even if the buyer did not purchase directly from the warrantor; no privity of contract is required. The problem for Mr. Ventura (P) in this case was that, though he could have sued Ford (D) directly under the Magnuson Act, he could not have sought the remedy of rescission under the Magnuson Act because Ford (D) had extended only a limited warranty for the car. The Magnuson Act does not provide for the remedy of rescission in cases where there is breach of a limited warranty. The court got around this limitation by finding that Mr. Ventura (P) had rights against Ford (D) without regard to the Magnuson Act. Though Mr. Ventura (P) had bought the car from Marino (D), the court nevertheless found that he also had a contractual relationship with Ford (D) and could therefore sue under the UCC. Ford (D), the court pointed out, extended a warranty in this case for the purpose of inducing a sale. Under the warranty agreement, Ford (D) agreed, through an authorized dealer, to repair or replace any parts found to be defective within the 12,000 miles or one year of the car's purchase. Ford (D) specifically advised that repairs would be made through any authorized Ford (D) dealer and that a buyer should consult Ford (D) itself should there be any difficulties in having a vehicle repaired. Thus the court found that the warranty created in Ford (D) a direct contractual obligation to Mr. Ventura (P). Because the court found that Mr. Ventura (P) had privity of contract with Ford (D), the court also found that Mr. Ventura (P) had available to him all remedies for breach of implied warranties, including rescission, provided by the UCC.

■ CASE VOCABULARY

PRIVITY: A legal connection between two parties which must be demonstrated before one party will by allowed to exercise contractual rights against the other.

Colonial Pacific Leasing Corp. v. McNatt, Datronic Rental Corp.

(Leasing Company) v. (Lessees)
268 Ga. 265, 486 S.E.2d 804 (1997)

A PARTY WHO ACTS AS AN AGENT OF A SUPPLIER CAN BE HELD LIABLE FOR BREACH OF THE IMPLIED WARRANTIES OF MERCHANTABILITY AND FITNESS FOR A PARTICULAR PURPOSE

■ **INSTANT FACTS** A lessee is attempting to sue the lessor of equipment for breach of the implied warranties of merchantability and fitness for a particular purpose. The lessor has filed countersuit against the lessee seeking payment on the lease.

■ **BLACK LETTER RULE** A supplier's agent may be held liable for breach of the implied warranties of merchantability and fitness for a particular purpose.

■ **PROCEDURAL BASIS**

Appeal to Georgia Supreme Court from Appellate Court's decision to reverse trial court's grant of summary judgment.

■ **FACTS**

Linda and William McNatt (P) needed to buy a computer printing system for their company, Quick-Trip Printers, but they could not afford it. In order to arrange financing, they turned to Burnham Leasing Company (Burnham). Under a lease finance agreement with Burnham, the McNatts (P) selected equipment to be purchased from Itex Systems Southeast, Inc. (Itex) and then negotiated with Itex's representatives for the purchase of the equipment. Once the purchase terms were negotiated, Burnham stepped in and actually bought the equipment from Itex. Burnham agreed to lease the equipment to the McNatts (P) for a monthly rental payment and then assigned its lease rights to Colonial Pacific Leasing Corporation and Datronic Rental Corporation (the Lessors) (D). Soon after taking delivery of the Itex equipment, the McNatts (P) discovered that it did not function as Itex representatives had promised; consequently, the McNatts (P) withheld lease payments to the Lessors (D) and, in turn, the Lessors (D) repossessed the equipment from the McNatts (P). The McNatts (P) filed suit seeking to rescind the leases. The McNatts (P) claimed that the leases should be rescinded because Itex and the Lessors (D) had not provided them with proper, working equipment as consideration, and had consequently also breached the implied warranties of merchantability and fitness. The Lessors (D) filed a countersuit against the McNatts (P) seeking payment under the lease agreement. The trial court granted summary judgment finding that the McNatts (P) had signed valid agreements which waived their right to sue the Lessors (D) as assignees of the lease agreement and that they had also waived any claims for breach of the implied warranties of merchantability and fitness. Specifically, the McNatts (P) had signed a "hell or high water clause" stating that the McNatts (P) would make lease payments regardless of the condition of the equipment and that the McNatts (P) could not assert against the Lessors (D) any claim they might have had against Burnham. Accordingly, the trial court held the McNatts (P) liable for all lease payments owed to the Lessors (D). The appeals court reversed the trial court's order of summary judgment, finding that the "hell or high water" clause could have no effect if Itex's agents had fraudulently induced them to enter the lease agreement. Because there was a genuine issue of material fact on the issue of whether the McNatts (P) had been

Colonial Pacific Leasing Corp. v. McNatt Datronic Rental Corp. (Continued)

fraudulently induced to sign the lease agreement, the appeals court reversed the trial court's order of summary judgment. The McNatts (P) appealed the appellate court's decision to the Georgia Supreme Court.

■ ISSUE

May a party who serves primarily as a financer between the supplier and the buyer nevertheless be held liable for a breach of the implied warranties of merchantability and fitness for a particular purpose?

■ DECISION AND RATIONALE

(Benham, J.) Yes. If it can be shown that the financer acted as an agent of the supplier, the financer can be held liable for a breach of warranty. Ordinarily, under a lease finance agreement, the court will not treat the lessor as a seller with warranty liability because, under such an arrangement, the lessor's role is limited to providing financing for the equipment. The lessor does not warrant that the goods leased will be free of defects and the lessor expects to be paid even though the equipment may be defective or totally unsuitable to the buyer's needs. In this case, the fact that the Lessors (D) did not intend to warrant the leased equipment was underscored by the hell or high water clause of the lease agreement. Courts will generally regard a hell or high water clause as valid unless there is a finding of fraud in the inducement of the contract. The clause in question in this case states that any defense to a claim for payment which might have been asserted against the original lessor, Burnham, could not be asserted against the Lessors (D); in essence, the McNatts (P) must pay "come hell or high water." We note, however, that in this instance, the McNatts (P) are not seeking to *defend* a claim by the Lessors (D), but are rather taking the offensive by seeking to exercise their right to rescind the lease agreement. Though we find that the hell or high water clause does not preclude the McNatts (P) from seeking rescission of the lease pursuant to a claim of fraud, we nevertheless reverse the appellate court's decision and find that the trial court properly granted the Lessor's (D) motion for summary judgment on the fraud claim. It is plain from the record that Itex's agents were not also acting as agents of the Lessors (D) and that any alleged fraud on the part of the Itex agents cannot therefore be imputed to the Lessors (D). Because there is no competent evidence in the record to show that the Lessors (D) acted fraudulently in this case, the McNatts (P) had no grounds to rescind the contract and the trial court properly granted summary judgment against the McNatts (P) on the fraud claim. We turn next to the McNatt's (P) claim of lack of consideration as a defense to the Lessors' (D) claim for payments. Essentially, the McNatts (P) argue that they should not have to pay the Lessors (D) because the equipment provided by Itex did not function properly. The McNatts (P) claim that not only did the Itex equipment fail to function properly, the equipment provided by Itex was not even the equipment described in the contract. We find that the McNatt's (P) defense of lack of consideration fails for several reasons. First, the hell or high water clause bars the McNatts (P) from asserting against the Lessors (D) any defense they might have originally asserted against Burnham. Absent a showing of fraud, which we have already concluded does not exist in this case, the hell or high water clause will be enforced. Secondly, the claim of lack of consideration is without merit on its face. The McNatts (P) do not allege that the equipment supplied by Itex differed in any material way from the equipment they had ordered. The McNatts (P) only claim that there were discrepancies between the serial numbers on the parts contracted for and the serial numbers on the parts actually delivered. Because the equipment ordered did not materially differ from the equipment delivered, we find that the McNatts (P) effectively waived any claims against the Lessors (D) for a breach of the implied warranties of merchantability or fitness of the equipment delivered. It is clear to us that the McNatts (P) cannot validly claim a defense of lack of consideration. We therefore find that the appellate court erred again when it reversed the trial court's grant of summary judgment to the Lessors (D) on this claim. We do however find that the appellate court ruled correctly when it found that the trial court erred when it granted summary judgment on the McNatt's (P) final claim that the Lessors (D) acted negligently when they released funds to Itex without the McNatts' (P) approval. Judgment affirmed in part and reversed in part.

Analysis:

Any party, even a financer, can be held liable for a breach of the implied warranties of merchantability and fitness for a particular purpose if it can be shown that the party acted as an agent of the supplier.

Colonial Pacific Leasing Corp. v. McNatt Datronic Rental Corp. (Continued)

With that conclusion of law in mind, the court navigates its way through a legal obstacle course before finding that the Lessors (D) were not liable to the McNatts (P) for any defects in the Itex equipment. The first obstacle the court confronts is the "hell or high water clause." Hell or high water clauses protect assignees of a lease from any legal claims a lessee might assert by stating that the lessee will have to pay the lessor "come hell or high water." Nevertheless, the court recognizes that the hell or high water clause would not have effect if the McNatt's (P) claim that Lessors (D) acted fraudulently proved to be true. And, the court notes, even if the hell or high water clause were held to be effective, it would still not necessarily bar the McNatts (P) from seeking to rescind the lease. This was true, stated the court, because the hell or high water clause prohibited the McNatts (P) only from asserting a *defense* to a claim for payments and not from taking the *offensive* by seeking rescission. Whether the court chose to invalidate the hell or high water clause or chose to find that the clause did not prohibit the McNatts (P) from seeking rescission of the lease, the court recognized that rescission would be inappropriate in either event absent a showing of fraud. Because the court found that the record did not support a claim of fraud, it held that the trial court had acted correctly when it ordered summary judgment for the Lessors (D) and denied the McNatts' (P) attempt to rescind the lease.

CHAPTER FOUR

Terms of the Contract

Landrum v. Devenport

Instant Facts: Buyer of pace car, Landrum (P), sued seller, Devenport (D), for breach of contract claiming that agreed price of car was sticker price, whereas seller contended that it was market value.

Black Letter Rule: The omission of the price term from a written contract does not make the contract unenforceable if both parties intended to be bound and there is a reasonably certain basis for giving an appropriate remedy.

Cook Specialty Co. v. Schrlock

Instant Facts: Buyer of machine, with delivery terms "F.O.B. seller's warehouse", tried to pass risk of loss back to seller for not ensuring that carrier had adequate insurance to transport machine.

Black Letter Rule: A seller, under a "F.O.B. seller's warehouse" delivery contract, does not have an obligation to investigate the amount and terms of insurance held by the carrier before the risk of loss will pass to the buyer.

Rheinberg–Kellerei GMBH v. Vineyard Wine Co.

Instant Facts: Contract entered into for the sale of wine from West Germany to the United States, but seller, Rheinberg (P), did not promptly notify buyer, Vineyard (D), of shipment.

Black Letter Rule: The risk of loss under a contract not requiring delivery to any particular destination does not pass to the buyer upon delivery to the carrier where the seller has failed to give the buyer prompt notice of shipment.

Landrum v. Devenport

(Pace Car Buyer) v. *(Pace Car Seller)*
616 S.W.2d 359, 32 UCC Rep. Serv. 8 (1981)

GAPS IN CONTRACT TERMS DO NOT AUTOMATICALLY RENDER A CONTRACT UNENFORCEABLE

■ **INSTANT FACTS** Buyer of pace car, Landrum (P), sued seller, Devenport (D), for breach of contract claiming that agreed price of car was sticker price, whereas seller contended that it was market value.

■ **BLACK LETTER RULE** The omission of the price term from a written contract does not make the contract unenforceable if both parties intended to be bound and there is a reasonably certain basis for giving an appropriate remedy.

■ **PROCEDURAL BASIS**

Appeal from judgment following granting of instructed verdict on breach of contract action seeking damages.

■ **FACTS**

Landrum (P) brought this action against Devenport (D) for breach of contract and violation of the State's Consumer Protection Act. Landrum's (P) son dealt with Devenport (D), owner of an automobile dealership, on behalf of his father, an automobile collector. Landrum's (P) son talked with Devenport (D) regarding the specific options he wanted on a certain Indy Pace Car that he was interested in buying from Devenport (D). He signed a purchase order but the price was left blank. Landrum's (P) son testified at trial that Devenport (D) told him the price would be the car's sticker price which they estimated would be between $14,000 and $18,000. When the car arrived months later, the sticker price was $14,688.21. However, by this time, the demand for the Pace Cars had increased to the point that the market value exceeded the sticker price. Davenport (D) [wanting to make lots of money on the deal] demanded $22,000.00 for the car. Landrum's (P) son offered to pay the sticker price, which was refused by Devenport (D). Landrum's (P) son [not wanting to disappoint his father] tried unsuccessfully to find another car. A letter from his attorney to Devenport (D) did not help resolve the situation. Landrum (P) then paid the price of $22,000.00, under protest, relying upon the letter from his attorney to Devenport (D). At trial, Devenport (D) testified that the price was to be the market value of the car at the time of delivery. The trial court granted Devenport's (D) motion for instructed verdict and Landrum (P) appealed.

■ **ISSUE**

Does the omission of the price term from a written contract make the contract unenforceable?

■ **DECISION AND RATIONALE**

(Cornelius) No. The omission of the price term does not make the contract in this case unenforceable. We begin by noting that the elements for breach of contract are: (1) the existence of a valid contract; (2) plaintiff performed or tendered performance; (3) the defendant breached the agreement; and (4) the plaintiff was damaged as a result of the breach. The trial court ruled that there was no valid contract entered into because, among other things, the price was not expressed in the contract. However, there was conflicting testimony concerning the agreed price with Landrum's (P) son testifying

Landrum v. Devenport (Continued)

that they agreed to the sticker price, and Devenport (D) testifying that they agreed to market value upon delivery. The fact that the price was not included in the written purchase order does not invalidate the agreement if both parties agreed on a price. Even if the price was not agreed upon, the contract may still be valid if both parties intended to be bound and there is a reasonably certain basis for giving an appropriate remedy. UCC § 2–204 [A contract does not fail for indefiniteness if one or more terms are left open if the parties have intended to make a contract and there is a reasonably certain basis for giving an appropriate remedy.] UCC § 2–305 [The parties if they so intend can conclude a contract for sale even though the price is not settled....] The law implies that a reasonable price was intended. UCC § 2-305(1)(a) [The price will be a reasonable price at the time for delivery if nothing is said as to price.] In this case, both parties signed the purchase order agreement, which was complete in all respects except for price. This is evidence that they intended to be bound. The question of the amount of the price was one for the jury. With respect to the necessary element that Landrum's (P) son perform or tender performance, it was undisputed that he tendered payment in the sum he believed had been agreed to, but which was refused by Devenport (D). The trial court concluded that certain defenses had been established relating to Devenport's (D) refusing the tender of the sticker price and payment by Landrum's (P) son of the higher price demanded by Devenport (D). We disagree with the trial court's conclusions. Because there was evidence that Landrum's (P) son paid the demanded price under protest and following the attorney's letter, it cannot be said that there was a valid novation or waiver. Both require that the parties intend that the new arrangement be a substitute for the old one. There were factual issues for the jury to determine the parties' intent. In addition, ratification cannot be inferred from the conduct by Landrum's (P) son where there was no satisfactory alternative, and such issues should be decided by the jury. Finally, estoppel was not established under the facts of this case. For these reasons, we conclude that the instructed verdict was improperly granted. Reversed and remanded.

Analysis:

Certain provisions of the UCC deal with the omission of essential terms of the contract, such as price. Such omission does not invalidate the contract if there is evidence that the parties intended to make a contract. The court here held that there was evidence of such intention by the signing of the purchase order, and the jury should have decided the issues. Thus, a "gap" in price may be "filled in" by the trier of fact, making the contract enforceable. Note that, the court cites to UCC § 1–207 to show that there was no intention on the part of Landrum's (P) son to ratify or waive when he paid the demanded price under protest, since he did so under the exigencies of the case, and with no satisfactory alternative. Here, the fact that there was no price specified in the written contract for purchase of cases of motor oil does not cause the contract to be unenforceable. The issue is whether the price should be determined based upon a reasonable price, market value, or past course of dealings.

■ **CASE VOCABULARY**

MOTION FOR INSTRUCTED VERDICT: Requesting the judge to instruct the jury to return a verdict for one party.

PAROL EVIDENCE RULE: Prior oral agreements cannot be used to change or modify the terms of a written agreement, unless mistake or fraud exists.

Cook Specialty Co. v. Schrlock

(Buyer of Machine) v. (Seller of Machine)
772 F.Supp. 1532, 16 UCC Rep. Serv. 2d 360 (E.D.Pa.1991)

CONTRACT FOR TRANSPORTATION OF GOODS IS REASONABLE EVEN THOUGH SELLER DOES NOT DETERMINE ADEQUACY OF CARRIER'S INSURANCE TO TRANSPORT THE GOODS

■ **INSTANT FACTS** Buyer of machine, with delivery terms "F.O.B. seller's warehouse", tried to pass risk of loss back to seller for not ensuring that carrier had adequate insurance to transport machine.

■ **BLACK LETTER RULE** A seller, under a "F.O.B. seller's warehouse" delivery contract, does not have an obligation to investigate the amount and terms of insurance held by the carrier before the risk of loss will pass to the buyer.

■ **PROCEDURAL BASIS**

Motion and cross-motion for summary judgment before trial court for breach of contract seeking damages for loss of goods.

■ **FACTS**

Machinery Systems, Inc. (MSI) (D1) entered into a contract to sell Cook Specialty Co. (Cook) (P) a hydraulic press brake machine valued at $28,000.00. The machine was lost in transit and the buyer, Cook (P), sued to recover the loss. The delivery terms of the contract were "F.O.B. MSI's warehouse in Schaumburg, Illinois." R.T.L. (D2) was the carrier used to deliver the machine from MSI's (D1) warehouse to Cook (P) in Pennsylvania. MSI (D1) obtained a certificate of insurance from the carrier, with a face amount of $100,000.00 and a $2,500.00 deductible. While R.T.L. (D2) was transporting the machine from the warehouse to Pennsylvania, the machine fell from the truck. The police cited R.T.L. (D2) for not properly securing the load. Cook (P) recovered damages from the carrier's insurer for the applicable policy limit of $5,000.00. Cook (P) contends that [by *stretching* the interpretation of the Code to the maximum] the contract MSI (D1) made for transporting the machine was not reasonable because it did not ensure that R.T.L. (D2) had sufficient insurance coverage to compensate Cook (P) for a loss in transit. Accordingly, Cook (P) asserts that the machine was never duly delivered to the carrier, and the risk of loss therefore never passed to Cook (P). Cook (P) and MSI (D1) each have motions for summary judgment pending before the court.

■ **ISSUE**

Does a seller, under a "F.O.B. seller's warehouse" delivery contract, have an obligation to investigate the amount and terms of insurance held by the carrier before the risk of loss will pass to the buyer?

■ **DECISION AND RATIONALE**

(Waldman) No. A seller is not required to investigate the amount and terms of insurance held by the carrier before the risk of loss will pass to the buyer. The contract delivery term was F.O.B. place of shipment. Under UCC Section 2–319, this means "the seller must at that place ship the goods in the manner provided in this Article (Section 2–504) and bear the expense and risk of putting them into the possession of the carrier." Thus, the seller, MSI (D1), bore the expense and risk of putting the machine into possession of the carrier. Once the carrier takes possession, the risk of loss shifts to the buyer

Cook Specialty Co. v. Schrlock (Continued)

pursuant UCC Section 2–509 [where the contract requires the seller to ship the goods by carrier and if it does not require him to deliver them at a particular destination, the risk of loss passes to the buyer when the goods are duly delivered to the carrier.] [So what kind of crazy legal theory had Cook (P) come up with?] Cook (P) contends that there was a duty or obligation on the part of the seller, MSI (D1), to ensure that the transportation carrier had adequate insurance coverage. Cook (P) relies upon certain language contained in Section 2-504(a) which provides that when the seller puts the goods in the possession of a carrier he must "make such a contract for their transportation as may be reasonable having regard to the nature of the goods and other circumstances of the case." Cook (P) argues that because the machine was never duly delivered to a carrier within the meaning of Section 2–509, the risk of loss never passed to him. Cook (P) relies on *La Casse v. Blaustein* [seller breached duty to make a reasonable contract for shipment by failing to obtain adequate insurance where package was underinsured, misaddressed, shipped by fourth class mail, and bore a theft-tempting inscription]. However, the actions in that case were utterly reckless. Here, MSI (D1) did not undertake the responsibility to insure the shipment and did not ship the machine at a lower cost than Cook (P) authorized it to pay. Cook (P) also relies upon *Miller v. Harvey* [failure to declare the actual value of goods shipped on applicable form]. This case is inapplicable because it was decided before the UCC was enacted. Cook (P) also places reliance on Official Comment 3 to Section 2–504 [it is an improper contract ... for the seller to agree with the carrier to a limited valuation below the true value and thus cut off the buyer's opportunity to recover from the carrier in the event of loss, when the risk of shipment is placed on the buyer]. However, Cook (P) misinterprets the meaning of both Comment 3 and Section 2–504. The clear implication is that the reasonableness of a shipper's conduct is determined with regard to the mode of transport selected. Thus, sending perishable goods without refrigeration would be unreasonable. No inference can be drawn that a seller has an obligation to investigate the amount and terms of insurance held by the carrier. MSI (D1) obtained the certificate of insurance from the carrier and did nothing to impair Cook's (P) right to recover for any loss from the carrier. Cook (P) therefore clearly bears the risk of loss in transit. MSI (D1) is entitled to judgment.

Analysis:

This case examines three UCC Sections: 1) § 2–319, the duty of the seller to "ship the goods in the manner provided in this Article (Section 2–504) and bear the expense and risk of putting them into the possession of the carrier"; 2) § 2–509, providing, "where the contract requires the seller to ship the goods by carrier and if it does not require him to deliver them at a particular destination, the risk of loss passes to the buyer when the goods are duly delivered to the carrier"; and, 3) § 2–504(a), stating that the seller must "make such a contract for their transportation as may be reasonable having regard to the nature of the goods and other circumstances of the case." The buyer, Cook (P), unsuccessfully attempted to avoid the loss by arguing that the seller did not comply with one of its duties under § 2–504. Take note that in the next case, *Rheinberg,* the buyer was held not liable for the loss of the goods where the seller failed to comply with its duty under subsection (c) of § 2–504 to give the buyer prompt notice of shipment. The failure to give notice prevented the buyer from obtaining insurance coverage during transit. In this case, there was a certificate of insurance provided, and the court held that the seller was not under a duty to go the extra mile of ensuring the adequacy of the insurance coverage.

■ CASE VOCABULARY

CONSEQUENTIAL DAMAGES: A loss which is not a direct result of the breach, but which is a consequence thereof.

Rheinberg-Kellerei GMBH v. Vineyard Wine Co.

(Seller of Wine) v. (Buyer of Wine)
53 N.C.App. 560, 281 S.E.2d 425, 32 UCC Rep. Serv. 96 (1981)

BUYER MAY REJECT GOODS FOR NOT BEING *DULY DELIVERED* TO THE CARRIER WHERE SELLER FAILS TO PROMPTLY NOTIFY BUYER OF THE SHIPMENT

■ **INSTANT FACTS** Contract entered into for the sale of wine from West Germany to the United States, but seller, Rheinberg (P), did not promptly notify buyer, Vineyard (D), of shipment.

■ **BLACK LETTER RULE** The risk of loss under a contract not requiring delivery to any particular destination does not pass to the buyer upon delivery to the carrier where the seller has failed to give the buyer prompt notice of shipment.

■ **PROCEDURAL BASIS**

Appeal from judgment following court trial seeking damages for breach of contract.

■ **FACTS**

In August, 1978, Vineyard Wine Co. (Vineyard) (D) agreed to purchase cases of wine from a West German wine producer and exporter, Rheinberg-Kellerei GmbH (Rheinberg) (P), through its importing agent/broker, Frank Sutton (Sutton). Vineyard (D) had received confirmation of the sale orders from the agent Sutton. For the next three to four months, Vineyard (D) made telephone inquiries to the agent concerning when the wine would be shipped and/or arrive. In late November, 1978, Rheinberg (P) issued notice to its agent Sutton of the date of shipment, port of origin, vessel, estimated date of arrival and port of arrival. Vineyard (D) was not given this information. The purchase contract did not request Rheinberg (P) to deliver the wine to any particular destination. Rheinberg (P) gave notice to its agent Sutton of the shipment of the wine, but Vineyard (D) was not given such notice. Vineyard (D) did not learn that the wine had been shipped until some weeks later when documents were sent from the bank to collect the invoice from Vineyard (D). However, prior to its learning of the shipment, the wine was lost at sea en route between Germany and the United States [resulting in a sea full of drunken fish]. Vineyard (D) did not receive the wine and did not pay. Rheinberg (P) brought this action to recover the purchase price of the wine. After a court trial, judgment was entered in favor of Vineyard (D). Both Rheinberg (P) and Vineyard (D) appealed.

■ **ISSUE**

Does the risk of loss under a contract not requiring delivery to any particular destination pass to the buyer upon delivery to the carrier where the seller has failed to give the buyer prompt notice of shipment?

■ **DECISION AND RATIONALE**

(Wells) No. The risk of loss under a contract not requiring delivery to any particular destination does not pass to the buyer upon delivery to the carrier where the seller has failed to give the buyer prompt notice of shipment. It is not disputed that the contract in question was a "shipment contract," i.e., one not requiring delivery of the wine at any particular destination. UCC Section 2-509(1)(a) dictates when the transfer of risk of loss occurs in this situation [risk of loss passes to the buyer when the goods are

Rheinberg-Kellerei GMBH v. Vineyard Wine Co. (Continued)

duly delivered to the carrier even though the shipment is under reservation....] Before a seller will be deemed to have "duly delivered" the goods to the carrier, certain duties owed to the buyer must be fulfilled. Section 2-504 sets forth the duties, and under subsection (c) the seller must "promptly notify the buyer of the shipment." The Section also provides that "[f]ailure to notify the buyer under paragraph (c) ... is a ground for rejection only if material delay or loss ensues." [A sinking ship constitutes a material delay or loss!] We agree with the trial court's conclusion that the failure of the seller, Rheinberg (P), to notify Vineyard (D) of the shipment until after the sailing of the ship and the ensuing loss, was not "prompt notice" within the meaning of Section 2-504. Therefore, the risk of loss did not pass to Vineyard (D) upon delivery of the wine to the carrier pursuant to Section 2-509(1)(a). When a buyer assumes the perils involved in carriage, he must have a reasonable opportunity to guard against these risks by independent arrangements with the carrier. The prompt notification requirement allows a buyer to be informed of the shipment in sufficient time for him to take action to protect himself from the risk of damage or loss to the goods while in transit. Whether notification has been "prompt" must be decided upon a case-by-case basis. Although Rheinberg (P) notified its agent of the shipment of wine, this information was not given to Vineyard (D). The bank did not receive the shipping documents for forwarding to Vineyard (D) until after the loss had already occurred. Therefore, Vineyard (D) was entitled under Section 2-504(c) to reject the shipment. Judgment in favor of Vineyard (D) is affirmed.

Analysis:

This case examines the seller's duties to the buyer under § 2-504 and when a risk of loss passes under a shipment contract pursuant to UCC § 2-509(1)(a). If the duties under 2-504 are not fulfilled, such as the duty to promptly notify the buyer of the shipment, then the risk of loss does not pass to the buyer. The court has treated the failure to perform a duty as meaning the goods were not "duly delivered" under § 2-509. The seller, Rheinberg (P), gave the information to its agent, but because neither Rheinberg (P) nor his agent gave the information to Vineyard (D), there was a lack of prompt notification. Under the Code, even if a material delay ensued, rather than a loss of the goods, this would have been a sufficient basis for Vineyard (D) to have rejected the goods. In the previous case, *Cook*, an argument was also made that the goods were not "duly delivered." However, rather than relying upon subsection (c) of § 2-504, the buyer argued that there was a breach of the duty under subsection (a), which requires that the seller make a contract with the carrier for transportation as may be reasonable with respect to the goods and other circumstances. Thus, Section 2-504, which imposes certain duties upon a seller, may be used as a basis to claim that the risk of loss does not pass to the buyer when the goods are "duly delivered to the carrier" under Section 2-509.

■ CASE VOCABULARY

BILL OF LADING: A written document from a carrier as evidence that certain identifiable goods have been accepted by it from another for transport and delivery to another person and location.

FINDINGS OF FACT: Court weighs the evidence and makes a determination as to the facts.

CHAPTER FIVE

Performance of the Contract

Cherwell–Ralli, Inc. v. Rytman Grain Co.

Instant Facts: Buyer (D) and Seller (P) entered into an installment contract for the sale of grain meal. Buyer (D) failed to make payments as required by the contract, and Seller (P) sued for damages.

Black Letter Rule: Failure to pay as required in an installment contract may constitute a breach of the entire contract under UCC § 2–612(3).

Wilson v. Scampoli

Instant Facts: Buyer (P) purchased a color television set from Seller (D). When the television failed to function properly, Seller (D) offered to repair the television. Buyer (P) refused and insisted on a new replacement. When Seller (D) refused, Buyer (P) brought suit seeking cancellation of the contract and a refund of the purchase price.

Black Letter Rule: A seller may cure a nonconforming delivery by either repairing or replacing the nonconforming good.

Ramirez v. Autosport

Instant Facts: The Ramirezes (P) contracted with Autosport (D) to buy a new camper van and to trade-in a van owned by the Ramirezes (P). After numerous attempts to have defects corrected and to take delivery of the new van, the Ramirezes rejected the van and sought cancellation of the contract.

Black Letter Rule: A buyer may reject defective goods no matter how minor or trivial the defect.

Plateq Corp of North Haven v. Machlett Laboratories, Inc.

Instant Facts: Machlett (D) contracted with Plateq (P) to purchase steel tanks used to test x-ray tubes. When the tanks were substantially completed, Plateq (P) promised to remedy some remaining defects in time for delivery. Machlett (D), in turn, promised to pick up the tanks, but instead, cancelled the contract.

Black Letter Rule: A buyer accepts goods when he signifies to the seller that they are conforming or that he will take them in spite of their non-conformity.

Waddell v. L.V. R.V.

Instant Facts: Waddell (P) purchased a motor home from Wheeler's (D), but tried to revoke acceptance after numerous repair attempts failed to correct the defects.

Black Letter Rule: A buyer may revoke acceptance of goods when a nonconformity impairs the value of the goods to the individual buyer, taking into account the needs and circumstances of the individual buyer.

Jakowski v. Carole Chevrolet, Inc.

Instant Facts: Jakowski (P) contracted with Carole Chevrolet (D) for the purchase of a Camaro with undercoating and a polymer coating finish. The car was delivered to Jakowski (P) without the coatings. Jakowski (P) returned the car to Carole (D) for the coatings, and while there, the car was stolen.

Black Letter Rule: The risk of loss remains on the seller for non-conforming goods until he cures the defects or the buyer accepts the goods.

Arabian Score v. Lasma Arabian Ltd.

Instant Facts: Arabian Score (P) contracted with Lasma Corporation (D) and Lasma Arabian Ltd. (D) to buy and promote an Arabian colt named Score. When Score died, Arabian (P) sued for the remaining funds set aside for Score's promotion.

Black Letter Rule: The commercial impracticability doctrine does not excuse performance for events that are reasonably foreseeable.

Louisiana Power & Light Co. v. Allegheny Ludlum Industries, Inc.

Instant Facts: Allegheny Ludlum Industries, Inc (D) contracted to furnish Louisiana Power & Light Co. (P) tubing for use at LP & L's (P) nuclear power plant. When prices increased, Allegheny (D) requested additional compensation. LP & L (P) denied the request and sought assurance from Allegheny (D) that it would perform under the contract.

Black Letter Rule: A party to a contract who is insecure about the other party's performance may demand assurance of performance and treat the failure to provide such assurance as a repudiation of the contract.

Cherwell-Ralli, Inc. v. Rytman Grain Co.

(Seller) v. (Buyer)
180 Conn. 714, 433 A.2d 984, 29 UCC Rep. Serv. 513 (1980)

A BUYER'S FAILURE TO PAY UNDER AN INSTALLMENT CONTRACT MAY CONSTITUTE A BREACH OF THE WHOLE CONTRACT

■ **INSTANT FACTS** Buyer (D) and Seller (P) entered into an installment contract for the sale of grain meal. Buyer (D) failed to make payments as required by the contract, and Seller (P) sued for damages.

■ **BLACK LETTER RULE** Failure to pay as required in an installment contract may constitute a breach of the entire contract under UCC § 2-612(3).

■ **PROCEDURAL BASIS**

Appeal from judgment awarding damages to seller in action for nonpayment of monies due under an installment contract.

■ **FACTS**

Cherwell-Ralli, Inc. (P) (Seller) and Rytman Grain Co. (D) (Buyer) entered into an installment contract for the sale of grain meal. The contract called for shipments according to weekly instructions from Buyer (D), with payments to made within ten days after delivery. Almost immediately, Buyer (D) was behind in payments. Seller (P) called these arrearages to Buyer's (D) attention but continued to make all shipments requested by Buyer (D). Shortly before the last shipment, Buyer (D) became concerned about Seller's (P) ability to perform under the contract but was assured by Seller (P) that deliveries would continue so long as Buyer (D) continued to make its payments. Buyer (D) sent Seller (P) a check but later stopped payment on it after a truck driver unaffiliated with Seller (P) told him that Seller's (P) future deliveries were in jeopardy. Buyer (D) made no further payments, either to replace the stopped check or to pay for the nineteen accepted shipments for which balances were outstanding. Seller (P) made no further deliveries after the stopped check. Due to its inability to deliver the goods, Seller (P) was forced to close its plant. Seller (P) sued for the money due and owing for the accepted deliveries, and Buyer (D) counterclaimed for damages arising out of Seller's (P) refusal to deliver the remaining installments under the contract. The trial court rendered judgment in favor of Seller (P) and dismissed Buyer's (D) counterclaim. Buyer (D) appealed.

■ **ISSUE**

May a buyer's failure to pay as required in an installment contract substantially impair the value of the whole contract so as to constitute a breach of the whole contract under UCC § 2-612(3)?

■ **DECISION AND RATIONALE**

(Peters, J.) Yes. A buyer's failure to pay as required under an installment contract may substantially impair the value of the whole contract so as to constitute a breach of the whole contract under UCC § 2-612(3). What constitutes impairment of the value of the whole contract is a question of fact, and the record below amply sustains the trial court's conclusion in this regard. Conduct by a Buyer (D) that is sufficiently egregious can constitute substantial impairment of the value of the whole contract and a

Cherwell-Ralli, Inc. v. Rytman Grain Co. (Continued)

present breach of the contract as a whole. An aggrieved Seller (P) is expressly permitted by § 2-703(f), upon breach of a contract as a whole, to cancel the remainder of the contract with respect to the whole undelivered balance. Further, § 2–612(3) does not affect Seller's (P) remedy to cancel since Seller's (P) lawsuit seeks not only damages, but also an end to the contract. Buyer (D) argues that Seller (P) was obligated to provide assurance of its further performance. The right to such assurance, however, is premised on reasonable grounds to be insecure. Buyer's (D) insecurity was not reasonable since it received all the goods that it had ordered and had received verbal assurances from Seller (P) of its continued deliveries. The Buyer (D) cannot rely on its own nonpayment as a ground for its insecurity. Affirmed.

Analysis:

In single delivery contracts, the seller must make a perfect tender under UCC § 2–601. That is, the seller's delivery must theoretically conform to the contract in every respect or the buyer may hold the seller in breach of contract. However, the UCC is more lenient with respect to installment contracts. In keeping with the common law, the seller is entitled to payment so long as his tender of the goods substantially conforms to the contract, even if his performance is not technically perfect. UCC § 2–612 illustrates this leniency by limiting the buyer's right to reject installments (or to cancel the entire contract) to those occasions where the value of the installments is substantially impaired (or where the defect in the installment substantially impairs the value of the whole contract). Problems arise, however, since the UCC does not specify how to determine whether a defect substantially impairs the value of the installment or the whole contract. Likewise, the court in the present case fails to adequately discuss the factors relevant in making such a determination other than to say it is a question of fact.

■ **CASE VOCABULARY**

INSTALLMENT CONTRACT: A contract that requires or authorizes the delivery of goods in separate lots to be separately accepted.

UCC § 2–612: Gives a buyer the right to reject a defective installment if the nonconformity substantially impairs the value of that installment and cannot be cured by the seller, or to cancel the entire contract if the defect in the installment substantially impairs the value of the whole contract.

Wilson v. Scampoli

(*Television Dealer*) v. (*Buyer*)
228 A.2d 848, 4 UCC Rep. Serv. 178 (D.C. 1967)

A SELLER MAY CURE HIS NONCONFORMITY BY EITHER REPAIR OR REPLACEMENT

■ **INSTANT FACTS** Buyer (P) purchased a color television set from Seller (D). When the television failed to function properly, Seller (D) offered to repair the television. Buyer (P) refused and insisted on a new replacement. When Seller (D) refused, Buyer (P) brought suit seeking cancellation of the contract and a refund of the purchase price.

■ **BLACK LETTER RULE** A seller may cure a nonconforming delivery by either repairing or replacing the nonconforming good.

■ **PROCEDURAL BASIS**

Appeal from order granting rescission of a sales contract and directing the return of the purchase price in action alleging breach of warranty.

■ **FACTS**

Buyer (P) purchased a color television set from Seller (D), a retail dealer, paying the total purchase price in cash. The sales ticket showed the purchase price and guaranteed replacement of any defective tube and parts for a period of one year. When the set was delivered to Buyer (P) two days later, it did not function properly. Two days later, a service representative on behalf of Seller (D) attempted unsuccessfully to repair the television set on site. The service representative advised that the television's chassis would have to be taken to the shop for repair. Buyer (P) refused to allow the chassis to be removed, asserting that she wanted another brand new set, not a repaired set. Buyer (P) later demanded the return of the purchase price, but Seller (D) refused. However, Seller (D) renewed his offer to adjust, repair, or, if necessary, to replace the set. Buyer (P) ultimately initiated this suit against Seller (D) seeking a refund of the purchase price. The trial court granted rescission of the contract and directed the return of the purchase price to Buyer (P). Seller (D) appealed.

■ **ISSUE**

May a seller cure his nonconforming delivery by either repair or replacement of the nonconforming good?

■ **DECISION AND RATIONALE**

(Myers, J.) Yes. A seller may cure his nonconforming delivery by either repair or replacement of the nonconforming good. A retail dealer would certainly expect and have reasonable grounds to believe that merchandise like color television sets, new and delivered as crated at the factory, would be acceptable as delivered, and that, if defective in some way, he would have the right to substitute a conforming tender. Prior cases indicate that minor repairs or reasonable adjustments are frequently the means by which imperfect tender may be cured. Removal of the television chassis presents no great inconvenience to Buyer (P). Buyer's (P) refusal to allow inspection essential to determine the cause of the defect defeated any effort by Seller (D) to provide timely repair, or if necessary, replacement. As

HIGH COURT CASE SUMMARIES 83

Wilson v. Scampoli (Continued)

such, Buyer (P) has failed to show a breach of warranty entitling him to a brand new set or to rescission. Reversed.

Analysis:

It is not entirely clear which subsection of UCC § 2–508 the court applies in this case. § 2–508(1) allows the seller an opportunity to cure his nonconforming tender or delivery, provided the time for performance has not yet expired. The point at which the contract in this case was fully performed was when Seller (D) delivered the television, since Buyer (P) had already paid for it. As a result, the time for performance had expired by the time Seller (D) offered to repair the television set two days later. Thus, § 2–508(1) seems to be inapplicable . . . the court seemingly relies on § 2–508(2), which only applies after the time for performance has expired, when it states that "[a] retail dealer would certainly expect and have reasonable grounds to believe that merchandise like color television sets, new and delivered as crated at the factory, would be acceptable as delivered, and that, if defective in some way, he would have the right to substitute a conforming tender." But § 2–508(2) refers to the situation where the seller delivers goods that he knows are nonconforming but reasonably believes will be acceptable to the buyer, for example, when the buyer contracts to purchase a year 2000 car and the seller delivers a 2001 model that is "new and improved" for the same price.

■ CASE VOCABULARY

UCC § 2–508: Gives a seller an opportunity to cure his nonconforming tender or delivery before the expiration of the time for the performance of the contract, or after that period if the seller had reasonable grounds to believe that the non-conforming tender would be acceptable, regardless of whether the seller makes a money allowance.

Ramirez v. Autosport

(Buyer) v. (Car Dealer)
88 N.J. 277, 440 A.2d 1345, 33 UCC Rep. Serv. 134 (1982)

A BUYER MAY REJECT GOODS FOR ANY DEFECTS

■ **INSTANT FACTS** The Ramirezes (P) contracted with Autosport (D) to buy a new camper van and to trade-in a van owned by the Ramirezes (P). After numerous attempts to have defects corrected and to take delivery of the new van, the Ramirezes rejected the van and sought cancellation of the contract.

■ **BLACK LETTER RULE** A buyer may reject defective goods no matter how minor or trivial the defect.

■ **PROCEDURAL BASIS**

Appeal from judgment canceling the contract and awarding buyer restitution in breach of contract action.

■ **FACTS**

On July 20, 1978, the Ramirezes (P) contracted with Autosport (D) for the sale of a new camper van and the trade-in of a van owned by the Ramirezes (P). The contract provided for delivery on August 3, 1978. When the Ramirezes returned on August 3, there were several defects in the van including scratched paint, missing hubcaps, and missing electric and sewer hookups. Several more weeks passed, and Autosport (D) finally notified the Ramirezes (P) that the van was ready. On August 14, the Ramirezes (P) went to Autosport (D) to accept delivery. At that time, workers were still touching up paint and cushions inside were rain soaked. The Ramirezes (P) again refused delivery. Between August 15 and September 1, Autosport (D), in response to the Ramirezes' (P) inquiries, constantly advised that the van was not ready. When the Ramirezes (P) returned to Autosport (D) on September 1, as instructed to do by Autosport (D), they were still unable to pick up the van. In October, the Ramirezes (P) requested the return of their trade-in. The Ramirezes (P) eventually sued Autosport (D) seeking rescission of the contract. Autosport (D) counterclaimed for breach of contract. The trial court ruled that the Ramirezes (P) rightfully rejected the van and awarded them the fair market value of their trade-in. The Appellate Division affirmed, and Autosport (D) appealed.

■ **ISSUE**

May a buyer reject the tender of nonconforming goods that have only minor defects?

■ **DECISION AND RATIONALE**

(Pollock, J.) Yes. A buyer may reject the tender of nonconforming goods that have only minor defects. Under UCC § 2–601, a seller has the duty to deliver goods that conform precisely to the contract, and before acceptance, a buyer has the right to reject goods for any defects. The Code mitigates the harshness of this rule, however, by allowing the seller the right to cure the nonconformity. After acceptance, under UCC § 2–608, the buyer may revoke acceptance only if the nonconformity substantially impairs the value of the goods to him. This provision protects the seller from revocation for trivial defects. However, because this case involves rejection of goods, we need not decide whether a seller has a right to cure substantial defects that justify revocation of acceptance. Because of a

Ramirez v. Autosport (Continued)

seller's right to cure, rejection does not automatically terminate the contract. However, after rejection, the buyer may cancel the contract pursuant to UCC § 2–711 if the defects remain uncured and seek the return of the purchase price that has been paid, Cancellation occurs when either party puts an end to the contract for breach by the other. The Code has discarded the word "rescission" in favor of the term "cancellation." Commercial reality permits the seller to cure imperfect tenders. Should the seller fail to cure the defects, whether substantial or not, the balance shifts in favor of the buyer, who has the right to cancel or seek damages. The trial court found that the Ramirezes (P) rejected the van within a reasonable time. We find that Autosport (D) did not cure the defects despite having ample time to do so. Because revocation of acceptance is not at issue here, the trial court correctly refrained from deciding whether the defects substantially impaired the van. The Ramirezes (P) are entitled to recover so much of the purchase price as has been paid, which the trial court set at the fair market value of the trade-in. Affirmed.

Analysis:

The court here is willing to interpret the "perfect tender" rule of UCC § 2–601 literally. The rule gives the buyer the right to reject goods that are defective "in any respect," no matter how minor. Note that this rule with respect to contracts for the sale of goods is contrary to the general rule regarding non-UCC contracts, where the breach must be material and the parties are only required to "substantially perform." Perhaps the court's willingness to interpret the perfect tender rule literally comes from its recognition that the seller is given a "second chance" in his limited right to cure the defects. However, some courts have not applied the perfect tender rule so strictly, generally allowing buyers to reject the seller's tender only if the defect was a substantial one. Such holdings seem to graft the common law into the UCC, which, in turn, virtually abolishes the perfect tender rule.

■ CASE VOCABULARY

UCC § 2–601: Gives the buyer in single delivery contracts the right to reject, accept, or accept and reject in part goods that fail to conform to the contract "in any respect."

UCC § 2–608: Allows the buyer to revoke his acceptance within a reasonable time if the nonconformity substantially impairs the value of the goods to him, provided that he accepted them on the reasonable assumption that the nonconformity would be cured and it has not been, or the nonconformity was undiscovered due to the difficulty of discovery or by seller's assurances.

UCC § 2–711: Specifies the buyer's remedies in general, including the right to cancel and to recover so much of the purchase price as has been paid.

Plateq Corp. of North Haven v. Machlett Laboratories, Inc.

(Seller) v. (Buyer)
189 Conn. 433, 456 A.2d 786, 35 UCC Rep. Serv. 1162 (1983)

ACCEPTANCE OCCURS WHEN A BUYER SIGNIFIES THAT THE GOODS ARE CONFORMING

■ **INSTANT FACTS** Machlett (D) contracted with Plateq (P) to purchase steel tanks used to test x-ray tubes. When the tanks were substantially completed, Plateq (P) promised to remedy some remaining defects in time for delivery. Machlett (D), in turn, promised to pick up the tanks, but instead, cancelled the contract.

■ **BLACK LETTER RULE** A buyer accepts goods when he signifies to the seller that they are conforming or that he will take them in spite of their non-conformity.

■ **PROCEDURAL BASIS**

Appeal from judgment awarding damages to seller in action for breach of contract.

■ **FACTS**

Machlett Laboratories, Inc. (D) ordered from Plateq Corp of North Haven (P) two lead-covered steel tanks to be constructed by Plateq (P) according to specifications supplied by Machlett (D). The tanks were specially designed for the purpose of testing x-ray tubes and were required to be radiation proof according to federal standards. The contract provided that the tanks would be tested for radiation leaks after their installation on Machlett's (D) premises and would be corrected at Plateq's (P) expense. When the tanks were substantially completed, Machlett (D) noted some remaining deficiencies. Plateq (P) promised to remedy these defects by the next day in time for delivery. Machlett (D) indicated that it would pick up the tanks within a day or two. Instead, Machlett (D) sent a notice of total cancellation, but failed to particularize the grounds upon which cancellation was based. Plateq (P) brought suit to recover the purchase price and incidental damages, and Machlett (D) counterclaimed. The trial court held for Plateq (P), and Machlett (D) appealed.

■ **ISSUE**

Does a buyer's general acquiescence in the seller's proposed tender, despite possible remaining minor defects, constitute an acceptance of the goods by the buyer?

■ **DECISION AND RATIONALE**

(Peters, J.) Yes. A buyer's general acquiescence in the seller's proposed tender, despite possible remaining minor defects, constitutes an acceptance of the goods by the buyer. The trial court determined that, pursuant to UCC § 2–606, Machlett (D) had accepted the tanks by signifying its willingness to take them despite their non-conformities or, in the alternative, by failing to make an effective rejection. In reaching that conclusion, the trial court necessarily found that Machlett (D) had had a reasonable opportunity to inspect the goods. The trial court rejected Machlett's (D) argument that the contract's post-installation test postponed its inspection rights until that time, concluding that the post-installation test clause was limited to adjustments to take place after tender and acceptance. Machlett (D) also accepted the tanks by failing to make an effective rejection. Machlett (D) did not

Plateq Corp. of North Haven v. Machlett Laboratories, Inc. (Continued)

reasonably notify Plateq (P) of its rejection since it failed to particularize the defects in its notice of rejection. Once the tanks had been accepted, Machlett (D) could rightfully revoke its acceptance only by showing substantial impairment of their value to Machlett (D). Such impairment is a question of fact and has not been proven, in part because Machlett's (D) conduct foreclosed any post-installation inspection. Machlett (D) has not shown that the trial court was clearly erroneous. As a result, there is no error in the trial court's conclusions. Since the specially manufactured tanks were not readily resalable on the open market, Plateq (P) was entitled to recover their contract price as well as incidental damages. Affirmed.

Analysis:

The court in the present case agreed with the trial court's finding that Machlett (D) had accepted the goods by signifying its willingness to take the tanks despite their nonconformities. However, the facts as reported reveal that Plateq (P) promised to remedy the defects prior to delivery, which seems to signify that Machlett (D) did not intend to pick up defective goods, but was expecting conforming goods on the delivery date. Nevertheless, Machlett (D) could have taken delivery of the tanks and revoked its acceptance shortly thereafter by showing a substantial impairment of the value of the tanks to him, assuming Plateq (P) was unable to cure the defect. Alternatively, Machlett (D) would have had a breach of warranty action, provided that he notified Plateq (P) of the breach within a reasonable time. An important question is the effect of a cancellation notice that did not specify the defects. Failure to specify the defects prevented Plateq (P) from making any needed repairs.

■ CASE VOCABULARY

UCC § 2–606: Acceptance of goods occurs when the buyer, after a reasonable opportunity to inspect the goods, signifies to the seller that the goods are conforming or that he will take or retain them in spite of their nonconformity; or when the buyer fails to make an effective rejection under § 2–602, but such acceptance does not occur until buyer has had a reasonable opportunity to inspect them; or when the buyer does any act inconsistent with the seller's ownership.

Waddell v. L.V. R.V.

(*Motor Home Purchaser*) v. (*Motor Home Seller*)
122 Nev. 15, 125 P.3d 1160 (2006)

ACCEPTANCE MAY BE REVOKED IF A NONCONFORMITY SUBSTANTIALLY IMPAIRS THE VALUE OF THE GOODS TO THE INDIVIDUAL BUYER

■ **INSTANT FACTS** Waddell (P) purchased a motor home from Wheeler's (D), but tried to revoke acceptance after numerous repair attempts failed to correct the defects.

■ **BLACK LETTER RULE** A buyer may revoke acceptance of goods when a nonconformity impairs the value of the goods to the individual buyer, taking into account the needs and circumstances of the individual buyer.

■ **PROCEDURAL BASIS:**
Appeal from a judgment for Waddell (P) entered after a bench trial.

■ **FACTS:**
Waddell (P) purchased a new motor home from L.V. R.V., d.b.a. Wheeler's (D). Before taking possession of the motor home, Waddell (P) specifically asked that Wheeler's (D) make certain repairs, including servicing the engine cooling system, installing new batteries, and aligning the door frames. Wheeler's (D) told Waddell (P) that the repairs had been made, and Waddell (P) took possession of the motor home.

Waddell (P) noticed problems with the cooling system and the doors on the motor home shortly after taking possession of it. Waddell (P) returned the motor home to Wheeler's (D) for repairs. Wheeler's (D) made several attempts to repair the motor home, but Waddell (P) continued to experience problems with it. Between September 1997 and March 1999, the motor home was in Wheeler's (D) service department for a total of seven months while Wheeler's (D) attempted repairs. Waddell (P) demanded a full return of the purchase price in March 1999, and attempted to resolve the matter during the summer of 1999. Wheeler's (D) did not respond until early 2000.

Waddell (P) filed a complaint to revoke acceptance of the motor home in June 2000. The court found that the motor home had nonconformities that included defective air conditioning and heating, failure of the batteries to stay charged, and a tendency of the engine to overheat. The court held that these nonconformities substantially impaired the RV's value to Waddell (P), and also held that Waddell (P) revoked acceptance within a reasonable time.

■ **ISSUE:**
Should Waddell (P) have been allowed to revoke acceptance?

■ **DECISION AND RATIONALE:**
(Gibbons, J.) Yes. A buyer may revoke acceptance of goods when a nonconformity impairs the value of the goods to the individual buyer, taking into account the needs and circumstances of the individual buyer. The test has two parts. The first part is a subjective inquiry into the needs and circumstances of the buyer who seeks to revoke. The court does not consider the "average" buyer. The second part of the inquiry is whether the nonconformity does in fact impair the value of the goods to the buyer. It is an

Waddell v. L.V. R.V. (Continued)

objective inquiry, and requires evidence that shows the buyer's needs were not met because of the nonconformity.

The value of the RV to Waddell (P) was based on plans to use the RV for extensive travelling. The RV was purchased based on those plans, and was purchased from Wheeler's (D) based in part on Wheeler's (D) advertisements. The advertising encouraged RV purchases as a way to find "unlimited freedom." The RV Waddell (P) purchased was recommended as one that would meet his needs. As a result of the defects in the RV, however, Waddell (P) was unable to use it as intended. The RV spent several months in Wheeler's (D) shop on repair attempts. This evidence shows a substantial impairment.

In addition, a nonconformity is a substantial impairment of value if the nonconformity undermines the buyer's confidence in the reliability of the item. Here, the chronic engine overheating undermined Waddell's (P) confidence in the RV. The overheating also made travel in the RV objectively unsafe. There was substantial evidence to support revocation of acceptance.

Wheeler's (D) also argued that Waddell (P) should not be allowed to revoke acceptance because the revocation was not made within a reasonable time. The trial court found that Waddell (P) noticed the defects immediately after the purchase. Waddell (P) always took the RV to Wheeler's (D) whenever he noticed a defect, and Wheeler's (D) always attempted to repair the defect. The RV was in Wheeler's (D) service department for seven of the eighteen months Waddell (P) owned the RV. Although a seller is entitled to try to cure a nonconformity before acceptance may be revoked, the seller may not continually postpone revocation by making repair attempts. Furthermore, a seller's attempts to cure do not count against a buyer regarding timely revocation. Tolling the reasonable time for revocation of acceptance is appropriate, given the buyer's obligation to act in good faith, and it also gives the seller a reasonable opportunity to cure defects. Waddell (P) gave several opportunities to repair, and when Wheeler's (D) was unable to make the repairs, Waddell (P) was entitled to revoke acceptance. Affirmed.

Analysis:

Article 2 of the U.C.C. does not explicitly state that a seller must be given an opportunity to cure defects before acceptance is revoked. In this case, the court seems to infer such an opportunity, based on the buyer's obligation to act "in good faith." Many consumer warranty laws, such as state motor vehicle "lemon laws," explicitly require that the seller be allowed to attempt repairs before there is any obligation to make a refund. Those laws often place a limit on the number of repair attempts required, so that the buyer is not strung along indefinitely, waiting for promised repairs to be effective.

Jakowski v. Carole Chevrolet, Inc.
(Buyer) v. (Car Dealer)
180 N.J.Super. 122, 433 A.2d 841, 31 UCC Rep. Serv. 1615 (1981)

THE SELLER BEARS THE RISK OF LOSS FOR DEFECTIVE GOODS

■ **INSTANT FACTS** Jakowski (P) contracted with Carole Chevrolet (D) for the purchase of a Camaro with undercoating and a polymer coating finish. The car was delivered to Jakowski (P) without the coatings. Jakowski (P) returned the car to Carole (D) for the coatings, and while there, the car was stolen.

■ **BLACK LETTER RULE** The risk of loss remains on the seller for non-conforming goods until he cures the defects or the buyer accepts the goods.

■ **CASE VOCABULARY**

UCC § 2–510(1): Provides that, where the seller delivers or tenders nonconforming goods, the risk of loss remains on the seller until he has cured the defects or until the buyer accepts the goods.

■ **PROCEDURAL BASIS**

Motion for summary judgment by buyer in breach of contract action.

■ **FACTS**

Jakowski (P) entered into a sales contract with Carole Chevrolet (D) for the purchase of a 1980 Chevrolet Camaro, Prior to delivery, the parties agreed that the car would be both undercoated and that its finish would have a polymer coating. The car was delivered to Jakowski (P) without the coatings. A few days later, Carole (D) notified Jakowski (P) of the mistake and instructed him to return the car for application of the coatings. While at Carole's (D) dealership, the car was stolen and was never recovered. Carole (D) refused to provide a replacement auto or to refund the purchase price. Jakowski (P) sued for breach of contract and now moves for summary judgment.

■ **ISSUE**

Does a seller who obtains possession of goods in an effort to cure defects in them bear the risk of loss of those goods while they are in his possession?

■ **DECISION AND RATIONALE**

(Newman, J.) Yes. A seller who obtains possession of goods in an effort to cure defects in them bears the risk of loss of those goods while they are in his possession. UCC § 2–510(1) provides: Where a tender or delivery of goods so fails to conform to the contract as to give the right of rejection the risk of loss remains on the seller until cure or acceptance. The contract clearly provided that the car would be delivered with undercoating and a polymer finish, and it was delivered without these coatings. Thus, the car was clearly nonconforming, and Jakowski (P) had a right to reject it under the "perfect tender"

Jakowski v. Carole Chevrolet, Inc. (Continued)

rule. No quantum of nonconformity is required by the "so fails to conform" language of § 2–510(1). Furthermore, Jakowski (P) cannot be held to have accepted the car since a buyer must be afforded a reasonable opportunity to inspect the goods. Jakowski (P) had no reason or opportunity to reject the car given Carole's (D) communication shortly after the sale advising of its mistake and exercising its right to cure the nonconformity. There was no acceptance by Jakowski (P) of this nonconforming auto. Lastly, there is no evidence that Carole (D) ever effected a cure of the defect. Accordingly, the risk of loss remained on Carole (D). Judgment is granted for Jakowski (P) for the purchase price and the finance charges incurred.

Analysis:

Note that UCC § 2–510 only applies when there has been a breach of contract and an ensuing loss. Where there has been no breach, UCC § 2–509 applies and provides that the risk of loss passes to the buyer on his receipt of the goods if the seller is a merchant, or on tender of delivery if the seller is a non-merchant. The risk of loss rules under § 2–509 are, however, altered if the contract requires shipment or if the goods are held by a bailee under certain circumstances.

■ CASE VOCABULARY

UCC § 2–510(1): Provides that, where the seller delivers or tenders nonconforming goods, the risk of loss remains on the seller until he has cured the defects or until the buyer accepts the goods.

Arabian Score v. Lasma Arabian Ltd.
(*Buyer*) v. (*Seller*)
814 F.2d 529, 3 UCC Rep. Serv. 2d 590 (8th Cir. 1987)

THE COMMERCIAL IMPRACTICABILITY DOCTRINE DOES NOT APPLY TO REASONABLY FORESEEABLE RISKS

■ **INSTANT FACTS** Arabian Score (P) contracted with Lasma Corporation (D) and Lasma Arabian Ltd. (D) to buy and promote an Arabian colt named Score. When Score died, Arabian (P) sued for the remaining funds set aside for Score's promotion.

■ **BLACK LETTER RULE** The commercial impracticability doctrine does not excuse performance for events that are reasonably foreseeable.

■ **PROCEDURAL BASIS**

Appeal from order granting summary judgment in favor of Lasma Arabian Ltd. (D) and Lasma Corporation (D).

■ **FACTS**

Arabian Score (P) entered into an agreement to purchase from Lasma Corporation (D) (Lasma) an Arabian colt named Score. The agreement provided that Arabian (P) would pay Lasma Arabian Ltd. (D)(Limited) $1 million for the purchase of Score and that Lasma (D) would spend $250,000 to advertise and promote Score as a 2 Star Stallion under a license agreement with Lasma Star Stallion, Inc., a separate corporation that is not a party to this suit. Paragraph 4 of the agreement provided that, for five years, Score would be a 2 Star Stallion, with Score's foals being eligible for nomination to all sales sponsored by Lasma (D). Paragraph 4 of the contract also provided that if Lasma Star Stallion, Inc., in its sole discretion, determined that Score was not eligible to participate in the Star Stallion Program, Lasma (D) would, at Arabian's (P) option, replace Score or refund the unused portion of the $250,000 earmarked for Score's promotion. The contract also provided that Arabian (P) accepted Score "as is," without any implied warranties, and that risk of loss passes upon closing. Arabian (P) subsequently obtained a mortality insurance policy insuring Score for his actual cash value. Score died shortly thereafter, and the insurance company went broke. Lasma (D) having expended only about $53,000 for the promotion of Score, Arabian (P) brought suit to recover the remaining $197,000. The trial court granted summary judgment in favor of Limited (D) and Lasma (D), and Arabian (P) appealed.

■ **ISSUE**

Does the doctrine of commercial impracticability apply when the frustrating event was reasonably foreseeable or when a party assumed the risk of the frustrating event?

■ **DECISION AND RATIONALE**

(Wollman, J.) No. The doctrine of commercial impracticability does not apply when the frustrating event was reasonably foreseeable or when a party assumed the risk of the frustrating event. Commercial frustration occurs as circumstances beyond the control of the parties render performance of the contract impossible, thereby exonerating the party failing to perform. The doctrine is not a general absolution to be used whenever performance becomes difficult or expensive. Here, the commercial

Arabian Score v. Lasma Arabian Ltd. (Continued)

frustration doctrine is inapplicable because Score's death was foreseeable, evidenced by Arabian's (P) purchase of insurance, and because Arabian (P) assumed the risk that Score might die prematurely. Furthermore, the party obligated to perform, Lasma (D), does not contend that it is unable or unwilling to complete its duty to promote Score. Also, Paragraph 4 of the contract does not obligate the return of the unspent portion of the promotion funds because Lasma Star Stallion, Inc. is not a party to this suit, and there is no evidence that Lasma (D) controls the discretion of Lasma Star Stallion, Inc. Furthermore, since Lasma Star Stallion, Inc. has not declared Score to be ineligible for the Star Stallion Program, the condition precedent to Lasma's (D) obligations under Paragraph 4 has not been satisfied. Even if it was within Lasma's (D) discretion to declare Score ineligible for the Star Stallion Program, we could not say that its decision not to do so would be an arbitrary or capricious abuse of discretion since Lasma (D) regularly promotes deceased horses. This is done to enhance the owner's reputation and to increase the value of the stallion's progeny. Although the thought of spending $197,000 promoting a dead horse sounds bizarre, we must agree with the trial court's dismissal of the complaint. Affirmed.

Analysis:
There are various unexpected events that can take parties to a contract by surprise and render performance literally impossible. In other situations, performance may become extremely costly, time consuming, or otherwise impracticable, though not literally impossible. The traditional view was that performance would not be excused unless it was literally impossible, even when it was extremely burdensome and the burden was unforeseen. Many modern courts, however, tend to equate extreme impracticability with impossibility and will excuse performance as if it were literally impossible. The UCC is in accord with this modern view at least on the seller's part. UCC § 2-615(a) provides that a seller's delay in delivery or non-delivery is excused "if performance as agreed has been made impracticable by the occurrence of a contingency the non-occurrence of which was a basic assumption on which the contract was made." Although on its face § 2-615 only excuses a seller's performance, the buyer may be exempt from performance in certain circumstances as discussed in Comment 9 to § 2-615. The common law supplements the UCC through the bridging provision of § 1-103 in those situations where the Code is silent, so a buyer could argue to equate extreme impracticability with impossibility to have his performance excused.

Louisiana Power & Light Co. v. Allegheny Ludlum Industries, Inc.

(*Buyer*) v. (*Seller*)
517 F.Supp. 1319, 32 UCC Rep. Serv. 847 (E.D.La.1981)

AN INSECURE PARTY TO A CONTRACT MAY DEMAND ASSURANCE OF PERFORMANCE

■ **INSTANT FACTS** Allegheny Ludlum Industries, Inc (D) contracted to furnish Louisiana Power & Light Co. (P) tubing for use at LP&L's (P) nuclear power plant. When prices increased, Allegheny (D) requested additional compensation. LP&L (P) denied the request and sought assurance from Allegheny (D) that it would perform under the contract.

■ **BLACK LETTER RULE** A party to a contract who is insecure about the other party's performance may demand assurance of performance and treat the failure to provide such assurance as a repudiation of the contract.

■ **PROCEDURAL BASIS**

Plaintiff seller moves for summary judgment in breach of contract action seeking "cover" damages.

■ **FACTS**

Louisiana Power & Light Co. (P)(LP&L) entered into an agreement with Allegheny Ludlum Industries, Inc (D)(Allegheny) in which Allegheny (D) agreed to furnish, fabricate, and deliver stainless steel condenser tubing to LP&L (P) for use at LP&L's (P) nuclear power plant. The agreement also included escalation clauses whereby the contract price would be increased by specified percentages if LP&L (P) delayed shipment beyond predetermined shipping dates. Prior to shipment, Allegheny (D), citing increased costs in materials and labor, requested additional compensation for performance under the contract. LP&L (P) advised that it considered these increased costs to be business risks that must be absorbed by Allegheny (D). In response, Allegheny (D) indicated that it would not perform under the contract. LP&L (P) responded by demanding written assurances within thirty days that Allegheny (D) would fully and properly perform under the contract. After the thirty-day time period elapsed and Allegheny (D) had not made the requested assurances, LP&L (P) notified Allegheny (D) that it considered the contract repudiated by Allegheny (D). Allegheny (D) subsequently offered to make delivery at Allegheny's (D) full cost of producing the material, a price higher than that specified in the contract. LP&L (P) rejected that offer and eventually entered into a contract with Trent Tube at a price some $600,000 higher than its contract with Allegheny (D). The evidence showed that Allegheny (D) plant's profit would be reduced from just over $1,000,000 to about $589,000. LP&L (P) seeks to recover from Allegheny (D) the costs of its "cover," the monetary difference between the Allegheny (D) contract and the Trent Tube contract, plus expenses. LP&L (P) moves for summary judgment.

■ **ISSUE**

Does a party to a contract have the right to demand adequate assurance of performance when he has reasonable grounds for insecurity and to treat the other party's failure to provide such assurance as a repudiation of the contract?

Louisiana Power & Light Co. v. Allegheny Ludlum Industries, Inc. (Continued)

■ **DECISION AND RATIONALE**

(Gordon, J.) Yes. A party to a contract has the right to demand adequate assurance of performance when he has reasonable grounds for insecurity and to treat the other party's failure to provide such assurance as a repudiation of the contract. The letter that LP&L (P) received from Allegheny (D) requesting additional compensation provided LP&L (P) with a reasonable basis for insecurity as to Allegheny's (D) performance under the contract. LP&L's (P) subsequent demand for written assurances within thirty days constituted an adequate demand on Allegheny (D) for an assurance of performance. Allegheny's (D) belated and qualified offer to make delivery at Allegheny's (D) full cost cannot be viewed as an assurance of performance under § 2-609. Allegheny's (D) failure to supply an assurance of performance within the allotted time operated as a repudiation of the contract. Accordingly, LP&L (P) is entitled to recover from Allegheny (D) the price of purchasing goods in substitution for the goods due from Allegheny (D), plus incidental and consequential damages. Allegheny (D), relying on UCC § 2-615, contends that its performance under the contract should be excused for commercial impracticability given the severe shortage of critical raw materials and an increase in labor costs. Allegheny (D) has the burden of proof of showing commercial impracticability. There are no facts to indicate that Allegheny (D) would have been unprofitable in the year in question. To the contrary, Allegheny (D) officials testified at deposition that a profit was anticipated even if Allegheny (D) had performed under the contract. Even if Allegheny (D) had suffered a loss, the loss must be especially severe and unreasonable. Allegheny's (D) cost of performance did not increase to the extent necessary to excuse its performance under the doctrine of commercial impracticability. Allegheny's (D) further assertion that claims of commercial impracticability cannot be resolved by summary judgment is also incorrect. To hold in such a way would allow sellers to hide behind the defense in order to be guaranteed a trial. Allegheny (D) also argues that the contractual provision allowing LP&L (P) alone the right to cancel is unconscionable. The question of unconscionability is a question of law to be decided by the court, not the jury. However, the court's determination of the issue cannot be made without a hearing. Accordingly, LP&L's (P) motion for summary judgment must be denied in this regard. Allegheny's (D) defense of bad faith based on LP&L's (P) failure to engage in renegotiation is without merit. LP&L (P) had no obligation to engage in renegotiation with Allegheny (D). However, Allegheny's (D) allegation of LP&L's (P) bad faith in its substitution of the goods relates to LP&L's (P) claim for damages. The court cannot say that there are no genuine issues of material fact surrounding LP&L's (P) claim for damages since the facts surrounding LP&L's (P) "cover," timeliness, and mitigation of damages cannot be decided at this time. As a result, that issue must be resolved at trial. The court hereby grants LP&L's (P) motion for summary judgment on the issue of liability and Allegheny's (D) defenses for commercial impracticability, mistakes of fact, and bad faith. The motion for summary judgment must be denied insofar as Allegheny's (D) defense of unconscionability and the issue of LP&L's (P) damages are concerned.

Analysis:

UCC § 2-609(1) requires that the reasonable grounds for insecurity "arise" from facts not known to the insecure party at the time the contract was entered into. This small detail prevents a party who is having second thoughts about his deal from using the demand for assurances to escape the contract. An insecure party could also consider using the demand for assurances in order to prevent repudiating the contract himself. Thus, instead of notifying the other party that he is in breach, assurances should be demanded. Then, if no assurances are made, it is clear that the other party repudiated.

■ **CASE VOCABULARY**

UCC § 2-609: This section provides, in pertinent part that "[a] contract for sale imposes an obligation on each party that the other's expectation of receiving due performance will not be impaired. When reasonable grounds for insecurity arise with respect to the performance of either party the other party may in writing demand adequate assurance of due performance .... After receipt of a justified demand failure to provide within a reasonable time not exceeding thirty days such assurance of due performance as is adequate under the circumstances of the particular case is a repudiation of the contract."

UCC § 2-615(a): This section provides that a seller's delay in delivery or non-delivery is excused "if performance as agreed has been made impracticable by the occurrence of a contingency the non-occurrence of which was a basic assumption on which the contract was made . . . ."

CHAPTER SIX

Remedies

Teradyne, Inc. v. Teledyne Industries, Inc.

Instant Facts: Teledyne (D) refused to purchase equipment it had ordered from Teradyne (P).

Black Letter Rule: All direct costs of producing a product, including the wages of testers and employee benefits, should be deducted from the contract price to determine a volume seller's lost profit.

Hughes Communications Galaxy, Inc. v. United States

Instant Facts: The government agreed to use its best efforts to launch 10 of a defense contractor's satellites on space shuttles. When the government stopped launching space shuttles, the contractor launched satellites through other, more expensive means and sought to recover its increased costs.

Black Letter Rule: In the event of a seller's breach of contract, under UCC § 2–712 the buyer may cover; if the cover is reasonable, the buyer may recover its increased costs from the seller.

Tongish v. Thomas

Instant Facts: Tongish (P) contracted to sell seeds to Coop (D) for a given price, but then failed to deliver when the price of seeds doubled.

Black Letter Rule: An injured buyer should receive market damages rather than its actual damages if there is no valid reason for the seller's failure to perform the contract.

Poli v. DaimlerChrysler Corp.

Instant Facts: A car buyer who also bought a seven-year warranty sued the dealer when the dealer was unable to repair the car. The dealer claimed the action was barred by the statute of limitations because the buyer did not bring the claim within four years after the buyer bought the car.

Black Letter Rule: Under UCC § 2–725, a breach of warranty claim accrues when the breach is or should have been discovered, not when the goods are delivered to the buyer.

Teradyne, Inc. v. Teledyne Industries, Inc.

(Seller) v. (Buyer)
676 F.2d 865 (1st Cir.1982)

ALL DIRECT COSTS OF PRODUCING A PRODUCT SHOULD BE DEDUCTED FROM A CONTRACT PRICE TO DETERMINE A VOLUME SELLER'S LOST PROFIT

■ **INSTANT FACTS** Teledyne (D) refused to purchase equipment it had ordered from Teradyne (P).

■ **BLACK LETTER RULE** All direct costs of producing a product, including the wages of testers and employee benefits, should be deducted from the contract price to determine a volume seller's lost profit.

■ PROCEDURAL BASIS

Appeal from the trial court's ruling primarily in favor of Teradyne (P) on its breach of contract case.

■ FACTS

Teradyne (P) accepted Teledyne's (D) purchase order to buy a T-347A transistor test system for the list price of $98,400 minus a discount of $984. This amount was also the system's fair market value. Teledyne (D), the buyer, canceled its order when the T-347A was packed and ready for shipment. Teradyne (P) refused to accept the cancellation despite Teledyne's (D) offer to purchase a $65,000 Field Effects Transistor System instead. Teradyne (P) spent an estimated $614 to dismantle, test, and reassemble the T-347A to prepare it for sale to another purchaser. Teradyne (P) had the purchase order from the other purchaser prior to the cancellation and sold the T-347A to the other purchaser for $98,400. The equipment involved here represented a standard product of Teradyne (P), and Teradyne (P) had the capacity to duplicate the equipment for a second sell had Teledyne (D) honored its purchase order.

■ ISSUE

Should the wages and benefits of testers, shippers, installers, and other employees be deducted from the contract price to determine Teradyne's (P) lost profit suffered by Teledyne's breach?

■ DECISION AND RATIONALE

(Wyzanski, J.) Yes. The parties agree that § 2–708(2) applies to this case. We concur in that agreement because § 2–708(2) applies only if the damages provided in § 2–708(1) are inadequate to put the seller in as good a position as performance would have done. Under § 2–708(1) the measure of damages is the difference between the contract price and the market price. Here the unpaid contract price was $97,416 and the market price was $98,400. Therefore, no damages would be recoverable under § 2–708(1). However, if Teledyne (D) had performed, Teradyne (P) would have had the proceeds of two sales, one to Teledyne (D) and another to the resale purchaser. The last sentence of § 2–708(2) provides a credit to the defaulting buyer for "proceeds of resale." A literal reading of this sentence would suggest that Teradyne (P) recover nothing because the proceeds of the resale exceeded the contract price. However, because of the statutory history of this section, it is universally agreed that when the seller resells the goods after the buyer's default, the proceeds of the resale should not be credited to the buyer if the seller is a lost volume seller. A lost volume seller is one who, had

Teradyne, Inc. v. Teledyne Industries, Inc. (Continued)

there been no breach by the buyer, would have had the benefit of both the original contract and the resale contract. Thus, Teradyne (P) is entitled to its § 2–708(2) expected "profit (including reasonable overhead)" on the broken contract. Teledyne (D) agrees that damages should be calculated under § 2–708(2) and pursuant to the formula approved in *Jericho Sash & Door Company v. Building Erectors Inc.* Under *Jericho*, the direct costs of producing and selling manufactured goods are deducted from the contract price in order to arrive at "profit." This formula is permissible provided that all variable expenses are identified. Teledyne (D) contends that all variable costs were not identified because the cost figures came from a catalog that did not fully reflect all direct costs. The trial court accepted Teradyne's (P) calculation of lost profit of $74,778. That figure was derived by deducting the direct labor costs associated with production, material charges, sales commission, and other expenses (for a total of $22,638) along with the $984 discount from the original contract price of $98,400. Teledyne (D) argues that a 10-K report Teradyne (P) filed with the SEC is a better index of lost profits than the catalog. The 10-K form showed that on average Teradyne's (P) revenues were distributed as follows: 9% profit, 26% administrative expense, 1% interest, and 64% costs of sales and engineering including research and development. Teledyne (D) specifically argues that a deduction should have been made for the wages paid to testers, shippers, and installers who directly handled the T-347A, as well as fringe benefits paid to those employees which amounted to 12% of wages. Teradyne (P) argues that the wages and benefits of the testers and other employees should not be deducted because they would not have been affected if each of the testers and other employees handled one product more or less. However, we find that the work of these employees entered directly into producing and supplying the T-347A as much as did the work of the fabricators which was a cost included by the trial court. The fringe benefits of 12% of wages should also have been deducted as a direct cost. Teledyne (D) also contends that Teradyne (P) was required to mitigate its damages by accepting Teledyne's (D) offer to purchase a Field Effects Transistor System instead of the T-347A. There is no right to mitigation of damages where the offer of a substitute contract is conditioned on surrender by the injured party of his claim for breach. Teradyne (P) had a valid contract with Teledyne (D) and was under no obligation to accept Teledyne's subsequent offer. Because the district court incorrectly calculated the lost profits, the judgment is vacated and remanded.

Analysis:

All of the remedies provided in the 2-700s should be read in light of § 1–106(1) which provides that remedies should be applied so that "the aggrieved party may be put in as good a position as if the other party had fully performed." This principle prompted the justices in this case to ignore the language of § 2–708(2), which provides a "due credit for payments or proceeds of resale." If the court were to take this sentence literally, Teledyne (D) would be given a credit of $98,400, because those were the proceeds Teradyne (P) received from its resale of the equipment to another buyer. Therefore, Teradyne (P) would not have lost any profits and would not be entitled to any damages. Most commentators agree that courts should simply ignore the "due credit" language in lost volume cases such as this one. Teradyne (P) was a "volume seller" because it would have made the sale to Teledyne (D), the breaching buyer, and to the party who purchased Teledyne's (D) equipment. Therefore, it should be entitled to its lost profits, calculated by deducting all direct costs from the contract price.

Hughes Communications Galaxy, Inc. v. United States

(Satellite Manufacturer) v. (Satellite Launcher)
271 F.3d 1060, 46 UCC Rep. Serv. 2d 453 (Fed.Cir.2001)

IF SELLER BREACHES, BUYER MAY SEEK REASONABLE SUBSTITUTE GOODS AND SUE SELLER FOR ITS INCREASED COSTS

■ **INSTANT FACTS** The government agreed to use its best efforts to launch 10 of a defense contractor's satellites on space shuttles. When the government stopped launching space shuttles, the contractor launched satellites through other, more expensive, means and sought to recover its increased costs.

■ **BLACK LETTER RULE** In the event of a seller's breach of contract, under UCC § 2–712 the buyer may cover; if the cover is reasonable, the buyer may recover its increased costs from the seller.

■ **PROCEDURAL BASIS**

Appeal of damages action for breach of contract in federal court.

■ **FACTS**

In 1985, NASA (D) and Hughes Communications Galaxy, Inc. (Hughes) (P) entered in to a Launch Services Agreement (LSA) which required NASA (D) to use its best efforts to launch all 10 Hughes (P) HS-393 satellites on space shuttles or until September 30, 1994, whichever came first. The LSA limited damages to direct damages only and excluded consequential damages. NASA (D) issued manifests assigning the Hughes (P) satellites specific slots on shuttles. After the space shuttle Challenger exploded in January 1986, NASA (D) suspended operation of the shuttles until September 1988. In August 1986, President Reagan announced that NASA (D) would no longer launch commercial satellites on shuttles. NASA (D) informed Hughes (P) that it would not launch any Hughes (P) satellites on shuttles. Hughes (P) then launched three of its HS-393 satellites on expendable launch vehicles (ELVs), which was more expensive than launching the satellites on shuttles. Hughes (P) also launched six HS-601 satellites on ELVs. HS-601 satellites are more powerful than HS-393 satellites and better suited for ELVs. Hughes (P) sued the U.S. (D) for breach of contract and for taking its property without just compensation. The Court of Federal Claims granted summary judgment to the U.S. (D) based on the sovereign act defense. The U.S. Court of Appeal reversed that summary judgment and remanded. On remand, the Court of Federal Claims granted summary judgment for Hughes (P). Before a trial on damages, the Court of Federal Claims ruled that the U.S. (D) could not produce evidence to reduce its damages by the amount Hughes (P) had passed on to its customers in increased prices. At the trial on Hughes' (P) damages, the Court of Federal Claims held that using its best efforts, NASA (D) would have launched only five HS-393 satellites. It averaged the actual costs of launching the three HS-393 satellites that were actually launched on ELVs and used that average for calculating the cost of launching the fourth and fifth satellites, rather than individually calculating the cost of launching each satellite. The court held that Hughes (P) developed the HS-601s because they were better suited for ELVs, not because the HS-601s were more marketable, as the U.S. (D) argued. The court held that the HS-601 launches were reasonable substitutes under the circumstances. The court awarded Hughes (P) $102,680,625 in damages for its increased launch costs. Hughes (P) and the U.S. (D) appealed.

Hughes Communications Galaxy, Inc. v. United States (Continued)

■ ISSUE

In the event of a seller's breach of contract, may the buyer seek substitute goods or services and recover its increased costs?

■ DECISION AND RATIONALE

(Rader, J.) Yes. In breach of contract cases the general rule is to award damages to put the injured party in as good as position as he or she would have been if there was no breach. The damages must be foreseeable. If a seller breaches a contract for goods, the buyer may "cover" or obtain substitute goods from another seller. The same is true for services contracts such as the LSA. When a buyer covers, the buyer's remedy for the seller's breach is the difference between the cost of the substitute services and the contract price plus other losses. The U.S. (D) argues that Hughes (P) may only recover damages for the three HS-393 satellites it actually launched. While Hughes (P) did not launch the fourth and fifth HS393, it did incur costs in launching the HS-601s. The lower court's holding that launching the HS-601s was a reasonable substitute was based on the witnesses' credibility. Such determinations are hardly ever clear error. This Court rejects the U.S.'s (D) cross-appeal. To determine damages, the lower court compared the costs of launching HS-393s on ELVs with the costs of launching the same HS-393s on shuttles. This provided a basis for assessing Hughes' (P) increased costs in launching the HS-601s. This was not an abuse of discretion. The increased costs are direct damages incurred by Hughes (P) in obtaining substitute launch services. They were not lost profits or consequential damages. The cost of cover is not the same as consequential damages. Before President Reagan's 1986 statement, NASA (D) gave equal priority to commercial and NASA payloads and could not have increased its launch rate. Therefore, the lower court did not err in holding that using its best efforts, NASA (D) would only have been able to launch five Hughes (P) satellites. The lower court used the same method to determine the shuttle launch costs and the ELV launch costs. This was a reasonable exercise of the court's discretion. The U.S. (D) sought to reduce Hughes' (P) damages by the amount Hughes (P) recouped by increasing prices to customers. Determining this pass-through damages reduction amount would be extremely difficult. It is nearly impossible to demonstrate that a plaintiff would not have increased prices absent the breach. Also, allowing such damages would destroy the symmetry between looking at proximity in both reduction and escalation of damages. The court did not abuse its discretion in disallowing pass-through damages reductions. Affirmed.

Analysis:

Despite its technical language, this case sets forth the basic rule in UCC § 2–712 that if a seller breaches a contract, the buyer may cover, i.e., buy substitute goods from another seller. The substitute goods do not have to be identical, but they must be a commercially reasonable substitute. This is a way the buyer mitigates damages. Here, the court held that launching the two different types of satellites on ELVs was a reasonable substitute for launching the one type on the space shuttles. When a buyer covers, the buyer can recover the amount that its increased costs exceed the contract amount. A buyer does not have to cover. If the buyer does not, under UCC § 2–712 he may recover the difference between the market price when the buyer learned of the breach and the contract price. Under UCC § 2–715, the buyer may recover consequential damages only if they could not be reasonably prevented by cover or otherwise.

■ CASE VOCABULARY

CONSEQUENTIAL DAMAGES: Damages that were caused as a direct foreseeable result of wrongdoing.

Tongish v. Thomas

(Seller) v. (Buyer)
16 Kan.App.2d 809, 829 P.2d 916 (1992)

WHERE A SELLER FAILS TO DELIVER OR REPUDIATES A CONTRACT WITHOUT A VALID REASON, MARKET DAMAGES RATHER THAN ACTUAL DAMAGES WILL BE AWARDED TO THE BUYER

■ **INSTANT FACTS** Tongish (P) contracted to sell seeds to Coop (D) for a given price, but then failed to deliver when the price of seeds doubled.

■ **BLACK LETTER RULE** An injured buyer should receive market damages rather than its actual damages if there is no valid reason for the seller's failure to perform the contract.

■ **PROCEDURAL BASIS**

Coop (D) appeals from a judgment which found that it was entitled to only actual damages on its breach of contract claim.

■ **FACTS**

The Dacatur Coop Association (D) contracted with Denis Tongish (P) to purchase all of the sunflower seeds grown by him. The seeds were to be delivered one-third by December 31, 1988, one-third by March 31, 1989, and one-third by May 31, 1989. The price for the seeds was $13 per one hundred pounds. Coop (D) also contracted with Bambino Bean & Seed to sell it all the sunflower seeds Coop (D) purchased from the farmers at the same price. Coop (D) would retain a handling charge of $.55 per hundred pounds as its only anticipated profit. In January, a disagreement arose between Tongish (P) and Coop (D) over the amount of waste material or dockage in the seeds. Also by January, the market price of sunflower seeds had doubled from the Tongish-Coop contract price. Tongish (P) then informed Coop (D) it was not going to honor the contract. Instead, Tongish (P) delivered 82,820 pounds of seeds to Danny Thomas (D) for a price of $14,714, or about $20 per hundred pounds. Tongish (P) would have received $5,153 more from Danny Thomas (D) than he would have by performing the contract with Coop (D). When Thomas (D) failed to pay the balance to Tongish (P) due on their sunflower seed sale, Tongish (P) sued Thomas (D) to collect. Thomas (D) later paid the balance and was dismissed as a party. Coop (D), however, intervened as a third-party defendant, alleging that Tongish (P) breached the contract and that it was entitled to damages.

■ **ISSUE**

Should an injured buyer receive market damages rather than its actual losses if there is no valid reason for the seller's breach?

■ **DECISION AND RATIONALE**

(Walton, J.) Yes. The only disagreement here is how the damages should be calculated. The trial court found that Coop (D) was entitled to damages of $455.51, the expected profit for handling charges in the transaction. Coop (D) argues that K.S.A. 64–2–713 (see *UCC* § 2–713) entitles it to collect as damages the difference between the market price and the contract price. Tongish (P) argues that K.S.A. 84–1–106 (see *UCC* § 1–106) provides that a party should be placed in as good a position as it would be had the other party performed. Which statute should prevail? If Tongish (P) had not

HIGH COURT CASE SUMMARIES 105

Tongish v. Thomas (Continued)

breached the contract, he would have received under the contract terms with Coop (D) nearly $5,153 less than what he received from Thomas (D). Coop (D) had a contract with Bambino to sell whatever seeds it received from Tongish (P) for the same price Coop (D) paid for them. Therefore, even if the contract had been performed, Coop (D) would have never received the extra $5,153. K.S.A. 84–2–713(1) provides that "the measure of damages for nondelivery or repudiation by the seller is the difference between the market price at the time when the buyer learned of the breach and the contract price together with any incidental and consequential damages provided in this article . . ." This is in conflict with K.S.A. 84–1–106 which would put the injured party in as good a position as if the other party had fully performed. A basic rule of statutory construction is that where there is a conflict between a statute dealing generally with a subject and one dealing specifically with a certain phase of it, the specific statute controls. Here, K.S.A 84–2–713 is the more specific statute dealing with damages. *Allied Canners & Packers, Inc. v. Victor Packing Co.* is some authority for Tongish's (P) position that lost profit should be the measure of damages. In that case, Allied contracted to purchase raisins from Victor for a small discount and then contracted to sell them to another party for a profit. Heavy rain damaged the raisin crop, the price of raisins rose, and Victor breached its contract. Allied's buyer agreed to rescind its contract so Allied was not bound to sell them raisins at a large loss. Therefore, the actual loss suffered by Allied was only the $4,462 profit it expected. The difference between the contract price and the market price was about $150,000. The *Allied* court found that in cases where the buyer has made a resale contract for the goods, which the seller knows about, it may be appropriate to limit damages to the actual loss. However, the Allied case and the present case are not alike because Victor could not deliver the raisins because the crop had been destroyed. In the present case, Tongish (P) could have delivered the seeds but chose not to and instead sold them to Thomas (D) for a higher price. There was no valid reason for Tongish's (P) breach. The majority of commentators and courts that have examined the issue have found that market damages should be awarded rather than actual loss. The market damages rule, or the difference between the contract price and the market price, discourages the breach of contracts and encourages a more efficient market. Therefore, we believe that the market damages rule of K.S.A. 84–2–713 should apply. It generates stability in the market by discouraging the seller from breaching when the market fluctuates to his advantage. This rule is further supported by the maxim of statutory construction that a specific statute should prevail over a more general one. The damage award is reversed.

Analysis:

Coop (D), even though it is the defendant here, is the injured buyer. It is entitled, the court found, to receive the benefit from the rise in sunflower seed prices. Section 2–713 provides a formula for measuring damages when there is nondelivery or repudiation. Section 2–712, on the other hand, applies when the buyer covers, or purchases goods as a substitute for those due from the seller. The formula of § 2–713 can be expressed as the market price (at the time the buyer learned of the breach), minus the contract price, minus expenses saved as a result of the breach, plus incidental and consequential damages. This section seems to fly in the face of the general principle of UCC § 1–106, which would put the buyer in the same position as he would have been had there been no breach, i.e., Coop (D) would have made only $455 in profit in handling charges. Therefore, market damages under § 2–713 often bear no relation to the buyer's actual loss. Nevertheless, most courts, as did the court in this case, adopt market damages because they discourage the breach of contracts and lead to more efficient markets.

Poli v. DaimlerChrylser Corp.

(*Buyer*) v. (*Seller*)
349 N.J. Super. 169, 793 A.2d 104 (2002)

BREACH OF WARRANTY CLAIM ACCRUES WHEN BREACH IS DISCOVERED, NOT WHEN BUYER RECEIVES GOODS

■ **INSTANT FACTS** A car buyer who also bought a seven-year warranty sued the dealer when the dealer was unable to repair the car. The dealer claimed the action was barred by the statute of limitations because the buyer did not bring the claim within four years after the buyer bought the car.

■ **BLACK LETTER RULE** Under UCC § 2–725, a breach of warranty claim accrues when the breach is or should have been discovered, not when the goods are delivered to the buyer.

■ **PROCEDURAL BASIS**

Appeal of grant of summary judgment for breach of warranty claims.

■ **FACTS**

On March 23, 1993, Poli (P) bought a new 1992 Dodge Spirit manufactured by DaimlerChrysler Corp. (Chrysler) (D). Poli (P) also bought a seven-year, 70,000-mile warranty. Over the next six years, Poli (P) had to have the car's timing belt replace about five times. In 1998, the failure of the timing belt caused the destruction of the engine's "short block," which Chrysler (D) took six months to repair. Chrysler (D) performed repairs pursuant to the warranty. On December 15, 1998, Poli (P) sued Chrysler (D) for breach of the warranty and violation of the New Jersey's lemon law, the Magnuson-Moss Warranty Act [federal act setting minimum standards for warranties], and the Consumer Fraud Act. Chrysler (D) moved for summary judgment on the ground that the claims were barred by the statute of limitations. Poli (P) dismissed his claim under the Consumer Fraud Act. The trial court granted Chrysler's (D) motion. It held that the claim under the lemon law was barred because Poli (P) did not give Chrysler (D) notice and an opportunity to correct the defect within the first 18,000 miles of operation. It held that the warranty claim and the claim under the Magnuson-Moss Warranty Act were untimely because they were not brought within four years after delivery of the car. Poli (P) appealed.

■ **ISSUE**

Does a breach of warranty claim accrue when the breach is or should have been discovered?

■ **DECISION AND RATIONALE**

(Skillman, J.) Yes. Under UCC § 2–725(1), the limitations period for breach of warranty claims is four years from when the cause of action accrued. The UCC provides that a cause of action accrues when the breach occurs, even if the aggrieved party did not know of the breach. It also provides that a breach of warranty occurs when the goods are delivered. However, under UCC § 2–725(2), a breach of warranty claim accrues when the breach is or should have been discovered. Here, the warranty was not a mere representation of the car's condition at the time of delivery, but was a promise that if a defect arose during the warranty period, Chrysler (D) would repair it. Otherwise, a buyer would be unable to

Poli v. DaimlerChrylser Corp. (Continued)

enforce any breach of the warranty that occurred during the last three years of the warranty. Courts in other jurisdictions agree with this view. Other jurisdictions hold that a repair warranty is not a warranty that extends to future performance of the goods, but that a cause of action for breach of the warranty does not accrue upon delivery because the promise to repair is an independent obligation that is not breached until the seller fails to repair. Under a proposed revision to the UCC, a promise by a seller to repair or replace a defective part during a warranty period is not a warranty at all and is therefore not subject to UCC § 2–725(1) or (2). Instead, a cause of action for breach of remedial promise would accrue when the remedial promise is not performed when due. Thus, we hold that Poli's (P) breach of warranty cause of action accrued in 1997 or 1998 when Chrysler (D) was unable to repair the timing belt problems. Under the Magnuson-Moss Warranty Act (the Act), if a seller warrants a product, the seller must comply with certain federal standards. The Act does not include a limitations period, so we look at the state statute of limitations most closely analogous to the federal action. The closest action is a breach of warranty claim under UCC § 2–725, which we discussed above. Therefore, we affirm the dismissal of Poli's lemon law claim, but reverse the dismissal of his breach of warranty and Magnuson-Moss Warranty Act claims.

Analysis:

If Chrysler's (D) argument that Poli's (P) cause of action began to accrue when Poli (P) received his car prevailed, then what good would a seven-year warranty be? Poli (P) would have no way to enforce the warranty after the fourth year. The cause of action on a warranty would begin to accrue when Poli (P) received the car if the warranty were merely a promise that the car was in great condition. Here, the warranty explicitly extended to Chrysler's (D) future performance. Under UCC § 2–725(2), Poli's (P) cause of action began to accrue when he discovered or should have discovered the breach.

■ CASE VOCABULARY

ACCRUE: The coming into being of the right to bring a lawsuit.

CHAPTER SEVEN

Negotiability

Triffin v. Dillabough

Instant Facts: American Express (D) refused to pay stolen money orders to Triffin (P).

Black Letter Rule: Money orders which contain a promise to pay on the front but state that they will not be paid if stolen, altered, or forged on the back still qualify as negotiable instruments under the UCC.

Woodworth v. The Richmond Indiana Venture

Instant Facts: Woodworth (P) gave a promissory note to Richmond (D) which then assigned it to Signet Bank (D).

Black Letter Rule: A promissory note containing a forfeiture provision exercisable only at the option of the original issuer makes the note non-negotiable for purposes of the UCC.

Triffin v. Dillabough

(Holder in Due Course) v. *(Payee)*
552 Pa. 550, 716 A.2d 605 (1998)

MONEY ORDERS STATING THAT THEY WILL NOT BE PAID IF ALTERED, STOLEN, UNENDORSED, OR FORGED ARE STILL NEGOTIABLE INSTRUMENTS UNDER THE UCC

■ **INSTANT FACTS** American Express (D) refused to pay Triffin (P) for stolen money orders.

■ **BLACK LETTER RULE** Money orders which contain a promise to pay on the front but state that they will not be paid if stolen, altered, or forged on the back still qualify as negotiable instruments under the UCC.

■ **PROCEDURAL BASIS**

Appeal from the reversal of a verdict in favor of American Express (D).

■ **FACTS**

American Express (D) sells money orders through its authorized agents. Typically, the agent collects cash from the purchaser, or sender, equal to the face value of the money order plus a small fee. The sender receives a partially completed money order embossed with the amount of money and blank spaces for the sender to fill in their own name and the name of the payee and date. On an unknown date, three American Express money orders were stolen from Chase Savings Bank. In an unrelated incident, numerous American Express money orders were also stolen while being shipped to an agent. On December 11, 1990, Stacey Dillabough (D) presented two stolen American Express money orders to Chuckie's, a check cashing business. They were for $550 and $650, and listed Dillabough (D) as the payee and David W. (last name illegible) as the sender. On February 25, 1991, Robert Lynn (D) presented a stolen American Express money order to Chuckie's for $200 which listed himself as payee and Michael Pepe as the sender. Charles Giunta, the owner of Chuckie's, recognized both Dillabough (D) and Lynn (D) from previous transactions. Dillabough (D) and Lynn (D) provided identification and endorsed the money orders. Unaware that the money orders had been stolen, Giunta paid them. Because American Express (D) had reported the money orders stolen on its fraud log, when they were presented for payment at the United Bank of Grand Junction, they were returned unpaid to Chuckie's stamped "Reported Lost or Stolen. Do not redeposit." Chuckie's then sold the money orders to Triffin (P), a commercial discounter. Triffin (P) then filed suit against Dillabough (D), Lynn (D) and American Express (D) seeking payment of the money orders. Triffin (P) obtained default judgments against both Dillabough (D) and Lynn (D), leaving only American Express (D) on appeal.

■ **ISSUE**

Does a money order stating that it will not be paid if it is altered, stolen, or forged constitute a negotiable instrument?

■ **DECISION AND RATIONALE**

(Newman, J.) Yes. The threshold question here is whether the money orders qualify as negotiable instruments under Division Three of Pennsylvania's version of the UCC. If the money orders are not negotiable instruments, Triffin's (P) claims against American Express (D) must fail. The purpose of

Triffin v. Dillabough (Continued)

negotiable instruments and the UCC is to enhance the marketability of instruments and stimulate financial interdependence. Division 13 Pa. C.S. 3104(a) sets forth a test to determine if a particular document is a negotiable instrument. To qualify as a negotiable instrument, a writing must: (1) be signed by the maker or drawer; (2) contain an unconditional promise or order to pay a sum certain in money and no other promise, order, obligation, or power given by the maker or drawer except as authorized by this division; (3) be payable on demand or at a definite time; and (4) be payable to order or to bearer. American Express (D) affixed a pre-printed signature of Louis Gerstner, its Chairman, to the front of the money orders. American Express (D) does not argue that Gerstner's signature was affixed to the money orders for any reason other than to authenticate them. Therefore, the first requirement for negotiability is met. American Express (D) argues the second requirement is lacking because the money orders do not contain an unconditional promise or order to pay. American Express (D) claims the legend on the back of the money orders qualifies the otherwise unconditional order on the front directing the drawee to "PAY THE SUM OF" a specified amount "TO THE ORDER OF" the payee. The legend on the back provides as follows: "Do not cash for strangers. This money order will not be paid if it has been altered or stolen or if an endorsement is missing or forged. Be sure you have effective recourse against your customers." We do not agree with American Express (D) that this language renders the order to pay conditional on the money order not being stolen, altered, or forged. In a similar case, the Louisiana Court of Appeals construed a similar legend on the back of a money order. The court found that the language on the form did not convert the money order into a conditional promise to pay, but merely operated as a warning to the party cashing the money order to protect itself. American Express (D) argues the legend in the present case is different in that it explicitly conditions payment on the money order not being altered, stolen, or forged. This misses the point because Comment 4, 13 Pa. C.S. 3104 provides that any writing which meets the requirements of subsection (a) and is not excluded under Section 3103 is a negotiable instrument, *even though it may contain additional language beyond that contemplated by this section.* Purported conditions in an otherwise negotiable instrument that merely reflect other provisions of the law do not destroy negotiability. The conditions on the back of the money orders do nothing more than restate the statutory defenses against payment. Whether these defenses are effective against Triffin (P) is a separate question. We hold that the second requisite of negotiability is met. The third and fourth requirements are not disputed by the parties, thus the money orders qualify as negotiable instruments. Triffin (P) has the rights of a holder in due course and takes the instruments free of American Express's (D) defenses. However, American Express (D) claims that even if Triffin (P) is a holder in due course it is only obligated to pay the instrument according to its "tenor." The word "tenor" is not defined in the Code, but the word "terms" was substituted for the word "tenor" in the Code, so we will treat these words synonymously. American Express (D) claims it is not obligated to pay the money orders according to their terms. However, as discussed previously, the legend is merely a warning that restates American Express's (D) defenses against those other than holders in due course. Because Triffin (P) is a holder in due course, those defenses are not available against him. Affirmed.

■ **DISSENT**

(Castille, J.) The money orders contained express conditional language which precludes a finding of negotiability. The statute distinguishes implied conditions and express conditions. An express condition renders an instrument non-negotiable. The use of the word "if" clearly and explicitly conditions payment on the money orders not being stolen, altered, or forged. The majority's reasons for departing from the statutory language are strained. The majority relies on a Louisiana case decided before the UCC was adopted. A decision by an intermediate Louisiana court interpreting French legal principles should not override the explicit language of a Pennsylvania statute. The majority supports its conclusion by claiming that the conditions on the back of the instruments merely reflect other provisions of the law rather than create a condition. The statutory defenses are ineffective against holders in due course. The language at issue here is operative even against holders in due course. Therefore, the language here sweeps beyond the statutory defenses and does more than reflect other provisions of the law. I respectfully dissent.

Analysis:

The language on the back of the money orders does seem to create a condition on their payment. Is it simply "additional language beyond that contemplated" by the Code and a restatement of other law as the majority finds? Or is it an express condition to payment that renders the money orders non-negotiable? Both justices make good arguments. In addition to finding that the money orders were negotiable instruments, the majority also found that Triffin (P) was a holder in due course who bought the money orders without notice of any claims or defenses against them. However, shouldn't Triffin (P) have known that something was wrong with the money orders because they were stamped "Reported lost or stolen. Do not redeposit"? Finally, who took a loss here? Clearly, American Express (D) did because it had to pay the full value of the stolen money orders. Chuckie's was also hurt, because it paid out the full value of the money orders but received less than their full value when it sold them at a discount to Triffin (P).

Woodworth v. The Richmond Indiana Venture

(*Maker of Promissory Note*) v. (*Partnership*)
13 UCC Rep. Serv.2d 1149, 1152 (Ohio Com.Pl.1990)

A FORFEITURE PROVISION IN A PROMISSORY NOTE CAN RENDER THE NOTE NON-NEGOTIABLE

■ **INSTANT FACTS** Woodworth (P) gave a promissory note to Richmond (D) which then assigned it to Signet Bank (D).

■ **BLACK LETTER RULE** A promissory note containing a forfeiture provision exercisable only at the option of the original issuer makes the note non-negotiable for purposes of the UCC.

■ **PROCEDURAL BASIS**

Hearing on Woodworth's (P) motion for partial summary judgment and Signet Bank's (D) motion for summary judgment.

■ **FACTS**

Woodworth (P) executed a promissory note in which he promised to pay The Richmond Indiana Venture (Richmond) (D), a Limited Partnership, or holder the sum of $655,625. This was to pay part of Woodworth's (P) investment in Richmond (D). The note contained a forfeiture provision which allowed Richmond (D), at its option, to forfeit Woodworth's (P) interest in Richmond (D) in the event of default. The note was then assigned or negotiated to defendant Signet Bank (D). Woodworth (P) is now in default and filed this action.

■ **ISSUE**

Does a forfeiture provision in a promissory note that is exercisable only at the option of the original issuer render the note non-negotiable?

■ **DECISION AND RATIONALE**

(Johnson, J.) Yes. In order to be negotiable, a promissory note must be a signed, unconditional promise to pay a certain amount of money payable on demand or at a stated time. The note must be payable to order or bearer and contain no other promise, order, obligation, or power given by the maker except as authorized by UCC §§ 3–101 to 3–805. The policy of both pre-Code law and of the Code is that instruments should be as concise as possible and uncluttered by other promises, orders, obligations or powers. The promissory note here contains a term which gives Richmond (D) the option to cancel Woodworth's (P) interest in Richmond (D) if he defaults on the note. The term also provides that Richmond (D) will have no obligation to repay any payments it has received. This term is clearly a promise by the maker, Woodworth (P), that his partnership interest will be forfeited in the event of default. It is more than a recitation of security or an agreement to protect collateral; it is a forfeiture provision. In the case of *Pacific Finance Loans v. Goodwin,* the court found that the requirement of an unconditional promise to pay was not met where a term provided for the repossession of collateral by a seller without judicial process. The present case is analogous. We find that the negotiability of this note is doubtful. Where there is doubt, the decision should be against negotiability. The note is not negotiable and Signet Bank (D) cannot claim the status of a holder in due course and is subject to contract defenses that Woodworth (P) may assert. On Signet Bank's (D) motion for reconsideration we

Woodworth v. The Richmond Indiana Venture (Continued)

maintain our decision. The forfeiture provision here can be exercised at the option of Richmond (D), not the holder of the instrument. The holder does not need to declare a default before Richmond (D) could exercise its option. A situation could develop where Richmond (D) exercises its option to forfeit Woodworth's (P) partnership interest before the holder declares a default. In such a case, Woodworth (P) might fail to cure the default because of the forfeiture. This shows the reason why negotiable instruments may not contain any other order, promise, or obligation. The forfeiture provision here is not analogous to collateral. Collateral follows the debt, but here the option to declare a forfeiture remains with Richmond (D). Including such forfeiture provisions clutters the unconditional promise to pay and thereby makes the commercial viability of this instrument uncertain. Signet Bank's (D) motion for summary judgment is denied and Woodworth's (P) motion is sustained.

Analysis:

The court here found that the UCC means what it says when it provides that the unconditional promise to pay may not contain any additional orders, promises, or obligations. These types of additional promises or obligations can clutter the note and make negotiability and marketability difficult. This is especially so where the original party to the note, Richmond (D), continues to hold an option to declare a forfeiture even after it has assigned the note to another party. Situations like this demonstrate why the promise to pay must be unconditional and may not contain additional promises or obligations.

■ CASE VOCABULARY

FORFEITURE PROVISION: A term in a contract or note which allows the divestiture of certain property without compensation as a result of nonperformance of some obligation.

CHAPTER NINE

Holders in Due Course

Falls Church Bank v. Wesley Heights Realty, Inc.

Instant Facts: Wesley Heights (D) made a check to a customer of Falls Church Bank (P) which advanced a portion of the amount of the check in cash to its customer.

Black Letter Rule: A bank may achieve the status of a holder in due course of negotiable paper deposited with it by a customer to the extent that the bank has acquired a security interest in the paper.

General Investment Corp. v. Angelini

Instant Facts: General Investment (P) purchased a note from Lustro who had failed to complete a home improvement project on the Angelinis' (D) home.

Black Letter Rule: A party cannot obtain holder in due course status where the circumstances show that he deliberately evaded knowledge out of a belief that investigation would disclose a defense to the instrument.

Any Kind Checks Cashed, Inc. v. Talcott

Instant Facts: Any Kind (P) cashed a large check made by Talcott (D) after Talcott directed his bank to stop payment, and Any Kind (P) claimed it was a holder in due course of the check.

Black Letter Rule: A holder in due course must act in good faith, which means acting according to reasonable standards intended to result in fair dealing.

Winter & Hirsch, Inc. v. Passarelli

Instant Facts: Winter & Hirsch (P) provided money to be loaned at a usurious rate by Equitable to the Passarellis (D).

Black Letter Rule: A co-originator of a loan is charged with knowledge of its terms and cannot claim the status of a holder in due course.

Jones v. Approved Bancredit Corp.

Instant Facts: Mrs. Jones (D) executed a promissory note for the purchase of a home which was destroyed before it was completed.

Black Letter Rule: A finance company will be denied holder in due course status where it maintains a close business relationship with the dealer from whom it buys paper.

Sullivan v. United Dealers Corp.

Instant Facts: United (P) purchased a promissory note from the contractor who had built a home for the Sullivans (D).

Black Letter Rule: A purchaser for value can become a holder in due course if, at the time the instrument was negotiated, the purchaser had no notice of defenses against the instrument.

Triffin v. Somerset Valley Bank

Instant Facts: A purchaser of forged checks claimed he was a holder in due course and entitled to payment for the checks.

Black Letter Rule: Under the shelter rule, a transferee of a negotiable instrument is a holder in due course if the transferor was, even if the transferee had notice of defenses to the instrument.

Federal Deposit Insurance Corp. v. Culver

Instant Facts: Culver (D) signed a blank promissory note believing he was signing only a receipt.

Black Letter Rule: Fraud in factum can be asserted as a defense against a holder in due course if the maker had no knowledge or reasonable opportunity to obtain knowledge of the instrument's character or essential terms.

Sea Air Support, Inc. v. Herrmann

Instant Facts: Herrmann (D) wrote a bad check to pay off gambling debts and Sea Air (P) tried to collect on the check.

Black Letter Rule: A promise to perform future services does not constitute taking "for value" for purposes of becoming a holder in due course.

Kedzie & 103rd Currency Exchange, Inc. v. Hodge

Instant Facts: Hodge (D) wrote a check and then stopped payment on it for work to be performed by an licenced plumber.

Black Letter Rule: Unless an instrument arising from a transaction is, itself, made void by statute, the illegality defense is not available to bar the claim of a holder in due course.

Virginia National Bank v. Holt

Instant Facts: Mrs. Holt (D) was sued on a note that she denied signing.

Black Letter Rule: The presumption that a signature on a negotiable instrument is valid can only be overcome by introducing evidence sufficient to support a finding that the signature is forged or unauthorized.

Herzog Contracting Corp. v. McGowen Corp.

Instant Facts: McGowen (D) issued promissory notes to a subsidiary of Herzog (P).

Black Letter Rule: Parol evidence may be introduced against a party other than a holder in due course to show that an unambiguous instrument was not intended to create a binding contract.

Falls Church Bank v. Wesley Heights Realty, Inc.

(*Holder in Due Course*) v. (*Payee*)
256 A.2d 915 (D.C. 1969)

A BANK WHICH HAS ACQUIRED A SECURITY INTEREST IN A CHECK DEPOSITED BY ITS CUSTOMER MAY BECOME A HOLDER IN DUE COURSE

■ **INSTANT FACTS** Wesley Heights (D) made a check to a customer of Falls Church Bank (P) which advanced a portion of the amount of the check in cash to its customer.

■ **BLACK LETTER RULE** A bank may achieve the status of a holder in due course of negotiable paper deposited with it by a customer to the extent that the bank has acquired a security interest in the paper.

■ **PROCEDURAL BASIS**

Appeal from judgment in favor of Wesley Heights (D) on the grounds that the bank was not a holder in due course.

■ **FACTS**

Wesley Heights Realty, Inc. (D) made a check for $1,400.00, payable to the order of a customer of Falls Church Bank (P). The customer deposited the check in his account and was given a provisional credit for that amount. The customer was allowed to withdraw $140.00 from his account before the bank discovered that Wesley Heights (D) had stopped payment on the check. The check was returned to Falls Church Bank (P) dishonored, and the customer had "skipped," leaving nothing in his account on which to charge the $140.00. Falls Church Bank (P) then demanded payment from Wesley Heights (D) and filed suit when Wesley Heights (D) refused.

■ **ISSUE**

May a bank achieve the status of a holder in due course of negotiable paper deposited with it by a customer if it has acquired a security interest in the paper?

■ **DECISION AND RATIONALE**

(Hood, J.) Yes. The UCC provides that a bank acquires a security interest in items deposited with it to the extent that the provisional credit given the customer on the item is withdrawn. See UCC § 4–210. It also provides that, for purposes of achieving the status of a holder in due course, the depository bank gives value to the extent that it acquires a security interest in the item. See UCC § 4–211. We agree that Falls Church Bank (P) is deemed by the UCC to be an agent of its customers, but under the scheme of the Code, a bank may be a holder in due course while acting as a collecting agent for its customer. As a holder in due course, Falls Church Bank's (P) claim cannot be defeated except by those defenses set out in UCC § 3–305(a)(1), none of which are alleged here. Judgment reversed with instructions to enter judgment for Falls Church Bank (P).

Analysis:

In order to qualify for "holder in due course" status, Falls Church Bank (P) had to take the check for value, in good faith, and without notice that it has been dishonored or is overdue or of any defense or

Falls Church Bank v. Wesley Heights Realty, Inc. (Continued)

claim against it. See UCC § 3-302(a). Section 4–211 provides that a bank has given value for an instrument to the extent it has a security interest in the item. Section 4–210 completes the argument by providing that a bank acquires a security interest in an item to the extent to which credit given on the item has been withdrawn. Because Falls Church Bank (P) paid value for the check (obtained a security interest in it) and met the other requirements for a holder in due course, it took the check free of personal defenses including failure or lack of consideration, breach of warranty, unconscionability, and regular fraud. The defenses referred to by the court in § 3-305(a)(1) are the so-called real defenses that a holder in due course must still face. Real defenses include infancy, duress, lack of legal capacity, illegality of the transaction, fraud that induced the obligor to sign the instrument without knowledge of its character or its essential terms, or discharge of the obligor in insolvency. Wesley Heights (D) did not allege any of these real defenses and lost.

General Investment Corp. v. Angelini

(Discounter) v. (Homeowners)
58 N.J. 396, 278 A.2d 193 (1971)

WHILE A HOLDER HAS NO DUTY TO INQUIRE AS TO POSSIBLE DEFENSES TO AN INSTRUMENT, IT CANNOT DELIBERATELY EVADE KNOWLEDGE OUT OF A BELIEF THAT INVESTIGATION WOULD DISCLOSE DEFENSES TO THE INSTRUMENT

■ **INSTANT FACTS** General Investment (P) purchased a note from Lustro who had failed to complete a home improvement project on the Angelinis' (D) home.

■ **BLACK LETTER RULE** A party cannot obtain holder in due course status where the circumstances show that he deliberately evaded knowledge out of a belief that investigation would disclose a defense to the instrument.

■ **PROCEDURAL BASIS**

Grant of certification after the trial court and appellate court found in favor of General Investment (P) on its breach of contract claim.

■ **FACTS**

Mr. and Mrs. Angelini (D) entered into a contract with Lustro Aluminum Products for repair work on their home. The contract provided that Lustro was a home repair contractor licensed in New Jersey, and that it would install certain siding and trim on the home. The total time payment price was $5,363.40 payable in 84 monthly installments of $63.85. They were to begin "60 days after completion of the work." The Angelinis (D) signed a note and agreed to pay the monthly installments "commencing February 19." Mr. Angelini (D) testified that a Lustro representative told him that the payments would not begin until he was completely satisfied with the job. The Angelinis (D) testified and the court found as fact that the note bore no other dates when it was signed. General Investment Corp. (P) arranges financing for home improvement loans. General Investment's (P) representatives testified that the Angelini (D) note was purchased for value on the day of its alleged execution, December 19, 1966. It was endorsed by Lustro without recourse except that as part of the endorsement it warranted that it had installed all materials and had completed all work under the contract. General Investment's (P) agent read the contract and was familiar with the terms in Lustro's contract. General Investment's (P) agent never inquired of the Angelinis (D) if the work had been completed, nor did he request from Lustro a certificate of completion signed by the Angelinis (D). Mr. Angelini's (D) undisputed testimony was that Lustro began work on his house on December 15. After that day, nothing more was done and the work was not completed. The portion of the work that was completed did not conform to the contract or meet workmanlike standards. On December 24, 1966 the Angelinis (D) received a payment book from General Investment (P) calling for payments to begin on February 19, 1967. The Angelinis returned the book stating that payment was to begin 60 days after the work was completed and that the work had not yet been completed. The Angelinis (D) assured General Investment (P) that they would begin payments as soon as the work was completed. Despite this, General Investment (P) filed this suit.

■ **ISSUE**

Can a party obtain holder in due course status if the circumstances reveal a deliberate desire to evade knowledge because of a fear that investigation would disclose a defense arising from the transaction?

General Investment Corp. v. Angelini (Continued)

■ **DECISION AND RATIONALE**

(Francis, J.) No. General Investment (P) argues that it is a holder in due course of the Angelini's (D) note, and as such it is immune from the defense of failure of consideration. The UCC defines a holder in due course as one who takes the instrument for value, in good faith, and without notice of any defense or claim to it on the part of any person. Good faith is to be determined by looking to the mind of the particular holder. The test is not freedom from negligence in entering into the transaction. Nor is awareness of circumstances that would arouse suspicions about the instrument the test. However, evidence of circumstances surrounding the negotiation which raise questions as to whether the obligation is dependant on performance of some duty by the payee is relevant if it supports a finding of a bad faith taking by the holder. Ordinarily, where the note appears to be negotiable in form and regular on its face, the holder has no duty to inquire as to possible defenses unless the circumstances of which he has knowledge rise to the level that the failure to inquire shows a deliberate desire to evade knowledge because investigation may disclose some defense or problem with the transaction. Here, General Investment (P) required that the home improvement contract be submitted with the note at the time it was purchased. General Investment (P) therefore knew that the February 19 date printed on the note as the date when the installment payments were to begin meant that they would begin 60 days after completion of the work. The obvious meaning is that the Angelinis' (D) liability to start payments was dependant upon completion of the work in a workmanlike manner 60 days before February 19. General Investment (P) could have requested a certificate of completion from Lustro according to New Jersey statute. Instead, it accepted Lustro's representation in the note endorsement form that he had fulfilled his contractual obligations. Such conduct shows that General Investment (P) wilfully remained ignorant because of fear that an inquiry would disclose a failure of consideration. Considering the evidence as a whole, General Investment (P) did not acquire the note in "good faith" and cannot claim the status of a holder in due course. Reversed.

Analysis:

While a holder has no duty to investigate possible defenses, it cannot remain purposefully ignorant out of fear that further investigation would reveal a problem with the instrument. It was clear from the note and its accompanying contract that the obligation to pay was conditioned on completion of the work. Therefore, General Investment (P) should have obtained proof, in the form of a certificate of completion, that the work had been satisfactorily completed. The court inferred that its failure to do so resulted from a belief or fear that inquiry would disclose a lack of consideration. Therefore, General Investment (P) did not obtain the note in good faith and cannot claim the status of a holder in due course. The good faith requirement at issue in this case has been the subject of a continuing dispute as to whether a subjective or an objective test should be applied. The trend today seems to be a move toward an objective standard of good faith, measured against reasonable commercial standards of fair dealing.

■ **CASE VOCABULARY**

GOOD FAITH: As defined by the Code, it is honesty in fact and the observance of reasonable commercial standards of fair dealing. See UCC § 3-303(a)(4).

Any Kind Checks Cashed, Inc. v. Talcott

(Check–Cashing Store) v. (Maker of Check)
830 So.2d 160, 48 U.C.C. Rep. Serv. 2d 800 (Fla.Dist.Ct.App.2002)

A HOLDER IN DUE COURSE MUST SHOW GOOD FAITH

■ **INSTANT** ■ **FACTS** Any Kind (P) cashed a large check made by Talcott (D) after Talcott directed his bank to stop payment, and Any Kind (P) claimed it was a holder in due course of the check.

■ **BLACK LETTER RULE** A holder in due course must act in good faith, which means acting according to reasonable standards intended to result in fair dealing.

■ PROCEDURAL BASIS
Appeal from a judgment for Talcott (D).

■ FACTS
Guarino (D) obtained check-cashing privileges at Any Kind Checks Cashed (P) in Florida by filling out a card and providing a Social Security number and a driver's license. Guarino (D) listed his occupation as "broker." He cashed a check for $450 without incident. Talcott (D), a ninety-three year old man who lived in Massachusetts, was persuaded by his "financial advisor" Rivera to send a check for $10,000 to Guarino (D), who was Rivera's partner. The check supposedly was for "travel expenses," to obtain a return on a valueless investment Rivera had previously sold to Talcott (D). Talcott (D) sent the check on January 10, and Guarino (D) received it on January 11. On January 11, Rivera told Talcott (D) that $10,000 was more than would be needed for traveling expenses, and that $5,700 would be sufficient. Talcott (D) called his bank, and stopped payment on the $10,000 check. The same day, Guarino (D) cashed the $10,000 check at Any Time (P).

Any Time (P) required a supervisor's approval before cashing a check over $2,000. There were no written guidelines to follow, and each supervisor used his or her discretion in deciding which checks to cash. Michael, a supervisor at Any Time (P), looked at Guarino's (D) driver's license and the envelope the check came in. Guarino (D) told her a client sent him the check for an investment. Michael tried to contact Talcott (D), but was unable to do so. Michael believed the check was good, based on her experience, and based on the Federal Express envelope the check came in. Michael testified that the envelope was important, because it showed that the maker sent the check to Guarino (D). She authorized cashing the check.

On January 15, Talcott (D) sent Guarino (D) a check for $5,700. He assumed that he knew the earlier check had been stopped. Guarino (D) took the check to Any Time (P) on January 17. Michael refused to allow the check to be cashed until she contacted the maker. She called the number on the back of Guarino's (D) check-cashing card. When there was no answer, she told Guarino (D) that she would not cash the check. He gave her another number, similar to the first, and Michael was able to speak to Taclott (D). Talcott (D) approved cashing the $5,700 check, but no mention was made of the $10,000 check.

On January 19, Rivera told Talcott (D) that Guarino (D) was a cheat and a thief, and Talcott (D) immediately called his bank to stop payment on the $5,700 check. Talcott's (D) daughter called Any Kind (P) and told them that payment on the check had been stopped.

Any Kind Checks Cashed, Inc. v. Talcott (Continued)

Any Kind (P) brought suit against Talcott (D) and Guarino (D), claiming that it was a holder in due course. There was no dispute at trial that Rivera and Guarino (D) pulled a scam on Talcott (D). No evidence was presented regarding the standard practices in the check-cashing industry. The court entered judgment for Any Time (P) on the $5,700 check, but found for Talcott (D) on the $10,000 check.

■ ISSUE

Was Any Kind (P) a holder in due course?

■ DECISION AND RATIONALE

(Gross, J.) No. A holder in due course must act in good faith, which means acting according to reasonable standards intended to result in fair dealing. The procedures followed by Any Kind (P) did not meet that test.

Formerly, the good-faith requirement for a holder in due course was met by honesty in fact in the conduct of the transaction. Honesty in fact meant a lack of actual knowledge of wrongdoing. The holder could be ignorant, but had to be "pure of heart." The law was amended, however, to define "good faith" as involving the observance of reasonable commercial standards of fair dealing. Fairness is measured by taking a global view of the transaction and considering what is fair to all of the participants in the transaction. The finder of fact must determine whether the holder acted in accordance with accepted industry standards and, if so, whether those standards were reasonable ones intended to result in fair dealing. If both requirements are met, the holder will be determined to have acted in good faith. It does not matter if the holder acted negligently, as long as the standards were followed.

The procedures followed in this case, even if they met industry standards, were not reasonably related to achieving fair dealing. There are statutory provisions that govern check-cashing businesses, and there is nothing in those statutes to show that the rules regarding holders in due course are to be bent to accommodate them. Check-cashing businesses occupy a niche in the financial services market that is not filled by traditional banks. They tend to service poorer areas and low-income customers. Typically, the checks cashed are not large ones, and they are usually not business-related checks. Check-cashing businesses offer convenience and speed. They are prohibited from placing a hold on a check, but it is expected that there will be some verification of a check before it is cashed.

In the context of this transaction, the trial court did not err in finding that the $10,000 check was suspicious. Checks of that size are not often cashed at check-cashing outlets. In addition, Guarino (D) was not the typical customer of a check-cashing business. Because of the fees charged, most businesspeople cash checks at banks. In addition, Guarino (D) did not have a history of cashing such large checks without incident. The need for speed in cashing such a large check is consistent with the payee's fear that payment on the check will be stopped. Fair dealing required some degree of caution before a $10,000 check was cashed.

The policy reason behind the holder in due course doctrine is to secure easy negotiability of checks. This policy cannot outweigh the reasons for caution in this case. Loose application of the objective requirement of good faith would make check-cashing businesses the easy refuge of scam artists. In most cases, verification of the identity of the payee will not be necessary to preserve the holder in due course status of check-cashing outlets. The verification requirement may slow down some transactions, but that requirement serves an important goal. The need for unquestioned negotiability has given way to the desire for reasonable commercial fairness. Affirmed.

Analysis:

The court takes some pains to note the limited nature of its opinion. The decision here was very fact-specific, holding that the trial court did not err in finding that the circumstances of the $10,000 check were suspicious and required further investigation. Most legitimate business transactions do not require large amounts of cash. When a broker claims to need a $10,000 check cashed for a client's investment, alarm bells should go off. For the usual run of business of a check-cashing store, nothing probably will need to change: regular customers, who present relatively small checks from reliable payors, will be able to cash their checks quickly and without the need for much verification. This is the type of trade check-cashing stores seem to be intended to serve.

■ CASE VOCABULARY

HOLDER IN DUE COURSE: A person who in good faith has given value for a negotiable instrument that is complete and regular on its face, is not overdue, and, to the possessor's knowledge, has not been dishonored. Under UCC § 3–302, a holder in due course takes the instrument free of all claims and personal defenses, but subject to real defenses.

Winter & Hirsch, Inc. v. Passarelli
(Lender) v. (Borrower)
122 Ill.App.2d 372, 259 N.E.2d 312 (1970)

A CO-ORIGINATOR OF A LOAN IS CHARGED WITH KNOWLEDGE OF ITS TERMS AND CANNOT CLAIM THE STATUS OF A HOLDER IN DUE COURSE

■ **INSTANT FACTS** Winter & Hirsch (P) provided money to be loaned at a usurious rate by Equitable to the Passarellis (D).

■ **BLACK LETTER RULE** A co-originator of a loan is charged with knowledge of its terms and cannot claim the status of a holder in due course.

■ **PROCEDURAL BASIS**

Appeal from an order denying the Passarellis' (D) motion to vacate a judgment by confession entered against them on a promissory note.

■ **FACTS**

Dominic and Antoinette Passarelli (D) approached the Equitable Mortgage & Investment Corporation ("Equitable") to borrow $10,000. The Passarellis (D) executed a note providing that they agreed to repay a total of $16,260 over a period of 60 monthly payments of $271 each. The note also contained a confession of judgment clause, provided for payment to the bearer, and was secured by a trust deed. It is uncontested that the maximum legal rate of interest was exceeded by Equitable on this note. Winter & Hirsch (P), a company in the business of purchasing loans, gave a check for $11,000 on February 18, 1963 to Equitable with a notation that the funds were for "the Passarelli deal." However, the Passarellis (D) did not receive the $10,000 until February 28, 1963, ten days later. The Passarellis (D) defaulted on the note and Winter & Hirsch (P) obtained a judgment by confession.

■ **ISSUE**

Can a co-originator to a usurious loan claim the status of a holder in due course?

■ **DECISION AND RATIONALE**

(McCormick, J.) No. The question here is whether the defense of usury is available to the Passarellis (D) where Winter & Hirsch (P) claims to be a holder in due course of the note and thus takes it free of such defenses. The Passarellis (D) argue that Winter & Hirsch (P) knew of the usurious interest rate being charged and thus could not have become a holder in due course. The Passarellis (D) point out that Winter & Hirsch's (P) name is on the loan application and that they were told by Equitable that Winter & Hirsch (P) might give them the $10,000. Also, the monthly payments on the note were to be made to the office of Ralph Brown, an attorney for Winter & Hirsch (P). The most compelling fact to this court is that Winter & Hirsch (P) issued its check to Equitable on February 18, ten days before the money was given to the Passarellis (D). Thus, Winter & Hirsch (P) gave the money to Equitable before the Passarellis (D) executed the note which Winter & Hirsch (P) claims to have bought from Equitable. This fact makes the entire line of cases cited by Winter & Hirsch (P) inapposite. The cases cited hold that a loan may be purchased at more than the usury rate if the purchaser is without knowledge that the original note was tainted with usury. In the instant case, Winter & Hirsch (P) provided the money for the

Winter & Hirsch, Inc. v. Passarelli (Continued)

usurious loan before the loan was actually made. In the cases cited, however, the innocent holder of the note had purchased it after the loan was made. Winter & Hirsch (P) argue there must have been a clerical error in the dates. However, the date on the check and the date of the note have been clearly established and must be accepted as accurate. Winter & Hirsch (P) was actually a co-originator of the note since it advanced the funds for the loan before the loan was formalized. As such, it was charged with knowledge of the terms of the loan, including the fact that a usurious rate of interest was being charged. Winter & Hirsch (P) maintains that it did not give the $11,000 to Equitable until after the note was executed. The facts do not sustain this contention, but even if they did, we would still hold for the Passarellis (D). If Winter & Hirsch (P) saw the note before they gave $11,000 to Equitable, they would have also seen the Passarelli (D) note promising to repay $16,260. This should have raised the question of why Equitable was willing to sell the note at such a large discount, and put Winter & Hirsch (P) on notice that the rate being charge was possibly usurious. They should have inquired as to how much the Passarellis (D) were actually being paid. We cannot allow parties to intentionally keep themselves ignorant of facts which would make the transaction unlawful. Furthermore, the UCC provides that when an instrument is so incomplete as to call its validity into question, a purchaser of that instrument is on notice of a possibility of a claim against it. See § 3-302(a)(1). By failing to include the principal amount loaned on the note, the note was incomplete and its validity was called into question. Therefore, Winter & Hirsch (P) was on notice of possible defenses to the note and cannot claim to be a holder in due course. Reversed and remanded.

Analysis:

This case rejects Winter & Hirsch's (P) "head in the sand" argument. While there is no duty for a holder to investigate the facts surrounding an instrument that appears normal on its face, a party cannot intentionally remain ignorant of facts that would make the transaction illegal. Here, the face of the document itself put Winter & Hirsch (P) on notice that the loan was usurious, so it cannot claim lack of notice. The "good faith" requirement is also missing here. Winter & Hirsch (P) cannot claim to have taken the note in "good faith" when it advanced the funds for the usurious loan before the Passarellis (D) even signed the note.

■ CASE VOCABULARY

CONFESSION OF JUDGMENT: Also called cognovit judgment. It is written permission from the debtor which allows the creditor on default to obtain a judgment against the debtor. Such agreements are either prohibited or greatly restricted in most states.

Jones v. Approved Bancredit Corp.
(Consumer) v. (Finance Company)
256 A.2d 739 (Del. 1969)

A BUYER OF COMMERCIAL PAPER THAT MAINTAINS A CLOSE BUSINESS RELATIONSHIP WITH THE DEALER FROM WHOM IT BUYS THE PAPER MAY BE DENIED HOLDER IN DUE COURSE STATUS

■ **INSTANT FACTS** Mrs. Jones (D) executed a promissory note for the purchase of a home which was destroyed before it was completed.

■ **BLACK LETTER RULE** A finance company will be denied holder in due course status where it maintains a close business relationship with the dealer from whom it buys paper.

■ **PROCEDURAL BASIS**

Appeal from a directed verdict in favor of Bancredit (P).

■ **FACTS**

Myrtle Jones (D) contacted Albee Dell Homes, Inc. ("Dell"), a sales agency for pre-cut homes, to purchase a home. Mrs. Jones (D) signed a series of documents evidencing an obligation of $3,250, to be paid in monthly installments over a number of years. The documents included a mortgage, a judgment bond, a promissory note, a construction contract, a request for insurance, and affidavits. Mrs. Jones (D) at first objected to signing the documents and stated that she would like to consult an attorney. Dell's representative told her she did not need an attorney, and that he would advise her. Dell's representative insisted that the papers be signed immediately, and Mrs. Jones (D) finally agreed and signed all of the documents. The paper was immediately endorsed and assigned by Dell to Approved Bancredit Corp ("Bancredit") (P) for $2,250. During construction of the house, an employee of Dell drove a bulldozer into the side of the house knocking it off its foundations. Dell refused to finish the work claiming the incident was "a work of God." After County authorities demanded that the unsafe condition be fixed, Mrs. Jones (D) removed the remains of the home at her own expense. Dell later closed its office and terminated nearly all of its business operations. Bancredit (P) then brought this action against Mrs. Jones (D) seeking foreclosure and collection of an unpaid balance of $2,560.23. During pretrial proceedings, the action developed into a suit on the promissory note, and Bancredit (P) contented it was a holder in due course. Dell and Bancredit (P) were both wholly owned subsidiaries of Albee Homes, Inc. ("Albee"). Ninety-nine percent of Bancredit's (P) business came from Dell and the other sales agency subsidiaries of Albee. Bancredit (P) supplied the contracts and financing documents to be used by each sales agency, including Dell. Albee and Bancredit (P) had the same officers and directors. Bancredit (P) received progress reports from Dell on the construction of new homes. Each new transaction by Dell was approved in advance by Bancredit (P), and Bancredit (P) had the exclusive power to approve or reject each transaction.

■ **ISSUE**

May a finance company that is closely involved in an underlying transaction for consumer goods claim the protected status of a holder in due course?

■ **DECISION AND RATIONALE**

(Herrmann, J.) No. In installment sales of consumer goods and household appliances, a conflict has developed between balancing the interests of the commercial community against the interests of

Jones v. Approved Bancredit Corp. (Continued)

installment buyers. The commercial community requires the free negotiability of instruments, while the installment community has an interest in preserving the normal remedy of withholding payment when there has been a misrepresentation or other valid reason to refuse payment. Many courts have solved this problem by denying holder in due course status to the finance company where it maintains a close business relationship to the dealer whose paper it buys. In such situations, the finance company should not be able to hide behind the UCC and obtain an unfair advantage over the purchaser. Other courts have justified this rule by arguing that a finance company is better able to bear the risk of the dealer's insolvency than the buyer and is in a better position to protect its interests against unscrupulous dealers. The cases look to factors which show that the finance company cannot claim that it was a good faith innocent purchaser of the instrument. Relevant factors include whether the finance company approves the standards of the dealer, whether it has agreed to take all or a predetermined quantity of the paper that meets such standards, and whether it investigates the credit of the purchaser. Under the facts of this case, the rule of balance should be adopted and should apply in favor of Mrs. Jones (D) because Bancredit (P) was so involved in the transaction that it may not be treated as a subsequent purchaser for value. Bancredit (P) is more accurately described as an original party to the transaction and cannot claim the protected status of a holder in due course. This rule should be applied carefully because of the delicate balance of interests involved. However, it is necessary in the proper case given the need for truth in lending, consumer protection, and in preventing the misuse of negotiable instruments to deprive installment purchasers of legitimate defenses. Reversed and remanded.

Analysis:

This case is typical of those using the "close connection" doctrine to protect consumers from parties who might otherwise qualify as holders in due course. Today, the Federal Trade Commission has abolished holder in due course status for consumer notes. The FTC rule requires that leases and contracts for the sale of consumer goods display a notice that the holder of the contract is subject to all claims and defenses that the debtor could assert against the seller. Before the FTC adopted this rule, however, courts had to invoke the "close connection" doctrine to protect consumers. The doctrine was originally developed in consumer transactions, but has also been applied in purely commercial settings.

Sullivan v. United Dealers Corp.

(*Home Buyer*) v. (*Finance Company*)
486 S.W.2d 699 (Ky.App.1972)

A PURCHASER CAN BECOME A HOLDER IN DUE COURSE IF IT HAS NO NOTICE OF PROBLEMS WITH THE NOTE AT THE TIME IT IS NEGOTIATED

■ **INSTANT FACTS** United (P) purchased a promissory note from the contractor who had built a home for the Sullivans (D).

■ **BLACK LETTER RULE** A purchaser for value can become a holder in due course if, at the time the instrument was negotiated, the purchaser had no notice of defenses against the instrument.

■ **PROCEDURAL BASIS**

Appeal from a judgment in favor of the finance company on its suit against the Sullivans (D) for breach of contract.

■ **FACTS**

Memory Swift Homes contracted with James and Norma Jean Sullivan (D) to construct a prefabricated house for them. The contract was dated March 26, 1963, and on April 9, 1963, the Sullivans (D) executed and delivered a promissory note and mortgage for $18,224.64 to Memory Swift. That same day, Memory Swift negotiated the note and assigned the mortgage to United Dealers Corp. (P), a finance company. On June 25, 1963, United (P) negotiated the note to a bank. After the negotiation of the note to United (P) but before it negotiated the note to the bank, the Sullivans (D) delivered a written statement to United (P) that the foundation of the house had been properly installed and that all framing on the house was sturdy and all work was performed in a workmanlike manner. Beginning in August 1966, the Sullivans (D) made monthly payments according to the terms of the note but then defaulted. In April 1966, the bank transferred the note back to United (P) for value, without recourse. United (P) then sued the Sullivans (D) for collection of the note and foreclosure of the mortgage. The Sullivans (D) argued that United (P) was not a holder in due course and claimed that the house was not constructed in a workmanlike manner by Memory Swift.

■ **ISSUE**

Is a purchaser for value a holder in due course if at the time the instrument was negotiated it had no notice of defenses against the instrument?

■ **DECISION AND RATIONALE**

(Reed, J.) Yes. The Sullivans (D) claim that United (P) knew at the time they purchased the note that no work had been performed on the house. They further argue that United (P) knew about the construction contract, and they were put on notice that there might be a defense on the note because of the faulty construction. Notice, in order to prevent one from becoming a holder in due course, means notice at the time the instrument was negotiated. To be effective, notice must be given in a time and manner to give the purchaser a reasonable opportunity to act on it. A close business association between the payee and the purchaser has been used to deny the purchaser holder in due course status. The insulation the holder in due course doctrine provides is primarily intended to protect

Sullivan v. United Dealers Corp. (Continued)

finance institutions acting independently to supply credit rather than a manufacturer who finances its own sales or through a controlled agency. In this case, there is no allegation of fraud, or any claim that any fact existed that United (P) could have discovered that would have indicated a problem with the instrument. The Sullivans (D) represented that the contractor complied with its duties under the agreement. Other than a frequent course of dealing, there was no direct connection between the contractor and United (P). The evidence shows a lack of notice to United (P) that would justify a finding that it failed to acquire holder in due course status. Affirmed.

Analysis:

The same facts that call a party's "good faith" into question may also give the party "notice" that the instrument has a problem. These factors are separate but related. A party with notice of possible defenses to an instrument cannot be said to take the instrument in "good faith." The focus in this case seems to be the relevant time when a party must have notice. The notice must arise at the time of the taking or at the time the instrument is negotiated. Notice arising subsequently is ineffective.

Triffin v. Somerset Valley Bank

(*Assignee of Checks*) v. (*Bank*)
343 N.J.Super. 73, 777 A.2d 993 (2001)

TRANSFEREE OF NEGOTIABLE INSTRUMENT ACQUIRES ALL RIGHTS OF TRANSFEROR, INCLUDING STATUS AS HOLDER IN DUE COURSE

■ **INSTANT FACTS** A purchaser of forged checks claimed he was a holder in due course and entitled to payment for the checks.

■ **BLACK LETTER RULE** Under the shelter rule, a transferee of a negotiable instrument is a holder in due course if the transferor was, even if the transferee had notice of defenses to the instrument.

■ **PROCEDURAL BASIS**

Appeal of summary judgment motion in action for negligence.

■ **FACTS**

In 1998, Alfred Hauser, the president of Hauser Contracting Company (Hauser) (D) was notified that people were cashing counterfeit Hauser (D) payroll checks. The checks were stamped with Mr. Hauser's facsimile signature, which was identical to the stamp used on Hauser (P) paychecks. Hauser (D) stopped payment on the checks. Somerset Valley Bank (the Bank) (D) received more than 80 forged Hauser (D) checks valued at $25,000. In 1999, Triffin (P) purchased 18 dishonored Hauser (D) checks from check cashing companies. The check cashing companies stated that they cashed the checks for value, in good faith, without notice of any claims or defenses to the checks, without knowledge that the signatures were unauthorized or forged, and with the expectation that the checks would be paid. All the checks were marked by the Bank (D) as "stolen" and stamped with the warning "do not present again." Triffin (P) then sued the Bank (D), Hauser (D), and each of the payees to enforce Hauser's (D) liability on the checks. Triffin (P) argued that Hauser (D) was negligent in failing to safeguard its payroll checks and its signature facsimile stamp and was therefore liable for payment of the checks. Triffin (P) filed a summary judgment motion, which the trial court granted. The trial court held that because the check cashing companies took the checks in good faith, Triffin (P) was a holder in due course as an assignee. The court also held that because the checks appeared to be genuine, Hauser (D) failed to show that the check cashing companies had notice that the checks were invalid.

■ **ISSUE**

Is an assignee of a negotiable instrument a holder in due course even if he has notice of defenses to the instrument?

■ **DECISION AND RATIONALE**

(Cuff, J.) Yes, an assignee of a negotiable instrument is a holder in due course even if he has notice of defenses to the instrument so long as the assignor was a holder in due course. First, the checks were negotiable instruments. They were payable to a bearer for a fixed amount on demand and did not state any other undertaking by the person promising payment aside from the payment of money. Each check appears to be signed by Mr. Hauser by a facsimile stamp. Whether the checks were authorized is a separate issue from whether they are negotiable. The next issue is whether Triffin (P) is a holder in

Triffin v. Somerset Valley Bank (Continued)

due course. Each of the check cashing companies were holders in due course. They submitted affidavits that they cashed the checks for value, in good faith, without notice of any claims or defenses, without knowledge that any of the signatures were unauthorized or fraudulent, and with the expectation they would be paid upon being presented to the drawer bank. Where a transferee does not take a check by indorsement, as here, the transferee still assumes all the rights of the transferor, so long as the transferor had valid rights to the instrument. There was no evidence that the appearance of the checks placed the check cashing companies on notice that the checks were not valid. The signature looked identical to Hauser's (D) authorized signature. Under the law, the signature is presumed to be authentic and authorized. The defendant, here Hauser (D), had the burden of proving otherwise. Here, Hauser (D) relied only on conclusory statements, but no actual evidence. Affirmed.

Analysis:

Because the check writing companies were holders in due course, they had the right to sue the purported maker, Hauser (D), for payment of the checks in this case. Under the shelter rule, the check cashing companies could assign these rights to Triffin (P), even if Triffin (P) had knowledge otherwise. Comments 2 and 3 to § 3–202 explain that it is inherent in the character of negotiable instruments that any person in possession of an instrument that is payable to that person or to the bearer is a holder. A holder in due course may even take the instrument from a thief and be protected against the claim of a rightful owner. While the equities may favor Hauser (D) over Triffin (P), the free negotiability of checks is a cornerstone of our longstanding banking practices.

Federal Deposit Insurance Corp. v. Culver
(Holder) v. (Borrower)
640 F.Supp. 725 (D.Kan.1986)

FRAUD IN FACTUM CAN BE ASSERTED AGAINST A HOLDER IN DUE COURSE WHERE THE MAKER HAD NO REASONABLE OPPORTUNITY TO OBTAIN KNOWLEDGE OF THE INSTRUMENT'S CHARACTER OR TERMS

■ **INSTANT FACTS** Culver (D) signed a blank promissory note believing he was signing only a receipt.

■ **BLACK LETTER RULE** Fraud in factum can be asserted as a defense against a holder in due course if the maker had no knowledge or reasonable opportunity to obtain knowledge of the instrument's character or essential terms.

■ **PROCEDURAL BASIS**

Ruling on the FDIC's (P) motion for summary judgment on its breach of contract case.

■ **FACTS**

Culver (D) entered a business relationship with Nasib Kalliel in which Culver (D) would operate his farm and Kalliel would manage the financial aspects of the farm. In July or August of 1984, Culver (D) notified Kalliel that he desperately needed money to avoid foreclosure. One week later, $30,000 was wired from the Rexford State Bank in Kansas to Culver's (D) bank in Missouri. Culver (D) knew where the money had come from, but thought Kalliel would be responsible for its repayment. Culver (D) was soon approached by Jerry Gilbert, who Culver (D) believed was working for Kalliel. Gilbert told Culver (D) that Rexford State Bank wanted to know where its money had gone for their records. Gilbert presented Culver (D) a document which he led Culver (D) to believe was merely a receipt for the money. Culver (D) signed the document without intending to commit himself to repay the money. In reality, the document Culver (D) signed was a form promissory note. The form contained blanks to insert the terms of the loan. At the time Culver (D) signed the note, the blanks had not been completed. Only the name of the payee, Rexford State Bank, was printed on the forms. Later, some unknown individual completed the note indicating the principal amount as $50,000, the execution date as August 2, 1984, the maturity date was February 2, 1985, and the interest rate as 14.5% until maturity and 18.5% thereafter. Although Culver (D) received only $30,000, the Rexford State Bank did deposit $50,000 into an account controlled by Kalliel. The $30,000 apparently came from that account. When Rexford State Bank became insolvent, the Federal Deposit Insurance Corporation ("FDIC") (P) purchased a number of the bank's assets, including the note at issue here. At that time, FDIC (D) had no notice of the events that occurred before it purchased the note. Culver (D) has made no payments on the note and the FDIC (D) brought this action.

■ **ISSUE**

Can fraud in factum be asserted as a defense against a holder in due course where the maker had a reasonable opportunity to learn of the instrument's character and terms?

■ **DECISION AND RATIONALE**

(O'Connor, J.) No. There is no doubt that the FDIC (P) has holder in due course status in this action. Culver (D) concedes that personal defenses such as fraud in the inducement, estoppel, and failure of

Federal Deposit Insurance Corp. v. Culver (Continued)

consideration are ineffective against a holder in due course. Culver (D), however, asserts the real defense of fraud in factum which is valid against a holder in due course. UCC § 3-305(a)(1)(iii) codifies the fraud in factum defense as a misrepresentation that "has induced the party to sign the instrument with neither knowledge nor reasonable opportunity to obtain knowledge of its character or its essential terms." Official Comment 7 to § 3-305 provides that fraud in factum often occurs when the maker is tricked into signing a note in the belief that it is merely a receipt or some other document. The test is that of excusable ignorance of the contents of the writing signed. The party must not only have been in ignorance, but must also have had no reasonable opportunity to obtain knowledge. The Kansas case of *Ort v. Fowler* is instructive. In *Ort*, a farmer signed a promissory note believing that he was merely signing an agency contract. The farmer could not read but relied on the agent to read it for him. The note was later sold to a third party. The Kansas Supreme Court found that this type of case presents a situation where one of two innocent parties must suffer. However, the holder in due course is not only innocent, it is free from all negligence. A party has a duty to read and understand what he signs. If he cannot read, he makes the stranger who reads for him his agent and adopts his reading as his own knowledge. Here, Culver (D) is able to read and understand English. Thus, under the rule announced in *Ort*, Culver (D) was negligent in relying on Gilbert's assurance that the note was only a receipt. Therefore, Culver (D) has failed to show "excusable ignorance" necessary to establish fraud in the factum. We find as a matter of law that Culver (D) had a reasonable opportunity to obtain knowledge of the document's character before he signed it. Culver's (D) second argument is that he had no opportunity to know of the note's "essential terms." The note's essential terms were left blank when he signed it; therefore, he had no opportunity at all to learn of those terms. Incomplete instruments are governed by K.S.A. 84-3-115 and 407. The former provides that when a paper is signed while incomplete it is effective when it is completed in accordance with the authority given. Because Culver (D) claims not to have authorized anyone to complete the note, we turn to K.S.A. 83-3-407 which provides that a "subsequent holder in due course may in all cases enforce the instrument according to its original tenor, and when an incomplete instrument has been completed, he may enforce it as completed." As a holder in due course, the FDIC (P) is entitled to enforce the note as it was eventually completed, not merely as Culver (D) would have authorized it to be completed. One who signs an instrument before its essential terms have been completed creates a "blank check" that may be enforced by a holder in due course according to any terms that are completed by an intervening holder. That is exactly what happened here. Culver's (D) only legal recourse is against the intervening holder who actually completed the note. We grant FDIC's (P) motion for summary judgment.

Analysis:

The court here followed the reasoning of the Kansas Supreme Court. One of two innocent parties had to lose: either Culver (D) or the FDIC (P). Because Culver (D) was negligent, he should bear the loss. The court held as a matter of law that Culver (D) had a reasonable opportunity to obtain knowledge of the document's character before he signed it. Generally, however, negligence is a factual issue to be determined by the finder of fact. It is rarely disposed of on summary judgment like it was here. As it is, Culver (D), a farmer who hired someone else to handle the financial affairs of his farm, is forced to pay back a $50,000 note for which he received only $30,000. His only avenue of recourse is against the unknown intervening holder who actually filled in the terms of the note.

Sea Air Support, Inc. v. Herrmann

(Holder) v. (Maker)
96 Nev. 574, 613 P.2d 413 (1980)

A PROMISE TO PERFORM FUTURE SERVICES DOES NOT CONSTITUTE TAKING THE INSTRUMENT "FOR VALUE" FOR PURPOSES OF BECOMING A HOLDER IN DUE COURSE

■ **INSTANT FACTS** Herrmann (D) wrote a bad check to pay off gambling debts and Sea Air (P) tried to collect on the check.

■ **BLACK LETTER RULE** A promise to perform future services does not constitute taking "for value" for purposes of becoming a holder in due course.

■ **PROCEDURAL BASIS**
Appeal after trial court dismissed Sea Air's (P) action to collect a gambling debt.

■ **FACTS**
Ralph Herrmann (D) wrote a check for $10,000 to the Ormsby House, a casino in Carson City, Nevada, to pay off counter checks he had written earlier that evening to acquire gaming chips. The Ormsby House was unable to collect the money for the check because Herrmann's (D) account had insufficient funds. The debt was then assigned to Sea Air Support (P) for collection. Sea Air (P) was also unable to collect and filed this action against Herrman (D) for $10,567.

■ **ISSUE**
Is Sea Air (P) a holder in due course where it did not pay value for the check and had notice that the check might be dishonored?

■ **DECISION AND RATIONALE**
(Per Curiam) No. Sea Air's (P) claim is barred by the Statute of Anne. Absent conflicting statutes, Nevada law incorporates the common law of gambling as stated in the Statute of 9 Anne. The Statute provides that notes drawn for the purpose of repaying any money lent for gaming are "utterly void, frustrate, and of none effect." Even though gambling in Nevada is legal, this court has long held that debts incurred or checks drawn for gambling purposes are unenforceable. If the law is to change, it must be done by the legislature. Herrmann's (D) check was clearly drawn to repay money advanced for gaming and is void and unenforceable. Sea Air (P) seeks to avoid this defense by claiming to be a holder in due course. Sea Air (P) took the check from the casino and promised to take "such legal action as may be necessary to enforce collection." The promise to perform services in the future does not constitute taking for value under the UCC. Furthermore, Sea Air (D) had constructive notice of a defense against collection because the check was payable to a casino, and Sea Air (P) knew the check was dishonored. Because Sea Air (P) did not take the check for value and without notice it cannot claim to be a holder in due course. Affirmed.

Analysis:
Soon after this decision, the Nevada legislature amended its laws to permit casinos to sue on credit instruments received in payment of gambling debts. The only thing surprising about this change was

Sea Air Support, Inc. v. Herrmann (Continued)

that it took until 1980 to make it. If Sea Air (P) had been a holder in due course, it still would have been unable to enforce the check, because under UCC § 3-305(a)(1)(ii), the defense of "illegality of the transaction which, under other law, nullifies the obligation of the obligor" would be available even against a holder in due course. Here, the Statute of Anne, still in force at the time in Nevada, made this type of debt void.

■ CASE VOCABULARY

PER CURIAM: An opinion from the whole court rather than one written by an individual justice.

Kedzie & 103rd Currency Exchange, Inc. v. Hodge

(Holder) v. (Payor)
156 Ill.2d 112, 619 N.E.2d 732, 189 Ill.Dec. 31 (1993)

THE "ILLEGALITY" DEFENSE IS AVAILABLE AGAINST A HOLDER IN DUE COURSE ONLY WHEN THE INSTRUMENT ARISING FROM AN ILLEGAL TRANSACTION HAS SPECIFICALLY BEEN MADE VOID BY STATUTE

■ **INSTANT FACTS** Hodge (D) wrote a check and then stopped payment on it for work to be performed by an unlicenced plumber.

■ **BLACK LETTER RULE** Unless an instrument arising from a transaction is, itself, made void by statute, the illegality defense is not available to bar the claim of a holder in due course.

■ **PROCEDURAL BASIS**

Appeal from the dismissal of the Currency Exchange's (P) action to collect a debt from Hodge (D).

■ **FACTS**

Fred Fentress (D) agreed to install a "flood control system" in the home of Eric and Beulah Hodge (D) for $900. In partial payment for the work, Beulah Hodge (D) wrote a check for $500 to "Fred Fentress-A-OK Plumbing." When Fentress (D) failed to appear on the date set for installation, Eric Hodge (D) telephoned him and announced the contract was "canceled." Hodge (D) also told Fentress (D) that he would order his bank, Citicorp Savings, not to pay the check. Hodge (D) stopped payment on the check that day. Fentress (D) then presented the check at Kedzie & 103rd Street Currency Exchange ("Currency Exchange") (P) and obtained payment. When the Currency Exchange (P) presented the check for payment at Citicorp, payment was refused. The Currency Exchange (P) then sued Hodge (D) and Fentress (D) for the amount stated. Fentress (D) was not a licensed plumber as was required under Illinois law.

■ **ISSUE**

May a holder in due course take an instrument free of the illegality defense where the instrument arising from the contract has not been specifically declared void by statute?

■ **DECISION AND RATIONALE**

(Freeman, J.) Yes. The Currency Exchange (P) claims to be a holder in due course of the check. However, Hodge (D) argues that its claim is barred, even as a holder in due course, based on the "illegality of the transaction" defense provided by UCC § 3–305. Hodge (D) contends Fentress (D) was not a licenced plumber, and his promised performance under the contract is illegal and bars the Currency Exchange's (P) claim for payment. Illegality arises under a variety of statutes and is left to local law. However, it is only when an obligation is made entirely "null and void" under local law that illegality exists as a real defense to defeat the claim of a holder in due course. Historically, this court has recognized illegality to arise only when there is a statute affecting both the underlying contract and the instrument exchanged upon it. A transaction which is void negates the obligation to pay arising from it between the contracting parties. However, unless the instrument memorializing the obligation is also made void by statute, an innocent third party may claim payment of it against the maker. Our

Kedzie & 103rd Currency Exchange, Inc. v. Hodge (Continued)

legislature has declared that any instrument involving gambling or the payment of gambling debts is void. The existence or absence of a legislative declaration is what controls. Our cases have recognized that for the illegality defense to prevail there must be a direct statutory expression that an instrument itself arising from a particular transaction is void. A plaintiff cannot recover on a suit involving an illegal contract because the plaintiff is a wrongdoer. But a holder in due course is an innocent third party without knowledge of the circumstances of the contract on which the obligation arose. If "illegality" means simply negation of the initial obligation to pay, a holder in due course enjoys no more protection than a party to the original transaction. The real defense of illegality would be reduced to a personal one. In adopting the UCC our legislature chose to give a holder in due course considerable protection against most claims. Our legislature continues to declare certain obligations void, such as payments for gambling debts, because of the circumstances of the agreements from which they arise. The legislature has selectively negated certain obligations. Thus, the legislature has indicated what will and what will not give rise to illegality. We find that unless the instrument arising from a contract is, itself, made void by statute, the "illegality" defense is not available to bar the claim of a holder in due course. The Currency Exchange (P), as a holder in due course, may claim payment for the check. Reversed.

■ DISSENT

(Bilandic, J.) The plain language of UCC § 3–305 and the comments make it clear that when the illegality of a transaction renders the obligation a nullity, the illegality of the transaction can be raised as a defense even against a holder in due course. Section 3–305 does not state that illegality is a defense only when the legislature has expressly declared that the instrument arising from an illegal transaction is void. The only inquiry then is whether the contract between Hodge (D) and Fentress (D) is void on the grounds of illegality. Here, it clearly is because Fentress (D) was not a licenced plumber as required by Illinois law. The rationale behind this law is to protect the public's health and safety from inadequate plumbers. The contract here between Fentress (D) and Hodge (D) represents the type of dangers the law intends to guard against. The majority asserts that it would be unfair to allow the illegality defense to prevail against the Currency Exchange (P) because the Currency Exchange (P) is an innocent third party. This argument is misplaced because § 3–305 provides that defenses such as infancy, duress, and illegality can be asserted even against an innocent third party. The policy disfavoring these type of transactions overrides the general policy favoring the free negotiability of instruments. The majority's reasoning would lead to the conclusion that all of the defenses listed in § 3–305 should be unavailable to defeat the claim of a holder in due course. Such a conclusion is obviously contrary to the provisions of § 3–305. I dissent and would affirm.

Analysis:

The rule adopted by the majority has the benefit of certainty. A purchaser of an instrument can easily tell if it will be enforceable by reference to the instrument itself and applicable statutes. The purchaser does not need to investigate the circumstances of the underlying contract to determine if the obligation is valid. However, the dissent makes a powerful argument. The UCC provides that even a holder in due course will take the instrument subject to "real defenses." One of these real defenses is "illegality of the transaction which, under other law, nullifies the obligation of the obligor." The UCC reads "illegality of the transaction" not "illegality of the instrument arising from the transaction." The UCC thus seems to clearly state that the illegality of the transaction, is what matters, contrary to what the majority held.

Virginia National Bank v. Holt

(Payee) v. (Maker)
216 Va. 500, 219 S.E.2d 881 (1975)

A SIGNATURE ON AN INSTRUMENT WILL BE PRESUMED VALID UNLESS SUFFICIENT EVIDENCE IS INTRODUCED TO SUPPORT A FINDING THAT THE SIGNATURE IS FORGED OR UNAUTHORIZED

■ **INSTANT FACTS** Mrs. Holt (D) was sued on a note that she denied signing.

■ **BLACK LETTER RULE** The presumption that a signature on a negotiable instrument is valid can only be overcome by introducing evidence sufficient to support a finding that the signature is forged or unauthorized.

■ **PROCEDURAL BASIS**

Appeal by Virginia National Bank (P) from the trial court's denial of its motion for summary judgment.

■ **FACTS**

Virginia National Bank (P) filed an action against Edgar and Gustava Holt (D), seeking recovery of the face amount of a promissory note plus interest and attorney's fees. The instrument was payable to the Bank (P) and was in the amount of $6,000. A default judgment was entered against Edgar Holt (D). However, Gustava Holt (D) in her pleadings specifically denied that the instrument was signed by her.

■ **ISSUE**

Must Mrs. Holt (D) introduce evidence sufficient to support a finding that her signature is forged or unauthorized to overcome the presumption that a signature on an instrument is valid?

■ **DECISION AND RATIONALE**

(Compton, J.) Yes. Witnesses for the Bank (P) testified that the signature on the note was in fact Mrs. Holt's (D). Mrs. Holt's (D) attorney attempted to show that she did not execute the note. During cross-examination, the loan officer was asked whether he was present during Mrs. Holt's (D) deposition when she "denied that she signed the note." The loan officer responded, "Yes, I was. Somewhat surprised." The only evidence offered on Mrs. Holt's (D) behalf was a set of answers the Bank (P) had filed in response to interrogatories made by her attorney. The answers indicate that the Bank (P) did not know of any witnesses who saw Mrs. Holt (D) sign the note. The trial court found that the question of whether the signature was genuine was for the jury. This was error. Section 3–308 establishes the burden of proof in an action in which issues arise challenging the genuineness of a signature. Under this section, a signature on an instrument is admitted unless the "effectiveness" of the signature is put at issue by a specific denial. The burden is then put on the other party to establish the genuineness of the signature, but such a party is aided by a presumption that the signature is genuine. The effect of the presumption is to eliminate the requirement that the plaintiff prove the signature is authentic until some evidence is introduced that would show that the signature is forged or unauthorized. Therefore, under § 3–308 the party denying the signature must make a showing of the grounds for denial before the plaintiff is put to his proof. Until the party denying the signature has introduced such sufficient evidence, the presumption requires a finding for the party relying on the signature. Here, the Bank (P) was entitled to summary judgment in its favor since no material issue of fact requiring resolution by the

Virginia National Bank v. Holt (Continued)

jury was presented. Mrs. Holt's (D) specific denial put the genuineness of her signature at issue. However, she failed to produce sufficient evidence to support her denial of genuineness. The loan officer's answer during cross-examination is insufficient to sustain a finding that the signature was forged or unauthorized. We hold that Mrs. Holt (D) has failed to make a sufficient showing to support a finding that she, or her representative, did not in fact sign the note. Reversed.

Analysis:

The word "presumed" is defined in § 1–201 and means that until some evidence is introduced that would support a finding that the signature is forged or unauthorized, the plaintiff is not required to prove that it is valid. The reason for this presumption is that forged or unauthorized signatures are quite uncommon, and normally any evidence is in the control of, or more accessible to, the defendant. Mrs. Holt (D) put the genuineness of the signature at issue. However, she failed the second requirement by not introducing any evidence that would support a finding that the signature was forged or unauthorized. What would have been sufficient evidence to overcome the presumption? What if Mrs. Holt (D) had taken the stand and denied the signature?

Herzog Contracting Corp. v. McGowen Corp.

(Payee) v. (Maker)
976 F.2d 1062 (7th Cir.1992)

PAROL EVIDENCE MAY BE INTRODUCED AGAINST A PARTY OTHER THAN A HOLDER IN DUE COURSE TO SHOW THAT THE PARTIES DID NOT INTEND TO CREATE A BINDING CONTRACT

■ **INSTANT FACTS** McGowen (D) issued promissory notes to a subsidiary of Herzog (P).

■ **BLACK LETTER RULE** Parol evidence may be introduced against a party other than a holder in due course to show that an unambiguous instrument was not intended to create a binding contract.

■ **PROCEDURAL BASIS**

Appeal from summary judgment granted in favor of Herzog (P) on its breach of contract suit to enforce two promissory notes issued by McGowen (D).

■ **FACTS**

In 1989 Herzog (P) bought the assets of Tru-Flex Metal Hose Corporation from McGowen (D), and formed a subsidiary of Herzog (P) (also called Tru-Flex) to hold them. Herzog (P) then assigned an asset purchase agreement to its wholly-owned subsidiary, Tru-Flex. The agreement required annual payments from Tru-Flex to McGowen (D) of $500,000 for five years. Later in 1989 two promissory notes were issued by McGowen (D) to Tru-Flex for the sum of $400,000. The parties disagree about the purpose of the notes. Herzog (P) claims it loaned McGowen (D) $400,000 and the notes are McGowen's promises to repay that loan. McGowen (D) admits having received the $400,000, but argues that it was not a loan but rather a partial prepayment of the next year's installment due under the asset purchase agreement. McGowen (D) believes that the only purpose of the notes it gave Tru-Flex was to enable McGowen (D) to postpone the realization of taxable income by making the $400,000 payment look like a loan. Herzog (P) soon refused to make further payments under the asset purchase agreement, and McGowen (D) brought an action against Herzog (P) in state court which remains pending. Tru-Flex has assigned McGowen's (D) promissory notes to Herzog (P) which has brought this suit to enforce them.

■ **ISSUE**

Are promissory notes enforceable solely on the basis that they are "clear and unambiguous" regardless of what the parties actually intended?

■ **DECISION AND RATIONALE**

(Posner, J.) No. The notes would be enforceable if Herzog (P) were a holder in due course, but Herzog (P) concedes it is not. Herzog (P) argues that the parol evidence rule dictates that the unambiguous notes cannot be varied by extrinsic evidence. However, a holder of a promissory note who is not a holder in due course takes the note subject to all defenses which would be available on an ordinary contract action. One of these defenses, notwithstanding the parol evidence rule, is that the parties did not intend to create an enforceable contract. Some cases enforce the parol evidence rule more broadly in suits on promissory notes where the plaintiff is not a holder in due course. Despite

Herzog Contracting Corp. v. McGowen Corp. (Continued)

these cases, the parties have tacitly agreed that the applicability of the parol evidence rule to this case is not governed by general contract law, but by a special doctrine that allows parol evidence to show that the negotiable instrument he is suing on was "for a special purpose." Herzog (P), however, argues that the special purpose doctrine is limited to allowing the promisor to defend by showing that his obligation on the note was subject to a condition precedent. There is no condition precedent here. McGowen (D) does not contend that something had to happen before payment was due, but rather than Herzog (P) could never demand payment. Based on our review of history, we do not believe the special purpose defense is limited only to "condition precedent" cases as Herzog (P) argues. Rather, the special purpose defense encompasses all cases in which the instrument was not intended to create an enforceable obligation. The trend of our law has been to relax strict rules. Furthermore, the purpose of the parol evidence rule is to prevent parties to a written contract from changing its terms by reference to side agreements. Here, McGowen is not trying to change the terms of the promissory note, but to show that the notes were not intended to create a legally enforceable obligation. Herzog (P) made no attempt to discount the notes to a third party who could have claimed the status of a holder in due course and enforced the notes against McGowen (D). Herzog (P) is not such a holder in due course and McGowen (D) may attempt to show an oral agreement that the notes were not intended to be enforced. Reversed and remanded.

Analysis:

The UCC has been revised since this case was decided. Under the revision, the outcome would likely be the same. Section 3-105(b) provides that "[a]n instrument that is conditionally issued or is issued for a special purpose is binding on the maker or drawer, but failure of the condition or special purpose is a defense." Official Comment 2 to this section states that it "continues the rule that nonissuance, conditional issuance or issuance for a special purpose is a defense of the maker or drawer of an instrument" and "can be asserted against a person other than a holder in due course." In addition, § 3–117 provides that "subject to applicable law regarding exclusion of proof of contemporaneous or previous agreements, the obligation of a party to an instrument to pay the instrument may be modified, supplemented, or nullified by a separate agreement of the obligor and a person entitled to enforce the instrument." This section goes on to provide that "[t]o the extent that an obligation is ... nullified by an agreement under this section, the agreement is a defense to the obligation." These two sections taken together would probably lead to the same result reached by Justice Posner.

CHAPTER TEN

The Nature of Liability

Ward v. Federal Kemper Insurance Co

Instant Facts: Insurance Co. cancelled policy for nonpayment after it mistakenly sent insured a refund check for too much, and then billed for the overage, but check was never cashed.

Black Letter Rule: Mere possession of a check, without negotiation, does not constitute acceptance of the funds.

Floor v. Melvin

Instant Facts: Owner of note improperly sued guarantor of contract guaranteeing collection without first attempting to collect from, or make allegation of insolvency against, the maker of the note.

Black Letter Rule: If a contract guaranteeing a note is one for collection, rather than payment, there must first be an effort to collect from, or a showing of insolvency of, the maker of the note before the guarantor may be sued.

Chemical Bank v. PIC Motors Corp.

Instant Facts: Siegel (D2), guarantor and former owner of car dealership, was sued under guaranty, and he argued that conduct by Bank (P) and current owner discharged the obligation.

Black Letter Rule: A guarantor's obligation under a payment guaranty cannot be discharged based upon impairment of collateral where the guarantor has expressly consented to the release of the collateral.

London Leasing Corp. v. Interfina, Inc.

Instant Facts: Corporate officer, who signed promissory note on behalf of corporation and personally endorsed it, attempted to discharge personal obligation based on non consent to agreement extending due date.

Black Letter Rule: Where the party personally endorsing the note consents to the agreement between the note's maker and payee to extend the time when payment is due, there is no discharge of the endorser on the obligation on the note.

Messing v. Bank of America, N.A.

Instant Facts: Messing (P), a non-account holder of a check, unsuccessfully attempted to cash the check, after refusing to provide a thumbprint signature as required by the bank's (D) policy.

Black Letter Rule: If presentment of a check is not in accordance with the agreement of the parties, the refusal to pay does not constitute dishonor of the instrument.

Makel Textiles, Inc. v. Dolly Originals, Inc.

Instant Facts: Two individual endorsers of corporate notes sought to have liability discharged for failure to present notes for payment and failure to give notice of dishonor.

Black Letter Rule: The requirements of presentment and notice of dishonor are not excused with respect to an endorser of subsequent notes who had no active participation or knowledge of the note maker's affairs.

Norton v. Knapp

Instant Facts: Buyer of equipment signed back of sight draft with the words ""Kiss my foot,"' and court held that this did not constitute an acceptance.

Black Letter Rule: The words "kiss my foot"' written on the back of a sight draft and signed by the drawee do not constitute an acceptance of the draft.

Galyen Petroleum Co. v. Hixson

Instant Facts: Payee of checks sued drawee bank for dishonor of drawer's checks presented to it for payment, although drawer had funds on deposit.

Black Letter Rule: A payee on a check has no cause of action against the drawee bank for dishonoring a check even though funds are in the account.

Mundaca Investment Corp. v. Febba

Instant Facts: Individual signed promissory notes as "trustee" borrower but did not identify the principal, and thus intent of the original parties was held to be the material issue of fact.

Black Letter Rule: When a principal is not expressly identified in an instrument signed by an agent, the agent can be personally liable to the holder of the instrument unless the agent proves that the original parties did not intend the agent to be personally liable.

Nichols v. Seale

Instant Facts: Nichols (D) signed his name to a note, below a fictitious business name, without showing that he signed on behalf of corporation doing business under the fictitious name.

Black Letter Rule: Where an instrument is signed by an agent or other representative, names the person represented, but does not show that the representative signed in a representative capacity, extrinsic evidence is admissible to establish the capacity of the signer and whether he is personally liable.

Ward v. Federal Kemper Insurance Co.

(*Insured*) v. (*Insurance Co.*)
62 Md.App. 351, 489 A.2d 91, 40 UCC Rep. Serv. 753 (1985)

TRUE OWNER OF MONEY, IN FORM OF CHECK DRAWN UPON BANK, IS DETERMINED BY WHETHER CHECK WAS PRESENTED FOR PAYMENT AND HONORED

■ **INSTANT FACTS** Insurance Co. cancelled policy for nonpayment after it mistakenly sent insured a refund check for too much, and then billed for the overage, but check was never cashed.

■ **BLACK LETTER RULE** Mere possession of a check, without negotiation, does not constitute acceptance of the funds.

■ **PROCEDURAL BASIS**

Appeal from judgment following ruling on hearing for declaratory judgment.

■ **FACTS**

Federal Kemper Insurance Company (Insurance Co.) (D) issued an automobile liability policy to Ward (P) and he paid the premium in full. After Ward (P) changed vehicles, Insurance Co. (D) sent him a refund check for overpaid premium in the amount of $12.00 drawn on Citizens National Bank (the Bank). Although Ward (P) received the check, he never negotiated it. Soon thereafter, the Insurance Co. (D) realized that it had made a mistake in the amount of the refund due Ward (P). It had sent Ward (P) [the whopping sum of] $7.50 too much. Ward (P) did not pay, nor does he recall receiving, the bill. Insurance Co. (D) cancelled the policy. Approximately one month later, Ward (P) was involved in an automobile accident. Ward (P) and others involved in the accident sustained injuries and property damage. Insurance Co. (D) declined to provide coverage. Ward (P) sued seeking a declaratory judgment as to coverage. The trial judge treated the cross motions for summary judgment as a hearing on the merits and issued a declaratory judgment in favor of Insurance Co. (D). Ward (P) appealed.

■ **ISSUE**

Does the mere possession of a check, without negotiation, constitute acceptance of the funds?

■ **DECISION AND RATIONALE**

(Adkins) No. The mere possession of a check, without negotiation, does not constitute the acceptance of the funds. A check is a draft or bill of exchange—an order by a drawer, the Insurance Co. (D), to a drawee, the Bank, to pay money to a payee, Ward (P). When the drawer draws a check on the drawee and delivers the check to the payee, the check is generally considered a conditional payment of the underlying obligation. The conditions are that the check be presented and honored. Until then, no one is directly liable on the check itself. The underlying obligation on the insurance policy is similarly suspended until those conditions are met. *UCC* Section 3-802(1)(b) [now Section 3-310] provides that in the case of an uncertified check, suspension of the obligation continues until dishonor of the check or until it is paid. Moreover, *UCC* Section 3-409(1) [now Section 3-408] provides: "A check or draft does not itself operate as an assignment of any funds in the hands of the drawee available for its payment, and the drawee is not liable on the instrument until he accepts it." Thus, mere possession of the check did not have the effect of transferring the funds to Ward (P). Insurance Co. (D) could have stopped

Ward v. Federal Kemper Insurance Co. (Continued)

payment, or closed its account at the bank [a highly unlikely option for the meager sum involved!], prior to presentment of the check. The overpayment thus has remained in control of the Insurance Co. (D). The delivery of the check to Ward (P) did not operate as an assignment to him of any funds from the drawee Bank. The check was never presented for payment, so it was never transferred to Ward (P). Therefore, Ward (P) did not owe any premium to the Insurance Co. (D). When the Insurance Co. (D) attempted to cancel the policy, the entire premium was in its bank account, and Ward (P) owed it nothing at that time. Thus, Insurance Co. (D) could not have lawfully cancelled the policy for nonpayment of the premium. Ward (P) is entitled to a declaratory judgment that the policy was in full force and effect when the accident occurred. Reversed.

Analysis:

This case examines who is considered the owner of the money presented by way of a check. The answer requires a determination of when a check is considered accepted for payment. The holding of the case shows that mere possession is not sufficient. There must be presentment of the check for payment. The court noted that the relationship between drawer and drawee is one of creditor and debtor, and the drawer does not own the funds it has on deposit with the drawee. Under former UCC § 3-409(1), now Section 3-408, a check alone does not operate as an assignment of the funds in the hands of the drawee Bank. The Bank is not liable on the instrument until it is accepted. Under UCC § 3-310(b), if a check is accepted as a conditional payment for an underlying obligation, the obligation cannot be the basis for a cause of action until the check is presented for payment and dishonored. Under former UCC § 3-802, now § 3-310, if the check is taken for an obligation, the obligation is suspended, and such suspension continues until the check is dishonored or paid.

■ CASE VOCABULARY

DONEE: One who receives a gift or bequest, or one who is given a power.

DONOR: One who gives something to another, or one who gives a power to another.

DRAWEE: The person ordered in a draft to make payment.

DRAWER: The person who signs or is identified in a draft as the one ordering payment.

GIFT CAUSA MORTIS: Gift made by one whose death is imminent, the donor, to one intended to survive him, the donee, so as to belong fully to the intended donee.

HOLDER IN DUE COURSE: One who takes a negotiable instrument that does not at the time of its issuance bear evidence of any doubt as to its authenticity, and is taken for value, in good faith, before it was overdue, without notice that it was previously dishonored and without notice of any defect in its title.

INSURER: An insurance company that has agreed under an insurance policy to indemnify another, called the insured.

PAYEE: The person to whom the negotiable instrument is made payable.

Floor v. Melvin

(*Owner of Note*) v. (*Guarantor*)
5 Ill.App.3d 463, 283 N.E.2d 303, 11 UCC Rep. Serv. 109 (1972)

A CONTRACT GUARANTEEING COLLECTION CARRIES GREATER PROTECTIONS FOR THE GUARANTOR THAN ONE GUARANTEEING PAYMENT

■ **INSTANT FACTS** Owner of note improperly sued guarantor of contract guaranteeing collection without first attempting to collect from, or make allegation of insolvency against, the maker of the note.

■ **BLACK LETTER RULE** If a contract guaranteeing a note is one for collection, rather than payment, there must first be an effort to collect from, or a showing of insolvency of, the maker of the note before the guarantor may be sued.

■ **PROCEDURAL BASIS**

Appeal from order dismissing claim for failure to state a cause of action to recover money due on a promissory note.

■ **FACTS**

Floor (P) sued the estate of Charles W. Melvin (D) to recover money allegedly due on a promissory note. Melvin's (D) company, Melco, Inc., made and issued a promissory note in the sum of $12,000.00 payable to Floor (P). The back side of the note contained the following language: "For and in consideration of funds advanced herein to Melco, Inc., we irrevocably guarantee Marjorie Irene Floor against loss by reason of nonpayment of this note." The signatures of Melvin (D) and others followed this language. Floor's (P) claim is against Melvin (D), not Melco, Inc., the maker of the note. There is no allegation that Melco, Inc. is insolvent. Melvin (D) contends that Melco, Inc., as the maker of the note, must be sued for the money allegedly due before a valid claim can be made against Melvin (D). It asserts that the guarantee on the back of the note is one for *collection*. Floor (P), on the other hand, asserts that the language of Melvin's (D) guarantee presents an absolute undertaking and is thus a guarantee of *payment*. The trial court granted Melvin's (D) motion to dismiss for failure to state a cause of action and Floor (P) appeals.

■ **ISSUE**

If a contract guaranteeing a note is one for collection, rather than payment, must there first be an effort to collect from, or a showing of insolvency of, the maker of the note before the guarantor may be sued?

■ **DECISION AND RATIONALE**

(Alloy) Yes. If the guarantee is one for collection, the guarantor may not be sued unless certain conditions have been met. UCC Section 3–416, now Section 3-419(d), provides that if the signature of the accommodation party is accompanied by words indicating unambiguously that the party is guaranteeing collection rather than payment of the instrument, liability is limited. The instrument may be enforced only if execution of judgment against the other party has been returned unsatisfied, the other party is insolvent or in an insolvency proceeding, the other party cannot be served with process or it is otherwise apparent that payment cannot be obtained from the other party. [This means try to squeeze the blood from the turnip.] Thus, if the guarantee is for collection, the owner of the note must

Floor v. Melvin (Continued)

first make use of legal means to collect it from the debtor and to no avail. Only then may it sue the guarantor. [Nothing is easy!] However, if the guarantee is for payment of the instrument, the guarantor may be sued at once, and liability is not dependent upon prosecution of the maker of the instrument. Therefore, the language of the guaranty must be construed as one for collection or payment. Other cases have held that a guarantee of payment exits from the following language: "I hereby guarantee this loan," "I guarantee payment of the within note at maturity," and agreeing to pay the note if the maker did not "retire" it at maturity. However, the language in these cases is different from the language in the case before us [and poor Ms. Floor (P) is therefore out of luck]. In our opinion the language of the guarantee in this case should be construed as for collection. Although the word "collection" was not used, the guarantee as against "loss" by reason of nonpayment is in effect a guarantee of collection. In another case with similar language, whereby the defendant agreed to indemnify the plaintiff against "any loss on account of any monies," it was held to be one for collection rather than payment. We also reject Floor's (P) contention that a subsection of Section 3–416, now Section 3–419, should apply to the effect that where words of guaranty do not otherwise specify, the guarantee is of payment. This subsection is limited to instances where no conditional language has been used. Therefore, the guarantee in this case is one for collection and not of payment. Since Floor (P) did not allege that her claim was prosecuted to judgment and execution unsatisfied, or that Melco Inc. was insolvent, the dismissal of the action was proper. Affirmed.

Analysis:

UCC § 3–416, now § 3–419(d), provides that an accommodation party is liable on the instrument in the capacity in which he signed the instrument. In most cases, that capacity will be either a maker or an endorser of a note. A guarantor is an accommodation party. The guarantee does not add anything to the obligation under the instrument unless the surety has guaranteed collection. If so, the guarantor is given extra protections. These protections, in the form of limitations, are set forth in subsection (d) and require that there be a determination as to whether the guarantee is one for collection or payment. As this case illustrates, if it is a guarantee for collection, one must first attempt to collect from the maker of the note before suit may be brought against the guarantor.

■ **CASE VOCABULARY**

GUARANTOR: A person who makes a promise of payment, or performance of an obligation, under a guaranty agreement.

OBLIGOR: A person who has entered into, and engaged to perform, an obligation.

Chemical Bank v. PIC Motors Corp.

(*Bank*) v. (*Car Dealership*)
87 A.D.2d 447, 452 N.Y.S.2d 41, 34 UCC Rep. Serv. 219 (1982)

GUARANTOR IS NOT DISCHARGED FROM OBLIGATION IF HE EXPRESSLY WAIVES DEFENSES

■ **INSTANT FACTS** Siegel (D2), guarantor and former owner of car dealership, was sued under guaranty, and he argued that conduct by Bank (P) and current owner discharged the obligation.

■ **BLACK LETTER RULE** A guarantor's obligation under a payment guaranty cannot be discharged based upon impairment of collateral where the guarantor has expressly consented to the release of the collateral.

■ PROCEDURAL BASIS

Appeal following entry of summary judgment in action to collect money due under contract of guarantee.

■ FACTS

PIC Motors Corp. (PIC) (D1), a car dealership, had a financing agreement with Chemical Bank (the Bank) (P) whereby the Bank (P) loaned PIC (D1) money under an established line of credit, with PIC's (D1) inventory of cars as collateral. The Bank (P) conducted periodic inspections of the car inventory to determine whether the financed vehicles were owned by PIC (D1) and whether the loan was reduced upon sale of the financed vehicles. The Bank (P) had a curtailment policy whereby any loan was reduced and ultimately paid in full for inventory remaining unsold over certain time periods. Siegel (D2), the owner of PIC (D1), had personally guaranteed the loans for many years. Siegel (D2) sold his interest to Robl (D3). However, Siegel's (D2) *payment* guaranty continued as agreed. Thereafter, the Bank (P) informed Siegel (D2) that PIC (D1) was "out of trust" because more than 50 percent of the inventory was unaccounted for. The Bank (P) sued PIC (D1), Siegel (D2) and the other guarantors for the balance due under the loans. Siegel (D2), by way of defense, asserted that the Bank (P) failed to conduct regular inspections and enforce its curtailment policy. In addition, Siegel (D2) claimed that the Bank's (P) employees either negligently or in complicity with Robl (D3) submitted incorrect or false inventory reports, and approved loans on nonexistent cars. Because of this and assurances made by the Bank (P) concerning regular inspections and enforcement of the curtailment policy, Siegel (D2) contends that there are triable issues which will cause the discharge of his obligations as guarantor under the written guaranty. [Siegel (D2) should have carefully read the language of the guaranty before signing it.] Nothing in the financing agreement or guaranty obligated the Bank (P) to conduct inspections or maintain the curtailment policy. The guaranty was fully integrated, and under its terms, the Bank (P) had the right to release the collateral without discharging the guarantor. Summary judgment was granted against Siegel (D2) and he appeals.

■ ISSUE

Can the guarantor's obligation under a payment guaranty be discharged based upon impairment of collateral where the guarantor has expressly consented to the release of the collateral?

■ DECISION AND RATIONALE

(Fein) No. A guarantor's obligation under a payment guaranty cannot be discharged based upon impairment of collateral where the guarantor has expressly consented to the release of the collateral.

Chemical Bank v. PIC Motors Corp. (Continued)

Because the guaranty is fully integrated, it cannot be modified by a parol promise or prior course of conduct. Siegel (D2) expressly consented that the security could be released at any time and he would remain liable under the guaranty notwithstanding such release. Thus, the Bank (P) had the right to release the collateral without discharging the guarantor. Negligence or dishonesty on the part of the Bank's (P) employees is irrelevant. There was no obligation under the terms of the guaranty to preserve and protect the collateral. Under the terms of the guaranty, the Bank (P) could release or surrender the collateral, and extend further credit to PIC (D1), without notifying or discharging Siegel (D2). Where the collateral is in the possession of the debtor, inaction by the creditor does not release a guarantor who has executed a waiver. A party may waive any obligation upon the part of a creditor, including the obligation of the creditor not to impair the security. The parties, by agreement, may determine the standards by which the fulfillment of the rights and duties of the secured party may be measured. [No amount of wrongdoing by others will help Siegel (D2) in this case.] Thus, entry of summary judgment against Siegel (D2) was proper. Affirmed.

■ DISSENT

(Milonas) Summary judgment was not proper since there is an issue of fact as to whether the Bank (P) can be held liable for the tortious acts of its employees. Where the bank's negligence has resulted in a breach of its duty to preserve and protect the collateral, a waiver will not be enforced so as to bar a viable setoff or counterclaim sounding in fraud, or where based upon the creditor's negligence in failing to liquidate collateral upon the guarantor's demand. To hold that a guarantor will always be bound on the underlying obligation, notwithstanding any negligent, fraudulent or tortious conduct on the part of the creditor, simply because a clause to that effect is inserted in the agreement undermines the spirit of the UCC.

Analysis:

Under UCC § 3–605 (e), formerly § 3–606, if the holder of a negotiable instrument, in this case the Bank (P), impairs the value of the interest in collateral, the obligation of the endorser or accommodation party is discharged to the extent of the impairment. The holder of the negotiable instrument has a duty to protect the collateral securing the debt. In this case, Siegel (D2) wanted to raise various defenses based upon the conduct of the Bank (P) and representations made, so that his obligation under the guaranty would be discharged. However, under subsection (i) of § 3–605, a party is not discharged if the agreement provides for waiver of discharge. After noting that a party may waive any obligation upon the part of a creditor, including the obligation of the creditor not to impair the security, the court found that Siegel (D2) had waived his right to discharge the obligation under the terms of the payment guaranty.

■ CASE VOCABULARY

CONDITION PRECEDENT: That which must first occur before something else may happen.

GUARANTY: An agreement whereby one promises payment, or performance of an obligation.

INTEGRATED: Where the parties to a written agreement intend it to be the final and complete expression of the agreement.

PAROL: Something expressed orally and not in writing.

SURETY: One who agrees to pay money or perform an obligation if another person who is obligated to pay or perform fails to do so.

TRIABLE ISSUE: A triable issue of fact will defeat a motion for summary judgment, so that the matter may proceed to trial.

London Leasing Corp. v. Interfina, Inc.

(Payee of Note) v. (Maker of Note)
53 Misc.2d 657, 279 N.Y.S.2d 209, 4 UCC Rep. Serv. 206 (1967)

SURETY'S CONSENT TO EXTENSION AGREEMENT PREVENTS DISCHARGE OF OBLIGATION

■ **INSTANT FACTS** Corporate officer, who signed promissory note on behalf of corporation and personally endorsed it, attempted to discharge personal obligation based on non consent to agreement extending due date.

■ **BLACK LETTER RULE** Where the party personally endorsing the note consents to the agreement between the note's maker and payee to extend the time when payment is due, there is no discharge of the endorser on the obligation on the note.

■ **PROCEDURAL BASIS**

Motion for summary judgment in trial court concerning action for money due on promissory note.

■ **FACTS**

Interfina, Inc. (D1) made and delivered to London Leasing Corp. (London) (P) a promissory note in the sum of $52,000.00. Interfina's (D1) President, Evans (D2), signed the note on behalf of the corporation, and he also personally endorsed the note. The note was not paid on its due date. Thereafter, Interfina, Inc. (D1), by its President Evans (D2) in his corporate capacity only, entered into letter agreements with London (P) extending the time for payment of the note. London (P) filed a motion for summary judgment against Interfina (D1) and Evans (D2) for the sum of $19,500.00 due on the note. Evans (D2) contends that the extension agreements, which were not signed by him in his personal capacity, discharged him from personal liability on the note because he did not personally consent to the extension.

■ **ISSUE**

Is a corporate officer who makes a note on behalf of his corporation, and also personally endorses the note, discharged from personal liability where he, in his corporate officer capacity, makes an agreement with the payee extending the corporation's time to pay the note?

■ **DECISION AND RATIONALE**

(Crawford) No. Where the party personally endorsing the note consents to the agreement between the note's maker and payee to extend the time when payment is due, there is no discharge of the endorser on the obligation on the note. There is no question that summary judgment should be granted against Interfina (D1). The issue presented is whether summary judgment should be entered against Evans (D2). UCC Section 3–605, formerly Section 3–606, provides, in part, that where one entitled to enforce an instrument agrees to extend the due date of the obligation to pay, the extension discharges an endorser or accommodation party to the extent that there is proof that the extension caused loss to the endorser or accommodation party with respect to the right of recourse. Although the Code does not explicitly define the term "consent", the Official Comment states that consent "may be given in advance, and is commonly incorporated in the instrument, or it may be given afterward. It requires no

London Leasing Corp. v. Interfina, Inc. (Continued)

consideration, and operates as a waiver of the consenting party's right to claim his own discharge...." As case law dictates, the accommodation party or surety must consent to any change in the maker's agreement with the payee concerning extending the due date of the obligation otherwise the accommodation party or surety will be discharged from his obligation. In other words, if the surety consents to a modification between the creditor and the principal, the surety will not be discharged. However, the consent for modification need not be expressly given, but may be implied from the surrounding circumstances or from conduct. In this case, Evans (D2) applied for, negotiated, signed in his corporate capacity, and received the agreements extending the time for payment. Although mere knowledge or acquiescence is not, in and of itself, sufficient to prevent discharge, Evans' (D2) conduct [without doubt, and by no stretch of the imagination] constituted consent to the extension. The motion for summary judgment is granted as to both Interfina (D1) and Evans (D2).

Analysis:

This case examines UCC § 3–605, subsections (c) and (i), formerly § 3–606. As the section provides, the endorser or accommodation party is discharged from an obligation if the party entitled to enforce the instrument and the principal agree to extend the due date for payment. Under subsection (i), there is no discharge of the obligation if the endorser or accommodation party has consented to the extension. Note on the consent need not be express, but may be implied. Evans (D2) made a farfetched argument that he did not *consent* to the extension of the due date because he did not sign the extension agreements in his personal capacity. However, he signed the agreements in the capacity as a corporate officer. If Evans (D2) had not signed the agreement as a corporate officer, or if he was unaware of the extensions, then summary judgment probably would not have been entered against him.

■ CASE VOCABULARY

LETTER AGREEMENT: Used informally to mean an extension agreement whereby the creditor gives the debtor additional time to pay the obligation due under a promissory note.

SURETYSHIP CONTRACT: An agreement whereby one party agrees to pay the debt or perform the obligation of another, known as the principal.

Messing v. Bank of America, N.A.

(*Non-Account Check Holder*) v. (*Bank*)
143 Md. App. 1, 792 A.2d 312 (2002)

IF "PRESENTMENT" OF A CHECK FOR PAYMENT IS NOT PROPER, THE REFUSAL TO PAY DOES NOT CONSTITUTE "DISHONOR"

■ **INSTANT FACTS** Messing (P), a non-account holder of a check, unsuccessfully attempted to cash the check, after refusing to provide a thumbprint signature as required by the bank's (D) policy.

■ **BLACK LETTER RULE** If presentment of a check is not in accordance with the agreement of the parties, the refusal to pay does not constitute dishonor of the instrument.

■ **PROCEDURAL BASIS**

Appeal from dismissal of complaint after entry of summary judgment in action for declaratory relief and order for cessation.

■ **FACTS**

Messing (P) attempted to cash a $976 check at Bank of America (D), which was made out to him and drawn on a Bank of America (D) customer checking account. Although Messing (P) provided identification by means of a driver's license and credit card, the Bank (D), upon learning that he was not a Bank of America (D) customer, required Messing (P) to provide a thumbprint signature, via an inkless fingerprinting device. Messing (P) refused, and the Bank (D) refused to cash the check. The thumbprint signature requirement for non-account holders was in accordance with the deposit agreement the Bank (D) had with its account holders. Messing (P) [feeling very indignant] sued the Bank (D) for declaratory relief, and sought a cease and desist order to prevent the Bank (D) from seeking thumbprint signatures. The court granted the Bank's (D) motion for summary judgment, and dismissed Messing's (P) complaint. Messing (P) appealed.

■ **ISSUE**

If presentment of a check is not in accordance with the agreement of the parties, does the refusal to pay constitute dishonor of the instrument?

■ **DECISION AND RATIONALE**

(Krauser) No. Section 3-501(b)(2) provides that the person making presentment of an instrument for payment must give "reasonable identification." We must determine whether a thumbprint signature requirement is a form of reasonable identification. We conclude that it is for a number of reasons. First, it is an effective, reliable, and accurate way to authenticate a writing on a negotiable instrument. Second, the process of providing such a signature is not unreasonably convenient in that an inkless device is used, which leaves no ink stains or residue. Third, the procedure is reasonable and necessary in light of the growing incidence of check fraud. We also reject Messing's (P) contention that the Bank (D) dishonored the check when it did not make payment on the date of presentment. There can be no dishonor if presentment fails to comply with the terms of the instrument, an agreement of the parties, or other applicable law or rule. It is undisputed that the Bank (D) had the authority to refuse

Messing v. Bank of America, N.A. (Continued)

payment in accordance with the deposit agreement it had with each account holder, including the drawer of the check in question. As such, the Bank (D) had the authority to set "physical and/or documentary requirements" for all those who seek to cash a check with the Bank (D). And because it had authority to refuse payment by agreement with its customer unless reasonable identification was presented, Messing's (P) failure to provide his thumbprint rendered the presentment ineffective and did not result in a dishonor of the check. Case remanded.

Analysis:

UCC § 3–501 defines and describes presentment, and § 3–502 describes dishonor. Dishonor of a check does not occur if the check was not properly presented for payment. In this case, Bank of America (D) had a deposit agreement with its customer, the account holder, which permitted the bank "to establish physical and/or documentary requirements" of payees who seek to cash a check drawn on the customer's account. The court rejected Messing's (P) argument that a thumbprint signature was not "reasonable identification," since he had already provided a driver's license and a credit card. The court also rejected Messing's (P) argument that the bank "dishonored" the check upon presentment of the check for payment, because the check—having been improperly presented without a thumbprint signature—was never accepted by the Bank (D), and thus there was no "dishonor" of the check. Note that the drawer's liability only comes into play if the check is first presented to the drawee bank and then dishonored by the bank; in other words, the drawer's liability is secondary, in that there must first be presentment of the check to the drawee.

■ CASE VOCABULARY

DECLARATORY RELIEF: Action merely to have court declare one's rights, such as under a contract or to specific property.

Makel Textiles, Inc. v. Dolly Originals, Inc.

(*Enforcer of Note*) v. (*Principal of Note*)
4 UCC Rep. Serv. 95 (N.Y.Sup.1967)

FAILURE TO PRESENT NOTES FOR PAYMENT AND FAILURE TO GIVE NOTICE OF NON-PAYMENT CAN DISCHARGE LIABILITY OF INDIVIDUAL ENDORSER UNDER CERTAIN CIRCUMSTANCES

■ **INSTANT FACTS** Two individual endorsers of corporate notes sought to have liability discharged for failure to present notes for payment and failure to give notice of dishonor.

■ **BLACK LETTER RULE** The requirements of presentment and notice of dishonor are not excused with respect to an endorser of subsequent notes who had no active participation or knowledge of the note maker's affairs.

■ **PROCEDURAL BASIS**

Motion to dismiss complaint in trial court concerning action to recover money on promissory notes.

■ **FACTS**

Dolly Originals, Inc. (Dolly) (D1) borrowed money from Makel Textiles, Inc. (Makel) (P) and executed a promissory note in favor of Makel (P). Other individual defendants signed the note as endorsers. Another promissory note was made to the order of Makel (P) by Dolly (D1), with two individual endorsers signing on the back of the note. An additional two notes were thereafter executed by Dolly (D1), and endorsed on the back by two individuals in lieu of the second promissory note. Five checks payable to Makel (P) were executed simultaneously with the most recent two notes. One of the checks was returned unpaid and the other four were never deposited. Finally, two additional corporate checks were given to Makel (P) by Dolly (D1), one of which was paid [weird methods for repaying loan]. At the end of trial, one individual defendant was dismissed, and judgment was entered against Dolly (D1) who offered no defense. The motion to dismiss the complaint by the individual endorsers on the notes, defendant Goldberg (D2) and defendant Kushner (D3), is before the court for determination. The grounds for the motion to dismiss are: 1) the promissory notes of the corporation had never been presented for payment and thus the obligation of the endorsers, Goldberg (D2) and Kushner (D3), was discharged, and 2) the subsequent checks given after the endorsement on the previous notes were taken by Makel (P) in payment of this obligation, and therefore relieved the Goldberg (D2) and Kushner (D3) of any further liability on the debt.

■ **ISSUE**

Are the requirements of presentment and notice of dishonor excused for an endorser of subsequent notes who had no active participation or knowledge of the note maker's affairs?

■ **DECISION AND RATIONALE**

(Spiegel) No. The requirements of presentment and notice of dishonor are not excused with respect to an endorser of subsequent notes who had no active participation or knowledge of the note maker's affairs. Initially it must be said that the contention that the subsequent checks were taken in payment of the obligation and therefore relieved the endorsers of further liability has no merit and is rejected. Pursuant to *UCC* Section 3-310(b), formerly Section 3–802, a check given in payment of an obligation is

Makel Textiles, Inc. v. Dolly Originals, Inc. (Continued)

merely a conditional payment and does not relieve the endorser of his liability on the obligation if the check is unpaid. With respect to the issue that the notes were never presented for payment and thus the endorser's obligation is dismissed, the obligation of Goldberg (D2) and Kushner (D3) must be considered separately. With respect to Goldberg (D2), the evidence at trial established that he was the president and principal officer of Dolly (D1), and he executed the notes and corporate checks on its behalf. He also endorsed the notes as an individual. By virtue of his active participation in the affairs of the business, he well knew that the notes could not be and were not paid from the corporate funds. Thus, it was unnecessary [and a waste of paper] to serve Goldberg (D2) with notice of dishonor and non-payment under *UCC* Section 3–504, formerly Sections 3–507 and 3–511. [Presentment and notice of dishonor excused under certain circumstances.] Makel's (P) failure to present the notes for payment and give the individual endorsers notice of non-payment could not and did not injure nor prejudice Goldberg's (D2) rights in any way. With respect to Kushner (D3), he was an endorser only on the two subsequent notes. There was no evidence presented at trial of notice of presentment and dishonor, nor was there any evidence of any activity or participation in the affairs of the corporation so as to excuse presentment or notice of dishonor. Thus, judgment may be had in favor of Kushner (D3) and against Makel (P). In addition, judgment may be entered in favor of Makel (P) and against Goldberg (D2).

Analysis:

Under UCC § 3–503, the obligations of the endorser and the drawer may not be enforced unless the endorser or drawer is given notice of dishonor of the instrument, or notice is excused. The court held that the notice of presentment and dishonor was not required for Goldberg (D2), because it would be a useless gesture to advise him of a fact with which he was already familiar. In other words, the requirements were excused because they were completely unnecessary. Kushner (D3) was in a different category because he, unlike Goldberg (D2), was only an endorser and there was no evidence that he had knowledge of the corporation's affairs. Accordingly, he was entitled to presentment and notice of dishonor.

■ CASE VOCABULARY

DISHONOR: The refusal of the presentee to pay.

ENDORSER: Called "indorser" under the UCC and defined as one who makes an indorsement.

PRESENTMENT: The demand for payment made by the holder of the instrument to the maker of a note or a drawee of a draft.

Norton v. Knapp
(*Seller Drawer*) v. (*Buyer Drawee*)
64 Iowa 112, 19 N.W. 867 (1884)

ACCEPTANCE OF THE DRAFT MUST OCCUR IN ORDER FOR DRAWEE TO BE LIABLE THEREON

■ **INSTANT FACTS** Buyer of equipment signed back of sight draft with the words "Kiss my foot," and court held that this did not constitute an acceptance.

■ **BLACK LETTER RULE** The words "kiss my foot" written on the back of a sight draft and signed by the drawee do not constitute an acceptance of the draft.

■ PROCEDURAL BASIS
Not Stated.

■ FACTS
Norton (P) sold and delivered to Knapp (D) a piece of equipment, and the purchase price was due and unpaid. Thereafter, Norton (P) drew a sight draft on Knapp (D) for the agreed price of the equipment, which provided that "at sight pay to the order of Exchange Bank of Nora Springs, Iowa, eighty dollars, value received, and charge the same to the account of Norton Keeler." Knapp (D) signed the back of the draft and wrote the [very vulgar] words, "Kiss my foot. Miles Knapp." The issue before the court concerned whether these words constitute a legal and valid "acceptance" of the draft.

■ ISSUE
Do the words "kiss my foot" written on the back of a sight draft and signed by the drawee constitute an acceptance of the draft?

■ DECISION AND RATIONALE
(Seevers) No. The words "kiss my foot" written on the back of a sight draft and signed by the drawee do not constitute an acceptance of the draft. The rule of law involved in this case is that if the drawee does anything with or to the bill, or writes thereon anything, which does not clearly negative an intention to accept, then he can or will be charged as an acceptor. The language, "kiss my foot," meant either an acceptance or a refusal to accept the bill. It cannot be that he meant to accept, therefore he must have meant to refuse to accept. We believe that Knapp (D) used these vulgar words to give emphasis to his intention not to accept, and to express contempt for the person to whom the words are addressed. [If in 1884, "kiss my foot" was a vulgar expression, what would the justices say about modern day expressions?]

Analysis:
UCC § 3-409(a) defines acceptance as the "drawee's signed agreement to pay as presented" Which involves more than a mere signature on the back of the draft. The court was required in this case to interpret the meaning of the words "kiss my foot" to determine whether Knapp (D) had accepted the draft. Note that UCC § 3-408 provides that the drawee is not liable on the instrument until the drawee

Norton v. Knapp (Continued)

accepts it. Since the court described the language as "vulgar" and opined that it was used to express contempt, it concluded that there was no *acceptance* of the sight draft. Accordingly, Knapp (D) was not liable on the draft.

■ CASE VOCABULARY

AMENDED ABSTRACT: Referring an amended *abstract of record* which presents a summary of the history of the case for use as a record on appeal.

SIGHT DRAFT: A draft that is payable at sight.

Galyen Petroleum Co. v. Hixson

(Payee of Checks) v. (Drawer of Checks)
213 Neb. 683, 331 N.W.2d 1, 35 UCC Rep. Serv. 1221(1983)

PAYEE HAS NO CAUSE OF ACTION AGAINST DRAWEE BANK FOR DISHONOR OF DRAWER'S CHECKS

■ **INSTANT FACTS** Payee of checks sued drawee bank for dishonor of drawer's checks presented to it for payment, although drawer had funds on deposit.

■ **BLACK LETTER RULE** A payee on a check has no cause of action against the drawee bank for dishonoring a check even though funds are in the account.

■ **PROCEDURAL BASIS**

Appeal from summary judgment entered in action for money due on dishonored checks.

■ **FACTS**

Galyen Petroleum Co. (Galyen) (P) sued Commercial Bank (Bank) (D1) to recover on three checks presented to drawee Bank (D1) but which were refused even though the drawer Hixson (D2) had funds on deposit with Bank (D1). Hixson (D2) had an account with Bank (D1), but owed it money on promissory notes. Hixson (D2) issued three checks to Galyen (P) on different occasions, but they were returned unpaid for insufficient funds. The evidence showed that at the time of presentment, Hixson (D2) had funds in the account, but the funds were setoff by the Bank (D1) to credit Hixson's (D2) promissory note account. However, at that time the credited notes were not then due. [Bank (D1) wanted to make sure that it got its money from that untrustworthy Hixson (D2).] The notes provided that the Bank (D1), as payee of the notes, had the right of setoff against any deposit balances of Hixson (D2), the maker of the notes, and that it could apply the deposit balances against payment of the notes, whether due or not. Summary judgment was entered in favor of Bank (D1) and against Galyen (P). On appeal, Galyen (P) contends that it was error to grant summary judgment. Galyen (P) asserts that the Bank (D1) should not have refused payment of the checks and that it had no authority to make a setoff to credit Hixson's (D2) promissory notes where the notes were not due.

■ **ISSUE**

Does a payee on a check have a cause of action against the drawee bank for dishonoring a check even though funds are in the account?

■ **DECISION AND RATIONALE**

(Colwell) No. A payee on a check has no cause of action against the drawee bank for dishonoring a check even though funds are in the account. Under UCC Section 3–408, a "check or other draft does not of itself operate as an assignment of funds in the hands of the drawee available for its payment, and the drawee is not liable on the instrument until he accepts it." Furthermore, it is well established that a check, of itself, and in the absence of special circumstances, is neither a legal nor an equitable assignment of the drawer's funds in the hands of the drawee. Therefore, the holder of the check has not right of action against the drawee, and no valid claim to the fund of the drawer in its hands, even though the drawer has on deposit sufficient funds. In this case, there are no special circumstances or

Galyen Petroleum Co. v. Hixson (Continued)

agreements claimed. [Bank (D1) took the money just in time. Hixson (D2) went bankrupt.] Thus, Galyen (P) had no standing to bring a cause of action against the Bank (D1) for the dishonor of any of the three checks. Summary judgment was properly granted. Affirmed.

Analysis:

The "no assignment" rule under UCC § 3–408 provides that the creation and issuance of a check or draft is not an immediate assignment of the drawer's funds in the possession of the drawee, and thus, the holder of the check has no cause of action against the drawee bank. Note that it is possible that liability could be established outside of the UCC. For example, if the drawee bank had made an agreement with the drawer to deliver the check's proceeds to the payee but did not do so, the payee would be a third-party beneficiary of this agreement and could sue to enforce it. Finally, the drawee bank, through its checking account with the drawer, has a private contract with the drawer, which can be enforced by the drawer. However, this contract confers no rights on other parties.

■ CASE VOCABULARY

HEARSAY: Evidence from a witness who is repeating what he heard others say, rather than from personal knowledge of the witness.

STANDING: Having a right to bring a legal proceeding.

Mundaca Investment Corp. v. Febba

(Holder of Instrument) v. (Agent)
143 N.H. 499, 727 A.2d 990, 38 UCC Rep. Serv. 2d 454 (1999)

AGENT CAN BE PERSONALLY LIABLE ON INSTRUMENT IF HE FAILS TO IDENTIFY THE PRINCIPAL AND INDICATE THAT HE IS ONLY SIGNING IN A REPRESENTATIVE CAPACITY

■ **INSTANT FACTS** Individual signed promissory notes as "trustee" borrower but did not identify the principal, and thus intent of the original parties was held to be the material issue of fact.

■ **BLACK LETTER RULE** When a principal is not expressly identified in an instrument signed by an agent, the agent can be personally liable to the holder of the instrument unless the agent proves that the original parties did not intend the agent to be personally liable.

■ **PROCEDURAL BASIS**

Appeal from entry of summary judgment in action for money due on promissory notes.

■ **FACTS**

Febba (D) and two other individual defendants were trustees under a trust. They purchased two condominium units for the trust. As part of the financing, they executed two promissory notes, secured by two mortgages, payable to Dartmouth Savings Bank (Bank). At the end of both notes below the signature lines, the names of the individuals were typewritten beside the preprinted term "Borrower." Following the signatures, Febba (D) and the other individual defendants [believing that they would be off the hook] handwrote the word "Trustee." The trust is not identified on the face of the notes, but the notes state that they are secured by a mortgage. The mortgages however identify the "Borrower" as the trust. Thereafter, Mundaca (P) acquired the two notes from the Federal Deposit Insurance Corporation, which was receiver for the Bank. Mundaca (P) notified Febba (D) that the two promissory notes were in default. Mundaca (P) foreclosed on the condominium units and filed suit against Febba (D) and the two other individuals for the remaining amount due on the notes. Mundaca (P) moved for summary judgment, and it was granted. The trial court ruled that the signatures of Febba (D) and the other individual defendants, followed by the word "Trustee" did not show unambiguously that they were signing in a representative capacity. [What other reason did they have for putting that word in the document?] The trial court also ruled that Febba (D) and the two other individual defendants did not prove that the Bank did not intend to hold them personally liable. Febba (D) and the others appeal, asserting no personal liability.

■ **ISSUE**

Can an agent be personally liable to the holder of an instrument where a principal is not expressly identified in an instrument signed by an agent and there is no showing that the original parties did not intend the agent to be personally liable?

■ **DECISION AND RATIONALE**

(Brock) Yes. When a principal is not expressly identified in an instrument signed by an agent, the agent can be personally liable to the holder of the instrument unless the agent proves that the original parties did not intend the agent to be personally liable. The contentions on appeal by Febba (D) and

Mundaca Investment Corp. v. Febba (Continued)

the others are twofold: one, the notes and mortgages, when read together, show unambiguously that Febba (D) and the others signed in a representative capacity for the trust, as principal, and therefore there is no personal liability, and two, there was a genuine issue of material fact regarding whether the original parties intended Febba (D) and the other signors to be personally liable so as to preclude summary judgment. UCC Section 3–402 subsection (b)(1) provides that if a representative, also known as an agent, signs an instrument on behalf of a represented person, also known as a principal, and the signature unambiguously shows that it is made on behalf of a principal, *who is identified in the instrument*, the agent is not liable. Subsection (b)(2) provides that if the signature does not show unambiguously that the agent's signature is made in a representative capacity, or the principal is not identified in the instrument, the agent is liable on the instrument to a holder in due course that took the instrument without notice that the agent was not intended to be liable on the instrument. With respect to a non-holder in due course, the agent is liable unless the agent proves that the original parties did not intend the agent to be liable on the instrument. The instruments in this case are two promissory notes. Febba (D) and the other defendants argue that the notes and mortgages must be read together to interpret the parties' intentions. However, *UCC* Section 3-402(b)(1) expressly provides that the principal must be identified in the instrument, which are the notes in this case. Since the trust is not identified in the notes as required by the Section, this case falls under subsection (b)(2). [Febba (D) and the others are pulling their hair out for failing to write just one important word.] Thus, Febba (D) and the other defendants could be personally liable in two situations: (1) to a holder in due course who takes the instrument without notice that Febba (D) and the other defendants did not intend to be personally liable, and (2) to any other party unless Febba (D) and the other defendants prove that the original parties did not intend them to be personally liable. We believe that there is a disputed issue of material fact as to the intent of the original parties, i.e., the Bank and Febba (D) and the other defendants. Although the notes do not refer to the trust, the mortgages show that the trust is the borrower and that the individuals signed in a representative capacity. Since the identity of the borrower is a material issue of fact in dispute, we reverse summary judgment and remand for further proceedings. Reversed and remanded.

Analysis:

The court was primarily considering the application of that portion of UCC § 3–402(b)(2) that concerns a non-holder in due course. The court in this case found issues of fact concerning whether the original parties intended Febba (D) and the others to be liable on the notes and these issues of material fact should be decided at time of trial by the judge or jury hearing the matter. Although not discussed in the case, under subsection (a) of Section 3–402, the principal is bound on an instrument if a representative with express, implied, or apparent authority signs it. For an agent to escape personal liability against all persons, including holders in due course, the agent must, within the instrument, identify the principal and indicate that the agent is only signing in a representative capacity. If both of these requirements are not met, then liability depends upon whether the holder of the instrument is a holder in due course. If a non-holder in due course is involved, then the intent of the original parties is determinative.

■ CASE VOCABULARY

AFFIDAVIT: A written statement declaring, by oath or affirmation, the truth of the matters contained therein.

JOINTLY AND SEVERALLY: A form of liability where the creditor may sue one or more, separately, or all together.

REPRESENTATIVE: An agent or any other person empowered to act for another.

REPRESENTED PERSON: A principal or any other person who empowers another to act on his behalf.

Nichols v. Seale

(Representative Signer) v. *(Holder of Note)*
493 S.W.2d 589, 12 UCC Rep. Serv. 711 (Tex.Civ.App.1973)

AN AGENT WHO SIGNS AN INSTRUMENT WITHOUT NAMING REPRESENTED PARTY NOR SHOWING IT WAS SIGNED IN A REPRESENTATIVE CAPACITY MAY BE HELD INDIVIDUALLY LIABLE ABSENT EXTRINSIC EVIDENCE TO THE CONTRARY

■ **INSTANT FACTS** Nichols (D) signed his name to a note, below a fictitious business name, without showing that he signed on behalf of corporation doing business under the fictitious name.

■ **BLACK LETTER RULE** Where an instrument is signed by an agent or other representative, names the person represented, but does not show that the representative signed in a representative capacity, extrinsic evidence is admissible to establish the capacity of the signer and whether he is personally liable.

■ **PROCEDURAL BASIS**

Appeal from summary judgment in action to collect money due under promissory note.

■ **FACTS**

Seale (P) sued Carl V. Nichols (Nichols) (D) for personal liability on a promissory note. Nichols (D) was sued "individually and doing business as The Fashion Beauty Salon." Nichols (D) had signed and wrote his name on the promissory note below the words "The Fashion Beauty Salon." He answered the complaint by denying that he signed the note in his individual capacity and alleging that he signed on behalf of a corporation, Mr. Carls Fashion, Inc. Seale (P) filed a motion for summary judgment and Nichols (D) filed an affidavit in opposition thereto wherein he stated that he was President of Mr. Carls Fashion, Inc. a corporation, and that it did business as The Fashion Beauty Salon. He further stated that he signed the promissory note in the capacity of officer of the corporation, and not in his personal capacity. [It was to no avail.] The trial court granted summary judgment in favor of Seale (P) and against Nichols (D). He appealed contending that extrinsic evidence existed to show that he signed for the corporation rather than himself.

■ **ISSUE**

Where an instrument is signed by an agent or other representative, names the person represented, but does not show that the representative signed in a representative capacity, is extrinsic evidence admissible to establish the capacity of the signer and whether he is personally liable?

■ **DECISION AND RATIONALE**

(Guittard) Yes. We hold that where an instrument is signed by an agent or other representative, names the person represented, but does not show that the representative signed in a representative capacity, extrinsic evidence is admissible to establish the capacity of the signer and whether he is personally liable. In this case, Seale (P) asserts that Nichols (D) is personally liable because the note neither "names" the corporation nor shows that Nichols (D) "signed in a representative capacity." However, the use of an assumed name does "name the person represented" within the meaning of *UCC* Section

3–403 (pre 1990 revision) [An authorized representative who signs his own name to an instrument is personally obligated if the instrument neither names the person represented nor shows that the representative signed in a representative capacity.] This Section must be read along with Section 3–401(2) [A signature is made by use of any name, including any trade or assumed name, upon an instrument, ...], which expressly authorizes use of an assumed name in a negotiable instrument. The official comment to this Section states that the signature "may be made in any name, including any trade name or assumed name, however false and fictitious, which is adopted for the purpose. Parol evidence is admissible to identify the signer, and when he is identified the signature is effective." This rule also applies to corporations using assumed names. Therefore, extrinsic evidence was admissible to show that "The Fashion Beauty Salon" was an assumed name for "Mr. Carls Fashion, Inc." Parol evidence is admissible to explain an ambiguity with respect to the capacity of the signer and to show that the signer was not personally obligated. [Nichols had a lot of parol evidence he wanted to offer to relieve him of personal liability, but the trial court didn't want to hear it.] An ambiguity exists where an instrument shows the name of the person represented but does not show that the representative signed in a representative capacity since the signature may be interpreted either as an individual signature, or as a signature on behalf of the person represented. Existing case law supports our opinion that parol evidence is admissible under these circumstances. In this case, the ambiguity is not removed by Nichols' (D) name in typewriting, which, whether above or below his signature, may have been used only to identify the signer in case his handwriting was not legible. In addition, the printed language at the beginning of the note. "I, we or either of us", only serves to increase the ambiguity. Reversed and remanded.

Analysis:

This case examines UCC § 3–403 (pre-1990 version), which pertains to signatures by authorized representatives. If one signs an instrument and wants to avoid personal liability, the signer had better make sure to name the principal and indicate that he or she is signing in a representative capacity. However, this case also shows that extrinsic parol evidence may be admitted to clear up any ambiguity concerning the capacity in which the representative or agent signed the instrument. In this case, the court stated that there was ambiguity because the Nichols' (D) name was typed and signed below "The Fashion Beauty Salon." In addition, the court briefly discussed and concluded that the use of an assumed name, i.e., "The Fashion Beauty Salon," constitutes the naming of the person represented in the instrument.

■ CASE VOCABULARY

EXTRINSIC EVIDENCE: Evidence external to, or not contained within, the written instrument.

CHAPTER ELEVEN

Banks and Their Customers

Twin City Bank v. Isaacs

Instant Facts: Bank wrongfully dishonored customers' checks for four years after account was frozen due to stolen checkbook, but it remained frozen even after the criminals were convicted.

Black Letter Rule: Damages for mental suffering and other intangible injuries are recoverable under a cause of action for wrongful dishonor of checks.

Walter v. National City Bank of Cleveland

Instant Facts: Bank (D) claimed right to setoff an unmatured note of insolvent depositor claiming priority over judgment creditor with garnishment order seeking funds from depositor's account.

Black Letter Rule: A bank does not have a right of equitable setoff of an unmatured indebtedness of its insolvent depositor, as against a judgment creditor seeking to reach the depositor's account by a garnishment order.

Parr v. Security National Bank

Instant Facts: Check maker attempted to have bank stop payment on a check and gave all requested information, except for 50-cent error in check amount.

Black Letter Rule: A bank is given reasonable opportunity to stop payment on a check when the description received is exact in all respects except for a single digit error in the check amount.

Canty v. Vermont National Bank

Instant Facts: Bank improperly paid customer's cancelled checks to the IRS for a second time, and customer sued to have the bank recredit his account.

Black Letter Rule: A depositor has the burden of proving actual loss due to the bank's improper payment of an item before the bank must recredit the account.

Patriot Bank v. Navy Federal Credit Union

Instant Facts: Navy Federal Credit Union (D) stopped payment on a cashier's check that had been deposited with Patriot Bank (P).

Black Letter Rule: A customer has no right to stop payment on a cashier's check.

Rock Island Auction Sales, Inc. v. Empire Packing Co.

Instant Facts: Payor bank held check without payment, return or notice of dishonor, beyond fixed time period.

Black Letter Rule: The failure of the payor bank to meet the statutory deadline for handling a check results in liability for the amount of the check.

First National Bank of Chicago v. Standard Bank & Trust

Instant Facts: Payor bank attempted to come within Regulation CC's extension of midnight deadline where bank officers returned checks to presenting bank's processing center.

Black Letter Rule: A presenting bank's return of the checks via bank officer's delivery to payor bank's processing center comports with Regulation CC sec. 229.30(c)(1).

Valley Bank of Ronan v. Hughes

Instant Facts: Hughes (D) deposited certain checks in his account at Valley Bank (P), but when the bank transferred funds from his account, they learned that the checks were fraudulent.

Black Letter Rule: The U.C.C. establishes a bank's standard of care for the processing of checks but does not preempt common law tort claims regarding communications about the processing of checks.

Twin City Bank v. Isaacs
(*Bank*) v. (*Customer*)
283 Ark. 127, 672 S.W.2d 651, 39 UCC Rep. Serv. 35 (1984)

DAMAGES FOR MENTAL SUFFERING AS WELL AS PUNITIVE DAMAGES ARE RECOVERABLE FROM A BANK FOR THE WRONGFUL DISHONOR OF CHECKS

■ **INSTANT FACTS** Bank wrongfully dishonored customers' checks for four years after account was frozen due to stolen checkbook, but it remained frozen even after the criminals were convicted.

■ **BLACK LETTER RULE** Damages for mental suffering and other intangible injuries are recoverable under a cause of action for wrongful dishonor of checks.

■ **PROCEDURAL BASIS**

Appeal from judgment entered on a jury verdict for damages for wrongful dishonor of checks.

■ **FACTS**

Kenneth and Vicki Isaacs (P) sued Twin City Bank (the Bank) (D) for damages sustained from the Bank's (D) wrongful dishonor of their checks resulting in a hold order against their account for approximately four years. The Isaacs' (P) checkbook was discovered missing and they promptly advised the Bank (D). They later learned that two forged checks totaling $2,050 had been written on their account and honored by the Bank (D) before they discovered the missing checkbook. The Bank (D) decided to freeze the checking account, which contained approximately $2,500 before the forgeries occurred, and approximately $2,000 after checks had cleared. The Bank (D) suspected Mr. Isaacs (P) might have been involved because he had been convicted of burglary, and it was this concern that caused the Bank (D) to initially place a hold on the account. A short time later, a person was charged and convicted of the forgeries. The police on two separate occasions advised the Bank (D) that there was no connection between Mr. Isaacs (P) and the forgeries. The Bank (D) [not believing the police and on advice of its overly suspecting attorney] continued to keep the account frozen, denying the Isaacs (P) their money, for four years. Isaacs (P) sued the Bank (D) for wrongful dishonor of their checks and wrongful withholding of their funds. They sought actual damages for the loss of their money, the loss of equity in repossessed vehicles, and damages for mental suffering resulting from the loss of good credit standing, loss of ability to purchase a home, and marital difficulties. The jury awarded Isaacs (P) $18,500 in compensatory damages and $45,000 in punitive damages. The Bank (D) appealed.

■ **ISSUE**

Are damages for mental suffering and other intangible injuries recoverable under a cause of action for wrongful dishonor of checks?

■ **DECISION AND RATIONALE**

(Steele Hays) Yes. Damages for mental suffering and other intangible injuries are recoverable under a cause of action for wrongful dishonor of checks. The jury was instructed that if they found the Bank (D) liable, they were to fix the amount of money that would compensate the Isaacs (P) for damages

Twin City Bank v. Isaacs (Continued)

sustained which were proximately caused by the Bank (D) including the following: 1) The amounts wrongfully held by the Bank (D) and remaining unpaid, 2) mental anguish and embarrassment suffered by Isaacs (P) and, 3) financial losses sustained by Isaacs (P). We find that there was sufficient evidence to sustain damages for mental suffering, loss of credit and loss attributable to the inability to pursue the purchase of a home. Under UCC Section 4–402 [payor bank is liable to customer for damages proximately caused by the wrongful dishonor of an item...], the mental anguish suffered does not need to rise to the level required for an intentional infliction of emotional distress. Damages for wrongful dishonor are of the type that are more difficult to assess with exactness. In *Northshore Bank v. Palmer,* actual damages were awarded for dishonor of checks, and part of the actual damages awarded was attributed to mental suffering for the embarrassment and humiliation suffered from having been turned down for credit for the first time. Other cases have permitted damages for financial embarrassment. In the case before us, the evidence showed that prior to the check forgeries, the Isaacs' (P) credit was impeccable, and the freezing of their funds had a traumatic effect on their lives. They lost their credit standing with the Bank (D) and were unable to secure credit with other institutions because of it. They did not have use of their $2,000 for four years, they lost the ability to purchase a home due to the dishonor of an earnest money check, the financial strain resulted in marital difficulties, and they lost equity in two vehicles repossessed due to the withholding of their funds. We hold that damages for mental suffering and other intangible injuries are recoverable under Section 4–402. Exactness of proof as to these damages is not required. With respect to the award of punitive damages, we reject the Bank's (D) contention that the amount awarded was grossly excessive, or prompted by passion or prejudice. [Holding onto the money for four years and believing the customer to be a thief was probably what ticked off the jury.] We believe that there was substantial evidence to support the verdict. Judgment affirmed.

Analysis:

UCC § 4–402 provides that a "bank is liable to its customer for damages proximately caused by the wrongful dishonor of an item. When the dishonor occurs through mistake liability is limited to actual damages proved...." The holding of this case shows that damages flowing from wrongful dishonors tend to produce intangible injuries of the kind that are difficult to assess with exactness. When damages for mental suffering are sought, it is not necessary to prove the damages with exactness. Thus, the evidence presented to the jury was sufficient to allow the Isaacs (P) to recover for the loss of their money, loss of equity in their vehicles, the humiliation and embarrassment of losing their credit, and the emotional upset resulting from loss of ability to purchase a home and marital difficulties. Note that § 4–402 also provides that if dishonor occurs through mistake, liability is limited to "actual damages proved."

■ **CASE VOCABULARY**

COMPENSATORY DAMAGES: Those that will compensate an individual for the losses sustained.

MOTION FOR NEW TRIAL: Motion made post verdict or post decision by court to have the matter tried again.

PROXIMATELY CAUSED: That which produces the harm without any break by an intervening cause, and without which the harm would not have occurred.

PUNITIVE DAMAGES: Damages awarded to injured party to punish the defendant for acting in a malicious, oppressive or fraudulent manner.

Walter v. National City Bank of Cleveland
(*Judgment Creditor*) v. (*Setoff Bank*)
42 Ohio St.2d 524, 330 N.E.2d 425 (1975)

COURT FAVORS JUDGMENT CREDITOR AND DISALLOWS BANK'S SETOFF OF UNMATURED LOAN AGAINST INSOLVENT DEPOSITOR

■ **INSTANT FACTS** Bank (D) claimed right to setoff an unmatured note of insolvent depositor claiming priority over judgment creditor with garnishment order seeking funds from depositor's account.

■ **BLACK LETTER RULE** A bank does not have a right of equitable setoff of an unmatured indebtedness of its insolvent depositor, as against a judgment creditor seeking to reach the depositor's account by a garnishment order.

■ **PROCEDURAL BASIS**

Appeal of judgment entered following granting of motion for summary judgment in action seeking damages for civil conversion.

■ **FACTS**

Walter (P) brought an action for civil conversion against National City Bank of Cleveland (the Bank) (D) after it setoff a bank account against the unmatured debt of its loan to its depositor Ritzer. Walter (P) claimed priority of right to Ritzer's bank account with the Bank (D) since he had a judgment against Ritzer, and had obtained a garnishment order in order to collect the judgment from the account. When Ritzer executed a 90 day promissory note in connection with the loan from the Bank (D), its balance sheet showed it to be insolvent. Walter (P) did not obtain his judgment against Ritzer until weeks after Ritzer had signed the promissory note in favor of the Bank (D). When the Bank (D) was served with the garnishment order, the debt by Ritzer was unmatured since the 90 days had not yet expired. Nevertheless, the Bank (D) sent the court a letter stating that it was setting off the amount of its loan, leaving only $25.50 to send to the court to apply towards Walter's (P) judgment against Ritzer. [Since he felt he had been ripped off by the Bank (D)] Walter (P) brought this action against the Bank (D) contending that it had no right to setoff the amount of the unmatured loan. The trial court entered summary judgment in favor of Walter (P), the appellate court affirmed, and the Bank (D) appeals to the Ohio Supreme Court.

■ **ISSUE**

Does a bank have a right of equitable setoff of an unmatured indebtedness of its insolvent depositor, as against a judgment creditor seeking to reach the depositor's account by a garnishment order?

■ **DECISION AND RATIONALE**

(Stern) No. Based upon the facts presented in this case, the Bank (D) does not have a right of equitable setoff of the unmatured indebtedness of its insolvent depositor, Ritzer, as against Walter (P), the judgment creditor. The right to setoff is based upon legal and equitable claims, and is not one based upon statute. As a general rule, a bank may setoff a bank account against the matured indebtedness of its depositor, even though the bank has been garnished by the efforts of the depositor's creditor seeking to collect a judgment. However, the bank does not have a priority right

Walter v. National City Bank of Cleveland (Continued)

where it seeks to setoff an unmatured indebtedness. The reason for this is that an unmatured debt is not due, and to permit a setoff would alter the contract made between the parties. [Exceptions always exist!] If the depositor is insolvent, an exception to the rule prohibiting a setoff for an unmatured debt exists. Nevertheless, the case at bar is distinguishable in that when the Bank (D) negotiated the terms of the promissory note with Ritzer, the balance sheet showed Ritzer to be insolvent. The Bank (D) cannot claim a right to priority to Ritzer's account based upon insolvency when at the time it loaned the money Ritzer was insolvent. [It can only claim stupidity!] The Bank (D) also claims a right to setoff based upon its rules and regulations which reserves to itself the right to apply any balance in the depositor's account to payment of any indebtedness, due or to become due. If this were permitted, it would have the affect of accelerating the due date of the promissory note. There was nothing in the note concerning acceleration, other than by lack of performance. There was nothing in the note stating that it was made upon the security in the account. Accordingly, the rules and regulations are in direct conflict with the promissory note contract. The terms of the note control over the language of the rules. The intent of the parties in executing the note was that it become due in 90 days, not upon demand. Thus, the Bank (D) had no contractual right to treat the note as a demand note and setoff the account against the debt before maturity. Judgment affirmed.

Analysis:

. . . that the UCC does not contain any provisions concerning rules to apply for setoff, although the term is mentioned in passing in certain sections of the Code. The right to setoff developed through common law and exists in virtually all states today. However, federal legislation places certain restrictions on the right of setoff. For example, setoff is generally prohibited in cases involving customers' credit card debts, so that the bank issuing the credit card may not setoff the bank account to satisfy overdue payment on the credit card. In addition, setoff may only be had against general accounts, such as checking and savings accounts, of the depositor. In this case, the court was reluctant to permit the Bank (D) to setoff the loan since Ritzer was insolvent when the loan was made. Thus, if the company had been solvent at the time the note was signed, and thereafter became insolvent, the Bank (D) may have prevailed. An exception to the general rule provides that if the depositor is insolvent, a right to setoff for an unmatured debt exists.

■ CASE VOCABULARY

CONVERSION: Taking the property belonging to another for one's own use.

EQUITY: As used to signify an equitable right, where the relief sought is one of decree, enforcement, administering, enjoining and the like, as opposed to damages under law.

GARNISHED: Where the money or property has been attached to satisfy a judgment.

SETOFF: The right of a bank, by self-help, to take priority over others claiming a right to the funds on deposit in the depositor's account.

Parr v. Security National Bank

(*Check Maker*) v. (*Bank*)
680 P.2d 648, 38 UCC Rep. Serv. 275 (Okl.App.1984)

HUMANS MAY ERR IN REPORTING INFORMATION FOR STOP ORDER EVEN IF BANK'S COMPUTER RELIES UPON ERROR AND, CONSEQUENTLY, PAYS THE CHECK

■ **INSTANT FACTS** Check maker attempted to have bank stop payment on a check and gave all requested information, except for 50-cent error in check amount.

■ **BLACK LETTER RULE** A bank is given reasonable opportunity to stop payment on a check when the description received is exact in all respects except for a single digit error in the check amount.

■ **PROCEDURAL BASIS**
Appeal from judgment seeking recovery for damages for failure to stop payment of check.

■ **FACTS**
Parr (P) wrote a check drawn on her account with Security National Bank (Bank) (D) and made payable to Champlin Oil. The following day, she telephoned the Bank (D) and ordered payment stopped on the check. Parr (P) gave the Bank (D) her account number, the check number, the date, the payee and the amount of the check. However, there was a 50-cent error in the amount of the check. Either the next day or the day thereafter, she went to the Bank (D) and issued a written stop order payment, which also contained the same error. [You'd think she could get it right the second time!] The Bank (D) paid the check the following day. Parr (P) sued the Bank (D) seeking recovery for the amount of the check, interest thereon, attorney's fees and costs. The Bank (D) defended on the ground that its computers were programmed to stop payment only if the reported amount of the check was correct. It asserted that the 50-cent error relieved it of liability. The Bank (D) argued that whether a stop payment order has been received so as to afford it a reasonable opportunity to stop payment should be determined after examining how the Bank (D) handles stop orders.

■ **ISSUE**
Is a bank given reasonable opportunity to stop payment on a check when the description received is exact in all respects except for a single digit error in the check amount?

■ **DECISION AND RATIONALE**
(Reynolds) Yes. We hold that a bank is given reasonable opportunity to stop payment on a check when the description received is exact in all respects except for a single digit error in the check amount. This is true in spite of the bank's computerized stop payment system that only searches for checks with the exact amount. UCC Section 4–403 [customer may stop payment by giving notice that reasonably identifies the item and is received sufficiently before payment that the bank has a reasonable opportunity to act on it] has not changed the common law rule, which requires that a stop payment order must identify the check with *reasonable accuracy*. Other cases have reached the issue of reasonable accuracy without consideration of the bank's computer system. For example, other courts have held that a 10-cent error in the amount of the check, plus the payee, check number and date,

Parr v. Security National Bank (Continued)

described it with sufficient accuracy to allow the bank to stop payment. However, in one case the opposite result was reached where the bank told the customer that a stop payment order would not be effective unless the exact amount of the check was provided. In the case before us, the Bank (D) does not contend that it gave Parr (P) such notice. In *Delano v. Putnam Trust Co.*, the bank had a computer program, which, as here, required an exact match of the check amount before it would stop payment. The court in *Delano* held that despite the error of a single digit in the check amount the bank was not relieved of liability where the customer supplied the bank with the correct check, number, date, payee, and account number of the check. The court further held that the bank had a duty to inform the customer of the need for accurate reporting of the check amount. In *FJS Electronics, Inc. v. Fidelity Bank*, a customer prevailed against the bank even though a 50-cent error in the check amount prevented the bank's computer from acting on the stop payment order. The court in *FJS* held that the bank invites liability when it chooses to use a system that increases the risk that checks will be paid when there is an outstanding stop payment order. We are persuaded by the holdings of *Delano* and *FJS*, and therefore conclude that Parr (P) described her check with reasonable accuracy and the Bank (D) was given a reasonable opportunity to act on the stop payment order. [The Bank (D) now wishes that it had told Parr (P) to accurately report the information.] If the banking industry wishes to avoid this type of result, it can do one of two things: (1) notify the customer at the time a stop order is given of the need for accurate information, or (2) seek legislative amendment of Section 4–403. Under UCC Section 4-407(b) [if bank pays item it is subrogated to any person connected with the instrument to prevent unjust enrichment], since the Bank (D) paid the check to Champlin Oil, the Bank (D) is subrogated to the rights of the payee, Champlin Oil, against the maker, Parr (P). In such a suit, an award of attorneys fees and costs to the Bank (D) would be proper, since Champlin Oil would have been suing Parr (P) on an open account if the Bank (D) had stopped payment on the check. The matter is reversed and remanded for award of the amount of the check plus reasonable attorney's fees and costs.

Analysis:

The issue presented here was what constitutes reasonable identification of the check so as to give a bank a reasonable opportunity to stop payment. Since Parr (P) had given the Bank (D) all the requested information, and there was only a one-digit error in the check, amounting to a fifty-cent difference, the court held that this was sufficient reasonable identification. The court imposed an objective standard, which ignores the bank's procedures in determining whether or not a customer provided sufficient correct information. Note that the court suggested that an option for the banking industry was to seek legislative amendment in order to prevent this type of liability. This case was decided in 1984, and the 1990 revisions to the Code have made changes. The revised section requires that the item be described with reasonable certainty, and Official Comment 5 provides that the customer "must meet the standard of what information allows the bank under the technology then existing to identify the item with reasonable certainty." Thus, the legislature was listening to the banking industry's argument that it was unfair to hold them liable for customers' mistakes in giving information.

■ CASE VOCABULARY

OPEN ACCOUNT: An indebtedness that has not been settled, and is subject to future adjustment.

SUBROGATE: Derived from the doctrine of subrogation where one person is substituted in place of another with respect to rights or a claim.

UNJUST ENRICHMENT: Derived from the doctrine of unjust enrichment that provides that one may not profit or enrich himself at the expense of another which is contrary to justice and equity.

Canty v. Vermont National Bank
(*Customer*) v. (*Bank*)
25 UCC Rep. Serv.2d 1184 (Vt.Super.1994)

BANK NEED NOT RECREDIT CUSTOMER'S ACCOUNT BEFORE EARNING SUBROGATION RIGHTS

■ **INSTANT FACTS** Bank improperly paid customer's cancelled checks to the IRS for a second time, and customer sued to have the bank recredit his account.

■ **BLACK LETTER RULE** A depositor has the burden of proving actual loss due to the bank's improper payment of an item before the bank must recredit the account.

■ **PROCEDURAL BASIS**

Motion for summary judgment in trial court to collect amount wrongfully paid to payee by bank.

■ **FACTS**

Canty (P) had a checking account with Vermont National Bank (the Bank) (D). Canty (P) had problems with the Internal Revenue Service and was asked [more likely told] by it to provide canceled checks to document the previous payment of certain obligations to the IRS. After Canty (P) forwarded the canceled checks to the IRS it [wanting to get even more money] redeposited the canceled checks and the Bank (D) paid them a second time. Canty (P) sued the Bank (D) contending that the checks were wrongfully paid the second time and the Bank (D) should recredit his account for the funds withdrawn. The Bank (D) argued that it did not have to recredit the account unless there was proof of actual loss to Canty (P) from the improper payment to the IRS. Canty (P) moved for summary judgment.

■ **ISSUE**

Must the depositor first prove actual loss due to the bank's improper payment of an item before the bank must recredit the account?

■ **DECISION AND RATIONALE**

(Katz) Yes. A depositor has the burden of proving actual loss due to the bank's improper payment of an item before the bank must recredit the account. If a bank has paid an item that is not properly payable, it may not charge the customer's account. If it has done so, it must recredit the account. Although this is the usual response by a bank, the law does permit a bank to refuse to recredit the customer's account after wrongful payment of an item by subrogating itself to the rights of the presenter of the improperly paid checks. Where a bank's payment of such an item discharges a legal obligation of the customer, the customer would retain a benefit, and recover the amount of the check as well, all to his profit at the bank's expense. Canty (P) asserts that there can be no subrogation until his account is first recredited. This is contrary to the provisions of UCC Section 4–407 [permits a bank to be subrogated to the rights of a payee, against its own customer, the drawer or maker]. A bank may assert its subrogation rights defensively when, as in this case, the customer brings an action for wrongful debit of the account. As with the case of a stop payment order, the issue of unjust enrichment is a factor. The depositor bears the burden of proving actual loss. In addition, the payee must be

Canty v. Vermont National Bank (Continued)

considered. Here the payee is the IRS. One's account with the IRS is never closed, even upon death. To avoid unjust enrichment, the issue is whether the customer suffered any loss by the improper payment. If he did not, he may not recover because to do so would enrich him twice, once to the payee and once on his satisfied judgment. The burden is shifted to the party who has best access to the facts. Since the Bank (D) would have difficulty obtaining information from the IRS about Canty's (P) account, there is a presumption of the regularity of its proceedings. [Isn't that a joke!] Thus, Canty (P) must prove actual loss. Other courts have described the burden of proof in these types of cases as follows. The customer initially must establish a prima facie case by showing that an item was improperly paid. The bank, exercising its subrogation rights, has the burden of presenting evidence of an absence of actual loss to the customer. When it does so, the customer must then show actual loss. Since the payee is the IRS, we will presume an absence of actual loss to the customer and the Bank (D) has met its burden. We reject Canty's (P) contention that the Bank (D) must first recredit his account, before earning any right to subrogation. To do so, would tend to see the funds disappear while the case is ongoing. Therefore, Canty's motion for summary judgment is denied, and partial summary judgment is granted to the Bank (D) unless, within a 60-day period, Canty (P) can obtain evidence to show actual loss by the improper payment of his canceled checks.

Analysis:

UCC § 4–407 governs a bank's subrogation rights. Whereas the previous case, *Parr*, concerned a bank wrongfully paying an item over a stop order, this case concerns the payment of cancelled checks "under circumstances giving a basis for objection by the drawer." Canty (P) objected to the payment of the canceled checks for a second time. The court held that in order to earn subrogation rights, the Bank (D) did not have to first recredit Canty's (P) account. The case sets forth a clear description of the burden of proof in these types of cases, with the ultimate holding that a customer must prove actual loss before it may prevail against the bank for wrongful payment of an item.

■ CASE VOCABULARY

AFFIRMATIVE DEFENSE: Facts which constitute a defense even if the allegations in the complaint are true.

BURDEN OF PROOF: Obligation of proving each necessary element of the cause of action or defense.

INTERLOCUTORY ORDER: An order made relating to an intervening matter and not deciding the case in final.

PRIMA FACIE CASE: When the evidence is sufficient to prove the case, unless contrary evidence is presented by the other side.

SUI GENERIS: Latin for "of its own kind or class."

Patriot Bank v. Navy Federal Credit Union

(Depository Bank) v. (Issuer of Check)
2002 WL 481129, 47 U.C.C. Rep. Serv. 2d 662 (Va.Cir.Ct.2002)

NO STOP PAYMENTS CAN BE ISSUED ON CASHIER'S CHECKS

■ **INSTANT FACTS** Navy Federal Credit Union (D) stopped payment on a cashier's check that had been deposited with Patriot Bank (P).

■ **BLACK LETTER RULE** A customer has no right to stop payment on a cashier's check.

■ **PROCEDURAL BASIS**

Decision on an appeal de novo from the General District Court.

■ **FACTS**

Peeso, a member of Navy Federal Credit Union (D), obtained a cashier's check for $7,000, payable to Peeso. He used the check to purchase a car from Nation's Auto. Peeso endorsed the check to Nation's Auto. Under Peeso's signature, the account number of Nation's Auto's account at Patriot Bank (P) was written, with nothing else being noted. The check was deposited in Nation's Auto's account at Patriot Bank (P), and the check was submitted for payment.

Navy FCU (D) returned the check to Patriot (P), giving as its reason "absence of endorsement guarantee required." Patriot (P) returned the check to Nation's Auto, which informed Peeso that the check he gave them was not good. Peeso did not retrieve the original check, but went to Navy FCU (D) and asked that payment be stopped on that check. Navy FCU (D) agreed to stop payment and issued another check to Peeso, made payable to Nation's Auto. Peeso agreed to indemnify Navy FCU (D) for any claims made against it for refusing payment of the first check.

Patriot (P) attempted to reverse the credit given to Nation's Auto for the first check. It found that the Nation's Auto account was overdrawn and that Nation's Auto had gone out of business. Patriot (P) filed suit against Navy FCU (D). Patriot (P) learned, during the litigation, that Navy FCU (D) returned the first check because of the absence of endorsement guaranteed. Patriot (P) stamped a guarantee on the check and returned it to Navy FCU (D). Navy FCU (D) refused to honor that check, because payment had been stopped on it, because the second check had been issued and paid, and because Nation's Auto was out of business.

■ **ISSUE**

Was Navy FCU (D) entitled to refuse payment of the first check?

■ **DECISION AND RATIONALE**

(Roush, J.) No. A customer has no right to stop payment on a cashier's check. A customer has the right to stop payment only on items drawn on his or her own account, but a cashier's check purchased by a bank customer is not a check drawn on the customer's account. When a bank issues a cashier's check, it becomes obligated to pay the check according to its terms. The bank essentially is assuming the obligations of the maker of a promissory note. It may refuse to pay the check based on any defenses it

Patriot Bank v. Navy Federal Credit Union (Continued)

may have, such as non-payment for the check, unless the check is held by a holder in due course. It may not assert any defenses the customer who purchased the check may have had.

Navy FCU (D) has no defenses to payment in this case. It received full payment for the check, and any other defenses, such as Nation's Auto being out of business, or that payment already was made, belong to Peeso.

Navy FCU (D) was not entitled to dishonor the check in the first place. The account number written on the check was a sufficient endorsement. An endorsement is defined as a "signature," which in turn is defined broadly to include any mark used to authenticate a writing. It is a reasonable inference that Nation's Auto intended its account number on the check as authentication of the check. The check was properly endorsed.

Even if the account number was not an endorsement, Navy FCU (D) should not have returned the check. When an item is delivered to a depository for collection, the bank becomes a holder of the item if the customer was a holder. The depository bank warrants that the amount of the item was paid to the customer. When Patriot (P) submitted the check to Navy FCU (D), Patriot (P) warranted that the check was paid to Nation's Auto. That warranty was the functional equivalent of an endorsement. Navy FCU (D) was not entitled to refuse payment.

Judgment for Patriot (P) in the amount of $7,000 plus interest, and $5,700 attorney's fees and $182.26 costs.

Analysis:

Nation's Auto seems to have gone out of business quite quickly, which may mean that it was on shaky ground to begin with. Knowing, or suspecting, what kind of financial state Nation's Auto was in may have made Navy FCU (D) reluctant to take checks presented by it. Of course, if Nation's Auto had not gone out of business, the whole case may never have come up: Patriot (P) could have successfully reversed the credit to the Nation's Auto account, and Nation's Auto would have been paid by the second check.

Rock Island Auction Sales, Inc. v. Empire Packing Co.

(Cattle Seller) v. (NSF Buyer)
32 Ill.2d 269, 204 N.E.2d 721, 2 UCC Rep. Serv. 319 (1965)

THE ROLE OF A PAYOR BANK IN THE COLLECTION PROCESS IS CRUCIAL, AND IGNORING TIME DEADLINES WILL RESULT IN LIABILITY

■ **INSTANT FACTS** Payor bank held check without payment, return or notice of dishonor, beyond fixed time period.

■ **BLACK LETTER RULE** The failure of the payor bank to meet the statutory deadline for handling a check results in liability for the amount of the check.

■ **PROCEDURAL BASIS**

Appeal from judgment on claim for damages for dishonored check.

■ **FACTS**

Rock Island Auction Sales, Inc. (Rock) (P) sold cattle to Empire Packing Co., Inc. (Empire) (D1) and received a check from it for the purchase price. On the day of the sale, Rock (P) deposited the check in the First Bank and Trust Company. The payor bank, Illinois National Bank and Trust Company (Illinois National) (D2), received the check three days later on Thursday, September 27. However, Empire's (D1) balance was inadequate to pay the check. Empire (D1) assured Illinois National (D2) that additional funds would be deposited, and Empire (D1) therefore agreed to hold the check until Tuesday morning, October 2. Since there were still inadequate funds to pay the check, Illinois National (D2) marked the check "not sufficient funds," placed it in the mail for return to the Federal Reserve Bank and sent notice of dishonor by telegram to the Federal Reserve Bank. The check was never paid and shortly thereafter, Empire (D1) was adjudicated bankrupt. Rock (P) sued Empire (D1) and Illinois National (D2). An officer of Empire (D1) who had signed the check was also sued, but was never served. The bankruptcy stay order prevented prosecution of Empire (D1), and thus Rock (P) proceeded solely against the payor bank, Illinois National (D2). Rock (P) asserts liability against Illinois National (D2) on the ground that as the payor bank it became liable for the amount of the check because it held the check without payment, return or notice of dishonor, beyond the time limit set forth in UCC Section 4–302. Illinois National (D2) defended on the ground that the amount for which it is liable should be determined instead by Section 4–103(5). [This means zero!]

■ **ISSUE**

Will the failure of the payor bank to meet its statutory deadline for handling a check result in liability for the amount of the check?

■ **DECISION AND RATIONALE**

(Schaffer) Yes. If the payor bank fails to pay, return or give notice of dishonor of a check within the time limit set forth in UCC Section 4–302 [payor bank accountable for the amount of an item if it does not comply with time limits to take action after receipt of item] it will be liable for the amount of the check. We are asked to determine whether the amount for which the Illinois National (D2) is liable should be determined by Section 4–302 or Section 4–103(5) [measure of damages is reduced by amount that item could not have been collected absent bad faith]. Illinois National (D2) argues that the word *accountable* as used in Section 4–302 means that "the defendant must account for what it actually had", which is zero because there were no funds on deposit sufficient to pay the check. We do not agree. The word *accountable* is synonymous with *liable*. [Playing semantic subterfuge with this court will get you nowhere.] The lower court correctly held that Section 4–302 imposes liability for the amount of the item. The role of the payor bank in meeting its time deadline is crucial. It knows whether or not the drawer has funds available to pay the item. It is possible that the relationship between the payor bank and its customer will so influence its conduct as to cause a conscious disregard of its statutory duty. In this case, Illinois National (D2) deliberately aligned itself with its customer, Empire (D1), in order to protect that customer's credit and consciously disregarded the duty imposed upon it. The legislative sanction imposed by Section 4–302 to prevent conscious disregard of deadlines is not arbitrary or unreasonable, nor is it a legislative encroachment on the functions of the judiciary. Affirmed.

Analysis:

Although the primary issue in this case involved statutory construction of the damage provisions of § 4–302 as read with § 4–103(5), the purpose of this case is to explain the rule regarding final payment and when the payor bank becomes *accountable*. There was no dispute that Illinois National (D2) had missed the deadlines for payment, return, or giving notice of dishonor of the check. The only issue was how the damages should be assessed. Under the pre-1990 revision of § 4–302, which was before the court in this case, if the payor bank missed its deadline to pay or return the item or send notice of dishonor, it was *accountable* for the amount of the check. The court concluded that the legislature intended to sanction payor banks for the amount of the check if they did not comply with their crucial duties concerning collection of an item.

■ CASE VOCABULARY

COLLECTING BANK: A bank handling an item for collection except the payor bank.

DEPOSITARY BANK: The first bank to take an item even though it is also the payor bank, unless the item is presented for immediate payment over the counter.

PAYOR BANK: A bank that is the drawee of a draft.

STAY ORDER: As used in bankruptcy proceedings, an order prohibiting any collection efforts or civil court proceedings against the debtor.

First National Bank of Chicago v. Standard Bank & Trust

(Presenting Bank) v. (Payor Bank)
172 F.3d 472, 38 UCC Rep. Serv. 2d 1 (7th Cir.1999)

REGULATION CC EXTENDS UCC'S MIDNIGHT DEADLINE

■ **INSTANT FACTS** Payor bank attempted to come within Regulation CC's extension of midnight deadline where bank officers returned checks to presenting bank's processing center.

■ **BLACK LETTER RULE** A presenting bank's return of the checks via bank officer's delivery to payor bank's processing center comports with Regulation CC sec. 229.30(c)(1).

■ **PROCEDURAL BASIS**

Appeal from judgment following granting of motion for summary judgment in action for declaratory judgment, and appeal from judgment on the pleadings.

■ **FACTS**

First National Bank of Chicago, formerly known as NBD Bank, (Chicago) (P) brought suit for declaratory judgment alleging that Standard Bank & Trust (Standard) (D) failed to return checks to Chicago (P) in a timely fashion under the Expedited Funds Availability Act (EFAA). Both parties were involved in a check-kiting scheme perpetrated upon them by an individual [and each wanted to pass the loss off to the other]. On November 18, an individual [with a criminal mind set] presented checks to Chicago (P), drawn on customer accounts maintained at Standard (D), valued at just under $4 million dollars. On the same day, the individual deposited over 4 million in checks at Standard (D), drawn on Chicago (P) customer accounts. The next day, November 19, Chicago (P) presented the checks it received to Standard (D), and vice versa. The collecting bank, La Salle Bank, charged both banks' accounts for the checks drawn on them, and provisionally credited each bank for the amount presented to them. On the following business day, Monday, November 22, Chicago (P) opted not to honor the checks and returned all of them to Standard (D). Standard (D) received notice of Chicago's (P) decision on Tuesday morning, November 23. That afternoon, Standard (D) attempted to dishonor the checks it had received. Three of its bank officers dashed off to Chicago's (P) Operations Processing Center carrying the checks. The checks were received by Chicago (P) at 3:58 p.m. that day, but Chicago (P) did not credit Standard's (D) account for that sum. On November 30, Chicago (P) filed suit, seeking a declaration that Standard's (D) return of the checks was not timely because it neither met the "midnight deadline," nor any of the deadline exceptions laid out in the Federal Reserve Board (the Board) Regulations appurtenant to EFAA. Standard (D) argued the return was proper, and counterclaimed for prejudgment interest. The district court found that the checks were returned in a timely fashion, granted summary judgment to Standard (D), and awarded it prejudgment interest on the returned checks. The district court granted Standard's (D) motion for judgment on the pleadings. Each party appealed.

■ **ISSUE**

Does a presenting bank's return of checks via bank officer's delivery to payor bank's processing center comport with Regulation CC sec. 229.30(c)(1)?

First National Bank of Chicago v. Standard Bank & Trust (Continued)

■ DECISION AND RATIONALE

(Flaum) Yes. The issue before us is whether Standard's (D) return of the checks comports with the Board's Regulation CC sec. 229.30(c)(1) [final payment does not occur where payor bank returns the item to the presenting bank before close of business on the next banking day or where a highly expeditious means of transportation is used], which extends the UCC's "midnight deadline" [final payment does not occur until after midnight of the next banking day following receipt] for return or notice of nonpayment. We hold that the method used came within the meaning of such Regulation. Chicago (P) argues that the Regulation CC extension is only available to banks that regularly or ordinarily use expedited delivery. [In other words, bank officers dashing off with the checks does not count.] However, the language of the Regulation, which refers to a returned "check" rather than "checks", suggests that it may apply to a one-time check transaction. In addition, use of the word "ordinarily" in the Regulation denotes that the bank's means of delivery must ordinarily result in return by the applicable deadline. We also reject Chicago's (P) argument that Standard's (D) efforts were not in "an effort to expedite delivery" of the dishonored checks. [What other reason would there be for a bunch of bank executives rushing off with checks worth millions of dollars?] The purpose of the regulation is to promote the speedy return of dishonored checks over the postmark conscious "midnight deadline" of the UCC. We affirm the judgment on the pleadings in favor of Standard (D) that the checks were properly returned, but vacate the award of interest and remand to determine proper amount of prejudgment interest.

Analysis:

This case examines Regulation CC Sec 220.30(c). The purpose of the Regulation is twofold. It attempts to correct the prior situations where the bank would place a dishonored check in the mail in order to meet the midnight deadline, even though the fastest way would be to wait until the bank's courier made its normal delivery the following day. In other words, a delivery that starts later but arrives sooner is encouraged. In addition, where the bank misses its midnight deadline, there is a further extension if the paying bank uses a "highly expeditious means of transportation." Chicago's (P) argument that the extension is only available to banks that regularly or ordinarily use expedited delivery is somewhat nonsensical. If the purpose of the Regulation were to permit a further extension for expedited delivery, whether such service is regularly or ordinarily used would not matter. Note that there is no clear-cut answer as to whether the "further" extension means more than one, two, or many more days. In any event, Regulation CC serves the purpose of extending the midnight deadline of the UCC if the necessary requirements are met.

■ CASE VOCABULARY

DE NOVO: As used by courts of appeal to denote reviewing the entire record and making its decision anew, and without regard to lower court's decision.

MIDNIGHT DEADLINE: Defined in the UCC as, "With respect to a bank, midnight on its next banking day following the banking day on which it receives the relevant item or notice or from which the time for taking action commences to run, whichever is later."

MOTION FOR JUDGMENT ON THE PLEADINGS: Deciding the case as a matter of law based upon the allegations contained in the complaint.

Valley Bank of Ronan v. Hughes

(*Bank*) v. (*Fraud Victim*)
334 Mont. 335, 147 P.3d 185 (2006)

THE U.C.C. DOES NOT PREEMPT ALL COMMON LAW CLAIMS REGARDING THE PROCESSING OF CHECKS

■ **INSTANT FACTS** Hughes (D) deposited certain checks in his account at Valley Bank (P), but when the bank transferred funds from his account, they learned that the checks were fraudulent.

■ **BLACK LETTER RULE:** The U.C.C. establishes a bank's standard of care for the processing of checks but does not preempt common law tort claims regarding communications about the processing of checks.

■ **PROCEDURAL BASIS:**

Appeal from an order granting summary judgment and granting a motion *in limine*.

■ **FACTS:**

Hughes (D) was the victim of a "Nigerian scam" that promised to pay him a commission for his help in importing agricultural equipment into Africa. As a part of the scam, Hughes (D) received four checks that he deposited into his account at Valley Bank (P) on Friday, March 22. Two of the checks were "official" checks, and two were personal checks. Prior to depositing the checks, Hughes (D) asked Smith, a cashier and officer of Valley Bank (P), if the checks were valid. Smith told him that the official checks were the "same as cash" and just like cashier's checks. Another bank employee told Hughes (D) that he should believe whatever Smith told him about the validity of the checks.

On Tuesday, March 26, Hughes (D) made a written request that Valley Bank (P) wire $800,000 to a bank in Amman, Jordan. Valley Bank (P) executed that transfer no later than 1:51 that day, and the transfer proceeded through intermediary banks in Denver and New York. Approximately ten minutes after the transfer was initiated, Valley Bank (P) and Hughes (D) learned that one of the personal checks Hughes (D) received was being returned for insufficient funds. Hughes (D) immediately requested that the wire transfer be stopped, and Valley Bank (P) requested that the transfer be stopped, but all of the efforts to reverse the transaction were unsuccessful. The "official" checks were discovered to be counterfeit, and Hughes's (D) account was overdrawn by $800,000.

Valley Bank (P) exercised its right to charge back the account and collect the $800,000 from Hughes (D). Hughes deposited $607,838 from his retirement account into his Valley Bank (P) account, and executed a promissory note for $400,000, secured by mortgaged property. Part of the note would pay off an existing mortgage on the property, and the balance was to satisfy the charge-back in Hughes's (D) account. Hughes (D) was under the impression, based on conversations with Valley Bank's (P) president, that the note and loan agreement were to satisfy government auditors, and that a new agreement might be reached after resolution of the "fraud situation." Hughes (D) also understood that the loan might not be forgiven. One (late) payment was made on the note, and when no other payments were made, Valley Bank (P) sent a notice of default and acceleration on October 15, 2000. Hughes (D) requested that Valley Bank (P) forebear foreclosure until the end of the year. Valley Bank (P) agreed, but when no further payments were made, an action for judicial foreclosure was initiated.

Valley Bank of Ronan v. Hughes (Continued)

Hughes (D) counterclaimed for negligence, negligent misrepresentation, constructive fraud, unjust enrichment, breach of contract, breach of the implied covenant of good faith and fair dealing, and promissory estoppel. Hughes (D) also asserted, but dropped, a claim for intentional infliction of emotional distress.

The trial court granted Valley Bank's (P) motion for summary judgment on Hughes's (D) counterclaims, holding that the U.C.C. preempted Hughes's (D) common law and equitable claims.

■ ISSUE:

Did the U.C.C. preempt Hughes's (D) common law negligence claims against Valley Bank (P)?

■ DECISION AND RATIONALE:

(Rice, J.) No. The U.C.C. establishes a bank's standard of care for the processing of checks but does not preempt common law tort claims regarding communications about the processing of checks. The U.C.C. preempts the common law if the U.C.C. has a specific provision on a subject. The U.C.C. does not set out any rules regarding bank communications with customers, so common law principles may be used to supplement the bank's duty of care.

The U.C.C. requires that a bank use "ordinary care" in processing checks. "Ordinary care" is defined as the "observance of reasonable commercial standards." Unless the bank's procedures require otherwise, and unless general banking usage dictates otherwise, there is no requirement that a bank examine a check. Hughes's (D) common law claims regarding the processing of the check are thus preempted by the U.C.C. His claims that Valley Bank (P) improperly charged back his account are also preempted. The U.C.C. permits a bank to charge back an account even if the nonpayment of an instrument was due to the bank's own negligence. It is irrelevant whether Valley Bank (P) exercised ordinary care in exercising its charge back rights. The common law claims regarding the processing of the checks are preempted.

Hughes (D) does not make claims regarding only the processing of the checks, but also about Valley Bank's (P) communications about the processing. Such communications are not addressed by the U.C.C., so common law and equitable principles supplement the U.C.C. and govern the legal rights and responsibilities that apply to the representations made by Valley Bank (P) and relied upon by Hughes (D). Case law cited by Valley Bank (P) does support the proposition that the U.C.C. preempts claims regarding the processing of checks, but language in those cases leaves open the possibility that the banks in those cases could have been liable for express representations made to customers. The trial court properly determined that Valley Bank (P) did not violate the duty of due care in processing the checks, but the court erred in failing to consider whether common law principles supplement the statutorily defined duty of ordinary care with respect to the representations about that process. Affirmed in part, reversed in part and remanded.

Analysis:

Since the court is reviewing a grant of summary judgment, it is only considering the evidence favorable to Hughes (D). In assessing Valley Bank's (P) negligence, it will be necessary to know what Hughes (D) said about the checks, or if he explained why he wanted to transfer such a large sum of money overseas. At the trial of this case, Valley Bank (P) should also be able to raise the usual defenses to Hughes's (D) claim, including, for example, comparative fault.

CHAPTER TWELVE

Wrongdoing and Error

Leeds v. Chase Manhattan Bank, N.A.

Instant Facts: Leeds (P) sued Chase Bank (D), a depositary bank, after it paid an altered check to the Leeds' (P) attorney.

Black Letter Rule: A depository bank is strictly liable for conversion on a forged endorsement check if it makes payment with respect to the instrument for a person not entitled to enforce the instrument or received payment.

Price v. Neal

Instant Facts: Price (P) paid two forged bills presented by Neal (D), and then sought to recover from Neal (D).

Black Letter Rule: A drawee who pays drafts with forged drawer signatures may not recover from the person paid.

Decibel Credit Union v. Pueblo Bank & Trust Co.

Instant Facts: Drawee bank, Decibel (P), sued presenting bank, Pueblo (D), for breach of presentment and transfer warranties, but court of appeal held that Pueblo (D) was not liable.

Black Letter Rule: Presenting bank does not extend a presentment warranty to a drawee bank, which warrants all signatures to be genuine, and thus is not liable for amounts paid by drawee bank on forged checks.

Wachovia Bank, N.A. v. Foster Bancshares, Inc.

Instant Facts: A customer of Foster Bancshares (D) deposited a check drawn on Wachovia Bank (P), but because Wachovia (P) did not keep a paper copy of the check, it could not be determined if it was forged or if it was altered.

Black Letter Rule: When there is doubt as to whether an instrument has been forged or merely altered, the court will assume that the instrument was altered.

Hutzler v. Hertz Corp.

Instant Facts: Hutzler's (P) attorney forged her signature and ran off with all the funds from a check the Hertz Corp. (D) made payable to Hutzler (P) and the attorney.

Black Letter Rule: Payee whose agent forges her signature and steals her money may not recover against the drawer of the check.

The Bank/First Citizens Bank v. Citizens and Associates

Instant Facts: In an action for negligence, drawer of checks and bank, Citizens & Assoc. (P), failed to exercise ordinary care in transactions and drawer was assessed 80% of the fault and Bank 20%.

Black Letter Rule: Section 3–406 precludes one who substantially contributes to an alteration or the making of a forged signature from asserting the alteration or the forgery against one who, in good faith, pays the instrument or takes it for value or for collection.

Travelers Cas. & Sur. Co. of America v. Wells Fargo Bank N.A.

Instant Facts: Schwab (D) accepted a forged check drawn on Allianz's (P) account for deposit, and Wells Fargo (D) refused to reimburse Allianz (P) for its loss.

Black Letter Rule: A bank or other institution that receives a check for deposit has a duty to exercise due care to make sure that the depositor is the intended recipient of the funds.

Falk v. Northern Trust Co.

Instant Facts: Falk (P) sued bank (D) for loss of sustained from embezzlement by assistant contending that Bank (D) was negligent in allowing her to cash checks.

Black Letter Rule: The time limitation set forth in Section 4–406(f)—which requires a customer to notify the bank within one-year of receiving a bank statement of any unauthorized signature or alteration—is not applicable where the bank is alleged to have paid items in bad faith.

Leeds v. Chase Manhattan Bank, N.A.

(*Payees*) v. (*Depositary Bank*)
331 N.J.Super. 416, 752 A.2d 332 (2000)

A DEPOSITARY BANK MAY BE SUED FOR CONVERSION IF IT MAKES PAYMENT OF AN INSTRUMENT TO ONE NOT ENTITLED TO RECEIVE PAYMENT

■ **INSTANT FACTS** Leeds (P) sued Chase Bank (D), a depositary bank, after it paid an altered check to the Leeds' (P) attorney.

■ **BLACK LETTER RULE** A depositary bank is strictly liable for conversion on a forged indorsement check if it makes payment with respect to the instrument for a person not entitled to enforce the instrument or receive payment.

■ **PROCEDURAL BASIS**

Appeal from entry of summary judgment in action for conversion.

■ **FACTS**

The Leeds (P), mother and son, hired an attorney (Egnasko) to represent them in a real estate matter. The Leeds (P) bought certain real property at a foreclosure sale, and thereafter entered into a contract to sell the property. Their attorney closed the sale and accepted a settlement check on their behalf in the sum of $87, 293.56, which was made payable to the Leeds (P). Unbeknownst to the Leeds (P), their attorney altered the check by typing his name "as attorney for" the Leeds (P) above the payee line. The attorney endorsed the check, and deposited it into his attorney trust account at Chemical Bank, which stamped the back of the check "Endorsement guaranteed." Chase Manhattan Bank (D), successor-in-interest to Chemical Bank, presented the check for collection to the drawer bank, now Summit Bank, which honored its own teller's check. Thereafter, attorney Egnasko drew a check for $92,050 payable to the Leeds (P) from an attorney trust account held at the Trust Company of New Jersey (Trustco), which covered the proceeds of the sale of the home. Trustco honored the check drawn to the Leeds (P), and they received payment on that check. [So, what's the problem you ask?— Well ...] Egnasko improperly used other funds from the Trustco account—which had come from a check made payable to another bank, Shrewsbury, for which he had similarly altered and deposited— and paid the Leeds (P), instead of paying the Shrewsbury bank to whom the funds should have been paid. Trustco—facing a claim of conversion by Shrewsbury—sued attorney Egnasko and the Leeds (P) seeking repayment of the monies traceable to Egnasko's fraud. The Leeds (P) cross-claimed admitting receipt of the Trustco check but denying that they owed Trustco the converted proceeds of the check. Their cross-claim alleged that Chase (D), the depositary bank, and Summit, the drawer/drawee/payor bank, were both strictly liable for conversion due to the payment on the altered settlement check. Chase (D) and Summit moved for summary judgment. The Court granted the motion, and Leeds (P) appeal.

■ **ISSUE**

Is a depositary bank strictly liable for conversion on a forged indorsement check if it makes payment with respect to the instrument for a person not entitled to enforce the instrument or receive payment?

■ **DECISION AND RATIONALE**

(Wecker) Yes. We first address Leeds' (P) cause of action in conversion against Chase (D). UCC Section 3-420a states in pertinent part: "An instrument is also converted if it is taken by transfer, other

Leeds v. Chase Manhattan Bank, N.A. (Continued)

than a negotiation, from a person not entitled to enforce the instrument or a bank makes or obtains payment with respect to the instrument for a person not entitled to enforce the instrument or receive payment. An action for conversion of an instrument may not be brought by the issuer or acceptor of the instrument or a payee or indorsee who did not receive delivery of the instrument either directly or through delivery to an agent or a co-payee." Although the check was not actually delivered to the Leeds (P), it was delivered to Egnasko as Leeds' (P) attorney, with intent that title be transferred to the Leeds (P), the payees. Thus, the Leeds (P) are entitled to bring this action for conversion as one who "received[d] delivery of the instrument ... through delivery to an agent." By crediting Egnasko's trust account for the face amount of the check, Chase (D) paid the check to "a person not entitled to ... receive payment." As a depository bank under the UCC, Chase (D) is strictly liable for conversion on a forged or stolen instrument, because it made or obtained payment with respect to the instrument for a person not entitled to enforce the instrument or receive payment. Thus, the motion court improperly entered summary judgment against the Leeds (P) and in favor of Chase (D). We next address Leeds' (P) cause of action in conversion against Summit, the drawer, the drawee, and the payor bank on the altered check. A drawee bank is also strictly liable for conversion when it pays on a forged endorsement. However, state law limits damages for conversion against a representative, other than a depository bank, who has in good faith dealt with an instrument or its proceeds on behalf of one who was not the person entitled to enforce the instrument, beyond the amount of any proceeds that it has not paid out. Summit has paid out the entire face amount of the forged check and is not alleged to have acted other than in good faith. Therefore, it cannot be liable to Leeds (P) for conversion under § 3–420. We affirm summary judgment dismissing the complaint against Summit, reverse summary judgment in favor of Chase (D), and remand for entry of partial summary judgment on liability against Chase (D).

Analysis:

This case concerns an action for "conversion," as set forth in UCC § 3–420, which expressly provides that the law of conversion applies to "instruments." It also partially defines conversion as the taking of an instrument "by transfer, other than negotiation, from a person not entitled to enforce the instruments." Thus, a bank that makes or obtains payment with respect to a check for one not entitled to enforce it or receive payments is liable for conversion. An official comment to the UCC states that a payee cannot sue for conversion if the check has not been delivered to the payee—such as where a thief steals the check before delivery to the payee, forges the indorsement, and obtains payment from a depository bank. Without delivery, the payee never becomes the holder of the check nor a person entitled to enforce it. However, if the check is delivered to an agent for the payee, which Egnasko was, then the payee does have a cause of action for conversion against the depository bank.

■ CASE VOCABULARY

INSTRUMENT: Referring to a "negotiable instrument" as defined in UCC § 3-104(a). An executed written document that contains an unconditional promise or order to pay a certain sum of money, payable on demand or at a certain time, to the order or to the bearer.

UNCLEAN HANDS: Referring to the equitable doctrine of "clean hands," which provides that one cannot seek equitable relief or assert an equitable defense if he or she had "unclean hands," such as where one does not act in good faith.

Price v. Neal
(*Drawee of Draft*) v. (*Bearer of Draft*)
3 Burr. 1354, 97 Eng. Rep. 871 (1762)

DRAWEE WHO PAYS OR ACCEPTS A DRAFT ASSUMES THE RISK OF A FORGED DRAWER'S SIGNATURE

■ **INSTANT FACTS** Price (P) paid two forged bills presented by Neal (D), and then sought to recover from Neal (D).

■ **BLACK LETTER RULE** A drawee who pays drafts with forged drawer signatures may not recover from the person paid.

■ **PROCEDURAL BASIS**
Appeal of jury verdict for money had and received.

■ **FACTS**
Price (P) agreed to pay any bills of exchange that Sutton drew on Price (P). Lee forged Sutton's name on two bills made payable to Ruding. After several people endorsed the bills, Neal (D) received them. Neal (D) gave Price (P) notice of the first bill and Price (P), through his servant, later paid it. When Neal (D) later presented the second bill to Price (P), Price (P) wrote "Accepted, John Price" on the back and ordered his bankers to pay the bill when it was presented for payment. Price (P) later learned that Lee forged Sutton's name on the bills. He sued Neal (D) for return of the money. Price (P) argued that he could recover from Neal (D) because he paid the bills by mistake and that he could not recover from Sutton or from Lee, who was hung for forgery [a good way to reduce prison overcrowding]. Neal (D) argued that he could keep the money because Price (P) was negligent in failing to check whether Sutton actually signed the bills.

■ **ISSUE**
When a drawee pays or accepts a bill with a forged drawer's signature, may the drawee recover from the person paid?

■ **DECISION AND RATIONALE**
No. Neal (D) was an innocent party who paid fair consideration for the bills with no privity or suspicion of any forgery. It was Price's (P) duty to be satisfied that Sutton had in fact signed the bills before he paid them. Price (P) was negligent in not confirming that Sutton had signed the bills. Price (P) had notice of the bills before he paid them. This is especially true with respect to the second bill insofar as Price (P) had time after receiving the first bill to confirm that Sutton had signed it.

Analysis:
The rule from this old English case remains in force today. It assures an innocent presenter of a draft finality once the presenter has received payment from the drawee. This finality puts an end to the transaction and defines the parties' liabilities. The drawee bank is presumed to know the drawer's signature, even in light of a perfect forgery job. The rule of *Price v. Neal* is incorporated in UCC § 3–

Price v. Neal (Continued)

418. Thus, if Harry Villain steals your checkbook and signs your name to a check he makes payable to himself, the bank paying the check may not recover against Harry Villain or against your account. This is a completely different result than if Harry Villain were to steal a check made out to you and forge your signature. In that case, your bank could sue the depository bank for conversion.

■ CASE VOCABULARY

DRAWER: A person ordering the drawee to pay a draft.

Decibel Credit Union v. Pueblo Bank & Trust Co.

(*Drawee Bank*) v. (*Presenting Bank*)
996 P.2d 784 (Colo.App.2000)

COURT HOLDS THAT PRESENTING BANK DOES NOT BEAR THE LOSS FOR AMOUNTS PAID ON FORGED CHECKS

■ **INSTANT FACTS** Drawee bank, Decibel (P), sued presenting bank, Pueblo (D), for breach of presentment and transfer warranties, but court of appeal held that Pueblo (D) was not liable.

■ **BLACK LETTER RULE** Presenting bank does not extend a presentment warranty to a drawee bank, which warrants all signatures to be genuine, and thus is not liable for amounts paid by drawee bank on forged checks.

■ PROCEDURAL BASIS

Appeal from judgment following the granting of a motion for summary judgment in action for breach of presentment and transfer warranties.

■ FACTS

A thief stole blank checks furnished by Decibel Credit Union (Decibel) (P) to one of its checking account customers. Over a 40-day period, the thief forged the customer's signature on a series of 14 checks totaling $2,350. Each of the checks was cashed at Pueblo Bank & Trust Co. (Pueblo) (D), where the thief had a bank account, sometimes at the rate of more than one check per day. [Not surprisingly], the thief's checking account did not have sufficient funds to cover the checks that were being cashed. Pueblo (D) processed the checks and Decibel (P) timely paid them. As soon as Decibel's (P) customer discovered the forgeries, he notified Decibel (P). In turn, Decibel (P) then made demand upon Pueblo (D) for reimbursement, but Pueblo (D) declined. Decibel (P) filed suit against Pueblo (D), contending that Pueblo breached both the presentment and transfer warranties. After both parties filed motions for summary judgment, the court entered judgment for Decibel (P), and Pueblo (D) appealed.

■ ISSUE

Does a presenting bank extend a presentment warranty to a drawee bank, which warrants all signatures to be genuine, so as to be liable for amounts paid by drawee bank on forged checks?

■ DECISION AND RATIONALE

(Ruland) No. We hold that a presenting bank does not extend a presentment warranty to a drawee bank, which warrants all signatures to be genuine, and thus is not liable for amounts paid by drawee bank on forged checks. It is undisputed that under the UCC, a drawee bank is liable to its checking account customer for payment of a check on which the customer's signature has been forged. Further, when the drawee bank honors the forged instrument, the payment is deemed final for a person who or an entity which takes the instrument in good faith and for value. Pueblo (D) asserts that in this case there were no presentment or transfer warranties made to Decibel (P). Presenting warranties appear in Section 4-208(a), which provides in subsection (1) that the warranty to a drawee assures only that there are no unauthorized or missing endorsements on the checks. If a warranty that all signatures were genuine applied, the final payment doctrine contained in Section 3–418 [when a drawer's name is

Decibel Credit Union v. Pueblo Bank & Trust Co. (Continued)

forged, the drawee who pays or accepts the draft bears the loss] would be meaningless. Thus, we hold that Pueblo (D) did not extend any presentment warranty to Decibel (P) by returning the checks to it through the Federal Reserve System. Hence, the trial court erred in concluding that presentment warranties applied in this case. Transfer warranties appear in Section 4–207 and warrant to a transferee, other than a payor, that all signatures are authentic and authorized. Even if we assume that a transfer is involved here, it is well established that a transfer warranty as to the genuineness of the drawer's signature does not apply for the benefit of the drawee bank. Hence, the trial court erred in relying on this section to enter judgment for Decibel (P). Judgment is reversed and the cause is remanded for further proceedings.

Analysis:

Under *Price v. Neal,* when a drawer's name is forged, the drawee who pays or accepts the draft bears the loss. Decibel (P), the drawee bank here, was therefore clearly liable to its customer for paying out on the forged check. Seeking to recoup its loss, Decibel (P) sued Pueblo (D), the presenting bank, contending that it warranted that the signature on the check was genuine, and thus it breached the presentment warranty under § 4–208 by submitting the check to Decibel (P) for payment. The court quickly rejected this argument because, such a holding would be contrary to the final payment doctrine, which provides that the drawee bears the loss for payment on a forged drawer's signature.

■ CASE VOCABULARY

FINAL PAYMENT DOCTRINE: A drawee who pays an instrument with a forged drawer's signature bears the loss.

PRESENTMENT BANK: The bank that presents a check to the drawee bank for payment.

PRESENTMENT WARRANTY: A promise concerning the credibility of a negotiable instrument made to a payor upon presentment for payment.

TRANSFER WARRANTY: A promise concerning the credibility of a negotiable instrument made by a transferor to a transferee.

Wachovia Bank, N.A. v. Foster Bancshares, Inc.

(Payor Bank) v. (Presenting Bank)
457 F.3d 619 (7th Cir. 2006)

ALTERATION WILL BE ASSUMED, UNLESS FORGERY CAN BE PROVEN

■ **INSTANT FACTS** A customer of Foster Bancshares (D) deposited a check drawn on Wachovia Bank (P), but because Wachovia (P) did not keep a paper copy of the check, it could not be determined if it was forged or if it was altered.

■ **BLACK LETTER RULE:** When there is doubt as to whether an instrument has been forged or merely altered, the court will assume that the instrument was altered.

■ **PROCEDURAL BASIS:**

Appeal from a grant of summary judgment in a declaratory judgment case.

■ **FACTS:**

Choi, a customer of Foster Bancshares (D), deposited a check for $133,026 that was drawn on Wachovia Bank (P), and which listed her as the payee. The check was drawn on the account of a company called MediaEdge. Foster (D) presented the check to Wachovia (P), and Wachovia paid Foster (D) and debited MediaEdge's account.

Choi was not the original payee of the check. The check was meant for a company called CMP Media, and when CMP did not receive the check, an investigation ensued, revealing that Choi had gotten her name substituted on the check. By the time this discovery was made, Choi had withdrawn the money from her account and disappeared. Wachovia (P) had, by that time, destroyed the paper copy of the checked deposited by Choi, pursuant to its normal policies. Wachovia (P) retained a computer image of the check, but it could not be determined whether the check was a forgery, or whether the check had been altered.

■ **ISSUE:**

When there is no evidence to clearly establish forgery, should it be assumed that the check was altered, rather than forged?

■ **DECISION AND RATIONALE:**

(Posner, J.) Yes. When there is doubt as to whether an instrument has been forged or merely altered, the court will assume that the instrument was altered. The bank on which a check is drawn—in this case, Wachovia (P)—warrants that the check is genuine (meaning that a check on which the drawer's name has been forged cannot be returned once it is paid), but the presenting bank—in this case, Foster (D)—warrants that the check has not been altered since it was issued. When checks were inspected by bank employees, and when cancelled checks were stored, rather than merely copied, this allocation of responsibility was consistent with the principle that the party who could prevent a loss at the lowest cost has the duty to avoid the loss. Foster (D) could not reasonably determine whether the signature on the check could be forged, but may have had reason to suspect that Choi was not the intended payee, and would have been just as capable of detecting an alteration as Wachovia (P). Wachovia (P), on the other hand, would have no way of knowing that Choi was not the intended payee.

Wachovia Bank, N.A. v. Foster Bancshares, Inc. (Continued)

Since the check that was presented no longer exists, an assumption must be made as to whether the check was forged or altered. Changing the name of a payee is the usual method of altering a check. Although a check could be forged by use of modern technology to create a new instrument, this is a novel method and there must be more proof than an assertion that it is possible. A drawee bank must take reasonable measures to prevent forgery of checks, but Foster (D) has not shown that retention of paper copies of checks would be a reasonable method of determining whether the drawee or the presenting bank should be liable for a loss. The court cannot accept the rule that a drawee bank cannot enforce the "presentment warranty" unless it retains a paper copy of the check. A depository bank may sometimes see an alteration, or the size of the check may give some warning to the bank to delay making funds available for withdrawal. If reform of the rule allocating the loss is necessary in light of modern copying technology, that is not something for a federal court, sitting in diversity, to decide. Affirmed.

Analysis:

The presentment warranty in U.C.C. § 4–208 (a)(1) is different from the warranty that a check has not been altered, although the effect of both provisions is the same. It is a warranty that the person presenting an instrument to the drawee for payment is the "person entitled to enforce the draft or authorized to obtain payment or acceptance of the draft." This warranty puts the obligation to detect a forgery squarely on the presenting bank. Reliance on this warranty would not have required the discussion of how to allocate a loss when there is no evidence.

Hutzler v. Hertz Corp.
(Payee of Check) v. (Drawer of Check)
39 N.Y.2d 209, 347 N.E.2d 627 (1976)

PAYEE WHOSE AGENT FORGES SIGNATURE AND STEALS MONEY MAY NOT RECOVER AGAINST DRAWER OF CHECK

■ **INSTANT FACTS** Hutzler's (P) attorney forged her signature and ran off with all the funds from a check the Hertz Corp. (D) made payable to Hutzler (P) and the attorney.

■ **BLACK LETTER RULE** Payee whose agent forges her signature and steals her money may not recover against the drawer of the check.

■ **PROCEDURAL BASIS**
Appeal of cross-motions for summary judgment.

■ **FACTS**
Hutzler's (P) husband was killed in a car accident. Hutzler (P) hired attorney Yudow to sue the Hertz Corporation ("Hertz") (D) on behalf of her husband's estate. Yudow settled the suit with Hertz (D) and Hertz (D) mailed Yudow a check made payable to Hutzler individually and as the administrator of her husband's estate and to Yudow. Yudow indorsed the check with his signature and forged Hutzler's (P) signature. He deposited the check into his account at Manufacturers Hanover bank. He later closed the account and closed his law practice [giving us all a bad name]. Hutzler (P) then sued Hertz (D) for negligence, claiming that Hertz (D) failed to compare her signature on the settlement agreement with her signature on the check. She also sued Manufacturers Hanover for conversion and breach of warranty. The trial court granted Hutzler's (P) motion for summary judgment against Hertz (D) and Manufacturers Hanover's motion for summary judgment against Hutzler (P). The appellate court reduced Hutzler's (P) judgment against Hertz (D) by the amount Yudow would have been entitled to for his services. Hertz (D) appealed the summary judgment and Hutzler (P) appealed the reduction of the judgment. Hutzler (D) did not appeal Manufacturer Hanover's summary judgment.

■ **ISSUE**
When an agent forges the principal's signature on a check and converts the funds, may the principal recover against the drawer of the check?

■ **DECISION AND RATIONALE**
(Jasen, J.) No. Here we are dealing with two separate areas of the law: agency and negotiable instruments. With respect to agency law, an attorney has at least apparent authority to receive payment from a settling tortfeasor. After paying the attorney, a tortfeasor is discharged from liability. The rule has long been that a debtor's liability is discharged when a check payable to the creditor is wrongfully indorsed by the creditor's agent and is paid by the drawee bank. Therefore, Hertz' (D) tort liability was discharged when it paid Yudow. Hertz (D), the drawer, had no obligation to look for a forged indorsement. Otherwise, there would be an element of risk and uncertainty whenever one pays by check to an authorized agent. Moreover, because it takes some time for a check to reach the drawer, even if the drawer discovered the forgery, this would be of little practical value to the payee. As

Hutzler v. Hertz Corp. (Continued)

between two innocent parties, Hutzler (P) and Hertz (D), Hutzler (P) must bear the loss here because she chose a dishonest person to represent her. Our holding is consistent with UCC § 3–404 [now § 3-403(a): unauthorized signature is inoperative unless ratified]. Since our decision is based on agency principles, we hold that Hutzler (P) is estopped from denying her agent's unauthorized signature. While this may seem harsh, Hutzler (P) is not left without a remedy. She could sue Yudow (although he is an unpromising defendant) or the drawee bank, Manufacturers Hanover, for conversion. Unfortunately, Hutzler (P) did not appeal the order dismissing her conversion action against Manufacturers Hanover. [So can she sue her current attorney for malpractice?] Reversed.

Analysis:

Here, while discussing the law of agency and negotiable instruments, the court ultimately based its decision on equity. Hertz (D) and Hutzler (P) were both innocent parties. Hertz (D) properly paid what it owed and should not have to pay again. However, the court's reliance on UCC § 3–403 is puzzling. Even though Yudow was Hutzler's (P) attorney, did she really ratify his forgery of her name? Usually, ratification requires knowledge that an act is occurring and silence with regard to it. Unless Yudow had previously forged Hutzler's (P) name, and Hutzler (P) had let it happen, it is hard to see how she ratified Yudow's forgery this time. Under the court's reasoning, a principal ratifies all acts of an agent based solely on their agency status. Under that section, Hutzler (P) could also sue the drawee bank (Hertz' (D) bank) for conversion. Under UCC § 3-420(a), an instrument is converted if a bank makes payment to a person not entitled to obtain payment.

■ CASE VOCABULARY

APPARENT AUTHORITY: Authority that arises when the principal causes a third party to reasonably believe that another has been authorized to act in the principal's behalf.

DRAFT: An instrument that is an order, i.e., a check, as opposed to a promise, i.e., a promissory note.

DRAWEE: Person ordered in a draft to make a payment.

The Bank/First Citizens Bank v. Citizens and Associates

(Negligent Bank) v. (Substantially Contributing Drawer Bank)
44 UCC Rep. Serv. 2d 1072 (2001)

COURT DETERMINES BANK'S LIABILITY BASED UPON "SUBSTANTIALLY CONTRIBUTES" TEST UNDER SECTION 3–406

■ **INSTANT FACTS** In an action for negligence, drawer of checks and bank, Citizens & Assoc. (P), failed to exercise ordinary care in transactions and drawer was assessed 80% of the fault and Bank 20%.

■ **BLACK LETTER RULE** Section 3–406 precludes one who substantially contributes to an alteration or the making of a forged signature from asserting the alteration or the forgery against one who, in good faith, pays the instrument or takes it for value or for collection.

■ **PROCEDURAL BASIS**

Appeal in action for negligence involving bank-cashing procedures following judgment entered after trial.

■ **FACTS**

Citizens and Associates (Citizens) (P) sued The Bank/First Citizens Bank (The Bank) (D) for negligence after The Bank (D) accepted checks from [big time embezzler] Frieda Gray—written on a [a so-called dumb, innocent, and negligent] drawer's account and payable to Gray's employer Allied Mortgage— and allowed them to be deposited into Gray's personal account in the name of Gray and her husband. The facts leading up the lawsuit are as follows. Mr. Wilburn, President of Wilcore, Inc., a partner of Citizens (P), learned that Gray had opened an office for Allied in Tennessee. He and another partner and principal went to Tennessee and observed the operation, with Allied's name on the door and with Gray as the Branch Manager. They decided to purchase a franchise and, over a one-month period, Wilburn wrote three checks made payable to Allied, which totaled $50,000.00. He had called Gray for the mailing address and she volunteered to "overnight" it for him to Texas. Someone on Gray's behalf picked up the check from Wilburn's office. [Can you guess what happened next?] The checks were not forwarded to Allied's office, but deposited by Gray in her personal bank account with endorsements which read "Allied Mortgage Co. #259" or "Allied Mortgage Branch #259." The Bank (D) delivered them to another bank for credit of the funds deposited into Gray's account, and the other bank paid over the money and debited the same from Citizen's (P) account. The trial court, relied upon Section 3–406 [customer who fails to exercise ordinary care regarding unauthorized signatures is precluded from asserting the forgery against person who, in good faith, pays the instrument] and found Citizens (P) 80% at fault and The Bank (D) 20% at fault. Specifically, the court found that Citizens (P) failed to exercise ordinary care by engaging in negligent or careless business practices, and that The Bank (D) also failed to exercise ordinary care in accepting the checks and allowing them to be deposited into Gray's personal account, and that The Bank's (D) failure substantially contributed to the loss suffered by Citizens. Citizens (P) appealed.

The Bank/First Citizens Bank v. Citizens and Associates (Continued)

■ ISSUE

Is one who substantially contributes to an alteration or the making of a forged signature precluded from asserting the alteration or the forgery against one who, in good faith, pays the instrument or takes it for value or for collection?

■ DECISION AND RATIONALE

(Franks) Yes. On appeal, Citizens (P) contends: (1) it was not negligent; (2) even if it was, the negligence did not substantially contribute to the forgery; and (3) The Bank (D) did not take the items in good faith. With respect to the first contention, under Section 3–406, The Bank (D) must prove that Citizens (P) failed to exercise ordinary care, defined as "observance of reasonable commercial standards, prevailing in the area in which the person is located, with respect to the business in which the person is engaged." Both Wilburn and his partner were very experienced businessmen, with Wilburn making investments and loans for over 37 years, and both of them holding realtor's licenses. Given their experience, we agree with the trial court that they failed to exercise ordinary care by delivering the checks to Gray without having any written documentation and without ever verifying her authority or the terms of the alleged agreement with Allied. It has often been held that a drawer is negligent or fails to exercise ordinary care when he entrusts a third party to deliver a check to the payee, and fails to adequately investigate the transaction. There is no evidence to negate the finding that Citizens (P) engaged in negligent and careless business practices. With respect to the second contention, Citizen's (P) negligence in issuing checks without verification and delivering them to Gray substantially contributed to Gray's forgery, because the checks were put at her disposal, and was a substantial factor in her ability to forge the endorsement. Finally, with respect to the third contention, the trial court's finding that The Bank (D) failed to exercise ordinary care is not the same as lack of "good faith." Without any showing that The Bank (D) did not take the checks in good faith, or that there was dishonesty or collusion involved, the trial court's holding was correct. Judgment affirmed.

■ CONCURRENCE AND DISSENT

(Susano) I concur with the majority opinion as it holds that Citizens (P) is precluded from raising an issue on appeal as to the dismissal of the other bank from the action. However, I disagree with the conclusion that the trial court's determination concerning the negligence and fault of the parties. In my judgment, Citizens (P) did not engage in conduct that substantially contributed to a forgery, and I would thus hold that The Bank (D) was clearly 100% negligent in allowing checks made payable to a business to be deposited directly into an individual's bank account. I would reverse and render judgment in Citizen's (P) favor against The Bank (D).

Analysis:

In this case, the issue is one of negligence. Section 3-406(a) provides protection for any person who pays in good faith or takes an instrument for value or collection in good faith. However, if the person paying in good faith asserts § 3-406(a), then under subsection (b) that person must exercise ordinary care in paying the instrument; if not, subsection (c) provides that the loss is allocated between the person precluded and the person asserting the preclusion under subsection (a). The burden of proving failure to exercise ordinary care under subsection (a) is on the person asserting the preclusion, and the burden of proving failure to exercise ordinary care under subssection (b) is on the person precluded. Thus, by affirming the trial court's judgment, the court of appeals held that the Bank (D) did meet its burden and proved that Citizens (P) failed to exercise ordinary care.

■ CASE VOCABULARY

GOOD FAITH: Honesty in fact in the conduct or transaction concerned.

Travelers Cas. & Sur. Co. of America v. Wells Fargo Bank N.A.

(*Insurer*) v. (*Bank*)
374 F.3d 521 (7th Cir. 2004)

BANKS MUST USE DUE CARE TO MAKE SURE A CHECK IS AUTHORIZED

■ **INSTANT FACTS** Schwab (D) accepted a forged check drawn on Allianz's (P) account for deposit, and Wells Fargo (D) refused to reimburse Allianz (P) for its loss.

■ **BLACK LETTER RULE** A bank or other institution that receives a check for deposit has a duty to exercise due care to make sure that the depositor is the intended recipient of the funds.

■ **PROCEDURAL BASIS:**
Appeal from a judgment for Wells Fargo (D).

■ **FACTS:**
Schwab (D), a brokerage firm that also offered checking services to its customers, opened an account for Carden. Carden deposited into the account a check for $287,651.23 made out to Schwab (D) and drawn on Allianz's (P) account with Wells Fargo (D). Two weeks later, Carden directed Schwab (D) to wire the funds in the account to accounts at other financial institutions. None of the other accounts were in Carden's name. Schwab (D) made the transfers after checking with Wells Fargo (D) to make sure that the check had cleared.

Within a few days, Allianz (P) determined that Carden had never been employed by Allianz (P). Allianz (P) believed that Carden, who had disappeared, forged the check. Allianz (P) asked Wells Fargo (D) to reimburse it for the amount of the check, but Wells Fargo (D) refused. Allianz (P) was insured by Travelers (P), so Travelers (P) paid the loss and brought suit against Wells Fargo (D) and Schwab (D). At trial, Travelers (P) attempted to introduce affidavit evidence that the check was not authorized, but the judge ruled that the affidavits were inadmissible hearsay. The judge dismissed the claim against Wells Fargo (D) on the grounds that Travelers (P) had not proven that the check was unauthorized.

Two earlier suspicious checks had been drawn on Allianz's (P) account with Wells Fargo (D). One check was for $26,500, and one was for $46,651.23. There was strong reason to believe that whoever forged the second check also forged the check deposited by Carden. The judge held that Travelers (P) was barred from bringing a claim against Schwab (D), because Allianz (P) allegedly failed to investigate the prior checks. Schwab (D) argued that Travelers' (P) claim against it was barred by U.C.C. § 4–406(d)(2), which provides that the drawer of a check cannot complain about alteration by someone who altered a prior instrument if the alteration could have been discovered by examining the drawer's bank statement.

■ **ISSUE:**
Did Schwab (D) have a duty to verify that the check was authorized?

■ **DECISION AND RATIONALE:**
(Posner, J.) Yes. A bank or other institution that receives a check for deposit has a duty to exercise due care to make sure that the depositor is the intended recipient of the funds. The duty is a matter of tort

Travelers Cas. & Sur. Co. of America v. Wells Fargo Bank N.A. (Continued)

law and is not imposed by the U.C.C. or any contractual relationship between the parties. The danger in such cases is that a depositor found, stole, or forged a check. The risk of such fraud is reduced if the bank must take steps to be sure that the check is authorized. The duty is not limited to cases in which a check or instrument is forged. The duty arises in any situation in which a depositor is not authorized to deposit a check—for example, if a genuine check was stolen and then deposited.

It does not matter that Schwab (D) is a brokerage and not a bank. The common law duty should be extended to any institution that offers bank-type services, such as checking accounts. Failure to extend the duty to non-banks would give these businesses an unfair competitive advantage, since there would be no need for them to incur the added cost of liability insurance to cover payment of unauthorized checks. There is no reason to confer such a competitive advantage on the brokerage industry.

The imposition of a common law duty of care on a bank that receives a check is unusual, because it imposes a form of "good Samaritan" liability. The duty imposed is a duty to "rescue" a third party with whom the payee institution has no prior relationship. Such common law duties are not unheard of, however, and, in any event, this is no reason not to impose liability on a payee.

Schwab (D) did not fulfill its duty of due care. The trial court judge thought that any duty was discharged when Schwab (D) verified that there were sufficient funds to cover the check, but Schwab (D) was only protecting itself. Schwab (D) should have made some effort to inquire, and its duty of care would be satisfied by the attempt, even if an answer was not received. Schwab (D) could also have warned Wells Fargo (D) of the unusual deposit. The warning would have prompted Wells Fargo (D) to check the matter with Allianz (P), to avoid liability.

Schwab (D) was not a holder in due course. A bank that receives a check made out to it by someone who owes it no money, for deposit in the presenter's account, does not take the check in due course. Moreover, U.C.C. § 4–406(d)(2) does not apply to this situation, since that section only provides a bank with a defense to a claim by a customer. Since Allianz (P) was not a customer of Schwab (D), that section does not apply. Similarly, the trial court erred in holding that Allianz (P) was barred by its own negligence from making a claim against Schwab (D). A bank customer has a duty to notify the bank when unauthorized checks are being drawn on its account. The breach of this duty is a defense to a negligence claim against the bank. It is not clear that a breach of this duty would provide a defense to a bank that is not the customer's bank. Reversed and remanded for a new trial.

Analysis:

The court states in passing that Wells Fargo (D) could limit its strict liability for payment of an unauthorized check pursuant to § 4–401 (a) of the U.C.C., and Wells Fargo (D) argues that it did just that. This argument is not discussed in detail, probably because the trial court did not reach this point. The cited language states that a bank "may charge against a customer's account" an instrument that is "properly payable." "Properly payable" is defined as an instrument that is authorized by the customer "and is in accordance with any agreement between the customer and the bank." Query whether this language refers only to an instrument, or whether it is broad enough to create a defense from strict liability for paying an unauthorized check.

■ CASE VOCABULARY:

SUBROGATE: To substitute (a person) for another regarding a legal right or claim.

Falk v. Northern Trust Co.

(*Employer Victim of Embezzlement*) v. (*Bank*)
327 Ill.App.3d 101, 763 N.E.2d 380, 261 Ill.Dec. 410 (2001)

BANK'S LIABILITY IS NOT LIMITED WHERE CUSTOMER DOES NOT GIVE NOTICE OF UNAUTHORIZED SIGNATURE WITHIN ONE-YEAR OF RECEIPT OF BANK STATEMENT IF BANK PAYS ITEM IN "BAD FAITH"

■ **INSTANT FACTS** Falk (P) sued bank (D) for loss sustained from embezzlement by assistant contending that Bank (D) was negligent in allowing her to cash checks.

■ **BLACK LETTER RULE** The time limitation set forth in Section 4-406(f)—which requires a customer to notify the bank within one-year of receiving a bank statement of any unauthorized signature or alteration—is not applicable where the bank is alleged to have paid items in bad faith.

■ **PROCEDURAL BASIS**

Appeal from order dismissing the complaint demanding an accounting and negligence.

■ **FACTS**

Falk (P) filed a complaint against The Northern Trust Co. (the Bank) (D) seeking an accounting and damages for negligence based upon the Bank's (D) failure to investigate and alert Falk (P) to fraudulent transactions involving accounts with the Bank (D). Falk (P) employed Ms. Podmokly as his personal assistant for over 13 years, and she was a signor on Falk's (P) demand accounts at the Bank (D). Ms. Podmokly held a position of fiduciary with respect to Falk (P), a fact which was known to the Bank (D). In 1993, Podmokly began misappropriating funds from Falk's (P) accounts for her own personal benefit. She drew large amounts from the accounts through checks payable to cash, which she used to pay her personal obligations including loans she had at the Bank (D) and obligations of her business associates and friends at the Bank (D). The sum misappropriated from 1993 to 1997 was the [not so small] sum of over two million dollars. Falk (P) contended that the Bank (D) ignored clear evidence of the misappropriation of his funds and allowed her to continue her misappropriations well into 1997. For example, there were a number of changes and irregularities in Falk's (P) account activity during these years. In addition, in 1995, the Bank (D) accepted an unsigned $2,000 check drawn on Falk's (P) account for payment of Podmokly's personal equity credit line at the Bank (D). Further, Podmokly maintained her own accounts at the Bank (D), including a mortgage and equity line of credit. In connection with these loans, the Bank (D) reviewed her tax returns and other personal information and was aware that her income was insufficient to support the account and loan activity she was generating. [But maybe she just won the lottery!] The Bank (D) moved to dismiss the complaint on the ground that the claims were time barred under UCC Section 4-406(f), which allegedly required Falk (P) to notify the Bank (D) within one year after receiving his bank statement of any unauthorized signature or alteration. Falk (P) opposed the motion arguing that said section was inapplicable to his claim because it did not apply to claims based upon "actual knowledge" or "bad faith" on the part of the Bank (D). The trial court granted the motion to dismiss the complaint, and Falk (P) appealed.

Falk v. Northern Trust Co. (Continued)

■ ISSUE

Is the time limitation set forth in Section 4-406(f)—which requires a customer to notify the bank within one-year of receiving a bank statement of any unauthorized signature or alteration—applicable where the bank is alleged to have paid items in bad faith?

■ DECISION AND RATIONALE

(Hall) No. We conclude that the time limitation set forth in Section 4-406(f)—which requires a customer to notify the bank within one-year of receiving a bank statement of any unauthorized signature or alteration—is not applicable where the bank is alleged to have paid items in bad faith. In order to come to a proper conclusion in this matter, we must look at not only the wording of the current applicable section of the UCC, but the prior wording before its amendment in 1992. Section 4-406 of the UCC provided prior to its 1992 amendment that when a bank sent a statement to a customer accompanied by items paid in "good faith," the customer was required to exercise reasonable care and promptness in examining the statement and promptly notify the bank of an unauthorized signature or alteration. It further provided that the customer had one-year from the time the statement was made available to him to report his unauthorized signature or alteration, or be precluded from asserting a claim against the bank, regardless of the care or lack of care on the part of either the bank or the customer. After its amendment in 1992, the requirement that the items be paid in "good faith" was eliminated. If further provided that the customer is precluded from asserting the unauthorized signature or alteration of an item if the customer failed to examine the statement with reasonable promptness. The "preclusion" is treated differently depending upon the bank's conduct. If the bank "failed to exercise ordinary care" in paying the item, then the customer and the bank share the loss. However, if the customer proves that the bank did not pay the item in "good faith," the preclusion does not apply. Whether the time limitations set forth in Section 4-406(f) bars an action against a bank where the bank is alleged to have paid items in bad faith is a case of first impression in this State. In the case of *Appley v. West*, decided prior to the 1992 amendments, the federal circuit court held that where it is alleged that the bank acted in bad faith in allowing a fiduciary to cash checks and make withdrawals by use of forged endorsements or no endorsements, the time limitation in section 4-406 did not apply because that section required that the bank pay the items in "good faith." In the case of *Euro Motors, Inc. v. Southwest Financial Bank and Trust Co.*, this court found that section 4-406(f) was not a statute of limitations, but a statutory prerequisite of notice. In that case, we held that the actions were time barred. In the present case, however, the facts are more akin to *Appley* than to *Euro Motors*, because the latter case did not deal with the issue of bad faith. Thus, we conclude that *Euro Motors* does not control the present case. We next must examine the statute to determine if the 1992 amendments require a result different than the one reached in *Appley*. Our examination of section 4-406, as amended, convinces us that it does not bar suits brought beyond the time limitations set forth in that section, where the customer alleges that the bank acted in "bad faith" in paying the items that are the subject of the suit. Under section 4-406(f), the bank escapes liability regardless of the "care" or lack thereof exercised by it or the customer, if the unauthorized signature or alteration is not reported to the bank within one-year of the customer's receipt of the statement from the bank. Unlike subsection (e), however, subsection (f) does not refer to "good faith." We believe that the legislature's use of the term "care" in subsection (f) cannot be read to include "good faith." The fact that in other parts of section 4-406, the legislature drew a distinction between "ordinary care" and "good faith" in describing the consequences suffered clearly indicates that the legislature did not intend to limit a bank's liability when it acted in "bad faith" as opposed to acting with a lack of care when paying an item. Thus, section 4-406(f) requires that a bank act in "good faith" when paying the items on the statement in order to claim the protection of the prerequisite of notice requirement contained in that section. However, Falk (P) must still plead sufficient facts to support the claim of negligence against the Bank (D). We believe he has done so. Falk (P) has alleged that the Bank (D) was placed on notice of Podmokly's misappropriates based upon the increased account activity. Section 3-307 provides that where an instrument is taken from a fiduciary for payment, and the taker has knowledge of the fiduciary status, then if the instrument is issued by the represented person or the fiduciary to the taker as payee, the taker has notice of the breach of fiduciary duty if the instrument is: "(i) taken in payment of or as security for a debt known by the taker to be the personal debt of the fiduciary, (ii) taken in a transaction known by the taker to be for the personal benefit of the fiduciary, or (iii) deposited to an account other than an account of the fiduciary, or an account of the represented person." Falk's (P) complaint alleges that the Bank (D) had actual knowledge of the fiduciary relationship between Podmokly and Falk (P), and that the Bank (D) accepted checks drawn by Podmokly on Falk's (P) account for payment of her loans at the Bank (D), for payment on her personal equity credit line at the Bank (D) and for deposit into her own account at the Bank. (D). These allegations are sufficient to state a claim that the Bank (D) acted in bad faith rather than with a lack of care. Judgment reversed and the case remanded.

■ DISSENT

(Cerda) I believe that the legislature could have inserted "good faith" if it had wanted to do so. Since the words were not included in the section, I do not believe that we can require the Bank (D) to pay the items in "good faith" in order for the one-year period to apply.

Analysis:

The Bank (D) in this case attempted to assert the one-year limitation period contained in § 4-406(f) as a defense to Falk's (P) action. In other words, it alleged that he failed to bring suit in a timely manner. Although the Bank (D) was successful in the trial court level, the court of appeal disagreed and reversed. Falk (P) had alleged that the Bank (D) acted in bad faith. The court's reasoning was based upon its interpretation of the legislative intent in amending § 4–406. In the revised statute, the words "good faith" were omitted, which was of significance because if a customer could show that a bank did not pay the item in "good faith," the customer was not bound by the one-year period. If the bank merely "failed to exercise ordinary care," then both the customer and the bank shared the loss. Thus, without the "good faith" language in the amended statute, the court of appeals was required to determine whether the legislature intended for a customer to proceed with a claim beyond the one-year period when "bad faith" on the part of a bank was alleged. The dissent took the position that had the legislature intended to require a bank to pay items in "good faith" in order for the one-year period to apply, it could have inserted the language. The majority, however, based its holding on the federal court case of *Appely*, decided prior to the amendment, and its own interpretation of the statute after the deletion of the "good faith" language.

■ CASE VOCABULARY

FIDUCIARY: When used as a noun, a person acting as a trustee, executor, administrator, or guardian etc. and having the duty to act for the benefit of another.

STATUTE OF LIMITATIONS: A statute used as a defense to bar untimely filed claims.

CHAPTER THIRTEEN

Electronic Banking

Grain Traders, Inc. v. Citibank, N.A.

Instant Facts: A company that issued a wire transfer order sought a refund from an intermediary bank in the transfer process on the ground the intermediary bank failed to reject the payment order because the intermediary bank should have known that the transfer would fail due to the insolvency of other intermediary banks.

Black Letter Rule: If an originator chooses to transfer funds through an intermediary bank that fails to complete the transfer due to insolvency, the risk of loss falls on the originator who chose the method of transfer.

Corfan Banco Asuncion Paraguay v. Ocean Bank

Instant Facts: A Florida bank inappropriately accepted a payment order that correctly identified the beneficiary by name, but identified a nonexistent account number.

Black Letter Rule: A beneficiary's bank cannot accept a payment order that identifies as the beneficiary's account number an account that is nonexistent.

Bank of America N.T.S.A. v. Sanati

Instant Facts: A bank sought to recover the portion of funds that it had transferred erroneously to the beneficiary.

Black Letter Rule: The "discharge for value" rule can not be invoked in a case where the alleged preexisting debt or lien is at best a probable yet undetermined interest in a portion of funds.

Grain Traders, Inc. v. Citibank, N.A.

(*Originator*) v. (*Intermediary Bank*)
960 F.Supp. 784 (S.D.N.Y.1997)

A PAYMENT ORDER IS A SERIES OF INDIVIDUAL TRANSACTIONS UNDER WHICH LIABILITY FOR PAYMENT OR REFUND DOES NOT EXTEND BEYOND THE PERSONS OR BANKS INVOLVED IN ONE PARTICULAR TRANSACTION IN THE CHAIN

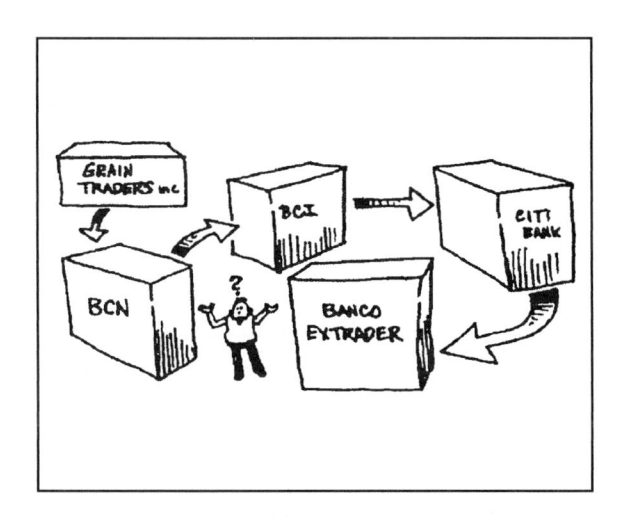

■ **INSTANT FACTS** A company that issued a wire transfer order sought a refund from an intermediary bank in the transfer process on the ground the intermediary bank failed to reject the payment order because the intermediary bank should have known that the transfer would fail due to the insolvency of other intermediary banks.

■ **BLACK LETTER RULE** If an originator chooses to transfer funds through an intermediary bank that fails to complete the transfer due to insolvency, the risk of loss falls on the originator who chose the method of transfer.

■ **PROCEDURAL BASIS**

Decision of the United States District Court denying the plaintiff's motion for summary judgment and granting the defendant's cross-motion for summary judgment.

■ **FACTS**

Grain Traders, Inc. (P) initiated a funds transfer to effectuate payment of $310,000 to Claudio Goidanich Kraemer. As per Grain Traders' (P) payment order instructions, the transfer was to be routed as follows: (1) Grain Traders' account at BCN was to be debited $310,000; (2) the $310,000 was to then be transferred to BCI by way of a $310,000 credit to BCI's account at Citibank New York (P) and a corresponding debit to BCN's account at Citibank (P); (3) Citibank (P) was then to instruct BCI to pay Banco Extrader, S.A.—the beneficiary Kraemer's bank—the total of $310,000 by way of an unspecified transaction; (4) finally, the Banco Extrader was to credit its client's account the sum of $310,000. The order proceeded as instructed until Citibank (P) credited BCI's account with instructions to pay Banco Extrader. At about the same time the transfer was to take place, Citibank (P) placed BCI's account on "hold for funds" status. Citibank (P) took the action because BCI's account was overdrawn by $12 million. BCI was eventually closed by Bahamian banking authorities. Kraemer never received the funds.

■ **ISSUE**

May the originator of a funds transfer recover from an intermediary bank the originator's loss suffered as a result of his choice of intermediary banks to complete the transfer?

■ **DECISION AND RATIONALE**

(Chin, D. J.) No. If an originator chooses to transfer funds through an intermediary bank that fails to complete the transfer due to insolvency, the risk of loss falls on the originator who chose the method of transfer. Grain Traders (P) argues that Citibank (D) knew or should have known that the next bank in the chain was experiencing financial problems, and should have, therefore, rejected the payment order. Grain Traders (P) seeks to recover under four causes of action: (1) a refund under UCC § 4A–402; (2)

Grain Traders, Inc. v. Citibank, N.A. (Continued)

a refund and attorney's fees under UCC §§ 4A–209, 4A-301, and 4A–305; (3) a breach of the duty of good faith under UCC § 1–203; and (4) conversion and money had and received under common law. Section 4A–402 of the UCC provides a "money back guarantee." In essence, it provides that if a sender of a payment was not obligated to pay all or any part of the amount it paid because the transfer was not completed, the receiving bank is obliged to refund the sender to the extent the sender was not obligated to pay. Thus, Grain Traders (P) argues that neither it nor its bank—BCN—were obligated to pay, and that Citibank (D) must refund the money it received. But Grain Traders has misread the statute, for § 4A–402 obliges the receiving bank to refund the sender from which the payment order was received. Consequently, Citibank (D) has a duty to refund only BCN, and no other participant in the chain. Under § 4A–402, Grain Traders must seek a refund from its bank, BCN. This requirement of "privity" is underscored by: (1) the plain language of § 4A–402, which treats a funds transfer as a series of separate transactions; (2) the Official Comment to § 4A–402, which limits the right of recovery to the parties to a specific payment order; (3) the fact that § 4A–402(5) gives the originator the right to sue an intermediary under different circumstances, a provision that would be unnecessary if the originator already had a right to seek a refund; and (4) the fact that when the drafters intended to provide an originator with the right to sue intermediary banks, they have done so expressly in other provisions. Grain Traders (P) second claim is premised on §§ 4A–209 and 4A–301, which govern *acceptance* and *execution*, respectively. Essentially, Grain Traders (P) argues that because Citibank (D) intended to use the transfer to set-off a debt owed to it by BCI, Citibank (D) improperly accepted and executed the payment order. This argument fails for two reasons. First, Citibank (D) did what it was supposed to do, debit one account and credit another. Second, even if Citibank's (D) intent to set-off a debt amounted to improper acceptance and execution, the Code sections upon which Grain Traders (P) relies do not provide for a cause of action, they are merely definitional. Grain Traders (P) cannot recover on its claim of a breach of the duty of good faith imposed by the UCC because that section applies only to contracts. Grain Traders (P) had no contractual relationship with Citibank (D). The common law claims must also fail because there is no evidence to support them. Citibank's (P) cross-motion for summary judgment is granted, and the complaint is dismissed with prejudice.

Analysis:

The court holds here that Citibank (D) is not liable under either of the causes of action based on Article 4A. According to the court, Citibank (D) did all that it was supposed to do, i.e., debit one account and credit another account. Citibank (D) did something it was not supposed to: frustrate the entire funds transfer process by using funds received to off-set a debt. Grain Traders' (P) biggest obstacle was that Article 4A did not provide it with a cause of action against Citibank (D) under these circumstances. The court's refusal to infer from Article 4A a cause of action by an originator against an intermediary bank is consistent with one of the statute's underlying policies. The relatively inexpensive cost of moving large sums of money in short periods of time makes it sensible to place much of the risk of loss on the parties who choose to transfer funds electronically, rather than on the banks who make the process possible.

Corfan Banco Asuncion Paraguay v. Ocean Bank

(Originator) v. (Beneficiary's Bank)
715 So.2d 967 (Fla.Ct.App.1998)

IF A BENEFICIARY'S BANK ACCEPTS A PAYMENT ORDER ON THE BASIS OF THE NAMED BENEFICIARY AND NOT THE ACCOUNT NUMBER IDENTIFIED, THE BENEFICIARY'S BANK BEARS THE RISK OF LOSS

■ **INSTANT FACTS** A Florida bank inappropriately accepted a payment order that correctly identified the beneficiary by name, but identified a nonexistent account number.

■ **BLACK LETTER RULE** A beneficiary's bank cannot accept a payment order that identifies as the beneficiary's account number an account that is nonexistent.

■ **PROCEDURAL BASIS**

Appeal from the Florida District Court's entry of summary judgment.

■ **FACTS**

Corfan Banco Asuncion Paraguay (Corfan) (P) originated a wire transfer via Swiss Bank to the account of its customer, Jorge Silva, in Ocean Bank (D). The transfer order bore Silva's name as recipient and identified as his account number 0100702 10400, which in fact was a nonexistent account. Ocean Bank (D) resolved the error on its own and deposited the funds in Silva's account. Neither Corfan (P) nor Swiss Bank were appraised of the error and subsequent correction. After realizing its error the next day, Corfan (P) issued another payment order, this time with the correct account number. Ocean Bank (D) was not notified that the second payment order was a correction. Ocean Bank (D) deposited the funds from the second order into Silva's account. Silva withdrew the funds from both transfers. Corfan (P) sued Ocean Bank (D) for refund basing its claim on § 4A-207 of the UCC as codified by the Florida Legislature and on principles of common law negligence. The trial court dismissed the complaint on the ground that Corfan (P) was in the best position to avoid the loss.

■ **ISSUE**

May a bank accept a payment order that identifies a non-existent account number?

■ **DECISION AND RATIONALE**

(Sorondo, J.) No. A beneficiary's bank cannot accept a payment order that identifies as the beneficiary's account number an account that is nonexistent. Section 4A-207(a) clearly provides that "if, in a payment order received by a beneficiary's bank, the name, bank account number, or other identification of the beneficiary refers to a nonexistent or unidentifiable person or account, no person has rights as a beneficiary of the order and acceptance of the order cannot occur." Because we must read this statute according to its plain language, we decline Ocean Bank's (D) invitation to look to legislative intent and conclude that the "or" should be read in the conjunctive. In this case, the payment order correctly identified the beneficiary, but referred to a nonexistent account. Under the clear and unambiguous terms of the statute, Ocean Bank (D) could not have accepted the payment order. As to Corfan's (P) claim for negligence, we hold that Corfan (P) may not recover. Article 4A was enacted on a clean slate in order treat funds transfers as a unique method of payment, governed by

Corfan Banco Asuncion Paraguay v. Ocean Bank (Continued)

unique rules addressing issues of risk of loss, liability, and the like. The statutory scheme preempts common law negligence in these circumstances. Reversed and remanded.

■ DISSENT

(Nesbitt, J.) The court has taken to restrictive an approach to the problem. It was Corfan's (P) own negligence that led to its loss, not any mistake by Ocean Bank (D). More importantly, nothing in the statute precludes Ocean Bank (D) from taking the action it did. The fact that the statute permits the bank to look at "other identification" surely allows for more flexibility than the majority have allowed. Ocean Bank's (D) actions comport with the statutory scheme and the policies underlying it. The primary purpose behind fund transfers is to enable the beneficiary to receive money quickly. Had Ocean Bank (D) refused to accept the payment order, the entire reason for the funds transfer may have been rendered moot. Consistent with the need for rapid transfers, Ocean Bank (D) resolved the discrepancy on its own, risking liability if its decision ultimately proved incorrect. Had Ocean Bank's (D) decision been incorrect, it would undoubtedly have been liable. However, Ocean Bank (D) should not face liability because it deposited the funds in the correct account.

Analysis:

Although Article 4A is meant to be read on a clean slate, the provisions of the statute should not be read without reference to the policies they are intended to carry out. The problem in this case was one of legislative oversight. Section 4A-207(a) provides that acceptance by a beneficiary's bank cannot occur if the payment order contains an unidentifiable or nonexistent name or account number. Subsection (b), however, provides a safe-harbor when the payment order identifies a beneficiary and an account number that do not coincide with each other, and the beneficiary's bank is aware of the discrepancy but nonetheless correctly deposits the funds. In such a case, the beneficiary's bank is shielded from liability, so long as its decision to deposit the funds was correct. The problem is that no such safe-harbor exists when the payment order contains an account number that is *nonexistent*. The situation presented by this case is simply not addressed. Consequently, the court refused to extend the safe-harbor to a situation where the beneficiary's bank correctly acts upon the beneficiary named in the payment order; thus equating legislative silence with an intent to impose liability on a beneficiary bank that acts reasonably.

Bank of America N.T.S.A. v. Sanati
(*Originator's Bank*) v. (*Beneficiary*)
11 Cal.App.4th 1079, 14 Cal.Rptr.2d 615 (1992)

AN ORIGINATOR'S BANK THAT HAS MADE AN ERROR IS ENTITLED TO RECOVER EXCESS PAYMENT TO A DESIGNATED BENEFICIARY UNDER COMMON LAW PRINCIPLES OF MISTAKE AND RESTITUTION

■ **INSTANT FACTS** A bank sought to recover the portion of funds that it had transferred erroneously to the beneficiary.

■ **BLACK LETTER RULE** The "discharge for value" rule cannot be invoked in a case where the alleged preexisting debt or lien is at best a probable yet undetermined interest in a portion of funds.

■ **PROCEDURAL BASIS**

Appeal from the trial court's decision to grant the plaintiff's motion for summary judgment on the ground that the defendant had no defense to a claim for restitution for an erroneous transfer of funds.

■ **FACTS**

While separated from his wife and living in Iran, Hassan Sanati had instructed Bank of America (P) in London to send interest, as it accrued monthly from his account, to an account held by he and his wife at Bank of America (P) in Tarzana, California. On April 30, 1990, Bank of America (P) in London erroneously sent the principal and accrued interest to the Sanati's account in Tarzana. The total amount of the erroneous transfer was $203,750. Upon receipt of the funds, Mrs. Sanati (D) authorized her children to withdraw $200,000 from the Tarzana account. These funds were then deposited in other bank accounts. In July, Bank of America (P) filed a complaint against the Sanati's (D) seeking restitution. Bank of America's (P) motion for summary judgment was granted on the ground that the Sanati's had no defense to the claim for restitution.

■ **ISSUE**

May the beneficiary of a wire transfer for an erroneously greater amount than authorized by the payment order defend an action for restitution on the ground that there the beneficiary has a quasi community property interest in the funds transferred?

■ **DECISION AND RATIONALE**

(Johnson, J.) No. The "discharge for value" rule can not be invoked in a case where the alleged preexisting debt or lien is at best a probable yet undetermined interest in a portion of funds. We must first note that the law in effect at the time of the transfer was not that of Article 4A. Rather, general common law principles govern this case. Under those principles, the recipient of an unauthorized transfer of funds could defend against a claim for restitution only if there had been detrimental reliance upon receipt of the funds by an innocent beneficiary or if the beneficiary had a good faith belief that the transfer was intended as a full or partial payment of a preexisting debt owed by the originator to the beneficiary, the latter defense known as the "discharge for value" rule. Even if Article 4A were to apply to this case, as Mrs. Sanati (D) argues, we believe that she has failed to raise a triable issue of fact as to whether Mr. Sanati owed her a preexisting debt. In essence, § 4A-303 provides that a receiving bank

Bank of America N.T.S.A. v. Sanati (Continued)

that executes a payment order in an amount greater than that of the sender's order, the bank is entitled to recover from the beneficiary of the erroneous order the excess payment received to the extent allowed by the law governing mistake and restitution. The commentary to this section adopts the discharge for value rule. Therefore, Mrs. Sanati (D) could retain the erroneously sent funds if she is able to prove that she harbored a good faith belief the funds were in payment of a preexisting debt. To this end, Mrs. Sanati (D) argues that she had a quasi community property interest in Mr. Sanati's London account. This maybe true, but such an interest does not create a preexisting debt for purposes of the discharge for value rule. In absence of any viable defense, the trial court was correct in granting summary judgment. Affirmed.

Analysis:

This case illustrates the general policy that a bank's liability under Article 4A should be kept to a minimum in order to keep the cost of wire transfers low. An executing bank ordinarily is bound by its execution errors that result in a completed funds transfer, but is expressly allowed to recover any unwarranted payment from the designated beneficiary. The California Court of Appeals was of the opinion that express adoption by Article 4A of the law of mistake and restitution—which permits executing banks that erroneously transfer a greater amount than that authorized to recover from the beneficiary—also incorporated the defenses available under that body of law. Therefore, the only defense available to Mrs. Sanati (D) was that of the "discharge for value" rule. But the court of appeals rejected the argument that an unliquidated debt, such as a "quasi community property interest," was sufficient to qualify as a "preexisting debt" under that rule.

CHAPTER FOURTEEN

Investment Securities

First American National Bank v. Christian Foundation Life Insurance Co.

Instant Facts: Recipients of church bonds, fraudulently issued in duplicate by the church's agent, sued for a declaratory judgment as to the validity of the bonds.

Black Letter Rule: Issuer is obligated to innocent purchasers for bonds containing authorized facsimile signatures even though bonds were fraudulently issued in duplicate by issuer's agent.

Jennie Clarkson Home for Children v. Missouri, Kansas and Texas Railway

Instant Facts: Defendant issuer of bonds demanded relief against defendant broker who witnessed the unauthorized signature of the registered owner's treasurer on a power of attorney purportedly authorizing the broker to sell the registered owner's bonds.

Black Letter Rule: When a stock broker represents a corporate owner of securities, the broker's indorsement guarantees that a signature purporting to transfer the securities was made by a person with authority to so obligate the corporation.

Powers v. American Express Financial Advisors, Inc.

Instant Facts: Powers (P) filed suit against American Express Financial Advisors (AEFA) (D) when, in contravention of an investment agreement, AEFA (D) permitted her former boyfriend to transfer $86,836.79 from the couple's joint investment account into a bank account from which he then withdrew the entire sum and absconded.

Black Letter Rule: When a securities intermediary has agreed that an entitlement order will only be effective when it is endorsed by both owners of a joint account, the intermediary cannot disregard the agreement and enforce an order signed by just one of the parties without making itself liable for damages.

First American National Bank v. Christian Foundation Life Insurance Company

(Bond Purchaser) v. (Bond Purchaser)
242 Ark. 678, 420 S.W.2d 912 (1967)

AN ISSUER IS LIABLE TO AN INNOCENT PURCHASER FOR BONDS CONTAINING AN AUTHORIZED FACSIMILE SIGNATURE EVEN THOUGH THE BONDS WERE FRAUDULENTLY PRINTED IN DUPLICATE BY THE ISSUER'S AGENT

■ **INSTANT FACTS** Recipients of church bonds, fraudulently issued in duplicate by the church's agent, sued for a declaratory judgment as to the validity of the bonds.

■ **BLACK LETTER RULE** Issuer is obligated to innocent purchasers for bonds containing authorized facsimile signatures even though bonds were fraudulently issued in duplicate by issuer's agent.

■ **PROCEDURAL BASIS**

Appeal from chancellor's decision that certain original and duplicate bonds were binding obligations of the issuer.

■ **FACTS**

In January 1964, the First Methodist Church of Mena [the "Church"] authorized a $90,000 construction bond issue. The Church hired Institutional Finance ["Institutional"] as the Church's fiscal agent. The Church gave the Church Treasurer's signature to Institutional's Vice-president Joe B. Springfield ["Springfield"] for use as a facsimile signature on the bonds. Springfield ordered bonds numbered 1 through 188 to be printed bearing the facsimile signatures of Springfield and the Church Treasurer. Inexplicably, the total value of the bonds was $94,000. Institutional was able to sell only $45,000 of the bonds to Church members. In July 1964, Institutional's President Lawrence Hayes ["Hayes"] borrowed $25,000 from First American National Bank ["First American"], using $27,000 worth of the Church's bonds as collateral. In February 1965, Hayes fraudulently had $25,000 worth of numbered Church bonds printed. These bonds had the same numbers as those securing Hayes' bank loan. Also in February 1965, Hayes had larger denomination Church bonds printed for sale to Christian Foundation Life Insurance Company ["Christian Life"]. Hayes' fraud was discovered when the duplicate bonds were presented for payment at the Church's bank, Union Bank of Mena [the "Bank"]. UCC § 202-3(c) states: "Except as otherwise provided in the case of certain unauthorized signatures on issue (Section 8–205), lack of genuineness of a security is a complete defense even against a purchaser for value and without notice." Section 8–205 provides that good faith purchasers may rely on signatures "either by a person entrusted by the issuer with the signing of the security or by an employee of such a person or of the issuer itself" even if the signature is unauthorized.

■ **ISSUE**

Is the issuer of an investment security liable to the purchaser for the value of duplicate bonds fraudulently printed by issuer's agent and containing authorized facsimile signatures?

■ **DECISION AND RATIONALE**

(Smith, J.) Yes. Because Christian Life and First American were both purchasers for value of the Church bonds with no notice of fraud or inauthenticity, the Church is liable to both for the value of the

First American National Bank v. Christian Foundation Life Insurance Company (Continued)

bonds. As far as First American knew, Hayes was employed by a Texas church bond dealer. First American did not know that Hayes was associated with Institutional. First American argued that Christian Life was not a good faith purchaser because they purchased the bonds at a 10 to 15 percent discount. This discount was not so low as to cause suspicion. The UCC § 8–205 governs this case. Section 8–205 states that issuers cannot escape liability to good faith purchasers with no notice of wrongdoing because securities have been signed by the issuer or issuer's agent entrusted with responsibility for the signatures. In this case, the Church carelessly entrusted the facsimile signature to Institutional. The Church's bond prospectus named Institutional as the Church's fiscal agent. The Church could have been more cautious by insisting on manual signatures, but did not. Hayes' fraud does not supersede § 8–205. Unlike the common law rule, which would have "held the church liable in contract to one purchaser and in damages to the other" in cases such as this, § 8–205 makes the bonds valid with regard to both purchasers. "[T]he chancellor should have found all bonds held by bona fide purchasers to be binding obligations of the church." Reversed and remanded.

■ DISSENT

(Jones, J.) I would hold that the fraudulently issued bonds are not "genuine" by the standard set forth in UCC § 1–201 (18): "'Genuine' means free of forgery or counterfeiting." According to UCC § 8-202(c), lack of genuineness of a security is a complete defense, even against a bona fide purchaser. Therefore, the Church should not be liable for the duplicate bonds. The majority decision is too broad because it does not protect issuers from an unscrupulous agent, even if the issuers revoke the agent's authority. "[A]s long as such [an unscrupulous] agent could find innocent purchasers and access to a printing press" he could continue to bind the issuer by creating fraudulent bond certificates.

Analysis:

The majority's interpretation of the Code has the effect of protecting the purchaser first and letting the other parties sort out the various liabilities. The dissent takes a different approach. According to the dissent, the majority opinion would give *carte blanche* to the fraud artists to continue producing forged bonds as long as they could find buyers. This, the dissent implies, potentially harms not only the issuer, but more purchasers as well. The dissent raises two issues that are worth considering. First, if the dissent's holding that lack of genuineness is a complete defense, even when the forged securities contained authorized signatures, were to stand, innocent purchasers likely would be left completely unprotected in those cases in which the forger was insolvent or had absconded. Second, the dissent's conclusion that the church should not have been liable for the duplicate bonds implies that the church did nothing wrong in this case. The majority opinion, however, asserts that the church was not completely blameless because it allowed Hayes to use facsimile signatures. Nothing in § 8–210 or § 8–250 indicates that the issuer's negligence or diligence should have any effect on liability, but here again we see the human faces of judges as they try to reach equitable decisions within the lines laid out by the Code.

■ CASE VOCABULARY

FACSIMILE SIGNATURE: An indorsement signature which the signer has authorized to be reproduced on the securities by machine or copier, usually used to avoid signing an enormous number of securities; facsimile signatures are more common on stocks than on bonds.

INNOCENT PURCHASER: Also referred to as a "protected purchaser" in Article 8, this is someone who buys a security for value, with no notice of an adverse claim, and who obtains control of the security; this status is somewhat analogous to a "holder in due course" in Article 3 on negotiable instruments.

ISSUER: The issuer is an entity—a corporation (in the case of equity securities), organization, municipality—that creates securities and offers them for sale; in the case of registered securities, the issuer or issuer's transfer agent must record registration changes.

Jennie Clarkson Home for Children v. Missouri, Kansas and Texas Railway

(Bond Owner) v. (Bond Issuer)
182 N.Y. 47, 74 N.E. 571 (1905)

A BROKER'S INDORSEMENT IS WORTHLESS IF IT DOES NOT GUARANTEE THAT THE SELLER HAS REALLY AUTHORIZED THE SALE

■ **INSTANT FACTS** Defendant issuer of bonds demanded relief against defendant broker who witnessed the unauthorized signature of the registered owner's treasurer on a power of attorney purportedly authorizing the broker to sell the registered owner's bonds.

■ **BLACK LETTER RULE** When a stock broker represents a corporate owner of securities, the broker's indorsement guarantees that a signature purporting to transfer the securities was made by a person with authority to so obligate the corporation.

■ **PROCEDURAL BASIS**

Appeal from an Appellate Division decision affirming a trial court judgment that a transfer agent was liable to the issuer when transfer agent incorrectly guaranteed the identity of a party claiming authority to transfer securities.

■ **FACTS**

A New York charity, the Jennie Clarkson Home for Children ["Jennie"] (P) was registered owner of four bonds issued by the Missouri, Kansas and Texas Railway Company [the "Railway"] (D). Each of the four $1000 par value bonds was secured by the Railway's (D) property, was payable in gold in 1990 and had four percent interest coupons. The bonds "were not transferable after registration, unless made on the books of the railway company by the registered holder, or by his attorney duly authorized, and noted on the bonds." In March 1902, Jennie's (P) treasurer George W. Lessels ["Lessels"] took the bonds from a safe deposit box with the intention of converting them for his benefit. Lessels took the bonds to a stockbroker, Robert Gibson ["Gibson"] (D) of H. Knickerbocker & Co., who told Lessels that the Railway's (D) transfer agent would have to change the registration on the bonds from "Jennie" (P) to "Bearer" in order for Lessels to convert the bonds. To comply with the Railway's (D) requirements for changing the bond registration, Lessels forged a resolution of Jennie's (P) Board of Directors authorizing sale of the bonds. The forged resolution was never passed by Jennie's (P) Board of Directors, did not have Jennie's (P) seal, and was not signed by Jennie's (P) secretary. Lessels also forged a power of attorney authorizing transfer of the bonds. Lessels signed the power of attorney on behalf of Jennie (P). The power of attorney was witnessed by H. Knickerbocker & Co.'s cashier, and was signed for H. Knickerbocker & Co. by Gibson (D). Gibson (D) had these documents sent to the Railway (D), whose transfer agent changed the registration to Bearer. Gibson (D) sold the bonds for Lessels. Lessels absconded with the proceeds of the sale. Jennie (P) sued the Railway (D) for improperly transferring the bond registrations. The Railway (D), in turn, sought relief from Gibson (D) on the grounds that the stock exchange had a rule that an indorsement by a member of the exchange guarantees the signature of the security owner. The trial court held that Gibson (D) was liable to the

Jennie Clarkson Home for Children v. Missouri, Kansas & Texas Railway (Continued)

Railway (D). The Appellate Division affirmed. On appeal, Gibson (D) argued that as a witness to Lessels' signature, he guaranteed that Lessels in fact signed, but not that Lessels had the authority to sign on behalf of Jennie (P).

■ ISSUE

Does the indorsement of a transfer agent who is a member of the stock exchange guarantee that the individual signing on behalf of the security owner corporation is duly authorized to transfer the corporation's securities?

■ DECISION AND RATIONALE

(Haight, J.) Yes. As a member of the stock exchange, Gibson (D)—by witnessing the signature of Lessels—guarantees not only the identity of Lessels, but also his authority to sign on behalf of Jennie (D), the bond owner. If the broker represents an individual, he guarantees not only the genuineness of the owner's signature, but also that the seller is really the owner of the securities. The rule protects purchasers from fraud by persons who do not really own the securities they offer for sale. Purchasers from corporate sellers need the same protection. If a broker's indorsement does not guarantee that the seller has really authorized the sale, then the guarantee is worthless. Brokers acting on behalf of corporate owners of securities are obliged to know their clients and to determine who in the corporation has the power to authorize transfers. It is no excuse that this may take time or delay completion of a securities sale. In the present case, Jennie (P) was not obligated by Lessels' actions because Lessels acted beyond the scope of his authority by signing the power of attorney authorizing transfer of Jennie's (P) securities. Registration of the bonds on the Railway's (D) books protected Jennie (P) in case the bonds were stolen or destroyed. By changing the registration without the proper authorization of Jennie (P), the Railway (D) violated its agreement with Jennie (P). Gibson (D) also knew that the bonds were Jennie's (P) property and could not be transferred without Jennie's (P) authorization. Lessels' fraud did not relieve the Railway (D) or Gibson (D) of their duties not to transfer Jennie's (P) property without Jennie's (P) permission. The issue of whether Gibson (D) is liable to the Railway (D) for his guarantee of Lessels' signature on the power of attorney does not really concern Jennie (P), which has a right to recover its property from the Railway (D) and Gibson (D). From the testimony of brokers and railway transfer agents, the trial court concluded that it was the custom and rule of the stock exchange that a broker's indorsement guaranteed the validity of a signature authorizing transfer of securities. Moreover, the trial court found that it was customary for transfer agents to require a member of the exchange to guarantee signatures on powers of attorney for transfers from corporate registered owners. Gibson (D) signed as a witness to Lessels' signature on the power or attorney and then gave the bonds, the power of attorney and the fraudulent resolution to the transfer agent. Custom dictates that Gibson (D) must be considered a witness to the power of attorney. As explained above, we hold that by witnessing Lessels' signature, Gibson (D) also guaranteed that Lessels was empowered to sign on behalf of Jennie (P). Thus Gibson (D) is liable to the transfer agent. Affirmed.

Analysis:

Although the Code no longer specifies that the guarantor must be a broker, in some markets brokers, commercial banks, and trust companies continue to guarantee signatures on securities. In other ways, *Jennie Clarkson* accurately reflects the law as it is currently codified in § 8–306. The person guaranteeing the signature still guarantees both that the signature is genuine and that the person signing was authorized to sign. The guarantor remains liable to a person dealing with the security who suffers a loss as a result of the inauthenticity of the signature. This case also gives one a practical example of the importance of registering securities. Only the registered owner, here the Jennie Clarkson Home for Children, could redeem the bonds or their coupons or sell the bonds. Fortunately for the Jennie Clarkson Home, the registration and guarantee of signature rules gives it an opportunity to recover its losses, since the case seems to indicate that Lessels successfully absconded.

■ CASE VOCABULARY

INDORSEMENT: As defined in § 8–102(11), a signature made on a registered security or on a transfer form specifically for the purpose of transferring or authorizing transfer (including assignment or redemption) of a security.

REGISTRATION: An entry on the books of the issuer indicating who is entitled to the security; although a registered security may be transferred, the issuer need honor only the owner registered in its books.

TRANSFER AGENT: The individual or office that maintains records of security registration and oversees the issuing of securities for an issuer; the transfer agent may be an employee of the issuer or a separate entity retained by the issuer.

Powers v. American Express Financial Advisors, Inc.

(Entitlement Holder) v. *(Securities Intermediary)*

238 F.3d 414 (4th Cir.2000)

A SECURITIES INTERMEDIARY WHICH TRANSFERS FUNDS PURSUANT TO AN INEFFECTIVE ENTITLEMENT ORDER IS LIABLE TO THE ENTITLEMENT HOLDER FOR DAMAGES RESULTING FROM THE IMPROPER TRANSFER

■ **INSTANT FACTS** Powers (P) filed suit against American Express Financial Advisors (AEFA) (D) when, in contravention of an investment agreement, AEFA (D) permitted her former boyfriend to transfer $86,836.79 from the couple's joint investment account into a bank account from which he then withdrew the entire sum and absconded.

■ **BLACK LETTER RULE** When a securities intermediary has agreed that an entitlement order will only be effective when it is endorsed by both owners of a joint account, the intermediary cannot disregard the agreement and enforce an order signed by just one of the parties without making itself liable for damages.

■ **PROCEDURAL BASIS**

Appeal to the Fourth Circuit Court of Appeals of a federal district court decision granting summary judgment.

■ **FACTS**

In 1994, Powers (P) and D'Ambrosia opened an investment account with American Express Financial Advisors (AEFA) (D). The couple opened the account as joint tenants with right of survivorship and added funds to the account over the next three years. The investment application that the couple used included the following language: "You understand that only one signature is required for redemption requests up to $50,000." In 1997, Powers (P) and D'Ambrosia parted ways. During the period of the separation a letter dated September 26, 1997, was sent to AEFA (D) directing them to transfer the entirety of the funds in the couple's investment account, $86,836.79, to a Prudential Securities account. The letter contained the signatures of both Powers (P) and D'Ambrosia, though Powers (P) later claimed that her signature was forged. A few weeks later, D'Ambrosia sent AEFA (D) a fax, dated October 16, 1997, which contained a memo from D'Ambrosia, a statement of the couple's account at AEFA, and a copy of the September 26 letter. The memo, which had only D'Ambrosia's signature, directed AEFA (D) to transfer the entirety of the couple's funds to a joint bank account held by Powers (D) and D'Ambrosia. AEFA (D) complied with D'Ambrosia's request and wired $86,836.79 to the requested account, from which D'Ambrosia promptly withdrew the funds and absconded. Upon discovering that the money was gone, Powers (P) filed suit against AEFA (D) seeking a recovery of the $86,836.79. In a motion for summary judgment, Powers (P) claimed that AEFA (D) had violated Maryland Commercial Code § 8-507(b), under which a securities intermediary which transfers funds pursuant to an ineffective entitlement order is liable to an entitlement holder for damages resulting from the improper transfer. Specifically, Powers (P) claimed that D'Ambrosia's fax was an ineffective entitlement order because the investment application required the signatures of both account holders when more than $50,000 was to be transferred out of the account. The district court granted Powers' (P) motion for summary judgment and awarded her the amount transferred plus pre-judgment interest. AEFA (D) appealed.

Powers v. American Express Financial Advisors, Inc. (Continued)

■ ISSUE

When a securities intermediary agrees that all holders of a joint financial account must approve an entitlement order before it is carried out, does it make itself liable for damages when it acts upon an order signed by only one of the joint tenants?

■ DECISION AND RATIONALE

(Per Curiam) Yes. The district court held that the fax dated October 16 constituted an ineffective entitlement order. The court recognized that Powers (P) and D'Ambrosia were entitlement holders, and because D'Ambrosia was an entitlement holder, AEFA (D) contended that he was an "appropriate person" to give an entitlement order under UCC § 8–107. The court also noted that when an "appropriate person" issues an entitlement order to an intermediary, the intermediary has a duty to execute the order under UCC § 8-507(a)(2). The court decided, however, that § 8-507(a)(2) cannot be read in a vacuum. The couple's investment application required the signatures of both investors for any redemption request above $50,000. Thus, the court held that when an intermediary has agreed that the "appropriate person" to make an order is both owners of a joint account, both owners must make the order. Because Powers (P), a joint owner, did not authorize the transfer at issue, the district court concluded that the transfer was ineffective. Based on this reasoning, the court granted Powers' (P) motion for summary judgment and concluded that she was entitled to damages caused by the improper transfer of funds. We are persuaded that the district court reached the correct result, and therefore affirm substantially on the court's reasoning.

Analysis:

Under UCC §§ 8–504–8–508, a securities intermediary has a number of obligations or duties with respect to the financial assets that it maintains for an entitlement holder. At issue in the present case is the specific duty of the securities intermediary to comply with an entitlement order made by the entitlement holder. An entitlement order can be defined as an order given by an entitlement holder that requires the securities intermediary to do a specific act with a particular financial asset. In the present case, that order was to transfer the $86,836.79 from the AEFA (D) account to another account held by the parties. The duty to comply with entitlement orders is contained in UCC § 8–507, which reads: "A securities intermediary shall comply with an entitlement order if the entitlement order is originated by the appropriate person, the securities intermediary has had reasonable opportunity to assure itself that the entitlement order is genuine and authorized, and the securities intermediary has had reasonable opportunity to comply with the entitlement order." In the present case, AEFA (D) violated the provisions of this section because it made the transfer of funds when such a transfer was not authorized under the terms of the securities agreement made at the time of the initial funding of Powers's (P) and D'Ambrosia's account.

■ CASE VOCABULARY

EFFECTIVE ENTITLEMENT ORDER: A valid entitlement order, or one which a securities intermediary is required by law to carry out.

ENTITLEMENT HOLDER: A person who holds or has the rights to a security entitlement.

ENTITLEMENT ORDER: An order given by an entitlement holder that requires a securities intermediary to do a specific act with a particular financial asset (such as sell the asset, transfer funds to another account, etc.).

INEFFECTIVE ENTITLEMENT: An invalid entitlement order, or one that a securities intermediary must not carry out.

SECURITIES ACCOUNT: An account to which a financial asset such as a security is or potentially may be credited.

SECURITIES INTERMEDIARY: A party or entity which holds a security or maintains a securities account on behalf of the entitlement holder.

SECURITY ENTITLEMENT: The power to control or exercise the rights that accompany the ownership of a particular financial asset.

CHAPTER FIFTEEN

Documents of Title

Procter & Gamble Distributing Co. v. Lawrence American Field Warehouse Corp.

Instant Facts: Bailor of soy oil sued the warehouse where the oil was stored after the oil disappeared.

Black Letter Rule: (1) A bailee is liable for the unexplained loss of goods for which he has issued a warehouse receipt. (2) When the date of loss or conversion of bailed goods cannot be established, damages are the highest market value of the goods between the date of bailment and the date that bailor becomes aware of the loss or conversion.

Dunfee v. Blue Rock Van & Storage, Inc.

Instant Facts: Bailor sued warehouse for the value of goods lost when a fire at the warehouse.

Black Letter Rule: Bailee may effectively limit his liability by clearly stating limitations "by article or item, or value per unit of weight" on the warehouse receipt, provided that bailor may purchase additional liability.

GAC Commercial Corp. v. Wilson

Instant Facts: Assignee, who took a straight bill of lading from consignor, sued the carrier for nondelivery of goods.

Black Letter Rule: On a straight bill of lading, carrier is liable for misdescription or nondelivery of goods only to the owner of goods, and is not liable to assignee's of the bill of lading.

Cleveland v. McNabb

Instant Facts: Landlord sued tenant for rent owing from farmland and sued other defendants to enforce landlord liens for the value of crops from the farmland.

Black Letter Rule: (1) Holder of a negotiable warehouse receipt acquires title to goods described therein when the warehouse receipts are "duly negotiated." (2) "Duly negotiated" means purchased in good faith, for value, without notice of claims or defenses, in the regular course of business, and not in satisfaction of a money debt.

Agricredit Acceptance, L.L.C. v. Hendrix

Instant Facts: An agricultural lender filed suit against a group of cotton buyers when a cotton grower to which it made a loan to help finance a cotton crop never repaid the loan.

Black Letter Rule: The general rule that a holder to whom a negotiable document of title has been duly negotiated takes priority over an earlier perfected security interest does not apply to duly negotiated electronic warehouse receipts when there has been no entrustment of the goods to another by the secured party.

Rheinberg Kellerei GmbH v. Brooksfield National Bank of Commerce

Instant Facts: Seller sued buyer's bank for failing to give notice of buyer's difficulties in making payments on a wine shipment for which payment was due "on arrival."

Black Letter Rule: Buyer's bank has a duty to inform seller's bank when buyer does not pay an "on arrival" draft presented by buyer's bank, even if the draft is not due at that time.

Procter & Gamble Distributing Co. v. Lawrence American Field Warehousing Corp.

(Bailor) v. (Bailee/Warehouser)
16 N.Y.2d 344, 213 N.E.2d 873, 266 N.Y.S.2d 785 (1965)

THE BURDEN OF PROOF TO EXPLAIN ANY LOSSES OR DAMAGE TO BAILED GOODS IS ON THE PARTY STORING THE GOODS

■ **INSTANT FACTS** Bailor of soy oil sued the warehouse where the oil was stored after the oil disappeared.

■ **BLACK LETTER RULE** (1) A bailee is liable for the unexplained loss of goods for which he has issued a warehouse receipt. (2) When the date of loss or conversion of bailed goods cannot be established, damages are the highest market value of the goods between the date of bailment and the date that bailor becomes aware of the loss or conversion.

■ **PROCEDURAL BASIS**

Appeal from trial court's grant of summary judgment in favor of bailor.

■ **FACTS**

Procter & Gamble Distributing Co. ["P & G"] (P) sold vegetable oils to Allied Crude Vegetable Oil Refining Corp. ["Allied"] "outright on sight draft with a bill of lading attached." Beginning in 1962, P & G (P) began "field warehousing" its oil at Allied's request. Field warehousing involved storing oil in tanks leased by Allied and sublet to Lawrence American Field Warehouse Corp. (D) who acted as a warehouser. Allied would purchase oil from P & G (P) or other producers. The oil was then shipped "to the seller's order, and stored for the seller's account" in Field's (D) tanks. Allied would make a 20% down payment at the time Field's (D) tanks received the oil. Allied paid the "balance by sight draft with a bill of lading attached, or cash in advance of shipment. . ." In March and April of 1963, P & G (P) shipped to its own account over 9,000,000 pounds of soybean oil to be stored in Field's (D) tanks. Field (D) issued warehouse receipts for the oil, and noted on monthly statements that Field (D) was warehousing the oil. Then, the oil disappeared. P& G (P) sued Lawrence (D) for conversion of the missing oil. The trial court granted summary judgment for P & G (P) and awarded it the value of the oil on the day P & G (P) discovered it was missing. On appeal, Field (D) argues that summary judgment was incorrect because there is a "triable issue respecting whether it exercised reasonable care as bailee of this oil [UCC § 7–204]." Field (D) also argues that P & G (P) was obligated to take a share of the products in the tanks to offset its damages. P & G (P) argues that its damages should be the highest market value of the oil during the time between its delivery and the discovery that it was missing.

■ **ISSUE**

Is a bailee who had issued a warehouse receipt liable for the market value of goods that disappear without explanation from bailee's warehouse?

Procter & Gamble Distributing Co. v. Lawrence American Field Warehousing Corp. (Continued)

■ DECISION AND RATIONALE

(Van Voorhis, J.) (1) Yes. Field's (D) warehouse receipts and month-end statements are evidence that Field (D) received and stored P & G's (P) soybean oil. Field (D) may suspect that P & G's (P) oil was stolen prior to arriving at Field's (D) tanks, but "mere suspicion ... is not sufficient to overcome this documentary evidence [the warehouse receipts and monthly reports]." Field (D) cited UCC § 7–204 and § 7–403 in support of its proposition that there is a triable fact in this case. Section 7–204 states that a warehouseman is liable for losses resulting from the warehouseman's "failure to exercise such care ... as a reasonably careful man would exercise under like circumstances ...." Section 7–403 states that the bailee must deliver the goods listed on a warehouse receipt to the consignee, unless the bailee can show that damage or loss occurred for which the bailee is not liable. Case law places the burden of proof on the warehouseman to explain any losses or damage to bailed goods. As the trial court in this case correctly stated, "it is self-contradictory for [Field (D)] simultaneously to assert due care and a total lack of knowledge of what happened." We do not want a decision that would reward bailees' ignorance by letting them off the hook in cases where merchandise in their warehouses just "disappears." Appellate division erred, however, "in directing an assessment of damages and in not awarding to plaintiff the undisputed market value of the [lost] merchandise ...at the time of its delivery ..." In a typical case, damages are calculated as of the date the property was converted. In this case, the conversion date is unknown since no one can determine exactly when the oil disappeared. Thus, the damages should be set at the oil's highest market value between the date that Field (D) issued a warehouse receipt for the oil and the date that P & G (P) discovered that its property was missing. Finally, Field's (D) contention that P & G (P) should accept the contents of Field's (D) tanks as offset for P & G's (P) losses fails because the contents were not vegetable oil, but rather "acid soap stock, fish oil and water." While P & G's (P) soy oil was fungible with the soy oil of other producers, this does not obligate P & G (P) to take completely different commodities in exchange. The judgment is affirmed, but the case is remanded for a calculation of damages per this decision.

Analysis:

This case alerts the future business lawyer to the fact that even in large-scale, routinized transactions, attention to detail is vital. The practitioner who represents the warehouse must advise his client on the level of care required for a warehouseman to avoid liability for loss or damage. Once the warehouse has the bailor's goods, the UCC establishes the standard of care as that of a reasonable person would exercise under similar circumstances. For the lawyer counseling a bailor, *Procter & Gamble* offers two important lessons. First, it is essential for the bailor-client to understand the importance of keeping warehouse receipts as documentation in the case that goods cannot be found or recovered. Second, bailors' attorneys must be aware of the damage rule from *Procter & Gamble*. If the market for the lost or damaged goods is in flux, calculating damages at the highest market value during bailment could be very important to the bailor.

■ CASE VOCABULARY

BAILMENT: The transfer of possession of personal property to another for storage, repairs, or transport; the party giving up possession is the "BAILOR," and the party receiving the property is the "BAILEE."

FUNGIBLE GOODS: Merchandise or commodities so similar in quality to those of another producer that they can be mixed or blended in storage; e.g., oils, gasoline, grains, etc.

Dunfee v. Blue Rock Van & Storage, Inc.

(Owner of Goods/Bailor) v. (Warehouse/Bailee)
266 A.2d 187 (Del.Super.Ct.1970)

BAILEE OWES BAILOR A DUTY OF REASONABLE CARE FOR GOODS RECEIVED, BUT MAY LIMIT LIABILITY FOR LOSS BY CLEARLY STATING LIMITATIONS ON THE WAREHOUSE RECEIPT

■ **INSTANT FACTS** Bailor sued warehouse for the value of goods lost when a fire broke out at the warehouse.

■ **BLACK LETTER RULE** Bailee may effectively limit his liability by clearly stating limitations "by article or item, or value per unit of weight" on the warehouse receipt, provided that bailor may purchase additional liability.

■ **PROCEDURAL BASIS**

Appeal from a trial court jury decision that defendant storage company was liable for goods destroyed in a fire.

■ **FACTS**

Dunfee (P) stored goods in Blue Rock Van & Storage, Inc.'s ["Blue Rock"] (D) warehouse in Wilmington. Following the assassination of Martin Luther King, Jr. in April 1968, riots broke out. During this unrest, a fire at Blue Rock's (D) warehouse destroyed Dunfee's (P) goods. Dunfee (P) sued Blue Rock (D) for the value of her goods. Blue Rock (D) argued that it was not liable because "arson by a public enemy" caused the fire. On the day of the trial, Blue Rock (D) moved to amend its answer by adding that the warehouse receipt limited its liability to $1,000. The warehouse receipt also contained language limiting Blue Rock's (D) liability to ".60 per pound, per article." Dunfee (P) signed the warehouse receipt at the time her goods, weighing 4,340 pounds, were picked up. Aware of the warehouse receipt, Dunfee (P) purchased $4,000 of additional insurance coverage for her goods. Dunfee (P) argued that Blue Rock's (D) attempt to amend its answer was not timely, and that the warehouse receipt did not comply with the content requirements of UCC § 7–202. Dunfee (P) also argued that the ".60 per pound, per article" language must be read to mean that the limitation was by pound and by article. The jury found in favor of Dunfee (P), awarding damages of $5,500.

■ **ISSUE**

Can a bailee effectively limit its liability by stating a limitation on liability "per pound, per article" on its warehouse receipt?

■ **DECISION AND RATIONALE**

(Per Curiam) Yes. Blue Rock's (D) warehouse receipt complied with the terms of § 7–204(2) by fairly describing the limitations on liability and including a provision for additional liability at an increased charge. UCC § 7–204(1) provides that the bailee must exercise "such care in regard to [bailor's goods] as a reasonably careful person would exercise under like circumstances." Section 7–204(2), however, provides that the warehouse may limit its liability by "setting forth a specific liability per article or item, or value per unit of weight." The purpose of § 7–204 is to allow "a bailee [to] limit his liability for loss of goods without impairing his obligation of reasonable care." To be effective, such a limitation must provide that the bailor can, by written request, increase the liability for an extra charge. Section

HIGH COURT CASE SUMMARIES 229

Dunfee v. Blue Rock Van & Storage, Inc. (Continued)

7–204 does not support Dunfee's (D) argument that the ".60 per pound, per article" language must be interpreted to mean that liability is limited by weight *and* by article. Section 7–204 does not require warehouse receipt limitations to be based on either item or weight and not on both. In the present case, Dunfee (P) understood that Blue Rock's (D) liability was limited to $1,000 in any event. Dunfee's (P) purchase of additional insurance supports this finding. For reasons not relevant here, Blue Rock (D) is allowed to amend it amend its answer to include the limitation of liability defense. Dunfee's (P) recovery is appropriately limited.

Analysis:

The court in *Dunfee* was careful to find evidence that the bailor knew of the limitations on the warehouse's liability. It is less clear, however, how the court in *Dunfee* arrived at the particular conclusion that the warehouse's liability was limited to $1,000 in this case. Section 7–204 states that the limitation statement must set forth "a specific liability per article or item, or value per unit of weight, beyond which the warehouseman shall not be liable." The limitation on Blue Rock's receipt—".60 per pound, per article"—is somewhat ambiguous. The court reads it to mean "per article" or "per pound," perhaps because that is the statutory language. The court then finds that regardless of the ".60 per pound, per article" language, both parties understood that the warehouse's liability was limited to $1,000.

G.A.C. Commercial Corp. v. Wilson
(*Commercial Lender*) v. (*Unidentified Party*)
271 F.Supp. 242 (S.D.N.Y. 1967)

A CARRIER IS LIABLE ONLY TO THE OWNER OF GOODS FOR MISDESCRIPTION OR NONDELIVERY OF GOODS DESCRIBED IN A STRAIGHT BILL OF LADING

■ **INSTANT FACTS** Assignee who took a straight bill of lading from consignor, sued the carrier for nondelivery of goods.

■ **BLACK LETTER RULE** On a straight bill of lading, carrier is liable for misdescription or nondelivery of goods only to the owner of goods, and is not liable to assignee's of the bill of lading.

■ **PROCEDURAL BASIS**

Decision on defendant's motion for a judgment on the pleadings.

■ **FACTS**

St. Lawrence Pulp & Paper Mill ["St. Lawrence"] borrowed over $254 thousand from G.A.C. Commercial Corp. ["GAC"] (P). As collateral, GAC took straight bills of lading issued to St. Lawrence, as consignor, by Norwood & St. Law. Railroad ["Norwood"] (D). The bills of lading indicated that St. Lawrence had shipped as yet undelivered products to various consignees. The railroad cars purporting to be carrying these products, however, were empty. Norwood (D) had allowed St. Lawrence to pack and seal freight cars on a spur track and to fill out bills of lading. Norwood's (D) agent signed the bills of lading, but made no indication that Norwood (D) was unaware of the actual contents of the cars. St. Lawrence subsequently went bankrupt. GAC (P) sued Norwood (D) for the value of the bills of lading. Norwood (D) sought a judgment on the pleadings.

■ **ISSUE**

Is a carrier liable to an assignee for issuing straight bills of lading in cases where no goods were delivered to consignee?

■ **DECISION AND RATIONALE**

(Bryan, J.) No. Norwood (D) is not liable to GAC (P) because the straight bills of lading in this case were non-negotiable and GAC (P) was not the "owner" or "consignee" of the goods. Bills of lading issued by a common carrier for interstate commerce are controlled by the Federal Bills of Lading Act 49 U.S.C. § 81, while those in intrastate commerce are governed by the UCC § 7–301. Prior to the federal act, the federal courts would have "held that a carrier was not liable for the act of its agent in issuing a bill of lading for goods where no goods had in fact been received." The federal act now distinguishes between straight bills of lading and order bills of lading. For order bills, the carrier may be liable for damages to a good-faith holder for value in cases where the carrier did not receive the goods by the date shown on the bill of lading. For straight bills, however, the carrier is liable only to the "owner" of the goods. Like straight bills generally, the bills at issue in this case were non-negotiable. GAC (P) was a transferee of the bills, and Norwood (D) owed GAC (P) only those duties it owed to St. Lawrence, the transferor. Since St. Lawrence never delivered any goods, Norwood (D) owed nothing. Moreover, GAC (P) could not be considered the "owner" of the goods described in the straight bills because

GAC Commercial Corp. v. Wilson (Continued)

those goods did not exist. Even a consignee cannot recover from a carrier for non-existent goods because a consignee must demonstrate "its title to specific property." GAC's (P) security interest in the bills does not make GAC (P) an owner of the goods for the purposes of the federal statute. Under the same rationale, GAC (P) cannot recover from Norwood (D) for the intrastate goods either. Although UCC § 7–301 substitutes "consignee" for "owner," the change is immaterial for GAC (P) in this case. This rule makes it dangerous for lenders to take straight bills of lading as security because of potential fraud by shippers. Lenders, however, may require order bills, if they so desire. The federal act anticipates that in the fast-paced world of modern commerce, shippers will load and count goods. Carriers may note "Shipper's weight, load, and count" on a bill of lading to avoid disputes. Nothing in the federal act or code, however, implies liability to carriers for not making such a note. Summary judgment on the pleadings entered for Norwood (D).

Analysis:

GAC Commercial involves non-existent goods. The court in *GAC* reasoned that it is typical for shippers to perform their own loading and counting, and that burdening carriers with responsibility for accurate counts would slow the pace of modern commerce too greatly. It was the shipper in this case who misidentified the contents of the boxcars. This raises two questions. First, why does the court not require the railroad to explicitly state on the bills of lading that the shipper did the loading and is responsible for the "weight, load, and count?" The court's reasoning seems to be simply that the statute does not require the railroad to state any such disclaimer. Second, would the result in *GAC* have been different if it was unclear who was responsible for the loss? In that case, the language disclaiming responsibility for the count would seem to be much more important. Perhaps the most distinguishing feature of *GAC*, however, is the fact that the documents in question were non-transferable "straight bills of lading." The court readily concedes that its interpretation of Federal Bills of Lading Act § 22 and the corresponding UCC provision in § 7–301 provide little protection for holders of "straight bills." The court concludes that this is not a problem, however, because G.A.C. is a sophisticated lender who is now just trying to reach the railroad, the one solvent entity remaining among the potential defendants.

■ CASE VOCABULARY

CONSIGNEE/OWNER: The recipient of goods given by a shipper to a carrier; the UCC uses the term "consignee," while the Federal Bills of Lading Act refers to same party as "owner" of the goods in the bill.

ORDER BILL OF LADING: A bill of lading that indicates that the goods are consigned to the order of the holder of the bill; order bills are negotiable.

STRAIGHT BILL OF LADING: A bill of lading that names the consignee or owner to whom the carrier must deliver the goods; straight bills are non-negotiable.

Cleveland v. McNabb

(*Landlord*) v. (*Tenant*)
312 F.Supp. 155 (W.D.Tenn.1970)

HOLDER OF A WAREHOUSE RECEIPT ACQUIRES TITLE TO GOODS WHEN THE RECEIPT IS "DULY NEGOTIATED" THROUGH GOOD FAITH PURCHASE FOR VALUE AND WITHOUT NOTICE OF DEFENSES

■ **INSTANT FACTS** Landlord sued tenant for rent owing from farmland and sued other defendants to enforce landlord liens for the value of crops from the farmland.

■ **BLACK LETTER RULE** (1) Holder of a negotiable warehouse receipt acquires title to goods described therein when the warehouse receipts are "duly negotiated." (2) "Duly negotiated" means purchased in good faith, for value, without notice of claims or defenses, in the regular course of business, and not in satisfaction of a money debt.

■ **PROCEDURAL BASIS**

Landlord's complaint for recovery of unpaid rent from tenant and enforcement of liens against recipients of tenant's crops.

■ **FACTS**

Jack McNabb ["McNabb"] (D) was a large-scale tenant farmer in Tennessee. McNabb (D) leased land from Dr. W.B. Cleveland ["Cleveland"] (P) on which McNabb (D) grew cotton and soybeans. Tennessee has a statute that gives a landlord a lien on all crops grown on his land up to the amount of rent owed by a tenant-farmer [the "Crop Lien Statute"] (T.C.A. §§ 64–1201 et. seq.), which allows a landlord to apply the lien to a purchaser of his tenant's crops "with or without notice." McNabb (D) took his cotton to a cotton gin. The tickets from the gin show that the cotton was grown on Cleveland's (P) land. After ginning, McNabb (D) took the cotton to a warehouse, which issued negotiable warehouse receipts. McNabb then took these receipts to the U.S. Agricultural Stabilization and Conservation Service ["ASCS"] and left them in exchange for a government loan. The ASCS clerk who executed the loan papers did not ask McNabb (D) where he grew the cotton. The papers indicated that McNabb (D) had said there were no liens against his cotton. McNabb (D) said ASCS had a copy of his lease. Cleveland (P) sued McNabb (D) for unpaid rent. Cleveland (P) also sued recipients of McNabb's (D) crops for enforcement of liens under the Crop Lien Statute. Among those sued under the Crop Lien Statute were the United States (D) and the Commodity Credit Corporation ["CCC"] (D), the branch of the Department of Agriculture that received the warehouse receipts from the ASCS loan transaction. The United States (D) argued that CCC (D) purchased the warehouse receipts in good faith and for value and therefore took the receipts free of Cleveland's (P) lien. UCC § 7–502 provides that a purchaser acquires title to goods described in warehouse receipts when the receipts have been "duly negotiated" as defined in § 7–501 (4). In addition to good faith purchase for value, however, § 7–501 also requires, in relevant part, that the receipts are taken "without notice of any defense . . . or claim," that the negotiation is "in the regular course of business." Cleveland (P) asserts that UCC (D) had notice of Cleveland's (P) lien and that UCC (D) did not receive the receipts in the regular course of business.

HIGH COURT CASE SUMMARIES 233

Cleveland v. McNabb (Continued)

■ ISSUE

Are warehouse receipts for cotton taken as security for a federal agricultural loan "duly negotiated" where cotton was grown by a tenant-farmer and the state has a statute giving landlords liens against tenant's agricultural products?

■ DECISION AND RATIONALE

(Brown, C.J.) No. The warehouse receipts held by CCC (D) were not "duly negotiated" under UCC § 7–501 and thus, CCC (D) did not acquire title to the cotton free of Cleveland's (P) liens. The warehouse receipts were not duly negotiated because CCC (D) had enough information to constitute notice of the landlord's liens on McNabb's (D) cotton. UCC § 1–210 (25) states that a person has "notice" when he has reason to know of a fact in light of "all the facts and circumstances." Several facts in this case give rise to a finding that CCC (D) had notice of the landlord's liens. First, the Department of Agriculture has a regulation providing that cotton taken under the CCC (D) loan program must be free of liens. This regulation obligates ASCS to make inquiry about possible liens on cotton before executing its loans. It would be unreasonable to expect tenant farmers to be completely familiar with statutory liens. Simply asking McNabb (D) about possible liens, therefore, was not sufficient inquiry. ASCS, however, had access to McNabb's (D) lease with Cleveland (P). ASCS also had the warehouse receipts that referenced the ginning tickets, which showed that McNabb (D) grew the cotton on Cleveland's (P) land. Given all the facts and circumstances, CCC (D) cannot be said to have taken the warehouse receipts without notice of Cleveland's (P) liens.

Analysis:

The ambiguities in *Cleveland* arise in the area of what constitutes notice. The UCC articulates a standard for notice akin to a totality of the circumstances test, but like a "knew or should have known" standard as well. In terms of fairness, it is difficult to fault the court's conclusion that the Commodity Credit Corporation and the ASCS should be familiar with state agricultural liens. After all, advancing credit for crops *is* what these large government programs do. On the other hand, it is difficult to imagine that a large-scale, commercial tenant farmer has had no occasion to encounter and understand these liens. It is perhaps not surprising that at the time of the *Cleveland v. McNabb* case—the late 1960s—federal courts would have been somewhat paternalistic with regard to farmers, who even today are considered by many to be "unsophisticated" or "uneducated." Still, it is interesting to consider whether the court would have held another holder to as high a standard of inquiry and research as it did with the government in this case.

■ CASE VOCABULARY

NEGOTIATION: The process of transferring the rights in a document of title; like Article 3 negotiable instruments, negotiation of a document of title payable to a named person requires indorsement and delivery, but negotiation of a bearer document requires only delivery.

Agricredit Acceptance, L.L.C. v. Hendrix

(Lender) v. (Borrower)
82 F.Supp.2d 1379 (S.D.Ga.2000)

THE RULE THAT A HOLDER TO WHOM A NEGOTIABLE DOCUMENT OF TITLE HAS BEEN DULY NEGOTIATED TAKES PRIORITY OVER AN EARLIER PERFECTED SECURITY INTEREST IS NOT AN ABSOLUTE RULE

■ **INSTANT FACTS** An agricultural lender filed suit against a group of cotton buyers when a cotton grower to which it made a loan to help finance a cotton crop never repaid the loan.

■ **BLACK LETTER RULE** The general rule that a holder to whom a negotiable document of title has been duly negotiated takes priority over an earlier perfected security interest does not apply to duly negotiated electronic warehouse receipts when there has been no entrustment of the goods to another by the secured party.

■ **PROCEDURAL BASIS**

Decision by the United States District Court for the Southern District of Georgia on a group of cotton merchants' motion for summary judgment against an agricultural lender.

■ **FACTS**

Thomas Hendrix (D) financed his 1997 cotton crop with a loan from Agricredit Acceptance Corporation (AAC) (P), using the crop as security for the loan. After making the loan, AAC (P) properly perfected its security interest by filing a Security Agreement with the appropriate agency. Hendrix (D) thereafter contracted with Sea Island Cotton Trading (Sea Island) to act as the selling agent, and AAC (P) notified Sea Island of its security interest in the crop. Prior to its sale, the cotton crop was stored in various warehouses, which issued electronic warehouse receipts (EWRs) for the cotton in the name of Sea Island. In 1997 and 1998, a number of merchants (D) purchased Hendrix's cotton. The merchants (D) paid Sea Island, and the EWRs were transferred into their names. Sea Island, however, never paid AAC (P) or Hendrix (D) for the cotton, and, as a result, AAC (P) filed suit against Hendrix (D) and the merchants (D) who had purchased the cotton. In its suit AAC (P) sought foreclosure of its security interest, a writ of possession against anyone in possession of the cotton, and a finding of conversion and an award of damages against the merchants (D). In response, the merchants (D) claimed that the cotton was no longer subject to AAC's (P) security interest because the EWRs were duly negotiated to them by Sea Island and because AAC (P) entrusted the cotton to Hendrix (D) with apparent authority to sell it. That is, the merchants (D) asserted that duly negotiated EWRs have priority over a prior perfected security interest, especially when the secured party entrusts the collateral to the borrower. The merchants (D) filed a motion to dismiss, which was denied, and then a motion for summary judgment.

■ **ISSUE**

Does a duly negotiated electronic warehouse receipt have priority over a prior perfected security interest in the goods when the secured party has not entrusted the goods to another party or acquiesced in the procurement of the document of title?

Agricredit Acceptance, L.L.C. v. Hendrix (Continued)

■ DECISION AND RATIONALE

(Nangle, J.) No. In Georgia a security interest in crops is perfected by the filing of a financing statement. Generally, a perfected security interest takes priority over other liens or claims to property and security interests perfected at a later date. This rule, however, is subject to some exceptions. For example, a buyer in the ordinary course of business takes free of a security interest created by the seller. Additionally, under Article 9, a holder to whom a negotiable document of title has been duly negotiated takes priority over an earlier perfected security interest. A warehouse receipt is a negotiable document of title if it provides that the goods are to be delivered to bearer or to the order of a named person. To be duly negotiated, it must be negotiated to a holder who purchases it in good faith for value in the regular course of business without notice of any defense against or claim to it. A holder to whom a negotiable warehouse receipt has been duly negotiated generally acquires title to the document and the goods and becomes the beneficiary of the warehouse's obligation to deliver the goods. However, per O.C.G.A. § 11-7-503, "[a] document of title confers no right in goods against [one who has a prior] perfected security interest in [the goods] and who neither: (a) [d]elivered or entrusted [the goods] ... to the bailor ... with actual or apparent authority to ship, store, or sell; nor (b) [a]cquiesced to the procurement by the bailor ... of any document of title." The UCC defines entrusted as any delivery and any acquiescence in retention of possession regardless of any condition expressed between the parties. However, Georgia courts have found that this definition only applies to owners of goods as one cannot entrust goods one does not own. The merchants' (D) motion for summary judgment is based on two theories: (1) that the EWRs were duly negotiated to the merchants (D) and their interest in the cotton therefore has priority over AAC's (P) interest; and (2) that AAC (P) waived the priority of its security interest by entrusting the cotton to Hendrix. It is undisputed that the merchants (D) purchased the EWRs for value. As for good faith, AAC (P) does not dispute that the merchants (D) acted with honesty in fact, the statutory definition of good faith. Rather, AAC (P) asserts that good faith requires the performance of a lien check on the cotton prior to purchase. We disagree. This does not end the inquiry, however. The merchants (D) must also be purchasers without notice of any defenses or claims to the EWRs. AAC (P) argues that the merchants' (D) experience with the cotton industry and willful ignorance as to the existence of the liens on the cotton constitute reason to know that AAC's (P) defense to the EWRs existed. While some jurisdictions have required suspicious circumstances for a finding of reason to know, others hold that willful or deliberate indifference to relevant information is a basis for such a finding. The evidence in the record indicates that a genuine issue of fact exists concerning the merchants' (D) notice of AAC's (P) claims. The merchants (D) testified that they do not perform lien searches on cotton. However, when buying directly from the producer or in a state with a central lien filing system, most do perform such searches. Further, when dealing with sales via contract for future delivery, they require the seller to warrant that there are no liens on the cotton. These facts imply that the merchants (D) certainly knew of the possibility of the existence of liens. Whether their failure to search for liens amounts to deliberate indifference or ignorance to their existence, however, is less clear. This is an issue for the jury. Even if the Court finds that the merchants (D) had no notice of AAC's (P) claims to the cotton, this finding would not automatically deem the merchants' (D) claims to be superior. O.C.G.A. § 11-7-503 expressly provides that EWRs confer no rights against security interests existing and perfected prior to the issuance of the EWR where there has been no entrustment or acquiescence on the part of the secured party. The merchants (D) argue that this Court is free to find that AAC (P) entrusted the cotton to Hendrix (D) by leaving it in his possession and allowing him to sell it. However, because Article 1 and Article 7 provide no definition for the term "entrusted," this Court must look to the Georgia courts' interpretation of that term. Because the Georgia courts have held in the context of § 11-2-403 that a secured party who does not own the goods cannot entrust them, this Court must hold similarly in the context of § 11-7-503. Consequently, the Court finds that AAC (P) did not entrust the cotton to Hendrix (D) as a matter of law. AAC (P) may, however, have acquiesced in the procurement of a document of title in the cotton (namely the EWRs) pursuant to § 11-7-303(1)(b). When a bank knows that a farmer is attempting to sell his collateral and it acquiesces in his procurement of documents of title to that collateral, the bank has waived its right to assert its security interest in the collateral. The evidence presently before the Court is not sufficient to support a ruling on this issue. The question of AAC's (P) acquiescence is better left to a jury. Motion for summary judgment denied.

Analysis:

The *Agricredit* court held that the above-stated rule does not apply to duly negotiated electronic warehouse receipts when there has been no entrustment of the goods to another by the secured party and no acquiescence in the procurement of the document of title. In terms of the facts of this case, that means that if AAC (P) cannot be shown to have entrusted the cotton to anyone and does not appear to have acquiesced in the procurement of the electronic warehouse receipts, it can collect from the merchants (D) as the electronic warehouse receipts at issue cannot be said to have been duly negotiated to the merchants (D). The purpose of this exception is to protect those owners of goods, or persons with prior perfected security interests in goods, whose goods or documents of title are wrongfully taken and thereafter duly negotiated to an innocent buyer. In such a case, the original owner is not responsible for the loss of the documents of title and therefore should be permitted to retain his or her documents or goods. On the other hand, if there has been entrustment to another or acquiescence in the procurement of documents of title, it can be said that the original owner is at least partially responsible for the loss and therefore does not deserve to take back property that has been transferred to another. Different jurisdictions potentially employ different definitions of the term entrusted, or, at least, have potentially different views on who can entrust goods to another, as is demonstrated by the fact that, in the present case, Georgia law is slightly different than a potentially relevant section of the Uniform Commercial Code.

■ CASE VOCABULARY

PERFECTED SECURITY INTEREST: A security interest that has been validated against and therefore takes precedence over the claims of other potential creditors.

SECURITY INTEREST: A property interest created for the purpose of guaranteeing the performance of an obligation, such as the repayment of a debt.

WRIT OF POSSESSION: A written court order issued or sought for the purpose of recovering possession of specific property.

WAREHOUSE RECEIPT: A document of title to goods being stored with a third party, generally in a warehouse.

Rheinberg Kellerei GmbH v. Brooksfield National Bank of Commerce

(*German Bank*) v. (*American Bank*)
901 F.2d 481 (5th Cir.1990)

BUYER'S BANK HAS A DUTY TO INFORM SELLER'S BANK THAT BUYER DID NOT PAY AN "ON ARRIVAL" DRAFT AT THE TIME BUYER'S BANK PRESENTED IT, EVEN IF THE GOODS HAVE NOT YET ARRIVED

■ **INSTANT FACTS** Seller sued buyer's bank for failing to give notice of buyer's difficulties in making payments on a wine shipment for which payment was due "on arrival."

■ **BLACK LETTER RULE** Buyer's bank has a duty to inform seller's bank when buyer does not pay an "on arrival" draft presented by buyer's bank, even if the draft is not due at that time.

■ **PROCEDURAL BASIS**

Appeal from a District Court decision holding that the American bank was not liable to German bank because the American bank had no duty to inquire about delivery of goods at issue.

■ **FACTS**

In January 1986, an American company, J & J Wine ["J & J"], ordered a shipment of wine from Rheinberg Kellerei GmbH ["Rheinberg"] (P). Frank Sutton & Co. ["Sutton"], an importer, arranged the deal. For this transaction, Edekabank—Rheinberg's (P) bank—sent a letter of collection, bill of lading and invoices to J & J's bank, Brooksfield National Bank of Commerce ["NBC"] (D). NBC (D) passed the letter, bill of lading and invoices on to J & J on March 27. The letter of collection stated that payment was due on receipt of the goods, which the invoices estimated would arrive early in April. The letter, in somewhat broken English, instructed NBC (D) to notify Sutton "in case of any difficulty of lack payment." In fact, the wine arrived on March 31. J & J never told NBC (D) that the wine arrived. J & J told NBC (D) that they could not pay and asked NBC (D) to hold the letter while J & J got together the money. Sutton told NBC (D) that the wine was still unclaimed at Houston harbor in May. NBC (D), in turn, sought instructions from Edekabank. [The wine actually sat out in metal containers until U.S. Customs auctioned it off. If J & J had consumed it, they might have had some excuse!] J & J went out of business. Rheinberg (P) brought suit against NBC (D) for negligently failing to tell Rheinberg (P) that J & J could not or would not pay. The District Court held for NBC (D) on the grounds that NBC (D) did not know that the wine had arrived, and therefore, did not know that J & J was in default. The District Court entered a take-nothing judgment in NBC's (D) favor. Rheinberg (P) appealed, arguing that the letter of collection and the International Rules for Collection [the "Rules"], properly construed, held NBC (D) liable. "Article 20 (iii)(c) of the Rules states ... collecting bank ... must send without delay advice on non-payment or advice of non-acceptance to the bank from whom the collecting order was received ...."

■ **ISSUE**

Do the instructions of a letter of collection and the International Rules for Collection obligate a buyer's bank to notify seller's bank of buyer's difficulties in payment only when buyer's bank has knowledge of buyer's default?

Rheinberg Kellerei GmbH v. Brooksfield National Bank of Commerce (Continued)

■ DECISION AND RATIONALE

(Garza, J.) No. Even though NBC (D) did not know that the goods had arrived, the letter of collection and the Rules created a duty for NBC (D) to inform Edekabank of any difficulties in collecting J & J's payment. The District court erred in finding that the letter called for NBC (D) to notify Sutton only in case of J & J's default. The Rules state that special instructions in letters of collection should be "complete and precise." Even though the letter could have been clearer, it was sufficient to alert NBC (D) to notify Sutton in case of any "difficulty" in payment. NBC (D) argues that it did not breach its duty under Article 20 (iii)(c) because it did not have actual notice of the wine's arrival. Essentially, this argument calls for the court to limit Article 20 (iii)(c) to apply only to cases where the buyer's bank has actual notice of buyer's default. The Rules serve the same function for international transactions that our UCC does domestically. UCC § 4–502 applies to "on arrival" drafts of the type at issue here. Under § 4–502, NBC (D) would have had a duty to notify Edeka when NBC (D) presented J & J with the "on arrival" draft on March 27 and J & J failed to pay at that time. Under the UCC, it does not matter that J & J would not yet have been in default or that the goods had not yet arrived; NBC (D) would still have had a duty to show "due care" by informing the seller's bank. Since the UCC and the Rules share this requirement of due care, we hold that the Rules have the same notice requirement as § 4–502. Without this interpretation, buyer's banks may try to avoid liability by remaining willfully ignorant of situations triggering their client's obligations to pay. Damages in this case are governed by UCC § 2–709(1), which states that seller may recover the price of goods lost or damaged after risk has passed to the seller. Risk of loss passed to J & J, in this case, when the wine arrived in Houston. Rheinberg (P) may recover the contract price and, under § 2-709(1)(a), the unpaid freight costs incidental to the loss. NBC's (D) damages should be offset by the auction price of the wine. The District Court used UCC § 2–708 to calculate damages. That section, "which figures damages as the difference between market value *at the time and place of tender* and contract price, plus incidental damages," does not apply in our case since the wine's value had decreased due to the delay before its sale. Reversed and remanded for calculation of damages.

Analysis:

The court here decided that the goals of the International Rules for Collection had the same purpose and policy as the corresponding provisions of the domestic UCC. Thus, the court concluded that a domestic financial institution should have the same obligations in international transactions as they would in domestic business. This holding fashions an equitable resolution of the present case. Some reading the decision might argue that it was unfair to hold NBC (the buyer's bank) liable under either statute, since the debt was really owed by J & J (the buyers). The statutes, however, actually keep the burden on financial institutions quite low by requiring only that they communicate to seller's bank that the buyer is having difficulty making payments. Like many of the rules governing documents of title, this kind of communication or notice requirement is necessary to prevent parties at various levels of complex transactions form avoiding liability simply by hiding their heads in the sand. All in all, the communication requirement on buyer's bank is easy to meet, but as the *Rheinberg* case reminds us, essential to avoid liability.

■ CASE VOCABULARY

"ON ARRIVAL" DRAFTS: A type of documentary draft that becomes payable after presentment and upon the arrival of the goods covered by the draft.

CHAPTER SIXTEEN

Letters of Credit

Voest–Alpine Trading Co. v. Bank of China

Instant Facts: A lawsuit arose when a bank refused to honor a letter of credit because of purported discrepancies between the letter and the presentation documents.

Black Letter Rule: The issuer of a letter of credit must honor a presentation of documents that appears on its face to comply with the terms and conditions of the letter of credit, and if the issuing bank chooses not to honor the presentation documents, it must provide a notice of refusal within seven banking days of receipt of the documents.

Sztejn v. Henry Schroder Bank Corp.

Instant Facts: After receiving a shipment of bogus goods, a merchant sought to restrain the payment of drafts under a letter of credit issued upon the merchant's application to secure the purchase price of the goods.

Black Letter Rule: Where the seller's fraud has been called to the bank's attention before the drafts and documents have been presented for payment, the principle of the independence does not prevent the bank from dishonoring the presentation.

Intrinsic Values Corp. v. Superintendencia De Administracion Tributaria

Instant Facts: A defaulting seller sought to have a court-ordered injunction dissolved which the proposed buyer obtained after the seller breached the sales contract.

Black Letter Rule: If a party claims that payment under a letter of credit would aid the beneficiary in facilitating a material fraud on the issuer or applicant, and can demonstrate that it is more likely than not to succeed under its claim, a court should enjoin payment.

Voest–Alpine Trading Co. v. Bank of China

(Payee) v. (Payor)

167 F.Supp.2d 940 (S.D.Tex.2000)

LETTERS OF CREDIT AND PRESENTATION DOCUMENTS ARE CONSIDERED TO BE CONSISTENT WHEN ALL OF THE DOCUMENTS CLEARLY RELATE TO THE SAME TRANSACTION

■ **INSTANT FACTS** A lawsuit arose when a bank refused to honor a letter of credit because of purported discrepancies between the letter and the presentation documents.

■ **BLACK LETTER RULE** The issuer of a letter of credit must honor a presentation of documents that appears on its face to comply with the terms and conditions of the letter of credit, and if the issuing bank chooses not to honor the presentation documents, it must provide a notice of refusal within seven banking days of receipt of the documents.

■ **PROCEDURAL BASIS**

Decision of the United States District Court for the Southern District of Texas following a 5-day bench trial.

■ **FACTS**

On June 23, 1995, Voest-Alpine Trading USA Corporation (Voest) (P) entered into a contract with Jiangyin Foreign Trade Corporation (JFTC) in which Voest (P) agreed to sell JFTC 1,000 metric tons of styrene monomer. JFTC then obtained a letter of credit through the Bank of China (BOC) (D) for the purposes of paying Voest (P), a letter which contained numerous typographical errors and misspellings. Following the execution of the contract, the market price of styrene monomer dropped significantly and JFTC asked for but was denied a reduction in the price. After the goods were shipped, Voest (P) presented the documents specified in the letter of credit to Texas Commerce Bank (TCB), the presenting bank. TCB then forwarded the documents to BOC (D) seeking payment. Shortly thereafter, on August 11, 1995, BOC (D) sent a telex to TCB stating that it would not pay because of the existence of discrepancies between the presentation documents and the letter of credit. TCB responded that the discrepancies were not an adequate basis to refuse payment and requested that BOC (D) honor its agreement. BOC (D) continued to refuse payment and a lawsuit was filed.

■ **ISSUE**

Is the issuer of a letter of credit required to honor a presentation of documents that appears on its face to comply with the terms and conditions of the letter of credit?

■ **DECISION AND RATIONALE**

(Gilmore, J.) Yes. The letter of credit is a method of payment that allows a buyer to tap into the resources of a superior credit source. A typical letter of credit transaction consists of three contracts: first, the issuing bank contracts with a customer to issue the letter; second, the issuing bank contracts with the party receiving the letter; and third, the customer who procured the letter contracts with the party receiving it. These contracts are independent of one another, and, as such, the issuing bank must pay on a draft properly presented by a beneficiary without reference to the rights or obligations of

Voest–Alpine Trading Co. v. Bank of China (Continued)

the parties to the underlying contract. The issuing bank need only make a facial examination of the presenting documents to determine whether the terms of the letter of credit have been complied with, however in doing so the bank bears the risk of any misinterpretation of the beneficiary's demand for payment. The current law requires an issuer to honor a presentation that, as determined by the standard practice of financial institutions that regularly issue letters of credit, appears on its face to comply with the terms and conditions of the letter of credit. In this case, in the letter itself the parties adopted the Uniform Customs and Practices for Documentary Credits 500 (UCP), a compilation of internationally accepted commercial practices, as the governing authority. Accordingly, we must look to the UCP for guidance in analyzing whether BOC's (D) actions were appropriate. BOC (D) claims that its August 11 telex to TCB constituted notice of refusal under UCP Article 14(d). Voest (P) disagrees, arguing that there is no clear statement of refusal. According to Article 14(d), if the issuing bank chooses not to honor the presentation documents, it must provide a notice of refusal within seven banking days of receipt and the notice must reference all discrepancies and state the disposition of the rejected documents. Here, BOC's (D) notice is deficient because it does not state that it is actually rejecting the documents or refusing to honor the letter of credit. This omission is compounded by the statement that BOC (D) would contact the applicant to determine if it would waive the discrepancies. Within the framework of Article 14, this additional piece of information holds open the possibility of acceptance upon waiver and indicates that BOC (D) has not refused the documents. BOC first mentions the possibility of refusal in an August 19 telex. Even if this second telex was sent as a notice of refusal, it came too late as it was not within the seven banking days allotted by the UCP. Accordingly, BOC (D) did not provide appropriate notice of refusal and is thus precluded from claiming that the documents are not in compliance with the terms and conditions of the letter of credit. On a different note, the UCP requires that the notice of refusal contain a list of discrepancies, and BOC's August 11 telex does contain such a list. We will now analyze those discrepancies. Voest (P) claims that these discrepancies are mere technicalities and typographical errors that do not warrant rejection of the documents. Voest (P) further contends that if the whole of the documents obviously related to the transaction covered by the letter of credit, the issuing bank must honor it. BOC (D) argues that the discrepancies were significant and that if the documents contain discrepancies on their face, it is justified in rejecting them. There are a range of interpretations regarding the standard banks should employ in examining document presentations for compliance. The most restrictive approach is to require that the presentation documents be a mirror image of the requirements. Second, there are also cases that support rejection only where the discrepancies are such that it would create a risk for the issuer if the bank accepted the presentation documents. A third standard analyzes the documents for risk to the applicant. The mirror image approach is troublesome because it absolves the bank reviewing the documents of any responsibility to use common sense to determine if the documents are related to the transaction or even to review an entire document in the context of the others presented. On the other hand, the second and third approaches employ a determination of harm standard that is too unwieldy. Such an analysis would improperly require the bank to evaluate risks that it might suffer or that might be suffered by the applicant and could undermine the independence of the three contracts that underlie the letter of credit payment scheme by forcing the bank to look beyond the face of the presentation documents. A more moderate standard lies within the UCP and the opinions issued by the International Chamber of Commerce Banking Commission (ICCBC). One of the opinions defined the term "consistency" between the letter of credit and the presentation documents to mean that the whole of the documents must obviously relate to the same transaction or bear a rational link to each other. Under this standard, the issuing bank must examine a document in light of all documents presented and use common sense but need not evaluate risks or go beyond the face of the documents. In this case, BOC's (D) listed discrepancies will be analyzed under this standard. First, BOC (D) claimed that the beneficiary's name in the presentation documents differed from the letter of credit, which had an inverted name. While the names did differ slightly, the inverted name bore obvious links to the documents presented by Voest (P). Additionally, the other documents bear the correct name and the addresses on all documents are identical. As such, this is not a discrepancy that warrants rejection of the presentation documents. Second, BOC (D) argues that the set of originals of the bill of lading should have been stamped "original" rather than "duplicate" and "triplicate," which is how they were stamped. Neither the letter of credit nor any provision in the UCP requires such stamping, and the ICCBC expressly ruled that a failure to label bills of lading as originals did not justify refusal. Third, BOC (D) claimed that the failure to stamp the packing list documents as "original" was a discrepancy.

Again, these documents are clearly originals and there is no requirement in the letter of credit or the UCP that original documents be marked as such. Fourth, BOC (D) argues that the date of the survey report is after the bill of lading and is therefore discrepant. The report may have been issued after the bill of lading, but it is clear that the survey itself was conducted before the ship departed. Fifth, BOC (D) claims that the letter of credit number listed in the beneficiary's certified copy of the fax is wrong, as an extra digit was added. Adding the letter of credit number to the document was gratuitous and in the numerous other places in the documents that the letter of credit was referenced by number, it was incorrect only in one place. Moreover, the seven other pieces of information contained in the document were correct. Finally, BOC (D) claims that the wrong destination is listed in the certificate of origin and the beneficiary's certificate as the city Zhangjiagang is misspelled in one of the certificates. The other information contained in the document was correct, and the document as a whole bears an obvious relationship with the transaction. The misspelling of the destination is not a basis for dishonor of the letter. The Court finds in favor of Voest (P).

Analysis:

One important duty that the issuer of a letter of credit must recognize is the duty to properly inspect the presentation documents before making payment on the letter of credit. In carrying out this duty, the issuer makes sure that the documents are in order and that the seller of the goods and beneficiary of the letter has acted in conformance with the terms and conditions of the letter of credit. As this case makes clear, if the issuer does not carefully perform this important duty, it can be held liable for any losses that result to the buyer and applicant for the letter. On a different note, the *Voest* opinion briefly addresses the issue of how strictly an issuing bank examines and compares the presentation documents with the letter of credit prior to adhering to or rejecting a demand for payment. The position that the *Voest* court adopts is not necessarily the majority position and, in fact, courts have adopted standards that span the entire spectrum from very strict comparison to a more lax comparison.

■ CASE VOCABULARY

APPLICANT: The party, usually a buyer of goods, who applies for a letter of credit to be issued on its behalf.

BENEFICIARY: The party, usually a seller of goods, who receives payment under a properly presented letter of credit.

ISSUING BANK: A bank that issues a letter of credit.

LETTER OF CREDIT: A financial instrument through which the issuer of the letter, generally a bank, promises to recognize and make payment on a draft or other demand for payment when that demand is made by a third party.

PRESENTATION DOCUMENTS: Documents such as invoices, inspection certificates, and others presented to the issuer of a letter of credit for the purpose of procuring payment under the letter.

PRESENTING BANK: A non-payor bank which presents a negotiable instrument to the proper entity for payment.

STYRENE: A liquid unsaturated hydrocarbon that is used in making synthetic rubber, resins, and plastics.

Sztejn v. Henry Schroder Bank Corp.

(*Letter of Credit Applicant*) v. (*Letter of Credit Issuer*)
177 Misc. 719, 31 N.Y.S.2d 631 (Sup.Ct.1941)

AN ISSUER OF A LETTER OF CREDIT MAY REFUSE TO HONOR IT IF THE BENEFICIARY HAS DEFRAUDED THE APPLICANT OR THE ISSUER

■ **INSTANT FACTS** After receiving a shipment of bogus goods, a merchant sought to restrain the payment of drafts under a letter of credit issued upon the merchant's application to secure the purchase price of the goods.

■ **BLACK LETTER RULE** Where the seller's fraud has been called to the bank's attention before the drafts and documents have been presented for payment, the principle of the independence does not prevent the bank from dishonoring the presentation.

■ **PROCEDURAL BASIS**

Motion to dismiss a state court action on the ground that the plaintiff has failed to state a cause of action.

■ **FACTS**

Mr. Sztejn (P) and his associate contracted with Transea Traders, Ltd. (Transea) (D), an Indian corporation, for the purchase of certain bristles. Mr. Sztejn (P) then contracted with J. Henry Schroder Banking Corporation (Schroder) (D) for the issuance of an irrevocable letter of credit to Transea. The letter provided that drafts by Transea for a portion of the purchase price would be paid by Schroder upon shipment of the bristles and presentation of an invoice and bill of lading. Transea (D) placed fifty crates filled with cow hair, and other worthless material on board a steamship, procuring a bill of lading from the steamship company. Transea (D) then drew a draft under the letter of credit to the order of Chartered Bank (D), delivering the draft and the documents to the same. Chartered Bank (D) then presented the draft and accompanying documents to Schroder (D) for payment. Mr. Sztejn (P) sought to prevent Schroder (D) from honoring the drafts and have the letter of credit declared null and void.

■ **ISSUE**

May a bank refuse to honor drafts drawn on a letter of credit in an effort to prevent a fraud from being perpetrated on the applicant?

■ **DECISION AND RATIONALE**

(Shientag, J.) Yes. Where the seller's fraud has been called to the bank's attention before the drafts and documents have been presented for payment, the principle of the independence does not prevent the bank from dishonoring the presentation. It is well established that a letter of credit is independent of the contract between the seller and the buyer. As a general rule banks are not permitted to delay paying drafts drawn on letters of credit on the ground that the merchandise shipped is inadequate. But this rule presupposes that the documents accompanying the draft are genuine and conform in terms to the requirements of the letter of credit. The fact that a bank is sheltered from liability if it pays a draft before receiving notice of the seller's fraud, does not prevent it from refusing to honor payment after

Sztejn v. Henry Schroder Bank Corp. (Continued)

receiving such notice. No hardship is caused by permitting a bank to refuse payment where fraud is claimed, where the merchandise is bogus, where the draft and documents are in the hands of one who is not a holder in due course, where the bank has been given notice of the fraud before presentment, and where the bank does not wish to pay until the parties have adjudicated their dispute. Because this court must assume that Chartered Bank (D) is not a holder in due course, the motion to dismiss is denied.

Analysis:

This case was decided well before the UCC was drafted, but presents the second of the two most litigated issues in the area of letters of credit. The most important exception to the independence principle—the notion that a letter of credit is wholly separate from the underlying commercial transaction—relates to enjoining payment of drafts drawn on a letter of credit on the ground of fraud by the beneficiary. It is obvious that the whole point of letters of credit is to generate the expectation that payment will be made upon the presentation of documents. Thus, a broad reading of the fraud exception threatens the commercial viability of letters of credit. Section 5–109 now addresses the issue of fraud. It allows, but does not require, an issuing bank to refuse payment if the documents are forged or materially fraudulent, or in order to prevent the beneficiary from perpetrating a material fraud on the issuer or the applicant. But the section requires the issuer to pay the draft if it is presented by certain good faith holders, i.e., *a nominated person*, a *confirmer*, et al. Notice that the fraud must also be material, which raises the applicant's burden of proof, and the fraud must be committed by the beneficiary.

Intrinsic Values Corp. v. Superintendencia De Administracion Tributaria

(*Defaulting Seller*) v. (*Intended Buyer*)
806 So.2d 616 (Fla.App.2002)

THE LAW PROTECTS AGAINST MATERIAL FRAUD IN THE PRESENTMENT AND HONORING OF LETTERS OF CREDIT

■ **INSTANT FACTS** A defaulting seller sought to have a court-ordered injunction dissolved which the proposed buyer obtained after the seller breached the sales contract.

■ **BLACK LETTER RULE** If a party claims that payment under a letter of credit would aid the beneficiary in facilitating a material fraud on the issuer or applicant, and can demonstrate that it is more likely than not to succeed under its claim, a court should enjoin payment.

■ PROCEDURAL BASIS

Appeal to the Florida Court of Appeals of a trial court's denial of a motion to dissolve a temporary injunction.

■ FACTS

Superintendencia de Administracion Tributaria (Superintendencia) (P), Guatemala's tax administration agency, contracted to purchase license plates, decals, and identification cards from Intrinsic Values Corporation (Intrinsic) (D). As a part of the transaction, the Bank of Guatemala issued irrevocable letters of credit with Intrinsic (D) as the beneficiary and First Union National Bank and Barclays Bank as the confirming banks. After Intrinsic (D) breached the contract, Superintendencia (P) petitioned a Guatemalan court for and received an injunction against payment on the letter of credit. After that, Superintendencia (P) filed suit in Florida seeking to prevent the confirming banks from honoring the letter. In doing so, Superintendencia (P) claimed that it had canceled the contract because of non-performance, and that any honoring of a presentment by Intrinsic (D) would facilitate a material fraud. An injunction was issued, Intrinsic (D) sought to have it dissolved, and the trial court ruled against Intrinsic (D). Intrinsic (D) then appealed.

■ ISSUE

If a party is able to demonstrate that payment on a letter of credit would facilitate a material fraud against the applicant or issuer, is a court permitted to enjoin payment?

■ DECISION AND RATIONALE

(Shevin, J.) Yes. Superintendencia (P) presented two bases for the injunction: (1) presentment would result in a material fraud; and (2) the principle of comity supports the injunction. Florida Statutes § 675.109(2) provides: "If an applicant claims that . . . [the] honor or . . . presentation [of a document] would facilitate a material fraud by the beneficiary on the issuer or applicant, a court . . . may . . . enjoin the issuer from honoring a presentation . . . only if the court finds that: (d) On the basis of the information submitted to the court, the applicant is more likely than not to succeed under its claim of . . . material fraud." Superintendencia (P) demonstrated that honoring a presentation would assist the

Intrinsic Values Corp. v. Superintendencia De Administracion Tributaria (Continued)

beneficiary in facilitating a material fraud on the issuer or applicant. The record demonstrates that Intrinsic (D) did not perform its obligations under the contract; Superintendencia (P) appropriately notified Intrinsic (D) of its cancellation and obtained an injunction against payment by the issuing bank; and Superintendencia (P) filed suit to prevent Intrinsic (D) from committing a material fraud by presenting documents for payment per the letter of credit. Superintendencia (P) also demonstrated that it would more likely than not succeed on the material fraud claim. The UCC Comment to § 675.109 addresses the propriety of awarding an injunction in this case. It reads: "Material fraud by the beneficiary occurs only when the beneficiary has no colorable right to expect honor and where there is no basis in fact to support such a right to honor." Here, Intrinsic (D) was aware that the contract had been cancelled prior to presentment. Under these circumstances, Intrinsic's (D) demand for payment had no basis in fact. Thus, the facts demonstrate the possibility of a fraud so serious that it would be unjust to permit Intrinsic (D) to obtain the money. Section 675.109, then, contemplates the issuance of an injunction. On this basis the motion to dissolve the injunction was properly denied. The temporary injunction is also properly granted under principles of comity. A foreign decree is entitled to comity where the parties have been given notice and the opportunity to be heard, where the foreign court had original jurisdiction, and where the foreign decree does not offend public policy. In the present case, all of these safeguards were met by the Guatemalan court and therefore its injunction must be given comity. The trial court properly enjoined payment on the letter of credit.

Analysis:

Intrinsic Values Corp. stands for the narrow yet significant principle that an issuer of a letter of credit has a legal duty to refuse payment when making payment would work a material fraud on the issuer or the applicant for the letter. This principle is the most significant exception to the independence principle, which holds that a bank's obligation to a beneficiary under a letter of credit is independent of the beneficiary's performance on the underlying contract. The holding of *Intrinsic* is an exception to the independence principle, because it forces the issuer to consider whether performance has in fact been made (or not made) on the underlying sales contract. The present case is a very basic example of why the issuer would not want to pay on the letter of credit. Clearly, Intrinsic (D) was looking to get paid for doing nothing-an obvious fraud.

■ CASE VOCABULARY

CONFIRMING BANK: A bank that agrees to honor a letter of credit issued by another bank or confirms that such a credit will be honored by the issuer or a third bank.

INDEPENDENCE PRINCIPLE: Principle of law applicable to letters of credit which holds that a bank's obligation to a beneficiary under a letter of credit is independent of the beneficiary's performance or lack thereof on the underlying sales contract.

PRESENTMENT: The presentation of documents to an issuer of a letter of credit or a confirming bank in an attempt to obtain payment under the letter.

CHAPTER SEVENTEEN

Introduction to Secured Transactions

Benedict v. Ratner

Instant Facts: After the Hub Carpet Company was adjudicated bankrupt, the trustee began collecting the company's accounts. Ratner (D) filed a petition as a creditor claiming that the accounts so collected had been assigned to him prior to the bankruptcy and demanding that the trustee pay over all collected amounts to him.

Black Letter Rule: An assignment of accounts that leaves the assignor with complete discretion as to the disposition of the proceeds is void.

Benedict v. Ratner
(*Trustee*) v. (*Creditor*)
268 U.S. 353, 45 S.Ct. 566 (1925)

AN ASSIGNMENT OF ACCOUNTS IS FRAUDULENT IF THE ASSIGNOR RETAINS UNRESTRICTED DOMINION OVER THE PROCEEDS

■ **INSTANT FACTS** After the Hub Carpet Company was adjudicated bankrupt, the trustee began collecting the company's accounts. Ratner (D) filed a petition as a creditor claiming that the accounts so collected had been assigned to him prior to the bankruptcy and demanding that the trustee pay over all collected amounts to him.

■ **BLACK LETTER RULE** An assignment of accounts that leaves the assignor with complete discretion as to the disposition of the proceeds is void.

■ **PROCEDURAL BASIS**

Grant of certiorari to examine an appellate affirmation of a District Court decision holding that the assignment of accounts was valid and was not fraudulent as to other creditors.

■ **FACTS**

The Hub Carpet Company entered into an agreement with Ratner (D) on May 23, 1921 by which Hub assigned to Ratner (D) all present and future accounts as collateral for certain loans. A list of the accounts outstanding at the time of the agreement was given to Ratner (D) and similar lists were provided to him every month. Under the terms of the agreement, Ratner (D) had the right to require all collections to be applied to the repayment of his loans at any time. However, until he did so, the company was allowed to use the monies it collected on the accounts in any way it deemed necessary. Hub continued to carry on its ordinary business and to incur indebtedness with no efforts made to repay the loans. There was no requirement that Hub make any effort to repay the loan or to account to Ratner (D) in any way unless Ratner (D) made an appropriate demand upon it. The arrangement was supposed to be kept secret. On September 17, 1921 Ratner (D) demanded that the proceeds of certain accounts be paid over to him and the company complied. On September 26, 1921, the company was adjudicated bankrupt in involuntary proceedings. Benedict (P) was named first as receiver and then as trustee. He began collecting the payments on the accounts receivable. Ratner (D) filed a petition with the court demanding that Benedict (P) turn over all the payments collected on the accounts, claiming that the monies belonged to him under the Agreement. Benedict (P) filed a cross-petition claiming that the original assignment was void under New York law and that the monies paid to Ratner (D) pursuant to his September 17 request constituted a voidable preference under the Bankruptcy Act. The District Court ruled that the assignment was valid and that Ratner (D) had a perfected interest in the accounts that was superior to the trustee's (Benedict's (P)) interest. The District Court ordered that the accounts collected be applied first to the repayment of Ratner's (D) outstanding loans and denied Benedict's (P) cross-petition. The Circuit Court of Appeals affirmed the District Court's order and Benedict (P) petitioned the United States Supreme Court for a writ of certiorari.

Benedict v. Ratner (Continued)

■ ISSUE

Is an assignment of accounts that allows the assignor to retain unrestricted control over the account proceeds a valid assignment?

■ DECISION AND RATIONALE

(Brandeis, J.) No. An assignment of accounts that provides that the assignor retains complete dominion over the proceeds is fraudulent in law. Under New York Law, a transfer of property as security that reserves to the transferor unrestricted control and dominion over the property is void as to creditors. The question in this case is whether this rule, which applies to chattels, also applies to an assignment of intangible book accounts. Although the New York Court of Appeals has not considered the question, we believe that the rule applies whether the collateral is accounts or chattels. If a party purports to transfer ownership of such items while at the same time retaining all the incidents of ownership, i.e. the ability to dispose of the property or to use the proceeds as he sees fit, the transfer is void as to creditors. Such a transfer creates the illusion that the party is the legal owner of the property, while in fact he is not. This is akin to the doctrine of ostensible ownership, which Ratner (D) argues is inapplicable to accounts. The doctrine, which usually applies to real or personal property, raises a presumption of fraud when property is sold to a party but the seller retains possession and control over it. The presumption may be avoided by recording the sale or mortgage in the appropriate recording office. We assume that this doctrine does not apply to an assignment of accounts, because there are no statutes governing the recording of a sale or assignment of accounts. Regardless, we still find that the New York rule stated above is applicable to accounts. In this case, the rule rests not on apparent ownership because of possession retained but on a lack of ownership because of dominion retained. A party that assigns its accounts to another but retains the ability to collect and control the proceeds has not made a valid assignment. The party's ability to retain unrestricted dominion over accounts that no longer belong to it is inconsistent with a true assignment. Instead, such an arrangement is fraudulent as to outside creditors. There is an analogous rule with regard to mortgages. A mortgagor's reservation of full control over the property might prevent the creation of an effective lien in the mortgagee, and New York's law holds such mortgages void. The law must be consistent regardless of the nature of the property given as collateral, i.e. whether the property is real, personal or intangible. In the instant case, the arrangement allowed the company to use the proceeds of its accounts in any way it chose, without requiring an accounting to Ratner (D). The arrangement was inconsistent with a transfer of title to the accounts, and was not effective to create a lien on the accounts in Ratner's (D) favor. Since the original assignment was fraudulent in law, the payments made to Ratner (D) pursuant to his September 17 request constituted voidable preferences under the Bankruptcy Act. Benedict (P), as trustee, can avoid the transfers and recover any monies paid to Ratner (D).

Analysis:

This case is actually much simpler than it appears. The arrangement between Ratner (D) and the company created a *secret lien*. That is, the agreement transferred the accounts to Ratner (D) and ostensibly made him the owner of those accounts. But to any outside creditor, it looked like the accounts still belonged to the company. Because the agreement was secret, there was no notice to any other creditor that the company no longer owned the accounts. The company continued to create new accounts and collect old accounts just at it had always done in the ordinary course of business. It used the money collected to do anything it wanted to do, and never had to account for anything to Ratner (D). To every other normal business creditor, it looked like the company still owned those accounts. Many probably extended further credit to the company on the strength of those accounts, because they had no way of knowing that the accounts actually belonged to someone else. Then, right before the company was declared bankrupt, Ratner (D) demanded that the collections from that month be paid to him. Presumably, he knew the company was going under and wanted to get his money out. If the original assignment was valid, then Ratner (D) had perfected his interest by taking possession of the list of accounts and was a secured creditor. If the original assignment was void, Ratner was just another unsecured creditor, so at a time when all of the company's unsecured creditors were getting in line and waiting to be paid a couple of cents on the dollar for their part, there was Ratner (D) claiming to be a secured creditor and demanding full payment for his loans out of the bankruptcy estate. This is what was bothering the Court. It simply does not make good commercial sense to allow creditors and debtors to create secret liens on property. Doing so would increase the costs and risks associated with commercial financing and the extension of credit because a creditor could never be assured that the collateral he accepted in return for a loan really belonged to the party seeking the loan. The Court in *Benedict v. Ratner* recognized the dangers of the secret lien, and Article 9 of the Uniform Commercial Code solves the problem by making sure that a creditor's interest in a debtor's property is obvious.

■ CASE VOCABULARY

BANKRUPTCY TRUSTEE: A person appointed by the bankruptcy court to collect all the assets of the debtor into a bankruptcy estate, to settle all the claims against the debtor and to defend against unwarranted claims.

PREFERENCE: When an insolvent debtor repays one creditor over another, it is said that he prefers that creditor and that the payment is an unlawful preference, which can be avoided (recovered and put back into the estate) by the trustee in bankruptcy.

CHAPTER EIGHTEEN

The Scope of Article 9

In re Fabers, Inc.

Instant Facts: An oriental rug merchant consigned carpets to Fabers, Inc. for retail sale. The oriental rug merchant did not comply with Article 9 requirements. When Fabers went bankrupt, the oriental rug merchant tried to reclaim the rugs, but the trustee claimed that the rugs were properly included in the bankruptcy estate.

Black Letter Rule: A consignment intended as security is subject to Article 9 of the Uniform Commercial Code.

In re Architectural Millwork of Virginia, Inc.

Instant Facts: Architectural Millwork (D) financed a truck and a forklift through agreements that appeared to be leases, but when it filed for bankruptcy and the lessor sought performance, it claimed they were not true leases.

Black Letter Rule: Whether an agreement is a true lease or a security agreement under the UCC depends upon factors such as whether the lessee can unilaterally terminate the agreement; whether the goods will have any significant residual value; whether the agreement includes an option to purchase; whether the option price is nominal; and whether the parties expect the lessee to build equity in the goods.

Philko Aviation, Inc. v. Shacket

Instant Facts: The Shackets (D) bought an airplane from Smith, who gave them possession of the airplane but not the title papers. Smith again sold the plane and the title papers to Philko (P), who subsequently filed the paperwork with the FAA.

Black Letter Rule: Some state commercial laws that would allow certain transactions are preempted by federal laws governing the same kinds of transactions.

In re Fabers, Inc.
(*Trustee in Bankruptcy*) v. (*Consignor*)
12 UCC Rep. Serv. 126 (Bankr.D.Conn.1972)

CONSIGNMENTS INTENDED FOR SECURITY ARE SUBJECT TO ARTICLE 9 FILING REQUIREMENTS

■ **INSTANT FACTS** An oriental rug merchant consigned carpets to Fabers, Inc. for retail sale. The oriental rug merchant did not comply with Article 9 requirements. When Fabers went bankrupt, the oriental rug merchant tried to reclaim the rugs, but the trustee claimed that the rugs were properly included in the bankruptcy estate.

■ **BLACK LETTER RULE** A consignment intended as security is subject to Article 9 of the Uniform Commercial Code.

■ **PROCEDURAL BASIS**

Petition to reclaim assets that were included in the debtor's bankruptcy estate.

■ **FACTS**

An oriental rug dealer (P) consigned oriental rugs to Fabers, a retail carpet merchant. The consignment agreement provided that title to the rugs remained with the oriental dealer (P) until the rugs were sold, and that Fabers held the proceeds of the sale of any rug in trust for the oriental dealer (P). Fabers was to remit the proceeds of any sale immediately to the dealer (P) with a report of sale. The agreement also provided that the risk of loss fell upon Fabers rather than the oriental dealer (P). The oriental dealer (P) did not comply with Article 9 filing requirements to perfect his interest in the rugs. Fabers went bankrupt and the trustee (D) apparently included the oriental rugs in the Fabers' estate. When the oriental dealer (P) petitioned to reclaim the rugs, the trustee (D) resisted, claiming that the consignment of the rugs was for security purposes and was subject to Article 9 of the UCC. The oriental dealer (P) claimed that the consignment was a "true consignment" and therefore was not subject to the requirements of Article 9.

■ **ISSUE**

Is a consignment that creates a security interest subject to the requirements of Article 9 of the UCC?

■ **DECISION AND RATIONALE**

(Seidman, Ref. Bankr.) Yes. Article 9 specifically covers consignments for security. The dealer (P) argues that this consignment agreement was not intended for security, but rather is a "true consignment." However, the language of the agreement does not support the dealer's (P) contentions. The agreement describes the rugs as belonging to the dealer (P) but the risk of loss or damage falls upon Fabers. Such an arrangement is inconsistent with the liability of a bailee. The agreement also states that Fabers holds the proceeds of sales in trust for the dealer (P). But a trustee has legal title to the property in trust. If Fabers had legal title to the rugs, this was not a true consignment, but rather a secured transaction. Aside from the agreement, the dealer's (P) main argument is that this transaction falls within an exception to the Article 9 requirements. A consignment for security purposes is termed by the Code a "sale or return" and goods so consigned are ordinarily subject to the claims of creditors. There are three ways a consignor can protect itself from the claims of the consignee's creditors, however. It can either comply with a state sign law (which would indicate that the goods were on

In re Fabers, Inc. (Continued)

consignment), it could establish that the consignee was "generally known by his creditors to be substantially engaged in selling the goods of others," or it could comply with Article 9's filing provisions. The dealer (P) in the instant case did not file according to Article 9 and there is apparently no applicable sign law. The dealer (P) argues that Fabers was "generally known by [its] creditors to be substantially engaged in selling the goods of others," and, as such, this transaction is a "true consignment" and is outside the scope of Article 9. To support his argument, the dealer (P) submitted that Fabers never sold oriental rugs before 1971 and that an advertisement placed by Fabers in the paper in October of 1971 included a picture of the dealer (P) with the narrative "By special arrangement, we proudly introduce: a distinctive collection of [oriental rugs.]" This one announcement does not meet the requirement that the consignee be "generally known by his creditors to be substantially engaged in selling the goods of others" as required for the exception. Furthermore, the evidence indicates that Fabers was *not* substantially engaged in selling the goods of others. To further support his argument, the dealer (P) claims that the members of the Oriental Rug Dealers Association usually sold their carpets on consignment. But there is no evidence that this was the universal practice in the trade, and the dealer (P) did not show that Fabers' creditors who did *not* deal in Oriental carpets were aware of this practice. As between the dealer (P) and Fabers, this was a consignment agreement. But as between the dealer (P) and other creditors of Fabers, it was a sale or return and bound by the provisions of UCC § 2–326 and Article 9. The consignment was intended to secure the payment of the sales price of the carpets. The dealer (P) did not establish that Fabers was "generally known by [its] creditors to be substantially engaged in selling the goods of others" and did not fall within the other exceptions to § 2–326. Therefore, the only way the dealer (P) could have protected his interest in the rugs was to perfect his interest by filing under Article 9. He did not do so. The goods are subject to the creditors' claims and the petition for reclamation is denied.

Analysis:

At common law, there was no filing requirement with respect to consignments. But the trouble with consignments is that they have the *Benedict v. Ratner* problem—the retailer appears to be the unfettered owner of goods that actually belong to someone else. Furthermore, some consignments are not really consignments. Instead they are disguised secured transactions. That was the problem in the instant case. The dealer (P) in *Fabers* only wanted the money from the sales of the rugs. The entire agreement was to secure Fabers' payment of the proceeds from the sale of the rugs to the dealer (P). In other words, the consignment of the rugs was intended as security for the payment of the sales price. It was not a "true consignment." To solve the problems associated with consignments, the drafters of the Code put all consignments into Article 9 and, with minimal exceptions, required the consignor to comply with Article 9 filing requirements to perfect a purchase money security interest in consigned goods.

■ **CASE VOCABULARY**

CONSIGNMENT: The delivery of goods to a consignee (an agent or bailee) for sale to others. See the 1999 version of the UCC § 9-102(a)(20) for the Code's precise definition of a consignment.

PURCHASE MONEY SECURITY INTEREST: A security interest retained by the seller in the goods sold to guarantee the payment of the purchase price, or the interest retained by a financing agency that makes a loan to enable a buyer to purchase an item.

In re Architectural Millwork of Virginia, Inc.
(*Bankrupt Lessee*)
226 B.R. 551, 39 UCC Rep.Serv.2d 36 (Bankr.W.D.Va.1998)

TO DETERMINE WHETHER AN AGREEMENT IS ONE FOR SECURITY OR A TRUE LEASE, COURTS USE FACTORS INDICATING WHETHER THE AGREEMENT LEAVES ANY RESIDUAL VALUE IN THE GOODS AND WHICH PARTY HAS A STAKE IN THAT VALUE

■ **INSTANT FACTS** Architectural Millwork (D) financed a truck and a forklift through agreements that appeared to be leases, but when it filed for bankruptcy and the lessor sought performance, it claimed they were not true leases.

■ **BLACK LETTER RULE** Whether an agreement is a true lease or a security agreement under the UCC depends upon factors such as whether the lessee can unilaterally terminate the agreement; whether the goods will have any significant residual value; whether the agreement includes an option to purchase; whether the option price is nominal; and whether the parties expect the lessee to build equity in the goods.

■ **PROCEDURAL BASIS**

Motion to compel assumption or rejection of leases and motion for payments of leases in Chapter 11 bankruptcy case.

■ **FACTS**

Motley, acting on behalf of Architectural Millwork of Virginia, Inc. (Architectural Millwork) (D), decided to buy a new truck and selected a Freightliner. After negotiating a purchase price and electing to finance the truck, Motley met with the seller's credit department. Motley decided that he could more easily obtain credit with a leasing company than with a bank, so he entered into a "Truck Lease Agreement" with Associates Leasing, Inc. (Associates) (P) for the Freightliner (Freightliner agreement). Under similar circumstances, Motley entered into a "Conditional Sales Contract" for a Komatsu forklift (Komatsu agreement) with River Ridge Supply. River Ridge assigned all of its rights under that agreement to Associates (P). Architectural Millwork (D) later filed for Chapter 11 bankruptcy. Architectural Millwork (D) still has possession of its assets and continues to operate its business. Associates (P) argues that the court should compel Architectural Millwork (D) to act pursuant to Bankruptcy Code § 365 [allows a bankrupt lessee to assume a lease and continue to make payments, or to reject it and return the leased goods]. Architectural Millwork (D) argues that § 365 does not apply because the transactions are not true leases.

■ **ISSUE**

If a party uses a lease agreement to finance equipment, is that agreement necessarily one for security rather than a true lease?

■ **DECISION AND RATIONALE**

(Anderson) No. Whether an agreement is a true lease or a security agreement depends upon state law. *Virginia Code § 8.1–201(37)* [UCC definition of "security interest"] explains that while the inclusion of an option to purchase does not alone make a lease agreement one intended for security, the agreement is intended for security if it gives the option for nominal or no additional consideration when

In re Architectural Millwork of Virginia, Inc. (Continued)

the lease term ends. Because the Komatsu agreement clearly provides for an option to purchase the forklift for one dollar upon completion of all scheduled payments, we find that this agreement is a security agreement. The characterization of the Freightliner agreement is more difficult. Architectural Millwork (D) argues that although the purchase option in this agreement is not for one dollar, it is still for nominal consideration. Associates (P) argues that the Freightliner agreement does not give an option to purchase at all, but has a final adjustment clause that requires Associates (P) to sell the truck at the end of the lease. This clause provides that if the proceeds of the sale are more than the residual value set forth in the agreement, then Architectural Millwork (D) will receive a credit for the excess, but if the proceeds are less, then Architectural Millwork (D) must pay the difference. We find that the final adjustment clause is simply an option to purchase the truck at the price set by the residual value, $9,625. However, the fact that the Freightliner agreement contains an option to purchase is only one step toward determining whether the agreement is a disguised security agreement or a true lease. § 8.1–201(37)(2) [describes factors that conclusively indicate a security agreement] states that a transaction creates a security interest if the consideration the lessee must pay for the right to possess and use the goods is an obligation which the lessee cannot terminate, *and* either (a) the lease term is at least as great as the remaining economic life of the goods; (b) the lessee must either renew the lease for the remaining economic life of the goods or buy them; (c) the lessee has an option to renew the lease for the remaining economic life of the goods for nominal or no additional consideration; or (d) the lessee has an option to purchase the goods for nominal or no additional consideration upon compliance with the lease agreement. It is subsection (d) that applies here. If (1) Architectural Millwork (D) cannot avoid paying Associates (P) the payments due under the lease, and (2) Architectural Millwork (D) can buy the Freightliner for nominal or no consideration upon compliance with the lease terms, then the Freightliner agreement creates a security interest. The first condition exists here. Architectural Millwork (D) could terminate the lease early, but it cannot terminate its obligation to pay Associates (P) the value of the consideration due under the agreement. As Architectural Millwork (D) argues, its obligation is to pay all the monthly payments plus the residual value of $9,625. If Architectural Millwork (D) pays the $9,625 at the end of the lease, Associates (P) would turn over the title. If Architectural Millwork (D) does not make this payment, then Associates (P) would sell the vehicle, and if the proceeds of the sale were less than $9,625, it would charge Architectural Millwork (D) for the difference. If Architectural Millwork (D) terminated the lease early, we find that the agreement would require it to pay the present value of the consideration that would be due at the natural conclusion of the lease. Therefore, Architectural Millwork (D) cannot avoid paying Associates (P) the value of the consideration due under the lease. As to the second condition, Associates (P) argues that the residual value of $9,625 is not nominal consideration. We agree, particularly since the agreement lists the capitalized cost of the truck as only $38,500. Further, the parties agree that $9,625 was their fair estimate of the truck's value at the end of the lease term. Thus, the parties did not clearly expect Architectural Millwork (D) to recognize any significant equity in the truck. It also is not clear that the only economically sensible course for Architectural Millwork (D) would be to exercise its option to purchase. We therefore find that the option price is not nominal. The fact that the Freightliner agreement does not satisfy any of § 8.1-201(37)(2)'s bright line tests for a security agreement does not necessarily mean it is not a true lease, but it is a factor we must consider. § 8.1–201(37)(3) [lists factors that alone do not indicate a security agreement] gives further guidance. This section states that a transaction does not create a security interest merely because (a) the present value of the consideration the lessee must pay is equal to or greater than the fair market value of the goods; (b) the lessee assumes the risk of loss or agrees to pay taxes, insurance, registration fees, or service costs; (c) the lessee has an option to renew the lease or purchase the goods; (d) the lessee has an option to renew the lease for a fixed rent that is equal to or greater than the reasonably predictable fair market rent for the term of the renewal; or (e) the lessee has an option to purchase the goods for a fixed price that is equal to or greater than the reasonably predictable fair market value of the goods at the time of the purchase. Here, (b) and (c) apply because Architectural Millwork (D) assumed the risk of loss, paid for insurance, taxes and maintenance on the truck, and had an option to purchase it. Associates (P) argues that Architectural Millwork's (D) responsibility for taxes, registration fees and insurance are not inconsistent with a true lease. We find many of the subsection (b) factors to be as consistent with true leases as with security interests. It makes sense that a lessee would provide insurance, pay taxes and maintenance, and assume some risk of loss while he is in possession of a vehicle. The most important remaining factors are whether Architectural Millwork (D) can purchase the truck for nominal consideration and whether the parties anticipated Architectural Millwork (D) developing equity in the truck. The fact that a lease contains an option to purchase for nominal consideration suggests that the lessor does not care, economically, whether or not the lessee exercises the option. Likewise, if the lessee develops equity in the goods, then the only economically sensible decision for him is to exercise the option, and the lessor will not likely expect the goods back. Here, Architectural Millwork (D) theoretically has the opportunity to build up equity in the truck if he can maintain its value over the lease term at an amount higher than the $9,625 option price. However, the parties' testimony indicates that when they executed the Freightliner agreement, the $9,625 residual value was a fair estimate of what the truck's value would be at the end of the lease, and they did not expect much, if any, equity to actually accrue to Architectural Millwork (D). Under these circumstances, the $9,625 option price is not nominal consideration. We find that the Freightliner agreement was a true lease. It transferred the right to possession and use of a truck to Architectural Millwork (D) for a term. It included an option to purchase the truck, but the option was for more than nominal consideration. Any equity created in the lessee is minimal, and therefore of only limited significance to Architectural Millwork's (D) argument that we should consider this lease as a security agreement. Granted in part and denied in part.

Analysis:

As this case demonstrates, courts deem the consideration for an option to be nominal if the only economically sensible decision for the lessee is to exercise the option. To make this determination, courts compare the original price of the goods, the total rent paid under the lease, and the fair market value of the goods at the time the lessee is to exercise the option. The characterization of an agreement as a security agreement or a true lease is important because it determines the application of Article 9 when a creditor or bankruptcy trustee makes a claim to the goods. If the agreement is a true lease, the lessor, as owner of the goods, will generally prevail, whether or not he files to record his interest according to Article 9. If a lessor wants to protect himself against the possibility that a court may decide his lease is really a security agreement, § 9–505 permits him to file a financing statement to notify other creditors of his interest in the goods. The court will not construe this filing as an admission that the agreement is a security agreement, but if it decides on other grounds that it is one, then the filing will protect the lessor's security interest.

■ CASE VOCABULARY

NOMINAL CONSIDERATION: Small or token consideration that has no relation to the value of the goods for which it is exchanged.

SECURITY: Something a debtor offers to ensure performance of his obligation, which his creditor can use to collect his debt if he fails to perform.

Philko Aviation, Inc. v. Shacket

(2nd Airplane Buyer) v. (1st Airplane Buyer)
462 U.S. 406, 103 S.Ct. 2476, 36 UCC Rep. Serv. 1 (1983)

FEDERAL STATUTES MAY PREEMPT STATE ENACTED UCC LAW

■ **INSTANT FACTS** The Shackets (D) bought an airplane from Smith, who gave them possession of the airplane but not the title papers. Smith again sold the plane and the title papers to Philko (P), who subsequently filed the paperwork with the FAA.

■ **BLACK LETTER RULE** Some state commercial laws that would allow certain transactions are preempted by federal laws governing the same kinds of transactions.

■ PROCEDURAL BASIS
Appeal to Supreme Court of lower court's declaratory judgment granting Shackets (D) title under state commercial law.

■ FACTS
On April 19, 1978, Smith sold a new airplane to the Shackets (D). The Shackets (D) paid the full sale price and took possession of the airplane. Smith did not give the Shackets (D) the title papers to the aircraft [red flag!], instead he gave them copies and told them that he would "take care of the paperwork." The Shackets (D) believed that Smith meant that he would file the paperwork with the FAA as mandated by the Federal Aviation Act. Smith did not do so, and the Shackets (D) never attempted to record their title with the FAA. Shortly after the sale to the Shackets (D), Smith fraudulently sold the same airplane to Philko (P). Smith told Philko (P) that the plane was in Michigan for servicing, and both Philko (P) and its financing bank were satisfied with that explanation. The bank checked the FAA records for information regarding the title and found the title good. At closing, Smith gave Philko (P) the title documents, which Philko (P) handed over to its bank. The bank subsequently recorded the title with the FAA. The Shackets (D) commenced a declaratory judgment action to quiet title when the scam was discovered. Philko (P) argued that it had title to the aircraft because the Shackets (D) never recorded their title with the FAA. Philko (P) relied on § 503 of the Federal Aviation Act, which provides that no conveyance or instrument affecting title to a civilian aircraft shall be valid against third parties not having actual notice of the sale unless such conveyance is recorded with the FAA. The District Court awarded summary judgment for the Shackets (D), however, reasoning that the federal statute did not preempt substantive Illinois commercial law regarding title transfers. Under Illinois state commercial law, the Shackets (D) had title to the aircraft. We granted certiorari to determine whether the federal law preempts the state law in this field.

■ ISSUE
Does the Federal Aviation Act provision regarding transfer of title to an aircraft preempt state commercial law regarding title transfers?

■ DECISION AND RATIONALE
(White, J.) Yes. A literal reading of the statute in question would seem to invalidate only unrecorded title instruments, rather than an unrecorded title transfer like the one that occurred between the

Philko Aviation, Inc. v. Shacket (Continued)

Shackets (D) and Smith. Smith did not give the Shackets (D) a title instrument when he purported to sell the aircraft to them. However, we find that such a literal interpretation would undermine Congress's purpose in enacting the Act. The legislative history surrounding the act indicates that Congress wanted to require the recordation of *every* transfer of *any* interest in a civil aircraft. The way we interpret the statute, then, *every* transfer of *any* interest in an airplane must be evidenced by an instrument, and every instrument must be recorded with the FAA before the rights of innocent third parties can be affected. Any other construction of the statute would defeat the congressional purpose for the act, that being to create one repository where any person could go to find out information relating to any claims against, or liens, or other legal interests in an aircraft. The state law in the instant case is in direct conflict with our interpretation of the federal law. The state law does not require any documentation for a valid transfer of title to be effected. We hold that state laws allowing undocumented or unrecorded transfers of interest in aircraft to effect innocent third parties are preempted by the federal act. The transfer must be documented and recorded with the FAA before third party rights can be affected. That is not to say that the state law does not apply with respect to priority. Priority of lien holders is not a concern of the federal law. Priority of lienholders may still be determined by state law, but in order to obtain that priority, it is at least clear that the interest in the aircraft must first be recorded with the FAA. The lower court erred by granting summary judgment in favor of the Shackets (D). There may still be a question as to whether Philko (P) had "actual notice" of the sale to the Shackets under the federal statute. If so, such notice would destroy Philko's (P) claim, because it would no longer be an innocent third party. However, this and other issues need to be addressed by the lower court. Reversed and remanded for further proceedings.

Analysis:

Some federal statutes displace state commercial laws, and some preempt state law completely. It is common for a federal law to affect some portions of state commercial law, but to be supplemented by state law in other regards. Such an effect is commonly seen with federal tax statutes. It is important for a legal practitioner to be aware that some commercial transactions need to be researched on both a state and federal level. As can be seen from the instant case, aircraft titles are in part regulated by federal statutes. The same situation may occur with ships, patents, trademarks, and railroad equipment, among other things. What it is most important to realize is that the UCC (state law) will apply to the extent that any federal law does *not* apply.

■ CASE VOCABULARY

ACTUAL NOTICE: When a party can be conclusively shown to have knowledge about a certain fact.

PREEMPTION: When a federal law is in direct conflict with a state law, the federal law prevails over the state law under the Supremacy Clause of the United States Constitution.

CHAPTER NINETEEN

The Creation of a Security Interest

In re Troupe

Instant Facts: Troupe (P) purchased a tractor and stated on the security agreement that it would be used for personal, household purposes, but later claimed it was used for business purposes and that the security interest had not been perfected.

Black Letter Rule: Representations made by a debtor in a purchase-money security agreement regarding the intended use of the collateral will be binding on the debtor and will determine whether the collateral is for business or personal purposes.

Morgan County Feeders, Inc. v. McCormick

Instant Facts: Morgan County Feeders, Inc. (P) claimed McCormick (D) purchased cattle from Allen subject to its security interest when Allen had originally purchased the cattle for recreational cattle drives.

Black Letter Rule: Collateral is classified based on the principal use of the goods.

In re Grabowski

Instant Facts: South Pointe (P) claimed that Bank of America's (D) financing statement was insufficient, because the address was incorrect and property covered by a lien was not identified.

Black Letter Rule: The description of collateral in a financing statement is sufficient if it notifies subsequent creditors that a lien may exist and that further inquiry is needed to learn the full state of affairs.

Border State Bank of Greenbush v. Bagley Livestock Exchange, Inc.

Instant Facts: Johnson (D) claimed that he owned cattle sold by Bagley Livestock Exchange (D) and Anderson (D), and Border State Bank (P) claimed a security interest in the cattle.

Black Letter Rule: A security interest may attach if the debtor has rights in the collateral, but there is no requirement that the debtor own the collateral.

In re Howell Enterprises, Inc.

Instant Facts: Howell (D) listed a letter of credit as an account receivable. Tradax (P) challenged whether First National's (D) security interest in Howell's (D) accounts receivable attached to the letter of credit.

Black Letter Rule: A security interest does not attach to a letter of credit in a debtor's possession but to which the debtor has no rights.

In re Troupe

(Debtor/Farmer)
340 B.R. 86 (Bankr. W.D. Okla. 2006)

REPRESENTATIONS IN A SECURITY AGREEMENT ABOUT THE INTENDED USE OF GOODS ARE BINDING ON THE DEBTOR

■ **INSTANT FACTS** Troupe (P) purchased a tractor and stated on the security agreement that it would be used for personal, household purposes, but later claimed it was used for business purposes and that the security interest had not been perfected.

■ **BLACK LETTER RULE** Representations made by a debtor in a purchase-money security agreement regarding the intended use of the collateral will be binding on the debtor and will determine whether the collateral is for business or personal purposes.

■ PROCEDURAL BASIS:

Bankruptcy court decision on cross-motions for summary judgment.

■ FACTS:

Troupe (P) purchased a tractor from Deere (D) and financed the purchase with a purchase-money security agreement. At the time the tractor was purchased, Troupe (P) and his wife (P) were employed full time, working at least sixty hours per week. When Troupe (P) purchased the tractor, he told the salesman that he wanted a tractor to fill in ditches on his property, and his wife (P) said that they wanted the tractor to move hay, dirt, and snow. Troupe (P) also said that he wanted a tractor small enough to go through the gate of a horse stall. The tractor that was purchased was marketed by Deere (D) as residential equipment.

The first page of the security agreement had boxes to classify the agreement as either "personal" or "commercial," and the "personal" box was checked. There was also a paragraph that stated that the agreement was a consumer credit transaction, and that the goods would be used primarily for personal, family, or household purposes unless otherwise stated. An affidavit on the agreement that the transaction was a commercial credit transaction was unsigned. The financing statement for the security agreement was not filed.

Troupe (P) and his wife (P) raised cattle and pigs on their property, and also boarded horses. They intended that the farming and ranching activities be profitable. While they were engaged in ranching and farming, Troupe (P) and his wife (P) both worked full-time at jobs away from their property. They estimated that they used the tractor for personal purposes ninety percent of the time, and for business purposes ten percent of the time. Troupe (P) and his wife (P) testified that they considered personal use to be work performed on their property.

It was undisputed that Deere (D) had to have a perfected security interest in order to prevail over the bankruptcy trustee's (P) claim to the tractor. It was also undisputed that, because the financing statement was not filed, Deere's (D) security interest would be deemed perfected only if the tractor was classified as consumer goods.

In re Troupe (Continued)

■ ISSUE:

Was Deere's (D) security interest in the tractor perfected?

■ DECISION AND RATIONALE:

(Weaver, J.) Yes. Representations made by a debtor in a purchase-money security agreement regarding the intended use of the collateral will be binding on the debtor and will determine whether the collateral is for business or personal purposes. Collateral is classified as business or non-business at the time the security interest is created. A classification does not change because of a later change in the manner in which collateral is used. When a debtor makes an affirmative representation in loan documents that goods are to be used primarily for personal, family, or household purposes, the creditor is protected, even if the representations are erroneous.

It is unclear what representations Troupe (P) and his wife (P) made regarding the use of the tractor. There is no evidence that they told Deere's (D) salesman that the tractor was for commercial purposes. Their credit application stated that they were both employed, and that neither Troupe (P) nor his wife (P) was self-employed. The security agreement stated that it was a "personal," rather than a "commercial," transaction. The body of the document stated that it was a consumer credit transaction, and that the tractor was intended to be used for personal, family, or household purposes. Troupe (P) and his wife (P) were involved in farming, but it was not profitable for them. The fact that the tractor was later used in an attempted profit-making venture does not change the original characterization of the tractor. Deere (D) is entitled to rely on the statements made by Troupe (P) and his wife (P).

The bankruptcy trustee (P) argued that Troupe (P) and his wife (P) should not be bound by the representations, since they did not know of them. But one who signs an agreement is bound by its terms, absent fraud or misrepresentation. There is no allegation of fraud or misrepresentation here. Deere's (D) motion for summary judgment is granted.

Analysis:

The rule that a debtor is bound by his or her classification of collateral has the advantages of simplicity and definiteness. The creditor does not, as the court noted, have to monitor the uses of collateral, and the creditor does not have to engage in lengthy discussions about what "commercial" or "personal" mean in this context. The decision is left to the debtor, and the debtor's word is final. This may work to the detriment of the debtor in cases in which the collateral does not have a solely "commercial" or "personal" use, or where, as here, the line between "commercial" and "personal" is unclear to the debtor.

Morgan County Feeders, Inc. v. McCormick
(*Lender*) v. (*Purchaser of Cattle*)
836 P.2d 1051, 180 UCC Rep. Serv. 2d 632 (Colo.App.1992)

COLLATERAL IS CLASSIFIED BASED ON ITS PRINCIPAL USE

■ **INSTANT FACTS** Morgan County Feeders, Inc. (P) claimed McCormick (D) purchased cattle from Allen subject to its security interest when Allen had originally purchased the cattle for recreational cattle drives.

■ **BLACK LETTER RULE** Collateral is classified based on the principal use of the goods.

■ **PROCEDURAL BASIS**
Appeal of action to seize collateral.

■ **FACTS**
Allen purchased cattle to be used primarily for recreational cattle drives. Morgan County Feeders, Inc. ("Morgan") (P) had a security interest in Allen's cattle. Allen sold McCormick (D) 56 head of cattle. If the cattle were Allen's inventory, they would pass to a business free of any security interest. Morgan (P) claimed the cattle were "equipment" and, therefore, McCormick (D) bought the cattle subject to Morgan's (P) security interest. McCormick (D) claimed the cattle were "inventory" and that, therefore, they passed to him free of any security interest. The trial court held in Morgan's (P) favor.

■ **ISSUE**
Are goods that have a relatively long period of use considered equipment?

■ **DECISION AND RATIONALE**
(Rothenberg, J.) Yes. Goods that are sold as inventory are not subject to any existing security interests, whereas goods sold as equipment are subject to existing security interests. Therefore, here, the classification of the cattle is key. To determine whether goods are inventory or equipment, we look at their primary use. Goods are equipment if they are fixed assets or have a relatively long period of use. Goods are inventory, even if they are not for sale, if they are used up or consumed in a short period of time to produce an end product. Here, Allen purchased the cattle for recreational cattle drives. These cattle have a relatively long period of use compared to rodeo cattle or feeder cattle. Accordingly, the cattle are "equipment" and not "inventory," and McCormick (D) bought the cattle subject to Morgan's (P) security interest. Affirmed.

Analysis:

This case illustrates that the classification of collateral determines the effect of the security interest. It also demonstrates how the same goods may be classified differently depending on the use to which they are put. For example, in this case, Allen used the cattle for recreational cattle drives. The court compared this to using cattle for rodeos or for feed, where the use of the cattle would be for a shorter period of time, and, therefore, would constitute inventory. The same goods may also be classified differently depending on who has possession of them. For example, milk in the hands of a farmer would be a farm product, whereas milk in a grocery store would be inventory. The same milk in a grocery store customer's hands would be a consumer good.

In re Grabowski
(Farmer/Debtor)
277 B.R. 388, 47 UCC Rep. Serv. 2d 1220 (Bankr.S.D.Ill.2002)

FINANCING STATEMENTS MUST GIVE NOTICE OF A POSSIBLE LIEN

■ **INSTANT** ■ **FACTS** South Pointe (P) claimed that Bank of America's (D) financing statement was insufficient, because the address was incorrect and property covered by a lien was not identified.

■ **BLACK LETTER RULE** The description of collateral in a financing statement is sufficient if it notifies subsequent creditors that a lien may exist and that further inquiry is needed to learn the full state of affairs.

■ PROCEDURAL BASIS

Decision on a motion to determine the priority of financing statements.

■ FACTS

The Grabowskis operated a farm. They also operated a farm equipment business at a different location. The Grabowskis obtained loans from Bank of America (D) and, at a later date, South Pointe Bank (P). The Grabowskis used their farm equipment as collateral for the loans. The financing statement filed by Bank of America (D) claimed a security interest in "[a]ll ... Equipment." The Bank of America (D) statement also listed the Grabowskis' address as the address of their farm equipment business, rather than their farming operation. The South Pointe (P) financing statement included a "JD 925 FLEX PLATFORM," a "JD 4630 TRACTOR," and a "JD 630 DISK." The South Pointe (P) statement gave the Grabowskis' address as a post office box.

The Grabowskis filed Chapter 11 bankruptcy. Agreement was reached regarding the disposition of all of their farm equipment, except for a John Deere 925 flex platform, a John Deere 4630 tractor, and a John Deere 630 disk. South Pointe (P) claimed that it had the priority claim to those items, even though Bank of America's (D) financing statement was filed first. South Pointe (P) claimed that Bank of America's (D) statement was insufficient because it did not notify subsequent creditors of its interest in the equipment. South Pointe (P) argued that the address on the financing statement was incorrect and did not refer to farm equipment or farm machinery so that a subsequent lender could reasonably conclude that the security interest included the property of the Grabowskis' business, rather than their personal farm machinery.

■ ISSUE

Was Bank of America's (D) financing statement sufficient to protect its security interest?

■ DECISION AND RATIONALE

(Meyers, J.) Yes. The description of collateral in a financing statement is sufficient if it notifies subsequent creditors that a lien may exist and that further inquiry is needed to learn the full state of affairs. A security agreement must contain a reasonable identification of the property covered, and blanket agreements, covering all the debtor's assets, are generally not sufficient. The identity of the collateral must be objectively determinable, and a description by category, or type of collateral, is

In re Grabowski (Continued)

permitted. A financing statement, however, may contain a broader description. U.C.C. § 9–504 specifically allows a financing statement that "covers all assets of all personal property." All that is required is that a subsequent creditor be notified that a lien may exist, and that further inquiry is needed to disclose the complete state of affairs.

Bank of America's (D) financing statement was sufficient to put South Pointe (P) on notice. It was not reasonable for South Pointe (P) to conclude that the only equipment subject to a lien was located at the farm equipment dealership. The address given was not a part of the description of the collateral, but was merely a way to contact the Grabowskis. Judgment for Bank of America.

Analysis:

The financing statement and the security agreement are two different types of documents and serve two entirely different purposes. The security agreement is the contract between the lender and the borrower. It is important that both parties know exactly what is covered—especially in the case of an individual debtor, who may be waiving exemptions. A financing statement, on the other hand, is just a way of providing public notice of the existence of a lien. All of the terms of the agreement are not put on the statement, because the only part that must be disclosed is the existence of the agreement. Further inquiry, if any, is left to the subsequent creditor.

■ CASE VOCABULARY

CHAPTER 11: 1. The chapter of the Bankruptcy Code allowing an insolvent business, or one that is threatened with insolvency, to reorganize under court supervision while continuing its normal operations and restructuring its debt. The vast majority of Chapter 11 cases involve business debtors. 2. A business reorganization conducted under this chapter.

FINANCING STATEMENT: A document filed in the public records to notify third parties, usually prospective buyers and lenders, of a secured party's security interest in goods or real property. *See* UCC § 9–102(a)(39).

LIEN: A legal right or interest that a creditor has in another's property, lasting usually until a debt or duty that it secures is satisfied. Typically, the creditor does not take possession of the property on which the lien has been obtained.

PRIORITY: The status of being earlier in time or higher in degree or rank; precedence. An established right to such precedence; especially, a creditor's right to have a claim paid before other creditors of the same debtor receive payment.

PRIORITY LIEN: A lien that is superior to one or more other liens on the same property, usu. because it was perfected first.

SECURITY AGREEMENT: An agreement that creates or provides for an interest in specified real or personal property to guarantee the performance of an obligation. It must provide for a security interest, describe the collateral, and be signed by the debtor. The agreement may include other important covenants and warranties.

Border State Bank of Greenbush v. Bagley Livestock Exchange, Inc.

(Bank) v. (Seller of Cattle)
690 N.W.2d 326 (Minn. Ct. App. 2004)

COLLATERAL DOES NOT HAVE TO BE OWNED BY THE DEBTOR

■ **INSTANT FACTS** Johnson (D) claimed that he owned cattle sold by Bagley Livestock Exchange (D) and Anderson (D), and Border State Bank (P) claimed a security interest in the cattle.

■ **BLACK LETTER RULE** A security interest may attach if the debtor has rights in the collateral, but there is no requirement that the debtor own the collateral.

■ **PROCEDURAL BASIS:**

Appeals from a directed verdict and from an order denying a motion for judgment notwithstanding the verdict.

■ **FACTS:**

Johnson (D) and Anderson (D) entered into a cattle-sharing agreement. Anderson (D) agreed to care for and breed cattle owned by Johnson (D), and Johnson (D) would receive a guaranteed percentage of the cattle crop. The agreement provided that the cattle would be owned by Johnson (D) and sold under his farm name. Johnson (D) and Anderson (D) would agree when calves were to be sold, and Johnson (D) would pay Anderson (D) his share of the proceeds "for his keeping of [the] cattle." Anderson (D) cared for cattle under these terms in 1998 and 1999.

Anderson (D) testified that, in October 1999, Johnson (D) asked him to care for additional cattle on the same terms. Anderson (D) declined at first, saying that he was ending his cattle business because of adverse personal and business circumstances. Anderson (D) testified that he and Johnson (D) continued to discuss their cattle-sharing agreement, and Anderson (D) said that he eventually agreed to continue, with certain modifications: the share percentage would be a straight 60/40 split; Johnson (D) would provide feed, including beet tailings; Johnson (D) would provide additional pasture; and the agreement would include approximately 500 cattle, instead of the original 151 cattle.

Johnson (D) testified as to a different understanding of the agreement. He agreed that he said he would provide beet tailings for feed, if Anderson (D) paid the cost of shipping. Johnson (D) also stated that the agreement was changed to provide that Anderson (D) would care for 500, rather than 151, cows. Johnson (D) denied that he promised to provide feed, other than the beet tailings.

In March 2000, Anderson (D) obtained loans from Border State Bank (P). To secure the loans, Anderson (D) granted to Border State (P) a security interest in, among other things, all of his "rights, title and interest" in all livestock then owned or thereafter acquired.

After the agreement between Johnson (D) and Anderson (D) was modified, Johnson (D) made a number of shipments of beet tailings to Anderson (D). When Johnson (D) stopped the shipments, he sent Anderson (D) a $55,000 check for the purchase of feed. In November 2000, Anderson (D) had difficulty caring for the cattle due to heavy rainfall and a lack of feed. Johnson (D) reclaimed the cattle, but Anderson (D) retained the calves for sale. Anderson (D) testified that some of the cattle taken by

Border State Bank of Greenbush v. Bagley Livestock Exchange, Inc. (Continued)

Anderson (D) belonged to Anderson (D), or to another person with whom Anderson (D) had a cattle-sharing contract.

In December 2000, the calves that remained with Anderson (D) were sold at the Bagley Livestock Exchange (D). The Exchange (D) knew of Border State's (P) security interest, but after discussing the agreement with Johnson (D), determined that the security agreement did not cover the calves. The Exchange (D) issued a check to Johnson (D) for $119,403. Johnson (D) then paid Anderson (D) $19,404, representing Anderson's (D) share of the proceeds, less $55,000 that Johnson (D) claimed as repayment for money advanced to Anderson (D) for feed.

Border State (P) sued Bagley Livestock Exchange (D) and Johnson (D), alleging that they converted Border State's perfected security interest in the cattle sold. Johnson (D) brought a third-party complaint against Anderson (D) seeking indemnity on the conversion claim. Anderson (D) counterclaimed for breach of contract. After Border State (P) presented its case to the jury, Johnson (D) and the Exchange (D) moved for a directed verdict. The trial court granted the motion, finding that Johnson (D) did not grant Anderson (D) an ownership interest in the cattle. Anderson's (D) counterclaim was submitted to the jury, and the jury found that the contract between Johnson (D) and Anderson (D) had been modified, and that Johnson (D) breached the contract. Johnson's (D) motion for judgment notwithstanding the verdict was denied.

■ ISSUE:

Did Anderson's (D) lack of an ownership interest prevent him from granting a security interest in the cattle?

■ DECISION AND RATIONALE:

(Lansing, J.) No. A security interest may attach if the debtor has rights in the collateral, but there is no requirement that the debtor own the collateral. Article 9 of the U.C.C. refers to "rights in the collateral," not just the "ownership" of the collateral. The term "rights in the collateral," as that term is used in Article 9, includes full ownership and limited rights that fall short of full ownership. A security interest attaches to collateral only to the extent of the debtor's rights in the collateral. While mere possession of the collateral is insufficient, the debtor need not have full ownership in order for a valid security interest to be created.

A security interest attaches to collateral when value has been given, the debtor has rights in the collateral or the power to transfer rights, and the debtor has signed a security agreement that contains a description of the collateral. The parties all agree that Anderson (D) signed a security agreement and that value was given. The parties also do not dispute the validity of the description of the collateral. What is disputed is whether Border State's (P) security interest attached to the calves sold. The trial court held that the cattle-sharing contract did not grant Anderson (D) an "ownership interest" in the calves, and specifically found that the modifications testified to by Anderson (D) did not modify the terms of the agreement to grant an ownership interest. The trial court apparently determined that, for Border State's (P) security interest to attach, Johnson (D) would have had to grant Anderson (D) an interest equivalent to ownership. This is an incorrect statement of the law, and the application of an incorrect standard of ownership prematurely terminated the analysis of the cattle-sharing agreement. Analysis of that agreement is necessary to determine whether Anderson's (D) rights in the collateral were sufficient for Border State's (P) security interest to attach. The finding that the security interest did not attach was thus influenced by an error of law and must be set aside.

On remand, the trial court must initially determine whether the cattle-sharing agreement is ambiguous. There is a suggestion of ambiguity because the agreement states that the cattle provided by Johnson (D) would continue to be "owned" by Johnson (D), but the agreement also required only that the calves bred from the cattle would be sold in Johnson's (D) "name." The parties whose interests are affected by this determination should have a full opportunity to argue whether the cattle-sharing contract is ambiguous. Reversed and remanded.

Analysis:

The court says that the interest in goods that a debtor must have before a security interest may attach is more than "mere possession," but may be less than ownership. The question then becomes, what does the creditor get? In this case, it is not clear whether there would be enough evidence to conclude that Anderson (D) had a claim to ownership of the cattle he raised. If Anderson (D) is ultimately found not to be the owner of the cattle, Border State (P) will have a security interest in his "right" to raise the cattle and sell it on behalf of Johnson (D).

■ CASE VOCABULARY:

CONVERSION: The wrongful possession or disposition of another's property as if it were one's own; an act or series of acts of willful interference, without lawful justification, with an item of property in a manner inconsistent with another's right, whereby that other person is deprived of the use and possession of the property.

In re Howell Enterprises, Inc.
(Rice Seller)
934 F.2d 969, 14 UCC Rep. Serv. 2d 1236 (8th Cir.1991)

NO ATTACHMENT OF SECURITY INTEREST BASED UPON DEBTOR'S POSSESSION OF LETTER OF CREDIT DUE TO LACK OF INTENT

■ **INSTANT FACTS** Howell (D) listed a letter of credit as an account receivable. Tradax (P) challenged whether First National's (D) security interest in Howell's (D) accounts receivable attached to the letter of credit.

■ **BLACK LETTER RULE** A security interest does not attach to a letter of credit in a debtor's possession but to which the debtor has no rights.

■ PROCEDURAL BASIS
Appeal of claim in bankruptcy action.

■ FACTS
Howell Enterprises, Inc. ("Howell") (D) and Tradax America, Inc. ("Tradax") (P) sell rice. First National Bank (D) had a security interest in Howell's (D) accounts receivable. Bar Schwartz Limited ("Bar Schwartz") wanted to buy rice and pay for it with a commercial letter of credit. Howell (D) would not accept the commercial letter of credit as payment and Bar Schwarz would not buy rice from Tradax (P). So Tradax (P) and Howell (D) [very creatively] agreed that Tradax (P) would sell rice to Bar Schwartz under Howell's (D) name. Howell (D) agreed to transfer the proceeds of the letter of credit to Tradax (P) once it matured. The companies' names were used interchangeably throughout the transaction. Howell (D) listed the Bar Schwartz transaction as an account receivable on its books. After the rice was delivered to Bar Schwartz, Howell (D) received Bar Schwartz' letter of credit. However, before the letter of credit matured, Howell (D) filed for bankruptcy. First National (D) claimed its perfected security interest in Howell's (D) accounts receivable, including the Bar Schwartz letter of credit. Tradax (P) brought this action claiming that the Bar Schwartz letter of credit was not one of Howell's (D) accounts receivable and, therefore, was not subject to First National's (D) security interest. Tradax (P) argued alternatively that the letter of credit was subject to a constructive trust in Tradax' (P) favor. The bankruptcy court held that First National (D) had a perfected security interest in the letter of credit, was a bona fide purchaser for value, and, therefore had an interest superior to Tradax (P). The district court affirmed.

■ ISSUE
Does a security interest attach to a letter of credit in the debtor's possession but to which the debtor has no rights?

■ DECISION AND RATIONALE
(Rosenbaum, J.) No. The facts of this case are complex, but most are not legally relevant. It is not relevant whether a letter of credit can ever be an account receivable. Under Arkansas Statutes § 4-9-203 (UCC § 9-203), a security interest cannot attach unless "the debtor has rights in the collateral." Here, Howell's (D) only claim to the Bar Schwartz account receivable is that Howell (D) recorded it on

In re Howell Enterprises, Inc. (Continued)

its receivables ledger. The rice was always owned by Tradax (P), so Howell (D) had no right in the account or in the letter of credit. Howell's (D) only role in this transaction was as a conduit for a sale by Tradax (P) to Bar Schwartz. We reject the equitable theory relied on by the lower courts that Tradax (P) was a "culpable" party and was responsible for the consequences it suffered. The arrangement by Tradax (P) and Howell (D) to hide the identity of the true seller is not legally relevant. Finally, while First National (D) was an innocent third party, it did not detrimentally rely (e.g., lend more money) on Howell's (D) accounting error.

Analysis:

In *Thrift*, the court held that the debtor's possession of the collateral (three cars) was sufficient for a security interest in the debtor's inventory to attach. Here, on the other hand, the court held that the debtor's possession of a letter of credit was not enough for a security interest in the debtor's accounts receivable to attach. The difference between these two cases lies in the difference between the parties' intents. In *Thrift*, the parties intended that the debtor would have title to the cars once the debtor paid for them. Here, the parties never intended that Howell (D) would have any rights to the Bar Schwartz proceeds. Howell (D) merely recorded the Bar Schwartz letter of credit as an account receivable. The court's holding makes sense, considering that how a debtor chooses to characterize an item does not determine the debtor's actual interest in it.

CHAPTER TWENTY

Perfection of the Security Interest

In re Short

Instant Facts: The Shorts (D) sought to avoid a loan secured by bedroom furnishings that was consolidated with a nonpurchase-money security interest.

Black Letter Rule: A purchase-money security interest remains a purchase-money security interest even if it is refinanced and consolidated with a nonpurchase-money security interest.

General Electric Capital Commercial Automotive Finance, Inc. v. Spartan Motors, Ltd.

Instant Facts: General Motors Acceptance Corporation advanced money to Spartan Motors, Ltd. after Spartan Motors, Ltd. purchased and obtained title to two Mercedes Benz automobiles.

Black Letter Rule: When a creditor reimburses a debtor for money used to purchase collateral, the creditor still has a purchase-money security interest.

In re Wood

Instant Facts: One attorney loaned money to another attorney and received an assignment of the contingency fees in two litigation matters as collateral.

Black Letter Rule: An attorney who received an assignment of an account receivable is not required to file a financing statement to perfect his security interest.

In re Short
(Furniture Buyer/Debtor)
170 B.R. 128, 24 UCC Rep. Serv. 2d 1020 (Bankr.S.D.Ill.1994)

PURCHASE MONEY LIEN SURVIVES DEBTOR'S REFINANCING

■ **INSTANT FACTS** The Shorts (D) sought to avoid a loan secured by bedroom furnishings that was consolidated with a nonpurchase-money security interest.

■ **BLACK LETTER RULE** A purchase-money security interest remains a purchase-money security interest even if it is refinanced and consolidated with a nonpurchase-money security interest.

■ PROCEDURAL BASIS
Motion in bankruptcy action to avoid lien.

■ FACTS
On June 20, 1992, the Shorts (D) bought bedroom furniture from Anderson Warehouse Furniture ("Anderson"). The Shorts (D) entered into a retail installment contract with Anderson under which they were not charged interest for one year and were required to pay the entire balance on June 20, 1993. Anderson assigned the contract to American General Finance, Inc. ("American"). The Shorts (D) did not make any payments under the contract. On July 16, 1993, the Shorts (D) executed a note with American in which they consolidated the June 20 contract obligation with another note to American for $3,642.33. The documentation for the July 16 note describes the security as a "continued purchase money interest" in the Shorts' (D) furniture and other household items. The Shorts (D) made one payment under the July 16 note of $248.38 and a partial payment of $146.00. On January 4, 1994, the Shorts (D) [who really liked their furniture] filed for bankruptcy. The Shorts (D) moved to avoid American's lien on the bedroom furniture pursuant to 11 U.S.C. § 522(f)(2) [bankruptcy debtor may avoid lien that is nonpurchase-money security interest on household furnishings]. American claimed that its lien was a purchase-money security interest and, therefore, could not be avoided under § 522(f)(2).

■ ISSUE
Does a purchase-money security interest remain a purchase-money security interest after it is refinanced and consolidated with a nonpurchase-money security interest?

■ DECISION AND RATIONALE
(Meyers, J.) Yes. Under UCC § 9–107 [now UCC § 9–103], a security interest is a "purchase money security interest" to the extent it is taken by the seller of the collateral to secure all or part of its purchase price or is taken by a person giving value to enable the debtor to acquire rights in the collateral. Under this definition, American clearly had a purchase-money security interest in the Shorts' (D) bedroom furniture pursuant to the June 20 note. There is a split of authority concerning whether a purchase-money security interest is extinguished when it is refinanced. One line holds that the new loan is "transformed" into a nonpurchase-money interest and may be avoided in its entirety under § 522(f)(2). The other line of cases applies the "dual status" rule, holding that the new loan may be

In re Short (Continued)

partially purchase-money and partially nonpurchase-money. This rule is in keeping with the language of § 9–107 that a lien is a purchase-money security interest "to the extent" it secures the purchase price of collateral. This rule also preserves the balance that Congress intended between debtors' and creditors' rights in exempt property by protecting a lender who enabled the debtor to purchase collateral in the first place. In this circuit, courts have adopted neither the transformation nor the dual status rule, but have taken a case-by-case approach to determine whether the refinanced loan substantially changes the debtor's obligation. This approach gives effect to the parties' intent. Under either the dual status rule or the case-by-case approach, American retained a purchase-money lien on the Shorts' (D) bedroom furniture. Since the Shorts (D) made no payments under the June 20 note, it is unlikely the parties intended to extinguish the Shorts' (D) obligation under that note. The July 16 note merely enabled the Shorts (D) to pay for the furniture over a longer period of time. In addition, the parties' intent was expressly stated in the July 16 note, which describes the security as a "continued purchase money interest" in the Shorts' (D) furniture. The only difficulty with holding that the new loan is both purchase-money and nonpurchase-money is in allocating payments to the two interests. Under the "first in, first out" allocation method, payments are applied to the oldest debts first. Accordingly, once the Shorts (D) pay the furniture's purchase price, any remaining debt becomes a nonpurchase-money security interest that is avoidable under § 522(f)(2). The purchase price includes the cost of the furniture along with any financing charges and sales taxes. Accordingly, the Shorts' (D) payments of $248.38 and $146.00 will be applied to reduce the unpaid purchase price of $2880.00, resulting in a purchase-money lien on the bedroom furniture of $2,485.62. The Shorts' (D) motion to avoid the lien is granted to the extent of the remaining amount of the lien.

Analysis:

Congress enacted 11 U.S.C. § 522(f) to permit bankruptcy debtors to avoid liens attached to household goods already owned by them, but not liens on collateral purchased with the money advanced. Congress thereby protected lenders who enabled the debtor to acquire the collateral in the first place. Therefore, someone cannot buy ten rooms of furniture on credit and avoid paying by filing for bankruptcy the next day. By allowing debtors to avoid nonpurchase-money liens, Congress protects against overreaching by lenders who encumber a debtor's existing property to secure loans. Under the current version of UCC § 9-103(f), in transactions involving nonconsumer goods, the dual status rule applies. UCC § 9-103(e) sets forth how payments are allocated between the purchase-money and nonpurchase-money components of the loan. However, because this case involves consumer goods, § 9–103 would not apply and the court would be free to apply any rule it deemed appropriate.

■ CASE VOCABULARY

EXEMPTION: Certain property that may be omitted from a bankruptcy estate, including homesteads, motor vehicles, household furnishings, animals and crops, jewelry, professional books and tools, life insurance, and professionally prescribed health aids.

NOVATION: The substitution of an entirely new agreement for an existing agreement.

General Electric Capital Commercial Automotive Finance, Inc. v. Spartan Motors, Ltd.

(*Automobile Finance Company*) v. (*Car Dealership*)
246 A.D.2d 41, 675 N.Y.S.2d 626 (1998)

FUNDS ADVANCED AFTER THE PURCHASE OF AN ITEM MAY QUALIFY AS PURCHASE-MONEY SECURITY INTEREST

■ **INSTANT FACTS** General Motors Acceptance Corporation advanced money to Spartan Motors, Ltd. after Spartan Motors, Ltd. purchased and obtained title to two Mercedes Benz automobiles.

■ **BLACK LETTER RULE** When a creditor reimburses a debtor for money used to purchase collateral, the creditor still has a purchase-money security interest.

■ **PROCEDURAL BASIS**
Appeal of summary judgment in action for conversion.

■ **FACTS**
In 1983, a predecessor of General Electric Capital Commercial Automotive Finance, Inc. ("GECC") (P) entered into an Inventory Security Agreement with Spartan Motors, Ltd. ("Spartan") (D). Under the agreement, GECC (P) acquired a blanket lien (a "dragnet" lien) on Spartan's (D) existing and after-acquired inventory to secure a debt in excess of $1,000.000. In 1991, Spartan (D) entered into a Wholesale Security Agreement with General Motors Acceptance Corporation ("GMAC") (D). Under that agreement, GMAC (D) agreed to finance or "floor-plan" Spartan's (D) inventory. This meant that GMAC (D) would advance funds to automobile manufacturers, distributors, or sellers on Spartan's (D) behalf and Spartan (D) would reimburse GMAC (D) after Spartan sold the automobiles. Both agreements were duly perfected. In 1992, Spartan (D) purchased two Mercedes Benz automobiles with its own money and was reimbursed days later by GMAC (D). A few months later, GECC (P) sued Spartan (D) for the money due under the Inventory Security Agreement. GECC (P) also sued GMAC (D) to determine lien priority in the two Mercedes. Spartan (D) then filed bankruptcy. GMAC (D) sold the two Mercedes. GECC (P) accused GMAC (D) of converting the two Mercedes in violation of GECC's (P) prior security interest. The trial court granted GECC's (P) motion for summary judgment, holding that GMAC (D) had a purchase-money secured interest in the two Mercedes only to the extent that it paid funds directly to the sellers in advance of the transfer of the cars to Spartan (D).

■ **ISSUE**
May a creditor that reimbursed the debtor after the debtor purchased and received possession of collateral have a purchase-money security interest in the collateral?

■ **DECISION AND RATIONALE**
(Friedmann, J.) Yes. A perfected purchase-money security interest has priority over prior security interests in the same inventory. Under UCC § 9–107 [now § 9–103], a security interest is a "purchase money security interest" to the extent it is taken by the seller of the collateral to secure all or part of its purchase price or is taken by a person giving value to enable the debtor to acquire rights in the

General Electric Capital Commercial Automotive Finance, Inc. v. Spartan Motors, Ltd. (Continued)

collateral. There is little law regarding whether a purchase-money security interest is created when title to and possession of the collateral have passed to the debtor before the loan is advanced. [So let's create some law!] Therefore, we look to the legislative history of UCC § 9–107. Professor Grant Gilmore, one of the drafters of Article 9, has explained that § 9–107 was meant to broaden the rules under which a creditor may obtain a purchase-money security interest. So long as the loan and the acquisition are "closely allied," the creditor may obtain a purchase-money security interest. One factor in whether a loan and an acquisition are closely allied is temporal proximity, i.e., whether the loan and the purchase occurred close in time. Here, GMAC (D) reimbursed Spartan (D) just days after Spartan (D) purchased the cars. Another factor is the parties' intent. To determine the parties' intent, we look at whether the availability of the loan was a factor in negotiating the sale and whether the lender was committed at the time of the sale to loan the purchase amount. Here, post-purchase reimbursements are common in the automobile trade generally, and between GMAC (D) and Spartan (D) specifically. GMAC (D) was committed to advance funds to enable Spartan (D) to acquire the two cars and Spartan (D) could not have purchased the cars without GMAC's (D) backing. The timing of the passing of title to Spartan (D) is not relevant. The fact that the Wholesale Security Agreement between GMAC (D) and Spartan (D) provides that GMAC (D) would advance the funds to automobile manufacturers, distributors, or sellers on Spartan's (D) behalf is not determinative. Generally, the express terms of an agreement and a different course of dealing are considered consistent with each other. Here, GMAC's (D) practice of sometimes reimbursing Spartan (D) and sometimes paying the seller directly are compatible with one another. In any event, the contract may have been modified by the parties' post-agreement course of conduct. Therefore, GMAC (D) may retain the proceeds of the sale of the two Mercedes and is granted summary judgment. Reversed.

Analysis:

In keeping with the holding in this case, Official Comment 3 to § 9–103 provides that a "purchase money security interest" requires a "close nexus" between the acquisition of the collateral and the secured obligation. While the Official Comment does not discuss the factors that are relevant in determining whether a close nexus exists, the court here held that the relevant factors include the closeness in time of the purchase and the loan and the parties' intent. The court easily distinguished a case relied on by GECC (P), *North Platte State Bank v. Production Credit Assn.* In *North Platte*, the debtor borrowed money from a bank one and one-half months after purchasing cattle and did not inform the bank that the loan was intended for any particular purpose. The *North Platte* court held that the bank did not have a purchase-money security interest in the cattle and that the debtor had merely borrowed money to pay an existing debt. Unlike in the present case, the bank was not obligated to enable the debtor to acquire the collateral and the purchase and loan transactions were not close in time. The court here rightfully focused on the actual substance of the arrangement between GMAC (D) and Spartan (D) rather than the form of a typical loan transaction or the language of the parties' written agreement.

In re Wood
(Attorney/Debtor)
67 Bankr. 321, 2 UCC Rep. Serv. 2d 1098 (W.D.N.Y.1986)

ATTORNEY ASSIGNEE OF ACCOUNT IS EXEMPT FROM FILING FINANCING STATEMENT UNDER § 9–309(2)

■ **INSTANT FACTS** One attorney loaned money to another attorney and received an assignment of the contingency fees in two litigation matters as collateral.

■ **BLACK LETTER RULE** An attorney who received an assignment of an account receivable is not required to file a financing statement to perfect his security interest.

■ **PROCEDURAL BASIS**

Motion in bankruptcy action to avoid lien.

■ **FACTS**

Larkin (P) and Wood (D) were attorneys. On March 15, 1977, Larkin (P) loaned $10,000 to Wood (D). Wood (D) executed a demand promissory note, but did not make any payment on the note for five years. On June 3, 1982, Wood (D) agreed to pay Larkin (P) $1000 to be applied to the accrued interest and that subsequent payments would be applied first to interest and then to principal. In the agreement, Wood (D) assigned to Larkin (P) his right to receive contingency fees in two litigation matters. On September 9, 1983, Wood (D) filed for bankruptcy. Wood (D) [a typical attorney] sought to avoid Larkin's (P) security interest in the contingency fees. The Bankruptcy Court found for Wood (D), holding that Larkin's (P) security interest was not perfected and was not exempt from filing under UCC § 9-302(1)(e) [now § 9–309(2)] [filing financing statement not required to perfect security interest in assignment of accounts which does not transfer a significant part of the assignor's outstanding accounts].

■ **ISSUE**

Does an attorney who received an assignment of an account receivable have to file a financing statement to perfect his security interest?

■ **DECISION AND RATIONALE**

(Telesca, J.) No. UCC § 9-302(1)(e) [now § 9–309(2)] provides that filing a financing statement is not required to perfect a security interest in an assignment of accounts which does not transfer a significant part of the assignor's outstanding accounts. Official Comment 5 [now Official Comment 4] explains that the section seeks to protect assignees who do not regularly take assignments. Courts use a "percentage test" and/or a "casual and isolated transaction" test to determine whether a "significant part" of the assignor's outstanding accounts have been assigned. Under § 9-302(1)(e), an assignee is required to file if the assignee received a large portion of the assignor's accounts, whether or not the transaction was an isolated one. The assignee has the burden of meeting each test. We agree with the Bankruptcy Court that Larkin (P) did not meet his burden on the percentage test, i.e., he did not prove that the size of the accounts assigned was insignificant in relation to Wood's (D) other outstanding accounts. However, under the "casual and isolated transaction" test, the Bankruptcy

In re Wood (Continued)

Court erred in holding that Larkin (P) was not protected under § 9-302(1)(e) because he is an attorney. Under this test, the assignee's status is relevant only with respect to whether the assignee is involved in commercial lending or regularly takes assignments of accounts. Just because Larkin (P) is an attorney does not make him ineligible to engage in casual and isolated assignments of accounts under § 9-302(1)(e). Larkin (P) was not involved in commercial lending and did not regularly take assignments of accounts. He made one loan and took one assignment of the proceeds of two cases. This clearly was a casual and isolated transaction. Therefore, Larkin (P) was exempt from filing a financing statement and he had a perfected security interest in the accounts. Reversed.

Analysis:

This case protects the security interest of an attorney who does not regularly take assignments of accounts. However, the court leaves open the question of how to decide whether an assignment is "casual and isolated." What if Larkin (P) had taken five assignments in his 20 years of practice? What if he had taken 20? Similarly, under the "percentage" test, what percent of an assignor's accounts must be assigned for the assignment to constitute a "significant" portion? Pursuant to § 9–309(2) Official Comment 4, the exemption from filing covers only transactions so isolated or insubstantial that "no one would think of filing." The best advice is, when in doubt, file a financing statement. Because filing is relatively easy and inexpensive, close cases should be resolved against the creditor, and the creditor should have the burden of proving that § 9–309(2) applies.

CHAPTER TWENTY–ONE

Multistate Transactions

Metzger v. Americredit Financial Services, Inc.

Instant Facts: Metzger (P) purchased a car without knowing that Americredit (D) had a perfected security interest in it.

Black Letter Rule: A buyer of goods not in the business of selling goods of that kind for which a certificate of title is required, who gives value for the goods and receives them after the certificate is issued, takes the goods free of a security interest perfected in another jurisdiction if the certificate of title does not show the security interest and the buyer did not know of the interest.

Metzger v. Americredit Financial Services, Inc.

(Car Buyer) v. (Finance Company)
273 Ga.App. 453, 615 S.E.2d 120 (2005)

SECURITY INTERESTS FROM OTHER JURISDICTIONS MUST APPEAR ON A CERTIFICATE OF TITLE

■ **INSTANT FACTS:** Metzger (P) purchased a car without knowing that Americredit (D) had a perfected security interest in it.

■ **BLACK LETTER RULE:** A buyer of goods not in the business of selling goods of that kind for which a certificate of title is required, who gives value for the goods and receives them after the certificate is issued, takes the goods free of a security interest perfected in another jurisdiction if the certificate of title does not show the security interest and the buyer did not know of the interest.

■ **PROCEDURAL BASIS:**

Appeal from an order granting partial summary judgment.

■ **FACTS:**

Strong purchased a car in New York, and the purchase was financed by Americredit (D). The New York certificate of title noted Americredit's (D) security interest. Strong later moved to Georgia and applied for a Georgia title for the car. As a result of a clerical error, the Georgia certificate of title did not reflect Americredit's (D) security interest. Strong later transferred the car to an automobile dealer, and the car was transferred to other owners. The car eventually was purchased by Metzger (P). None of the certificates of title reflected Americredit's (D) security interest.

After Metzger (P) purchased the car, Americredit (D) located it, repossessed the vehicle, and sold it at auction. Metzger (P) reported the car as stolen, and then learned that it had been repossessed. Metzger (P) sued Americredit (D) for conversion, negligence, deceptive trade practices, breach of the peace, breach of good faith, racketeering, unjust enrichment, and breach of sale. Metzger (P) moved for partial summary judgment, and Americredit (D) made a cross-motion for summary judgment on all of Metzger's (P) claims. The trial court granted Americredit's (D) motions.

■ **ISSUE:**

Was Americredit's (D) security interest valid against Metzger (P)?

■ **DECISION AND RATIONALE:**

(Bernes, J.) No. A buyer of goods not in the business of selling goods of that kind for which a certificate of title is required, who gives value for the goods and receives them after the certificate is issued, takes the goods free of a security interest perfected in another jurisdiction if the certificate of title does not show the security interest and the buyer did not know of the interest. Ordinarily, a security interest in a motor vehicle is perfected when the application documents for a certificate of title are delivered to the Department of Motor Vehicles or the local tag agent, provided that the application documents properly reflect the security interest. Perfection occurs on the date of delivery of the documents, even if the

Metzger v. Americredit Financial Services, Inc. (Continued)

certificate of title issued does not reflect a security interest. There are exceptions to this rule, and the one applicable in this case provides protection for some good-faith purchasers who are likely to have relied on a "clean" certificate of title. Metzger (P) meets all of the requirements for the exception: the security interest in the car was perfected in another state, the certificate of title did not reflect the security interest, Metzger (P) is not in the business of selling automobiles, Metzger (P) gave value for the vehicle, she received the vehicle after the issuance of the Georgia certificate of title, and Metzger (P) had no knowledge of the security interest.

Americredit (D) argued that the statutory exception does not apply to Metzger (P), because the perfected New York security interest did not apply once application was made for a Georgia certificate of title. However, another Georgia statute provides that a security interest perfected in another state may remain perfected even if goods are covered by a Georgia certificate of title. When read together, the two statutes give protection to a good faith purchaser for value when there is continued perfection of the security interest, but the certificate of title does not reflect that interest. Furthermore, a specific statute will govern over a more general one. The statutes addressing continued perfection of an out-of-state security interest are general statutes, while the statute that provides protection to Metzger (P) is a limited one, addressing a specific circumstance. Americredit's (D) interpretation is incorrect. Reversed and remanded with directions to enter summary judgment for Metzger (P).

Analysis:

The good faith requirement of the statute only extends to the buyer of the goods. A buyer in Metzger's (P) situation would still be protected even if the applicant for the certificate of title had somehow managed to fraudulently conceal the existence of a security interest. Of course, an applicant would seldom have a motive to do so. Failing to record the security interest on the certificate of title would not make the security interest or the debt go away, as far as the original debtor is concerned. The protection does not apply if the subsequent purchaser knew of the security interest, so the applicant would not be helping anyone who knew of the scheme.

■ CASE VOCABULARY:

IN PARI MATERIA: On the same subject; relating to the same matter; loosely, in conjunction with. It is a canon of construction that statutes that are *in pari materia* may be construed together, so that inconsistencies in one statute may be resolved by looking at another statute on the same subject.

CHAPTER TWENTY-TWO

Priority

In re Wollin

Instant Facts: Wollin (P) and the Moodys (P) each gave their vehicles as collateral to secure their vehicle loans, but OFCU (D) claimed that under a dragnet clause the vehicles also secured their visa charges.

Black Letter Rule: A dragnet clause will only apply to a future advance if it is of the same class as the primary loan and so related to it that one may infer the debtor's consent to its inclusion, and it will only apply to antecedent loans if it specifically references them.

Galleon Industries, Inc. v. Lewyn Machinery Co.

Instant Facts: While Galleon's (D) current and after-acquired inventory and equipment was subject to a security interest held by Central (D), Lewyn (P) failed to perfect a purchase money security interest in a machine it sold to Galleon (D).

Black Letter Rule: An unperfected purchase money security interest does not have priority over an existing perfected security interest.

Kunkel v. Sprague National Bank

Instant Facts: Hoxie (D) obtained a purchase money security interest in Morken's cattle while Sprague (D) had a prior security interest in all Morken's inventory.

Black Letter Rule: A creditor with a purchase money security interest in inventory has "superpriority" over prior security interest if the creditor with the purchase money security interest gives proper notice to the competing secured creditors.

International Harvester Co. v. Glendenning

Instant Facts: Glendenning (D) purchased three tractors in which International Harvester Co. (P) had a security interest.

Black Letter Rule: A buyer in the ordinary course of business is one who acts in good faith and does not have knowledge that the sale violates a security agreement.

First National Bank and Trust Co. of El Dorado v. Ford Motor Credit Co.

Instant Facts: Two creditors both claimed the proceeds from the sale of two vehicles that were on the debtor's lot but that had been sold in a sham sale to two of the debtor's principals.

Black Letter Rule: Only a buyer acting in good faith is a buyer in the ordinary course of business who takes free of existing security interests.

Clovis National Bank v. Thomas

Instant Facts: Bunch sold cattle with the implicit knowledge and consent of his secured creditor, Clovis National Bank (P). Clovis National Bank (P) did not demand payment, thereby waiving its security interest.

Black Letter Rule: By consenting to the sale of collateral and not demanding payment, a secured creditor waives its security interest.

Farm Credit Bank of St. Paul v. F & A Dairy

Instant Facts: F & A Dairy (D) bought milk that was subject to Farm Credit Bank of St. Paul's (P) security interest.

Black Letter Rule: Under the Food Security Act, a buyer of collateral takes subject to a security interest if a creditor complies with the Act's notice requirements.

In re Arlco, Inc.

Instant Facts: Galey (P) demanded reclamation of goods it sold to Arley (D), but CIT had a perfected security interest in Arley's (D) inventory, and the goods Galey (P) sought were sold to satisfy CIT's claim.

Black Letter Rule: A creditor with a security interest in after acquired property who has acted in good faith and for value, which includes acquiring rights as security for a preexisting claim, is a good faith purchaser with a claim superior to that of a reclaiming seller.

George v. Commercial Credit Corp.

Instant Facts: A bankruptcy trustee claimed that the debtor's mobile home was a motor vehicle, not a fixture, and was not subject to a real estate mortgage.

Black Letter Rule: A mobile home may be a fixture subject to a real estate mortgage.

Lewiston Bottled Gas Co. v. Key Bank of Maine

Instant Facts: Lewiston Bottled Gas Co.'s (P) purchase money security interest did not have priority over Key Bank of Maine's (D) real estate mortgage because the fixture filing did not state the name of the record owner of the real property.

Black Letter Rule: A purchase money security interest in a fixture has priority over a real estate mortgage if the fixture filing includes all the required information.

Maplewood Bank & Trust v. Sears, Roebuck & Co.

Instant Facts: Sears (D) had a security interest in kitchen fixtures and argued that it had priority over the mortgage holder to the funds recovered on foreclosure.

Black Letter Rule: Upon the debtor's default, a secured party's only remedy is to remove the fixtures from the real estate, and it must reimburse the mortgage holder for the cost of repair.

United States v. Estate of Romani

Instant Facts: Pursuant to the federal priority statute, the federal government claimed its tax claim was entitled to preference over a judgment creditor's lien on the real property in a decedent's estate.

Black Letter Rule: Pursuant to the Federal Tax Lien Act, the federal government's tax claim is not valid over a judgment creditor's prior perfected lien on real property.

Plymouth Savings Bank v. U.S. I.R.S.

Instant Facts: After Dionne defaulted on her loan, the Bank (P) tried to recover contract proceeds in which it held a security interest, but the IRS (D) claimed that its tax lien had priority over the security interest.

Black Letter Rule: Where a contract is made within 45 days after a tax lien filing, the rights under that contract and all the proceeds of those rights fall within § 6323 (c)'s safe harbor giving a security interest in those rights and proceeds priority over the tax lien.

In re Wollin
(*Consumer Debtor*)
249 B.R. 555, 41 UCCRep.Serv.2d 1257 (Bankr.D.Or.2000)

COURT NARROWLY CONSTRUES THE "SAME CLASS" TEST FOR FUTURE ADVANCES IN DRAGNET CLAUSES AND ADOPTS THE "SPECIFIC REFERENCE" TEST FOR ANTECEDENT DEBT

■ **INSTANT FACTS** Wollin (P) and the Moodys (P) each gave their vehicles as collateral to secure their vehicle loans, but OFCU (D) claimed that under a dragnet clause the vehicles also secured their visa charges.

■ **BLACK LETTER RULE** A dragnet clause will only apply to a future advance if it is of the same class as the primary loan and so related to it that one may infer the debtor's consent to its inclusion, and it will only apply to antecedent loans if it specifically references them.

■ **PROCEDURAL BASIS**

Objection by creditor to confirmation and objection by debtors to proofs of claim in Chapter 13 bankruptcy.

■ **FACTS**

In 1992, the Oregon Federal Credit Union (OFCU) (D) gave Steven Moody (P) a $3,000 LoanLiner line of credit, and Moody (P) pledged $5 of credit union shares as security. In April 1996, OFCU (D) gave the Moodys (P) a $3,900 advance under a LoanLiner agreement for debt consolidation. To secure this loan, the Moodys (P) gave OFCU (D) a security interest in a 1978 Ford Bronco. (The Moodys (P) have agreed to surrender the Bronco, and OFCU (D) has waived any deficiency claim.) In July 1996, OFCU (D) gave the Moodys (P) a $31,850.50 advance under another LoanLiner agreement for the purchase of a Ford pickup (the Pickup), and the Moodys (P) gave OFCU (D) a security interest in the Pickup to secure this loan. In 1998, OFCU (D) issued a visa card to Steven Moody (P). In 1988, OFCU (D) gave Wollin (P) a $2,000 line of credit and issued him a visa card. In 1996, OFCU (D) gave Wollin (P) a $9,000 advance under a LoanLiner agreement to purchase a Ford Probe (the Probe), and Wollin (P) gave OFCU (D) a security interest in the Probe to secure this loan. In 1999, the Moodys (P) and Wollin (P) each filed a petition for Chapter 13 bankruptcy. OFCU (D), maintaining a perfected security interest in the vehicles, filed a secured claim in each case, and both the Moodys (P) and Wollin (P) filed plans to modify OFCU's (D) secured claim. OFCU (D) objected to confirmation in both cases, and the Moodys (P) and Wollin (P) objected to OFCU's (D) proofs of claim. After a joint hearing on these objections, the Chapter 13 trustee recommended confirmation in both cases. All of the vehicle loan security agreements here contain identical "dragnet" clauses under which the security interest secures not only the original loan and any extensions, renewals or refinancings of that loan, but also any other loans under the LoanLiner agreement and "any other amount [the debtor owes] the credit union for any reason now or in the future." [That should about cover it.]

■ **ISSUE**

Can a "dragnet" clause make a vehicle that secures a consumer vehicle loan also secure all the debtor's past and future debt to the creditor?

In re Wollin (Continued)

■ DECISION AND RATIONALE

(Radcliffe) No. We first address the loans that occurred subsequent to the vehicle loans, namely, the Moodys' (P) visa charges. OFCU (D) argues that under the plain meaning of their dragnet clause, the Bronco and the Pickup secure the Moodys' (P) visa charges, which are "any other amount" they owe "in the future." Alternatively, OFCU (D) argues that the visa charges are of the "same class" as the Bronco and Pickup loans because they are all consumer debt, and that the vehicles therefore secure the visa charges. We reject both arguments. The Oregon Supreme Court has held that no matter how a dragnet clause is drafted, it will only apply to a future advance that is of the same class as the primary obligation and so related to it that one may infer the debtor's consent to its inclusion. Clearly, the Court has rejected OFCU's (D) "plain meaning" argument. The courts vary in their application of the "same class" test, at least in the business context. Some find it sufficient if the loans are all of a business nature, while others require a closer relation. However, we could find no Oregon decision applying the "same class" test in the consumer loan context. Some jurisdictions find that all consumer debt meets the test. Others hold that if the primary loan is a purchase money transaction, then only subsequent purchase money loans meet the test. Still others require that each consumer transaction be for the same use and not involve separate debt instruments. It appears that the Oregon Supreme Court would apply the test at least as strictly in the consumer context as it does in the business context. In *Community Bank v. Jones* [applies "same class" test in business context], the Court decided that a subsequent loan to cover business checking overdrafts was not of the "same class" as loans provided to finance inventory, which the inventory secured. Although they were both business related and conformed in form to the security agreement, in substance the loan for the checking account was different and not related to the intended purpose of the security agreement. Under the Community Bank standard, then, loans do not necessarily meet the "same class" standard simply because they are all business loans or all consumer loans. We also decline to adopt a per se test based on the status of the loans as purchase money transactions. In *Community Bank* the Court held that the future transaction must be "so related to" the primary loan "that the consent of the debtor to its inclusion may be inferred." Although we presume that Moodys' (P) visa charges are purchase money transactions, we cannot find that they are sufficiently related to the Pickup loan to satisfy the "same class" test. A vehicle loan differs both in scope and solemnity from typical visa charges. We cannot infer the Moodys' (P) consent to have their vehicle secure the visa charges. As to the loans that predated the vehicle loans (the Moodys' (P) 1992 line of credit and Wollin's (P) 1988 line of credit and visa charges), OFCU (D) again argues that the plain meaning of the dragnet clauses should apply. The Moodys (P) and Wollin (P) argue that the dragnet clauses must specifically reference the antecedent loans to be applicable to them. Again, we find no Oregon authority on this issue. Many jurisdictions apply the "plain meaning" test, while others apply the "same class" test, and still others apply the "specific reference" standard that the Moodys (P) and Wollin (P) offer. As with future advances, we reject the "plain meaning" test for antecedent debt. The Oregon Supreme Court has adopted a standard stricter than "plain meaning" for future advances, and we cannot conclude that it would lessen that standard for antecedent debt, especially in the consumer context. Guided by the policy that dragnet clauses are generally disfavored and strictly construed, we adopt the "specific reference" standard as effectuating the parties' true intent. If the parties truly intend a security agreement to cover antecedent debt, they have no good reason not to identify it. Here, the dragnet clauses do not specifically reference the antecedent debts, so the vehicles do not secure them. OFCU's (D) objections to confirmation are overruled, and the Moodys' (P) and Wollin's (P) objections to OFCU's (D) claims are sustained.

Analysis:

The court declined to construe the "same class" test as distinguishing only between the broad classes of consumer and business debt. It also refused to recognize purchase money debt as a class for purposes of this test. Instead, the court took a stricter approach to better effectuate the mutual intent of the parties. The court would infer that the parties intended to include a subsequent debt in their security agreement if the subsequent debt was related closely enough to the primary debt to permit such an inference. For antecedent debts, the court was even more strict, requiring the parties to specifically reference the debts in the security agreement before it would make the agreement applicable to them. The court could have applied the "same class" test to antecedent debt as well, but since the parties know about preexisting debts and could easily include them in their security agreement, the court opted to give consumers this broader protection.

■ **CASE VOCABULARY**

CONFIRMATION: Court approval of Chapter 13 bankruptcy plan after a hearing to determine whether the plan is feasible and to set forth the elements necessary for such approval.

"DRAGNET" CLAUSE: Provision in a security agreement that gives a creditor a security interest to secure not only the present debt but also past and future debt.

PROOF OF CLAIM: A statement a creditor files with a bankruptcy court to set forth the amount and basis for his claim against a bankrupt debtor.

Galleon Industries, Inc. v. Lewyn Machinery Co.

(*Equipment Purchaser*) v. (*Equipment Seller*)
50 Ala.App. 334, 279 So.2d 137, 12 UCC Rep. Serv. 1224 (1973)

PERFECTED SECURITY INTEREST IN EQUIPMENT HAS PRIORITY OVER UNPERFECTED PURCHASE MONEY SECURITY INTEREST

■ **INSTANT FACTS** While Galleon's (D) current and after-acquired inventory and equipment was subject to a security interest held by Central (D), Lewyn (P) failed to perfect a purchase money security interest in a machine it sold to Galleon (D).

■ **BLACK LETTER RULE** An unperfected purchase money security interest does not have priority over an existing perfected security interest.

■ **PROCEDURAL BASIS**

Appeal of action to recover personal property.

■ **FACTS**

Galleon Industries, Inc. ("Galleon") (D) and Central Bank and Trust Company ("Central") (D) entered into a security agreement whereby Central (D) obtained a security interest in all the equipment and inventory Galleon (D) owned or thereafter acquired. Lewyn Machinery Company ("Lewyn") (P) offered to sell Galleon (D) certain machinery. After investigating Galleon's (D) credit, Lewyn (P) notified Galleon (D) that it would not extend Galleon (D) credit, and that Galleon (D) could pay cash for the machines and pick them up at Lewyn's (P) office. Galleon (D) went to Lewyn's (P) office, paid cash, and took delivery of all the items except one that Lewyn (P) did not have on hand. Lewyn (P) ordered the machine from J.M. Lancaster ("Lancaster") and Lancaster was supposed to deliver it to Lewyn's (P) office. Through a mistake or a misunderstanding, Lancaster delivered the machine directly to Galleon (D). Upon learning of the delivery, Lewyn (P) sent Galleon (D) an invoice for the machine with payment due in 30 days. Galleon (D) then defaulted on the loan to Central (D) and Central (D) foreclosed its security agreement and took possession of Galleon's (D) inventory, including the machine from Lewyn (P). Lewyn (P) sued Galleon (D) and Central (D), claiming that title to the machine did not pass to Galleon (D) because Galleon (D) never paid for the machine and that, therefore, Galleon (D) did not have sufficient rights in the machine for Central's (D) security interest to attach. The trial court found for Lewyn (P).

■ **ISSUE**

Does an unperfected purchase money security interest have priority over an existing perfected security interest?

■ **DECISION AND RATIONALE**

(Wright, J.) No. Although Lewyn (P) and Galleon (D) originally agreed that the machine would not be delivered to Galleon (D) until Galleon (D) paid for it, that agreement was modified or waived when the machine was delivered to Galleon (P) and Lewyn (P) sent Galleon (D) an invoice requiring payment in 30 days. Galleon (D) then became a credit buyer subject to Article 9 of the UCC. Pursuant to UCC § 9–204, Central's (D) security agreement in the machine attached as soon as Galleon (D) acquired

Galleon Industries, Inc. v. Lewyn Machinery Co. (Continued)

"rights" in it. A credit buyer acquires rights in collateral when it receives possession of the collateral from the seller. Therefore, Galleon (D) acquired sufficient rights in the machine for Central's (D) security interest to attach when Galleon (D) received the machine. Pursuant to § 9–312(4) [now § 9-324(a)], Lewyn (P) could have perfected its purchase money security interest and received priority over Central (D) by filing a financing statement within 10 days [now 20 days] of delivery of the machine. Because it did not, Central (D) has priority and a superior right of possession. Reversed.

Analysis:

According to UCC § 9-103(a), a security interest is a "purchase money security interest" to the extent it is taken by the seller of the collateral to secure all or part of its purchase price, or by a person giving value to enable the debtor to acquire rights in the collateral. To have priority over existing security interests, the purchase money security interest must be perfected. Here, Lewyn (P) failed to perfect its purchase money security interest, probably because it did not believe Galleon (D) had any rights in the machine yet, or because it believed it had a purchase money security interest. Lewyn (P) had ten days [twenty days today] after Galleon (D) received the machine to file a financing statement. It's interesting to note that Lewyn's (P) security interest was temporarily perfected during that ten-day period, so long as it filed a financing statement before the ten-day period elapsed.

■ CASE VOCABULARY

DETINUE: An action to recover wrongfully detained personal property.

Kunkel v. Sprague National Bank

(*Bankruptcy Trustee*) v. (*Lender*)
128 F.3d 636, 33 UCC Rep. Serv. 2d 943 (8th Cir.1997)

PURCHASE MONEY SECURITY INTEREST HAS "SUPERPRIORITY" OVER PRIOR SECURITY INTEREST IN INVENTORY IF CREDITOR WITH PURCHASE MONEY SECURITY INTEREST GIVES NOTICE TO COMPETING SECURED CREDITORS

■ **INSTANT FACTS** Hoxie (D) obtained a purchase money security interest in Morken's cattle while Sprague (D) had a prior security interest in all Morken's inventory.

■ **BLACK LETTER RULE** A creditor with a purchase money security interest in inventory has "superpriority" over prior security interest if the creditor with the purchase money security interest gives proper notice to the competing secured creditors.

■ **PROCEDURAL BASIS**

Appeal of summary judgment in adversary proceeding in bankruptcy.

■ **FACTS**

Sprague National Bank ("Sprague") (D) loaned money to the Morkens and obtained a security interest in the Morkens' currently owned and after-acquired inventory. Sprague (D) perfected its security interest. In five transactions, Morken purchased interests in cattle from Hoxie Feeders, Inc. ("Hoxie") (D). For each transaction, Morken granted Hoxie (D) a purchase money security interest ("PMSI") in the cattle. Hoxie (D) perfected its security interests by taking possession of the cattle. The feedlot agreement between Hoxie (D) and Morken provided that Hoxie (D) would sell the cattle in its own name for slaughter, would receive direct payment from the packing house, would deduct the feeding and purchase expenses from the sale proceeds, and remit the balance to Morken. However, Hoxie (D) needed Morken's authority to sell the cattle and Morken determined the sales price. Morken then filed for bankruptcy. Hoxie (D) then sold the cattle to Iowa Beef Processors ("IBP") and deducted the care and feeding expenses. Sprague (D) and Hoxie (D) both claim the remaining $550,000 in sale proceeds. While this case was pending, Hoxie (D) gave Sprague (D) notice of its competing security interest. Hoxie (D) and Sprague (D) filed cross-motions for summary judgment. The bankruptcy court granted Hoxie's (D) motion for summary judgment, holding that both parties had perfected security interests and that Hoxie (D) had "superpriority" because it was a PMSI. The court held that Hoxie's (D) notice was sufficient even though it was given after the cattle had been slaughtered and sold. The district court affirmed, holding that notification of a PMSI is not necessary when the creditor perfects its security interest by possession rather than by filing. In the alternative, the district court held that Sprague (D) did not have a security interest in the cattle because delivery to Morken had not been completed and, therefore, Morken did not have "rights in the collateral" sufficient for Sprague's (D) security interest to attach.

■ **ISSUE**

If a creditor with a purchase money security interest in inventory gives proper notice to the competing secured creditors does it have "superpriority" over the prior security interests?

HIGH COURT CASE SUMMARIES

Kunkel v. Sprague National Bank (Continued)

■ DECISION AND RATIONALE

(Gibson, J.) Yes. Under UCC § 9–203(1), a security interest does not attach unless the debtor has rights in the collateral. The debtor need not have title or possession of the collateral. Under Article 2 of the UCC, delivery is not necessary for a sale to take place. Here, the cattle were specifically identified in the invoices and the parties agreed that delivery would be made to Morken by delivery to Hoxie (D). Morken bore the risk that the venture would not generate a profit. Hoxie (D) was solely a bailee and a secured party. Hoxie (D) claims that the sales were not completed because it had the right to stop delivery of the cattle. However, Hoxie (D) lost this right when the cattle were constructively delivered to Morken. Therefore, Morken had sufficient rights in the collateral for Sprague's (D) security interest to attach, and Sprague (D) had a perfected security interest in the cattle. With respect to priority, according to UCC § 9–312(3) [now § 9-324(b)], a PMSI in inventory has "superpriority" over an earlier perfected interest if the PMSI creditor gives written notification to all holders of competing security interests, the other secured creditors receive the notification within five years before the debtor receives possession of the inventory, and the notification states that the person giving the notice has or expects to acquire a PMSI in the debtor's inventory. Although § 9–312(3) does not expressly refer to perfection by possession, creditors that perfect by possession rather than by filing can obtain "superpriority" status. Section 9–312(3) does not refer to perfection by possession because this is a rare way for a creditor to perfect a security interest in inventory. But the UCC controls even if it does not expressly address every possible factual situation. Therefore, Hoxie's (D) PMSI was able to attain "superpriority" over Sprague's (D) interest. With respect to the requirement that the PMSI creditor give notice to other secured creditors within five years before the debtor receives possession of the inventory, we follow Professor Gilmore's comments and look at when the debtor had actual possession, not constructive possession. Here, Morken never had actual possession of the cattle, so Hoxie's (D) notice to Sprague (D) after the cattle were sold and slaughtered was timely. Sprague's (D) argument that pre-perfection notification is required is without merit. Section 9-312(d) provides that the creditor giving notice must state that it has or expects to have a PMSI. Therefore, the PMSI creditor can wait to notify other secured creditors after it has acquired and perfected its security interest. Finally, Sprague (D) argues that Hoxie (D) does not have "superpriority" in the proceeds of the cattle sales because Hoxie (D) received payment two or three days after delivering the cattle to IBP. Section 9–312(3) provides that a PMSI's "superpriority" extends to "identifiable cash proceeds received on or before the delivery of the inventory to a buyer." This language is meant to distinguish cash sales, to which "superpriority" applies, from credit sales, to which it does not apply. Here, the sale to IBP was a cash sale, and Hoxie's (D) receipt of the cash proceeds was reasonably contemporaneous with the delivery of the cattle. Accordingly, Hoxie's (D) "superpriority" extends to those proceeds. We reverse the district court's holding that Sprague (D) did not have a security interest in the cattle, but we affirm its judgment that Hoxie's (D) security interest has priority over Hague's (D).

Analysis:

This case is in sync with the current version of § 9–324. Official Comment 5 provides that if a debtor never receives possession of the collateral, as Morken never did here, the five-year period never begins, and the PMSI has priority even if the creditor does not give notice. Notice is required when the collateral is inventory, but not when the collateral is consumer goods. This is because in inventory financing, debtors often ask their general creditors for new extensions and offer new collateral. The notice requirement protects general creditors from dishonest debtors that seek a secured loan against new inventory from the original creditor when the debtor had already granted a PMSI to another creditor. The priority extends to cash proceeds only to the extent the proceeds are received on or before the delivery of the inventory to a buyer. The inventory purchase money lender's priority does not carry over into accounts receivable that arise when the inventory is sold. This rule is based on the commercial expectations of creditors that lend against inventory and creditors that lend against accounts.

■ CASE VOCABULARY

PLEDGE: Perfection of a security interest by possession.

International Harvester Co. v. Glendenning

(Secured Creditor) v. (Purchaser of Collateral)
505 S.W.2d 320, 14 UCC Rep. Serv. 837 (Tex.Civ.App.1974)

BUYER WHO DOES NOT ACT IN GOOD FAITH BUYS SUBJECT TO SECURITY INTEREST

■ **INSTANT FACTS** Glendenning (D) purchased three tractors in which International Harvester Co. (P) had a security interest.

■ **BLACK LETTER RULE** A buyer in the ordinary course of business is one who acts in good faith and does not have knowledge that the sale violates a security agreement.

■ PROCEDURAL BASIS

Appeal from damages action for conversion.

■ FACTS

For 20 years, Glendenning (D) bought, sold, and traded tractors. He had previously owned an International Harvester Co. ("International") (P) dealership and been an International (P) salesman. He was familiar with International's (P) custom of "floor-planning" tractors whereby International (P) would supply tractors to dealers who would then give International (P) a note and security interest in the tractors. When a dealer sold a tractor, he would pay International (P) the amount due. Glendenning (D) agreed to buy three tractors from Barnes, an International (P) dealer, for $16,000 cash. Glendenning (D) believed the tractors were worth $22,500. International (P) had a perfected security interest in the tractors. In connection with the sale, Barnes filled out a Retail Order Form stating that Glendenning (D) had traded in four tractors worth $8,700 and paid $16,000 cash, making a total purchase price of $24,700. Barnes and Glendenning (D) signed the form. Glendenning (D) did not ask Barnes or International (P) whether the tractors were subject to a security interest. A few days later, Glendenning (D) told an International (P) representative that he had traded four tractors to Barnes. Glendenning (D) subsequently sold the three tractors in Louisiana. International (P) sued Glendenning (D) claiming that he was not a buyer in the ordinary course of business and that the sale was subject to International's (P) security interest. Glendenning (D) argued that he was a buyer in the ordinary course of business and that the purchase was made in good faith without any knowledge of International's (P) security interest. The jury verdict was in favor of Glendenning (D).

■ ISSUE

To be a buyer in the ordinary course of business, must a buyer act in good faith?

■ DECISION AND RATIONALE

(Williams, C.J.) Yes. Section 9–307 (now § 9–320(a)) provides that a buyer in the ordinary course of business takes free of any security interests taken by the buyer's seller. However, a buyer in the ordinary course of business must act in good faith and without knowledge that the sale violated a third party's security interest. Good faith requires honesty in fact in the transaction. Glendenning (D) purchased the tractors for considerably less than their value, did not inquire into International's (P) interest, acquiesced in the falsification of a retail order form, and lied to International's (P) representa-

International Harvester Co. v. Glendenning (Continued)

tive. Clearly, Glendenning (D) did not act in good faith and was not a buyer in the ordinary course of business. Reversed.

Analysis:

Section 1–201(9) defines "buyer in the ordinary course of business" as a person who buys in good faith and without knowledge that the sale to him is in violation of the ownership rights or security interest of a third party. Section 9-320(a) provides that a buyer in ordinary course of business takes free of a security interest created by the buyer's seller, even if the security interest is perfected and the buyer knows of its existence. While these sections may seem to conflict, they do not. Official Comment 3 to § 9–320 explains that a buyer takes free of the security interest if the buyer merely knows that a security interest covers the goods, but takes subject to the security interest if the buyer also knows that the sale violates a term in an agreement with the secured party. One who buys dishonestly is not within the definition of "buyer in the ordinary course of business," even if the dishonesty is not related to the buyer's knowledge about the security interest.

First National Bank and Trust Co. of El Dorado v. Ford Motor Credit Co.

(Bank/Creditor) v. (Credit Company/Creditor)
231 Kan. 431, 646 P.2d 1057, 34 UCC Rep. Serv. 746 (1982)

ONLY BUYER ACTING IN GOOD FAITH IS BUYER IN THE ORDINARY COURSE WHO TAKES FREE OF EXISTING SECURITY INTERESTS

■ **INSTANT FACTS** Two creditors both claimed the proceeds from the sale of two vehicles that were on the debtor's lot but that had been sold in a sham sale to two of the debtor's principals.

■ **BLACK LETTER RULE** Only a buyer acting in good faith is a buyer in the ordinary course of business who takes free of existing security interests.

■ **PROCEDURAL BASIS**

Appeal of action to turn over personal property.

■ **FACTS**

In 1978, Heritage Ford Lincoln Mercury, Inc. ("Heritage") entered into a "floor plan" loan agreement with Ford Motor Credit Company ("Ford") (D). Under the agreement, Heritage gave Ford (D) a purchase money security interest ("PMSI") in all the vehicles it owned or acquired. Heritage was required to repay Ford (D) when Heritage sold a car. Ford (D) perfected its security interest. The floor plan agreement provided that Heritage would sell the cars in the ordinary course of business, which the agreement defined as a bona fide retail sale to a purchaser for his own use at fair market value. In 1981, Heritage was in financial trouble, and the officers of Heritage decided to double finance several new cars. Tom Overton, president of Heritage, and Robert Magill, vice-president of Heritage, issued dealer papers to themselves and obtained financing from First National Bank and Trust Co. of El Dorado ("Bank") (P). (Another car was at issue too, but the excerpt of the opinion does not discuss the third car.) The cars were sold for less than their fair market value. The loan proceeds were deposited directly into Heritage's account at the Bank (P) and were never paid to Ford (D). One security interest was perfected; the other was not. Overton and Magill did not obtain licenses for the cars. The cars remained on Heritage's lot and were available for sale. A couple of weeks later, Heritage quit business and surrendered its entire inventory, including the two cars at issue, to Ford (D). The Bank (P) sued to establish its claim to the two cars. The trial court held that the Bank (P) had a prior purchase money security interest. The Bank (P) then obtained the cars and sold them.

■ **ISSUE**

Must a buyer act in good faith to be a buyer in the ordinary course of business who takes free of existing security interests?

■ **DECISION AND RATIONALE**

(Fromme, J.) Yes. UCC § 9–312 [now § 9–324(b)] provides that a perfected PMSI in inventory has priority over a conflicting security interest. Therefore, Ford (D) had priority subject to the rights of a buyer in the ordinary course of business. Section 9–307 [now § 9–320] provides that a buyer in the

First National Bank and Trust Co. of El Dorado v. Ford Motor Credit Co. (Continued)

ordinary course of business takes free of a security interest created by his seller. Section 1–201(9) defines "buyer in ordinary course of business" as a person who buys in good faith and without knowledge that the sale violates a security interest. There is no question that Overton's and Magill's sham sales violated the security agreement with Ford (D). Overton and Magill did not obtain licenses for the cars, and the cars remained available for sale. The cars were sold for less than their fair market value. Thus, Overton and Magill were not buyers in the ordinary course of business. Moreover, § 9–307 protects only buyers. The Bank (P) was not a buyer; it was a financier. Therefore, § 9–307 did not provide any protection to the Bank (P). Official Comment 3 to § 9–306(2) (now § 9-315(a)(1)) provides that when a debtor makes an unauthorized disposition of collateral, as Heritage did here, the security interest continues in the collateral. Accordingly, Ford's (D) security interest continued in the vehicles and in the proceeds. Reversed.

Analysis:

To purchase free of a prior security interest, a buyer must be a buyer in the ordinary course who (1) does not buy in bulk and does not take the interest as security for or in total or partial satisfaction of a preexisting debt, (2) buys from one in the business of selling goods of that kind, (3) buys in good faith and without knowledge that the purchase violates another's ownership rights or security interest, and (3) does not buy farm products from a person engaged in farming operations. The competing security interest must be created by the seller. Basically, § 9–307 covers the simple situation where a customer buys a car from a dealer. Even though the car is covered by a floor plan security agreement, as the cars here were, and the buyer knows about the security agreement because they are common in the industry, the sale does not violate the security agreement. Therefore, the customer buys the car free and clear of the floor plan security interest. Section 9–307 was not meant to protect dishonest buyers like Glendenning, Overton, and Magill.

Clovis National Bank v. Thomas

(Bank) v. (Cattle Auctioneer)
77 N.M. 554, 425 P.2d 726, 4 UCC Rep. Serv. 137 (1967)

BY CONSENTING TO SALE OF COLLATERAL AND NOT DEMANDING PAYMENT, CREDITOR WAIVES ITS SECURITY INTEREST

■ **INSTANT FACTS** Bunch sold cattle with the implicit knowledge and consent of his secured creditor, Clovis National Bank (P). Clovis National Bank (P) did not demand payment, thereby waiving its security interest.

■ **BLACK LETTER RULE** By consenting to the sale of collateral and not demanding payment, a secured creditor waives its security interest.

■ **PROCEDURAL BASIS**

Appeal of damages action for conversion.

■ **FACTS**

Clovis National Bank ("Clovis") (P) made several loans to Bunch and obtained a security interests in Bunch's cattle branded "W D Bar." The security agreement between Clovis (P) and Bunch provided that Bunch would not sell the cattle without Clovis' (P) prior written consent. Bunch deposited with Clovis various checks for the proceeds from the sale of the cattle covered by the security agreements. Two checks were given by Thomas (D), a licensed cattle auctioneer, who handled the sales for Bunch. Clovis (P) was aware that Bunch was selling cattle covered by the security agreements. Bunch then consigned cattle to Thomas (D) for sale. Clovis (P) had no actual knowledge of these sales. Bunch's son, Bunch Jr., owned a brand of cattle called "Swastika K." Bunch or his son acquired cattle that were branded Swastika K. No security agreement was given by Bunch or his son to Clovis (P) for these cattle. Clovis (P) thereafter requested that Bunch sell the remainder of his cattle, including the Swastika K cattle. With Clovis' (P) knowledge, Bunch trucked cattle to Thomas' (D) place of business. Clovis (P) told Thomas (D) that it had an interest in the cattle. After the cattle were sold, Clovis told Thomas (D) that it would be "nice" if the check for the cattle would be made payable to the Bunches and to Clovis (P). Clovis (P) did not demand payment or ask Thomas (D) not to pay Bunch. Bunch Jr. demanded payment from Thomas (D) and Thomas (D) paid him. Clovis (P) first sued Bunch and Bunch Jr. for garnishment, but that suit was unsuccessful. Clovis (P) then sued Thomas (D) for conversion. The trial court held for Thomas (D) on the grounds that (1) Clovis (P) consented to the sales of the W D Bar cattle and to the receipt by Bunch of the proceeds, and, thus, waived any possessory rights it may have had in the cattle, and (2) Clovis (P) did not have a security interest in the Swastika K cattle.

■ **ISSUE**

By consenting to the sale of collateral and not demanding payment, does a secured creditor waive its security interest?

■ **DECISION AND RATIONALE**

(Oman, J.) Yes. Through its course of conduct, Clovis (P) permitted, acquiesced in, and consented to Bunch's sales of the W D Bar cattle. Clovis (P) never demanded that Bunch give Clovis (P) prior written

Clovis National Bank v. Thomas (Continued)

consent before selling the cattle. Clovis (P) relied on Bunch to turn over the proceeds of the sales. When Clovis (P) consented to the sales and to Bunch's collection of the proceeds, Clovis (P) waived its security interests. UCC § 9–307(1) (now § 9-320(a)) expressly excludes livestock and other farm products from the rule that a buyer in the ordinary course of business takes free of a security interest created by the seller. The weight of authority holds that auctioneers are personally liable when they sell property subject to a lien unless the creditor is estopped from recovery or consents to the sale. Thus, ordinarily, Thomas (D) would be liable to Clovis (P) for conversion of the cattle. Here, while Clovis (P) may not be estopped from recovery (it did not expressly consent to the sales), it impliedly acquiesced and consented to the sales. The UCC does not have a provision regarding waiver; therefore, the common law applies. Accordingly, Thomas (D) is not liable for conversion of the W D Bar cattle because Clovis (P) consented to and acquiesced in the sale of the cattle, and thereby waived its rights in it. Affirmed.

Analysis:

The court here did not consider § 1–205(4), which provides that the express terms of an agreement and a course of conduct are to be construed as consistent with one another. When they cannot be so construed, the express terms control. UCC § 1–205(1) defines "course of conduct" as a sequence of previous conduct between the parties to a particular transaction which establishes a common basis for interpreting their expressions and other conduct. While, technically, course of conduct includes only the conduct between the parties before they entered into the agreement, § 2–208(1) provides that any course of performance accepted or acquiesced in without objection is relevant to determine the meaning of an agreement. Section 9-320(a) provides that a buyer of farm products, unlike a buyer of other inventory, does not take free of security interests in the products. This reflects the national policy to encourage lenders to lend money to farmers. Farm lenders also convinced the UCC drafters that buyers of farm products are more sophisticated than other consumers and could, therefore, be expected to check for financing statements and remit proceeds to secured creditors. However, a 1985 federal statute now preempts the § 9-320(a) farm products exclusion. Section 1324 of the Food Security Act allows a buyer of farm products to take free of a bank's security interest so long as the buyer complies with certain notice provisions.

■ CASE VOCABULARY

CONVERSION: The unauthorized and wrongful assumption and exercise of dominion and control over another's personal property, to the exclusion of, or inconsistent with, the other person's rights.

ESTOPPEL: Knowing and express oral or written consent to conduct that gave rise to an injury, thereby precluding a claim based on that conduct.

Farm Credit Bank of St. Paul v. F & A Dairy

(*Secured Creditor*) v. (*Buyer of Collateral*)
166 Wis.2d 360, 477 N.W.2d 357, 16 UCC Rep. Serv. 2d 885 (1991)

UNDER FOOD SECURITY ACT, BUYER TAKES SUBJECT TO SECURITY INTEREST IF CREDITOR COMPLIES WITH NOTICE REQUIREMENTS

■ **INSTANT FACTS** F&A Dairy (D) bought milk that was subject to Farm Credit Bank of St. Paul's (P) security interest.

■ **BLACK LETTER RULE** Under the Food Security Act, a buyer of collateral takes subject to a security interest if a creditor complies with the Act's notice requirements.

■ **PROCEDURAL BASIS**

Appeal of damages action for conversion.

■ **FACTS**

The Bonneprises own and operate a dairy farm. Farm Credit Bank of St. Paul ("Farm Credit") (P) loaned them $300,000 and obtained and perfected a security interest in the Bonneprises' milk. The Bonneprises sold milk to Land O' Lakes Dairy. In exchange for waiving its lien, Farm Credit (P) entered into an assignment agreement whereby Land O' Lakes would pay Farm Credit (P) $4333 per month from the Bonneprises' milk proceeds. In August 1988, the Bonneprises switched dairies and began selling milk to F&A Dairy ("F&A") (D). The Bonneprises refused to enter into an assignment agreement requiring F&A (D) to pay Farm Credit (P). In August 1988, Farm Credit (P) sent F&A (D) a letter demanding $4333 per month and enclosing a product lien notification statement and a copy of the filed financing statement. Four days later, Farm Credit (P) notified F&A (D) of its perfected security interest and enclosed a copy of the security agreement. F&A (D) refused to pay Farm Credit (P) during August, September, October, and November. The trial court held that Farm Credit (P) had a perfected security interest in the milk and that, under § 1631 of the Food Security Act, F&A (D) bought the milk subject to Farm Credit's (P) security interest. It also held that F&A (D) converted $4333 per month for proceeds from the August, September, October, and November milk sales.

■ **ISSUE**

Under § 1631 of the Food Security Act, does a buyer take subject to a creditor's security interest?

■ **DECISION AND RATIONALE**

(Cane, J.) Yes, if the creditor gives proper notice. Section 1631 preempts UCC § 9–307 [now § 9–320(a)] [buyers of farm products take subject to security interests]. Under § 1631(e), a buyer of farm

Farm Credit Bank of St. Paul v. F&A Dairy (Continued)

products takes subject to a security interest if, within one year before the sale, the buyer has received from the seller written notice of the security interest containing certain required information, including notice of any payment obligation. Here, Farm Credit (P) sent proper notice to F&A (D). F&A (D) argues that Farm Credit's (P) notice of the $4333 payment obligation was ambiguous. We hold that it was not ambiguous. In fact, Farm Credit (P) was entitled to all the sale proceeds, not just $4333 a month. The requirement that the creditor provide notice of any payment obligation allows the creditor to accept less of the proceeds if it desires. We also disagree with F&A's (D) argument that an assignment agreement was required before it had to pay Farm Credit (P). While Farm Credit's (P) notice requested an assignment, § 1631(e) does not require an assignment. Section 1631(e) requires that the notice be given within one year before the sale of the farm products. The Bonneprises began selling milk to F&A (D) in early August and Farm Credit (P) sent its notice in late August. Thus, the notice was untimely for the August sales, but was timely for the September, October, and November sales. With respect to Farm Credit's (P) claim for conversion, Farm Credit (P) must prove that it was entitled to immediate possession of the milk. When the Bonneprises defaulted on their August payment to Farm Credit (P), under UCC § 9–503 [now § 9–609] [secured party may take possession after default], Farm Credit (P) was entitled to immediate possession of the milk. Therefore, F&A (D) is liable for conversion. Affirmed in part, reversed in part.

Analysis:

The Food Security Act allows buyers of farm products to take free of security interests created by the seller even if the security interest is perfected and the buyer knows of the security interest. A security interest is protected in three situations. Two situations depend upon a state establishing a central filing system whereby buyers can obtain information about financing statements filed for products they tend to buy. The other exception is the notice at issue here. The notice required by the Food Security Act is much more detailed than that required in a financing statement, and includes the debtor's social security number or taxpayer identification number, and the type, county, crop year, and amount of the farm products. While § 1631 of the Food Security Act preempts the UCC with respect to defining a buyer in the ordinary course, the UCC still applies with respect to perfecting a security interest against an attack by a bankruptcy trustee and in analyzing whether a creditor waived a security agreement or is estopped from asserting its terms.

■ CASE VOCABULARY

PREEMPTION: Occurs when federal law expressly or implicitly replaces state law. Implicit preemption may occur when federal law comprehensively occupies an entire field of regulation or when state law conflicts with federal law and makes it impossible to carry out Congress' objectives.

In re Arlco, Inc.
(Bankrupt Debtor)
239 B.R. 261, 39 UCC Rep.Serv.2d (Bankr.S.D.N.Y.1999)

SECURED CREDITOR WITH A FLOATING LIEN ON INVENTORY IS A GOOD FAITH PURCHASER WHOSE RIGHTS ARE SUPERIOR TO THOSE OF A RECLAIMING SELLER

■ **INSTANT FACTS** Galey (P) demanded reclamation of goods it sold to Arley (D), but CIT had a perfected security interest in Arley's (D) inventory, and the goods Galey (P) sought were sold to satisfy CIT's claim.

■ **BLACK LETTER RULE** A creditor with a security interest in after-acquired property who has acted in good faith and for value, which includes acquiring rights as security for a preexisting claim, is a good faith purchaser with a claim superior to that of a reclaiming seller.

■ **PROCEDURAL BASIS**

Motions for summary judgment in bankruptcy adversary proceeding seeking reclamation of goods.

■ **FACTS**

Arley Corporation (Arley) (D) was a wholesaler of home furnishings. Since 1995, CIT Group/Business Credit Inc. (CIT) has held a perfected security interest in substantially all of Arley's (D) assets, including accounts receivable and inventory. Galey & Lord, Inc. (Galey) (P), in its ordinary course of business, sold textile goods on credit to Arley (D). On May 16, 1997, Galey (P) sent a letter to Arley (D) (May 16th letter) demanding that Arley (D) return the goods it received during the prior 10 days and notifying Arley (D) that it should protect and segregate all goods subject to its reclamation right and not use them for any purpose. On June 6, 1997, Arley (D) filed for chapter 11 bankruptcy, and on June 9, Galey (P) commenced an adversary proceeding against Arley (D) for reclamation of the goods it referred to in its May 16th letter. In September 1997, the court approved an asset purchase agreement for the sale of substantially all of Arley's (D) assets. Pursuant to this agreement, Arley (D) changed its name to Arlco, Inc. In August 1998, the court converted Arley's (D) chapter 11 case and appointed a chapter 7 trustee (Trustee). Galey (P) now moves for summary judgment in its adversary proceeding, arguing that it has complied with all the statutory requirements for reclamation. The Trustee opposes this motion and moves for summary judgment in Arley's (D) favor, arguing that Galey's (P) right to reclamation is subject to CIT's perfected security interest.

■ **ISSUE**

Does a secured creditor with a security interest in after-acquired inventory have a claim superior to that of a reclaiming seller?

■ **DECISION AND RATIONALE**

(Gonzalez) Yes. The purpose of *11 U.S.C. § 546(c)* [makes trustee's powers in bankruptcy subject to seller's nonbankruptcy reclamation rights] is not to create a new right to reclamation, but only to give the seller an opportunity to use any reclamation right it has under nonbankruptcy law. Under § 546(c), a seller may reclaim goods it has sold to an insolvent debtor if it establishes by a preponderance of the

In re Arlco, Inc. (Continued)

evidence (1) that it has a statutory or common law right to reclaim the goods; (2) that it sold the goods in its ordinary course of business; (3) that the debtor was insolvent when it received the goods; and (4) that the seller made a written demand for reclamation within 10 days of the debtor's receipt of the goods. To be subject to reclamation, goods must be identifiable and cannot have been processed into other products, and they must be in the debtor's possession or control when the seller makes his demand for reclamation. Sellers usually base their reclamation demand on *UCC § 2–702* [seller's reclamation right]. Under *§ 2–702(3)* [good faith purchaser's right is superior to reclamation right], the seller's right to reclamation is "subject to" the rights of a good faith purchaser from the buyer. This does not automatically extinguish the reclamation right, but only makes it subordinate to the good faith purchaser's right. Most courts treat a holder of a prior perfected, floating lien on inventory as a good faith purchaser. Galey (P) points out that to define "good faith purchaser," these courts have referred to the definitions of *UCC § 1–201* [general definitions]. However, Galey (P) argues that because § 2–702(3) makes the reclaiming seller's interest subject to the interest of a good faith purchaser "under this Article," only a party that acquires its secured interest in inventory under Article 2 is a good faith purchaser that receives § 2-702(3)'s protection. Therefore, Galey (P) argues, § 2–702(3) does not cover parties that acquire security interests under Article 9. § 2–702(3) states that the reclamation right is "subject to the rights of a buyer in the ordinary course or other good faith purchaser under this Article (Section 2–403)." However, neither *§ 2–403* [power to transfer; good faith purchase of goods; entrusting] nor any other section in Article 2 defines "good faith purchaser." One must refer to § 1–201 for this definition, which provides general definitions for the entire UCC. *§ 1–201(19)* ["good faith"] defines "good faith" as "honesty in fact in the conduct or transaction concerned." When dealing with a merchant, *2-103(1)(b)* [defines "good faith" for a merchant] requires "observance of reasonable commercial standards of fair dealing in the trade." *§§ 1–201(32), (33)* ["purchase," "purchaser"] define a purchaser as one who takes "by sale, discount, negotiation, mortgage, pledge, lien, issue or re-issue, gift or any other voluntary transaction creating an interest in property." This definition is broad enough to include an Article 9 secured party, which then qualifies as a purchaser under § 2–403. The language of § 2–702(3) does not imply that reclaiming sellers are only subject to interests acquired under Article 2, but rather focuses on the parties' rights under Article 2. Its reference to § 2–403 is meant to help define those rights. § 2–403 provides that a person with voidable title can transfer good title to a good faith purchaser for value. *§ 1–201(44)* ["value"] considers "value" to be given for rights if they are acquired "as security for or in total or partial satisfaction of a pre-existing claim." Thus, under § 2–403, a party who qualifies as a "good faith purchaser" and gives "value" under § 1–201 acquires greater rights than the party transferring the goods to it had. Here, if CIT qualifies as a good faith purchaser and gave value, then under § 2–403, even if Arley (D) had only voidable title to the goods, it could still transfer good title to CIT. If CIT obtained the goods this way, then under § 2–702(3) the demand of a reclaiming seller would be subject to CIT's interest. Galey (P) also argues that although many courts hold that perfected lienholders are good faith purchasers, legal scholars still debate this issue. According to one view, *§ 2–702(2)* [gives seller right to reclaim goods from insolvent buyer within 10 days after buyer's receipt of the goods] gives a seller the rights of a purchase-money security holder for 10 days, and the purchase-money lender has priority over a creditor with a security interest in after-acquired inventory. The premise of this view is the idea that we should only consider the secured creditor as a good faith purchaser for value if he has suffered detrimental reliance by extending new value. Scholars that hold this view acknowledge that prior secured lenders with an after-acquired property interest meet the literal requirements of a good faith purchaser for value, but argue that § 2–403 and a weighing of the equities justify a more flexible approach. However, if the language of a statute is plain, the court should enforce it according to its terms. Based on our earlier analysis of the relevant UCC sections, we find that a creditor with a security interest in after-acquired property who acted in good faith and for value, which includes acquiring rights as security for or in total or partial satisfaction of a preexisting claim, is a good faith purchaser with a claim superior to that of a reclaiming seller. We now must decide whether CIT acted in good faith. § 1–201(19) defines good faith as "honesty in fact," which, for Article 2 purposes, means "reasonable commercial standards of fair dealing." Galey (P) argues that a factual issue as to CIT's good faith prevents us from deciding this issue on summary judgment. However, Galey (P) does not challenge the validity of the lien, assert any misconduct by CIT, or allege that CIT acted in bad faith in its dealings with Arley (D). Galey (P) argues that CIT knew Arley (D) was having financial problems and stopped advancing funds to Arley (D) without informing Galey (P). However, a secured creditor with a floating lien remains a good faith

In re Arlco, Inc. (Continued)

purchaser even if it terminates funding knowing that sums are owed to third parties, as long as the decision to terminate funding was commercially reasonable. It is clearly reasonable to stop funding a business with enormous debt and continuous losses. An entity that advances funds secured by a valid lien on the borrower's assets is a good faith purchaser absent a showing of misconduct by the secured creditor, and it is the reclaiming seller's burden to show such misconduct. Galey's (P) conclusory statements about CIT's absence of good faith do not create the fair doubt necessary to present a genuine issue of material fact. There is also no factual dispute about whether CIT gave value and qualifies as a good faith purchaser for value. We therefore grant summary judgment on the issue of CIT's good faith and find that CIT qualifies as a good faith purchaser for value. As we have previously noted, although a seller's reclamation right is subject to the rights of a good faith purchaser, the good faith purchaser's rights do not automatically extinguish the reclamation right. Therefore, Galey (P) argues that it is entitled to an administrative claim or lien in lieu of its right to reclamation because otherwise the presence of a good faith purchaser would effectively extinguish its claim. Galey (P) argues that because there will be surplus collateral after CIT is paid in full, payment of its administrative claim or lien should come from that collateral. The Trustee does not argue that Galey's (P) claim is extinguished, but that once the goods subject to a reclamation demand are liquidated and the proceeds used to pay the secured creditor's claim, the subordinated reclamation right becomes valueless. The Trustee argues that once the secured creditor is paid in full, the reclaiming seller can only reclaim surplus collateral if it consists of the very goods that it sold or the traceable proceeds from those goods. The court has broad discretion under § 546(c) to substitute an administrative claim or lien in place of a right to reclaim. This gives the court the flexibility it needs to recognize the reclaiming creditor's rights while allowing the debtor to keep the goods to help his reorganization effort. However, courts differ on how to treat reclaiming sellers subject to the rights of good faith purchasers. Some award them an administrative claim or replacement lien for the full amount of the goods they seek to reclaim. The majority, however, give the seller only what he would have received outside the bankruptcy context after the superior claim was satisfied. Thus, only when the reclaiming seller's goods or traceable proceeds from those goods exceed the value of the good faith purchaser's claim can the seller either reclaim the goods that remain after the superior claim has been paid or receive an administrative claim or lien for their value. While the reclaiming seller's claim is not automatically extinguished when his rights are subject to those of a good faith purchaser, he also is not automatically granted an administrative claim or lien for the full amount sought. His right to reclaim depends on the value of the goods that remain after satisfaction of the secured creditor's claim. Since a bankruptcy filing does not enhance the reclaiming seller's rights, we should determine what would have happened to his claim in a nonbankruptcy context. The secured creditor would have the option to proceed against any of its collateral, including by foreclosing on the goods sold by the reclaiming seller. When those goods are used to pay the secured creditor's claim, the seller's right to reclaim becomes valueless. Here, CIT did not seek to liquidate all assets, but supported Arley's (D) efforts to sell its inventory, including Galey's (P) goods, in the ordinary course of its business. All of the goods Galey (P) sought to reclaim were sold, and the proceeds went to CIT. Galey's (P) reclamation claim, and any administrative claim or replacement lien it might have, has therefore been rendered valueless. Galey's (P) motion for summary judgment is denied, and the Trustee's motion for summary judgment in Arley's (D) favor is granted.

Analysis:

This case demonstrates that a secured creditor with a floating lien on inventory is a good faith purchaser who gets to fully satisfy his claim from the inventory before a reclaiming seller can enforce his rights at all. Only if there are goods left over after the secured creditor's claim is satisfied, and those goods happen to include the very goods or proceeds the reclaiming seller has a right to, can the seller enforce his reclamation right. The reclaiming seller has no rights in any other goods, so if his goods do not remain, he must resort to standing in line with all the other While preservation of the UCC priority system may require tolerating occasional minor inequities, equity will intervene in extraordinary situations. As discussed in this case, bad faith will except a case from the general rule governing priority of claims.

In re Arlco, Inc. (Continued)

■ **CASE VOCABULARY**

FLOATING LIEN: A lien against a set of assets, some of which the debtor owns and some of which he will acquire later (such as a lien on inventory).

RECLAMATION: The right to or process of demanding the return of goods that a seller has delivered to an insolvent buyer.

George v. Commercial Credit Corp.

(Bankruptcy Trustee) v. (Secured Creditor)
440 F.2d 551, 8 UCC Rep. Serv. 1315 (7th Cir.1971)

MOBILE HOME MAY BE FIXTURE SUBJECT TO A REAL ESTATE MORTGAGE

■ **INSTANT FACTS** A bankruptcy trustee claimed that the debtor's mobile home was a motor vehicle, not a fixture, and was not subject to a real estate mortgage.

■ **BLACK LETTER RULE** A mobile home may be a fixture subject to a real estate mortgage.

■ **PROCEDURAL BASIS**

Appeal of a bankruptcy court order.

■ **FACTS**

Foskett owned five acres of land. In December 1968, he purchased a mobile home from Highway Mobile Home Sales, Inc. ("Highway") on an installment contract. The mobile home was set on cinder blocks and was hooked up to a septic tank and to gas and electrical lines. Foskett asked the seller to remove the wheels. Foskett did not apply for a certificate of title from the Wisconsin Motor Vehicle Department, but he did apply for a homeowner's insurance policy. He also applied for a building permit. Also in December 1968, Foskett executed a real estate mortgage to Highway, who then assigned the mortgage to Commercial Credit Corporation ("CCC") (D). After Foskett filed for bankruptcy, the trustee in bankruptcy (P) claimed that the mobile home was personal property and was not subject to CCC's (D) mortgage. The bankruptcy court sustained CCC's (D) interest in the mobile home. The district court affirmed.

■ **ISSUE**

Can a mobile home become a fixture and thereby be subject to a real estate mortgage?

■ **DECISION AND RATIONALE**

(Duffy, J.) Yes. In Wisconsin, we apply a three-part test to determine whether personal property becomes a fixture. We look at (1) actual physical annexation to the realty; (2) application or adaption to the use or purpose to which the realty is devoted; and (3) the intention of the person annexing to make a permanent accession to the real property. The party's intention is the main consideration; physical annexation is relatively unimportant. Here, Foskett treated the mobile home like part of the real estate. He applied for a building permit, bought homeowner's insurance, and requested that the wheels be removed from the mobile home. Therefore, Foskett clearly intended that the mobile home be part of the realty. In addition, the mobile home was adapted to use as Foskett's permanent residence. The fact that the mobile home could have been more securely attached to the ground is not relevant. It was attached to cinder blocks and was connected to electricity, sewage, and gas. Also, the home was large and difficult to transport. This holding is consistent with UCC § 9-334(b) which provides that the UCC does not prevent encumbrances upon fixtures under real estate law. Affirmed.

George v. Commercial Credit Corp. (Continued)

Analysis:

UCC § 9-334 covers fixtures and recognizes three categories of goods: "pure goods" that retain their chattel character and are not part of the real property; "pure realty," i.e., ordinary building materials that have become an integral part of the real property; and "fixtures," an intermediate class that has become real property for certain purposes, but as to which chattel financing may be preserved. The American Law of Property defines a fixture as a former chattel that is so connected with the realty that a disinterested observer would consider it a part thereof. Whether personal property has become a fixture depends specifically on what would be included in a deed in that state. Most courts look at the intention of the parties, as the court here did. However, intention may be manifested in various ways, such as how the parties attached the goods to the real estate and how the goods are related to the use of the real property.

■ **CASE VOCABULARY**

FIXTURE: Goods that have become so related to particular real property that an interest in them arises under real property law. (UCC § 9-102(a)(41)).

Lewiston Bottled Gas Co. v. Key Bank of Maine

(Seller of Collateral/Secured Creditor) v. (Mortgage Holder)
601 A.2d 91, 17 UCC Rep. Serv. 2d 282 (Me.1992)

FIXTURE FILING MUST INCLUDE NAME OF RECORD OWNER OF REAL PROPERTY TO HAVE PRIORITY OVER REAL ESTATE MORTGAGE

■ **INSTANT FACTS** Lewiston Bottled Gas Co.'s (P) purchase money security interest did not have priority over Key Bank of Maine's (D) real estate mortgage because the fixture filing did not state the name of the record owner of the real property.

■ **BLACK LETTER RULE** A purchase money security interest in a fixture has priority over a real estate mortgage if the fixture filing includes all the required information.

■ **PROCEDURAL BASIS**

Appeal of summary judgment.

■ **FACTS**

In July 1986, DiBiase borrowed money from Key Bank of Maine ("Key Bank") (D). The loan was secured by a mortgage on real property owned by DiBiase on which he was going to build the Grand Beach Inn. The mortgage included after-acquired fixtures. The mortgage was properly recorded. In June 1987, Grand Beach purchased 90 heating and air-conditioning units from Lewiston Bottled Gas Co. ("LBG") (P). The contract between Grand Beach and LBG (P) provided that the units would remain Grand Beach's personal property notwithstanding their attachment to the real property. LBG (P) obtained a purchase money security interest in the 90 units. LBG (P) filed a financing statement identifying the debtor as "Grand Beach Inn, Inc., William J. DiBiase, Jr., President." The statements were indexed under the name "Grand Beach Inn, Inc." Nothing was indexed under DiBiase's name. Later in June 1987, Key Bank (D) made another loan to DiBiase secured by a second mortgage on the same property. Key Bank's (D) title search failed to disclose LBG's (P) financing statement. In 1989, Key Bank (D) foreclosed on both the mortgages. LBG (P) was not joined as a party because Key Bank (D) did not know of LBG's (P) interest in the units. LBG (P) filed this action seeking a declaratory judgment that its purchase money security interest in the units had priority over Key Bank's (D) mortgages. The trial court granted summary judgment for Key Bank (D), holding that the units were fixtures and that Key Bank's (D) mortgages had priority over LBG's (P) unperfected security interest.

■ **ISSUE**

Does a purchase money security interest in fixtures have priority over a real estate mortgage?

■ **DECISION AND RATIONALE**

(Clifford, J.) Yes, if the fixture filing includes all the required information. Whether the units were fixtures is based on a three-prong test. Goods become fixtures when they are (1) physically annexed to the real estate; (2) adapted to the use to which the real estate is put; and (3) annexed with the intent to make them part of the real estate. Here, the units were part of the walls of the Grand Beach Inn and were, therefore, physically annexed to the real estate. The units helped create a livable atmosphere for guests of the Inn and, therefore, were adapted to the use of the real estate. With respect to the intent of the parties, LBG (P) argues that the units were not fixtures because the agreement between LBG (P) and DiBiase specifically stated that the units would remain personal property. However, in determining the intent of the parties, we look at the external facts, such as the structure and mode of attachment, not at the parties' hidden subjective intent. The agreement between LBG (P) and DiBiase cannot be used against Key Bank (D) because Key Bank (D) was not a party to the agreement and was not aware of it. The physical annexation of the units to the walls of the building clearly indicates that the units were intended to be fixtures and part of the Grand Beach real estate. Because the units were fixtures, pursuant to § 9–313, Key Bank's (D) mortgage would take priority over LBG's (P) security interest. The only exception to this is found in § 9-313(4)(a) (now § 9-334(d)) which provides that a perfected purchase money security interest has priority over a conflicting real estate mortgage. However, here, LBG's (P) purchase money security interest was not properly perfected. Section 9–402(5) (now § 9-502(b)) requires that a fixture filing must include, not only the general requirements for financing statements, but must also include the name of the record owner of the real estate if the debtor does not have an interest of record in the real estate. Here, LBG's (P) fixture filing failed to identify DiBiase as the record owner of the property. Moreover, the fixture filing failed to give a title searcher sufficient notice to make further inquiry concerning the lien. Therefore, because LBG (P) failed to properly perfect its security interest in the units, Key Bank's (D) mortgage takes priority over LBG's (P) security interest.

Analysis:

The court here made two key rulings. First, it decided that the heating and air conditioning units are fixtures. Next it decided that LBG's (P) security interest was not properly perfected and that, therefore, LBG's (P) purchase money security interest in the units did not have priority over Key Bank's (D) mortgage. With respect to whether the units are fixtures, the court rejected out of hand LBG's (P) argument that the agreement between LBG (P) and DiBiase specifically states that the units are to remain personal property. Instead, the court determined the parties' intent by looking at how the units were attached to the real estate and the purpose for the attachment. With respect to the priority issue, pursuant to § 9-334(c), ordinarily a security interest in fixtures is subordinate to a conflicting real estate mortgage. However, § 9-334(d) provides that a perfected purchase money security interest has priority if the real estate mortgage arises before the goods become fixtures and the security interest is perfected before the goods become fixtures or within twenty days thereafter. But § 9-502(b) provides that a financing statement for fixtures must provide the name of the record owner of the real property if the debtor does not have an interest therein. Section 9-519(d) requires the financing statement to be indexed in the name of that owner. Because LBG (P) failed to include the name of the owner of the real property, it lost its security interest.

Maplewood Bank & Trust v. Sears, Roebuck & Co.
(*Mortgage Holder*) v. (*Secured Creditor*)
265 N.J.Super. 25, 625 A.2d 537, 21 UCC Rep. Serv. 2d 171 (1993)

SECURED CREDITOR'S ONLY REMEDY IS TO REMOVE FIXTURES

■ **INSTANT FACTS** Sears (D) had a security interest in kitchen fixtures and argued that it had priority over the mortgage holder to the funds recovered on foreclosure.

■ **BLACK LETTER RULE** Upon the debtor's default, a secured party's only remedy is to remove the fixtures from the real estate, and it must reimburse the mortgage holder for the cost of repair.

■ PROCEDURAL BASIS
Appeal of summary judgment on counterclaim for declaratory relief.

■ FACTS
The Capers borrowed money from Maplewood Bank & Trust Company ("Maplewood") (P) to purchase a house. They then bought a new kitchen, including, countertops, cabinets, sinks, an oven, and a dishwasher from Sears, Roebuck and Company ("Sears") (D). Sears (D) installed the kitchen and filed a financing statement on its security interest in the kitchen. Later that year, the Capers executed a second mortgage to New Jersey Savings Bank ("New Jersey") (D). When the Capers defaulted on the loans, Maplewood (P) filed a foreclosure action. Sears (D) filed a counterclaim for a declaration that, pursuant to § 9–313 (now § 9–334) [purchase money security interest in fixtures has priority over conflicting mortgage], its lien was a purchase money security interest and, therefore, had priority over Maplewood's (P) mortgage. The trial court dismissed Sears' (D) counterclaim.

■ ISSUE
Upon a debtor's default, may a secured creditor institute judicial foreclosure proceedings and recover proceeds for fixtures?

■ DECISION AND RATIONALE
(Coleman, J.) No. It is undisputed that the kitchen is a fixture and that Sears (D) obtained and perfected a purchase money security interest. It is also undisputed that Sears (D) has "super priority" as to the kitchen fixtures. The dispute here is over Sears' (D) remedy. Sears (D) argues that it is entitled to file a judicial foreclosure action and recover the difference between the value of the realty with the new kitchen and the value of the realty after the new kitchen has been removed. Louisiana is the only state that has adopted Sears' (D) position, and there it was based on the legislature's modification of § 9–313(8) (now § 9–604) [lists creditor's remedies on default]. Sears' (D) argument that it may initiate a judicial foreclosure action is supported only by a journal article written by Professor Morris Shanker. We reject Sears' (D) argument because it is not authorized by statute, and we are not in a position to legislate long-established rights of purchase money mortgage holders. Section 9–313(8) provides that, upon the debtor's default, a secured party's only remedy is to remove the fixtures from the real estate, and it must reimburse the mortgage holder for the cost of repair. The fact that the fixtures are custom made is not relevant. Even based on equity, Sears (D) is not entitled to a different

Maplewood Bank & Trust v. Sears, Roebuck & Co. (Continued)

remedy. Sears (D) knew its remedy was limited to repossessing the kitchen upon default, and its own security agreement so provides. Thus, Sears (D) may either remove the kitchen and reimburse Maplewood (P) or not remove the kitchen. It is not entitled to any funds from the foreclosure. Affirmed.

Analysis:

The 1999 amendments to Article 9 overrule this case and adopt Sears' (D) and Professor Shanker's argument. Section 9–604 now provides that a creditor may enforce a security interest in fixtures by either removing the fixtures from the real property and reimbursing the mortgage holder for the cost of repair or by following real property law, including sale or other disposition of the property. Official Comment 3 states that the revised § 9–604 overrules cases such as this one that hold that a secured creditor's only remedy is the removal of the fixtures from the real property. Thus, now a secured creditor may not be entitled to sell the real property, but it may probably claim the amount of the debt owed to it or the value of the fixtures out of the proceeds of a sale of the property.

■ CASE VOCABULARY

JUDICIAL FORECLOSURE: An action by a creditor alleging the existence of a debt, default by the debtor, and the existence of a deed of trust or other lien. A foreclosure judgment directs a sheriff or constable to seize and sell the land in satisfaction of the judgment.

United States v. Estate of Romani
(*Federal Government*) v. (*Tax Debtor*)
523 U.S. 517, 118 S.Ct. 1478 (1998)

TAX CLAIM IS NOT VALID OVER PRIOR PERFECTED JUDGMENT LIEN

■ **INSTANT FACTS** Pursuant to the federal priority statute, the federal government claimed its tax claim was entitled to preference over a judgment creditor's lien on the real property in a decedent's estate.

■ **BLACK LETTER RULE** Pursuant to the Federal Tax Lien Act, the federal government's tax claim is not valid over a judgment creditor's prior perfected lien on real property.

■ **FACTS**

In 1985, Romani Industries' $400,000 judgment was recorded against Romani (D) in Cambria County, and thereby became a lien against all his real property in that county. Thereafter, the Internal Revenue Service (the "Government") (P) filed a series of notices of tax liens, totaling about $490,000, on Romani's (D) property. When Romani (D) died in 1992, his real estate was worth only about $53,000. When the administrator of Romani's estate (D) sought to transfer Romani's (D) real property to Romani Industries, the Government (P) acknowledged that its tax claims were not valid against the earlier judgment lien, but it argued that the federal priority statute, 31 U.S.C. § 3713(a) [establishes preference for federal claims when person indebted to government is insolvent or otherwise unable to pay debts], gave it the right to be paid first. The trial court ruled against the Government. The appellate court and the Supreme Court of Pennsylvania affirmed. The Supreme Court of Pennsylvania noted the inconsistency between § 3713(a) and the Tax Lien Act of 1966 [federal tax lien not valid against judgment lien creditor]. The court held that the Tax Lien Act modified the Government's (P) preferred position and limited § 3713(a) as to tax debts.

■ **ISSUE**

Does a federal tax claim have priority over a judgment creditor's perfected lien on real property?

■ **DECISION AND RATIONALE**

(Stevens, J.) No. It is undisputed that Romani Industries had a prior perfected lien on Romani's (D) real property. Congress amended the statutes regarding federal tax liens several times since 1865. Each amendment, culminating in the Tax Lien Act of 1966, limited the Government's (P) ability to enforce tax liens. By the terms of § 6323 of the Tax Lien Act, the Government's (P) liens are not valid against Romani Industries' judgment lien. The federal priority statute, § 3713, has remained unchanged since 1797. The statute does not create a lien in favor of the Government (P); it merely provides that the Government (P) will be paid first. Dicta in *Concord v. Atlantic Ins. Co.* [Section 3713 creates right of prior payment] supports this view. While *Thelusson v. Smith* holds that § 3713 gives the Government (P) priority, that case is not controlling because, when it was decided, no procedure for recording a judgment and creating a lien on a specific parcel of real estate existed. In addition, in *Thelusson*, unlike in the present case, the judgment creditor had not perfected his lien. Cases cited by the Government (P) where the competing claims were unsecured are not relevant. On several occasions, the Court has concluded that a specific policy set forth in a later federal statute controls the earlier priority statute, even though the priority statute was not expressly amended. For example,

United States v. Estate of Romani (Continued)

pursuant to the National Bank Act, the Court concluded that the priority statute does not apply to federal claims against national banks and, pursuant to the Transportation Act of 1920, the priority statute does not apply to federal claims against railroads. In addition, the Bankruptcy Act of 1898 treats the Government (P) like any other general creditor. Like these statutes, the Tax Lien Act is the later and more specific statute, and its provisions are comprehensive. It reflects the strong policy objections against secret liens. The two cases the Government (P) cites to support its position that the priority statute controls, *United States v. Key* [priority statute trumps Chapter X of the Bankruptcy Act] and *United States v. Emory* [priority statute trumps National Housing Act], are distinguishable from the present case. In both cases, the priority statute was not inconsistent with the other federal acts at issue and applying the priority statute would not frustrate Congress' intent. The Government (P) argues that when Congress amended the Tax Lien Act in 1966 and in 1970, it did not modify the federal priority statute. However, there are a myriad of reasons why Congress did not amend the priority statute, and this failure to amend does not mean that Congress endorses the Government's (P) position. Indeed, the 1966 amendments to the Tax Lien Act reflect Congress' condemnation of secret liens because they unfairly defeat the expectations of innocent creditors and create commercial instability. Affirmed.

Analysis:

The federal priority statute, 31 U.S.C. § 3713, gives priority to all federal government claims, whether arising from tax liens, contract debts, or something else. This conflicts with the Federal Tax Lien Act of 1966, 26 U.S.C. § 6321, which gives a tax lien priority, except with respect to a purchaser, holder of a security interest, mechanic's lienor, or judgment creditor. Under the Tax Lien Act, the tax lien must be filed in the proper place to be effective. Thus, the Court ruled here that the Tax Lien Act trumps the federal priority statute for several reasons. First, the Tax Lien Act is the more recent and more specific statute. Second, § 3713 does not require the Government (P) to file anything, thereby allowing secret liens, going against the public policy to promote full disclosure of liens. While § 3713 provides absolute federal priority, courts have granted priority to earlier liens that are choate, as the Court acknowledged Romani Industries' lien was here. A choate lien is one that is definite with respect to the identity of the lienor, the amount of the lien, and the property to which the lien attaches. Lower federal courts have held that most security interests perfected under Article 9 are choate and, under the Tax Lien Act, have priority over tax claims.

Plymouth Savings Bank v. U.S. I.R.S.

(*Secured Creditor*) v. (*Tax Lienholder*)
187 F.3d 203, 39 UCC Rep.Serv.2d 543 (1st Cir.1999)

FOR PURPOSES OF THE 45-DAY SAFE HARBOR, THE ACQUISITION OF CONTRACT RIGHTS AND PROCEEDS OCCURS AT THE FORMATION OF THE CONTRACT

■ **INSTANT FACTS** After Dionne defaulted on her loan, the Bank (P) tried to recover contract proceeds in which it held a security interest, but the IRS (D) claimed that its tax lien had priority over the security interest.

■ **BLACK LETTER RULE** Where a contract is made within 45 days after a tax lien filing, the rights under that contract and all the proceeds of those rights fall within § 6323(c)'s safe harbor giving a security interest in those rights and proceeds priority over the tax lien.

■ **PROCEDURAL BASIS**

Appeal from summary judgment granted in action for declaratory relief.

■ **FACTS**

Dionne owned and operated the Greenlawn Nursing Home (Greenlawn). In 1993, Plymouth Savings Bank (the Bank) (P) filed a financing statement for its security interest in Greenlawn and other Dionne assets, and in 1994, it loaned her $85,000. Dionne gave the Bank (P) a security interest in all of her tangible and intangible personal property individually and as owner of Greenlawn, including all cash and non-cash proceeds arising from her rendering of services; all general intangibles including proceeds of other collateral; and all of Dionne's inventory, receivables, contract rights or other personal property. Later that year, Dionne defaulted on her loan leaving $65,465 unpaid. Dionne also failed to make FICA payments. On February 2, 1995 the IRS (D) assessed her liability at $62,767, and filed a tax lien on February 14. Exactly 45 days later, on March 31, 1995, Dionne signed a contract whereby she agreed to help Jordon Hospital (the Hospital) obtain a license to operate a nursing home, and the Hospital agreed to pay her $300,000 in three installments. Dionne fully performed as agreed, but the Hospital did not pay her the final installment of $75,000. The Bank (P) sued the Hospital to recover this sum. The court ruled that the Bank (P) had security interest in the $75,000 because it was proceeds arising from Dionne's personal services. However, the court did not award the Bank (P) this money, but instead directed the Bank (P) to bring a declaratory judgment action to determine whether its security interest had priority over other lien-holders. The Bank (P) therefore brought this action, and in came the IRS (D). On cross-motions for summary judgment by the Bank (P) and the IRS (D), each asserting priority, the court ruled in favor of the IRS (D). The court reasoned that the Bank's (P) right to recover depended on when Dionne performed the services required by the contract. Since Dionne did not help the Hospital secure approval of a nursing home license within the 45 days following the tax lien filing, the court concluded that the IRS's (D) lien was superior to the Bank's (P).

■ **ISSUE**

Does a security interest in the proceeds of a contract fall within FTLA's 45-day safe harbor if the contract was signed within 45 days of the tax lien filing, but performance did not occur until later?

Plymouth Savings Bank v. U.S. I.R.S. (Continued)

■ **DECISION AND RATIONALE**

(Cudahy) Yes. When a person fails to pay her taxes, the *Federal Tax Lien Act, 26 U.S.C. §§ 6321, 6323(c) (FTLA)* [tax liens and their priority] grants a tax lien upon all the person's property, real or personal, presently owned and after-acquired. However, under *§ 6323(c)* [45-day safe harbor], these tax liens are subordinate to a security interest in "qualified property" covered by a "commercial transactions financing agreement" [a security agreement] that existed before the filing of the tax lien if the taxpayer acquires the property within 45 days after the filing. § 6323(c) defines a "commercial transactions financing agreement" as an agreement between a lender and the taxpayer to make loans secured by "commercial financing security" that the taxpayer acquires in the ordinary course of her business. Under § 6323(c), "commercial financing security" can include accounts receivable and documents giving contract rights. Under *26 C.F.R. § 301.6323(c)-(1)(c)(2)* [Treasury regulations/definitions], an "account receivable" is a right to payment for goods sold or services rendered, while a "contract right" is a right to payment under a contract that is not yet earned by performance. Dionne's agreement with the Bank (P) was a "commercial transactions financing agreement," and her contract with the Hospital was "commercial financing security." Dionne signed her contract with the Hospital exactly 45 days after the IRS (D) filed notice of its tax lien. Therefore, if Dionne "acquired" rights to the proceeds of the contract simply by signing it, then the Bank's (P) lien trumps the IRS's (D) because it would fall within the safe harbor for after-acquired property. If Dionne did not acquire rights to the money when she signed the contract, then the IRS's (D) lien takes priority. Because, under *§ 301.6323(c)-1(d)* [acquiring contract rights and proceeds], a taxpayer acquires a contract right when the contract is made, Dionne acquired the right to payment when she signed the contract. The Bank (P) had a security interest in this contract right, and since Dionne acquired it within 45 days of the tax lien filing, it falls within the safe harbor for after-acquired property. However, it is not just the contract right, but the money, that the Bank (P) wants. § 301.6323(c)-1(d) defines "proceeds" as "whatever is received when collateral is sold, exchanged, or collected." Under this section, the taxpayer acquires identifiable proceeds from qualified property when he acquires the qualified property itself if the secured party has a continuously perfected security interest in the proceeds. Therefore, where, as here, the collateral is a contract giving contract rights, the proceeds of the rights, like the rights themselves, are deemed acquired when the contract is made. This is so even though the right to proceeds does not become unconditional until the contract is performed. The conditional right to the proceeds relates back to the formation of the contract. Thus, Dionne acquired the right to the proceeds of her contract with the Hospital exactly 45 days after the tax lien filing. These proceeds, however, are simply an account receivable, the right to payment for services rendered. The IRS (D) therefore argues that under the regulations, a taxpayer only acquires an account receivable when and to the extent the right to payment is earned by performance. Dionne did not earn the right to payment with the 45 days after the tax lien filing. However, the contract and the rights under it are the "qualified property" here [not just the account receivable], and the regulations provide that the proceeds of qualified property are deemed acquired when the qualified property is acquired. The regulations do not distinguish between forms of proceeds. The IRS (D) also argues that the account receivable cannot be "proceeds" because the contract was not "sold, exchanged or collected," but performed. However, Dionne's performance effectively "exchanged" her contract right for an account receivable. The account receivable is the proceeds of the contract right. The IRS (D) complains that we are expanding the safe harbor for after-acquired property too much, and argues that Congress only intended it to cover property that was collected within 45 days of the tax lien filing. However, the legislative history the IRS (D) cites does not directly address a security interest in contract rights. It does, on the other hand, indicate that the FTLA was an attempt to conform the tax laws governing liens to UCC concepts, and the Treasury regulations defining FTLA terms closely track UCC definitions. Our conclusion that the Bank's (P) security interest in the contract rights covers the proceeds of those rights, even if those proceeds are accounts receivable, is compatible with the UCC. Finally, the IRS (D) argues that Dionne did not enter into her contract with the Hospital in the ordinary course of her business as § 6323(c) requires. Because trade-or-business determinations are fact-intensive and the record is undeveloped on this point, we decline to affirm on this ground, but allow the parties to develop the record on remand. Because the Bank's (P) lien may trump the IRS's (D), we reverse the summary judgment in favor of the IRS (D). Reversed and remanded.

Analysis:

Under § 6323, the IRS has priority over a secured interest in accounts receivable or contract rights that come into existence (1) after the secured creditor learns of the tax lien filing, or (2) more than forty-five days after the tax lien filing. The secured creditor retains its priority over accounts receivable and rights that arise within the forty-five day safe harbor. In practice, then, secured creditors should search for tax lien filings not only at the beginning of their security agreement, but every 45 days while the agreement is in force.

■ CASE VOCABULARY

CHATTEL PAPER: Writings that set forth both an obligation of payment for and a security interest in specific goods.

CHAPTER TWENTY-THREE

Bankruptcy and Article 9

In re Smith's Home Furnishings, Inc.

Instant Facts: U.S. Trustee contending that payments to a floating-lien creditor made during the 90-day preference period were preferential, is held not to have met his burden of proving that the creditor was undersecured at some time during the preference period.

Black Letter Rule: Payments made to a creditor secured by a floating lien, who is fully secured on the petition date, are not preferential unless it is shown that the amount of indebtedness under the floating lien was greater than the amount of collateral at some point during the preference period.

In re Smith's Home Furnishings, Inc.

(*Debtor*)
254 F.3d 959 (1990)

TRANSFERS MADE DURING THE PREFERENCE PERIOD TO A CREDITOR SECURED BY A FLOATING LIEN FOUND NOT PREFERENTIAL WHERE THE CREDITOR WAS NEVER UNDERSECURED

■ **INSTANT FACTS** U.S. Trustee contending that payments to a floating-lien creditor made during the 90-day preference period were preferential, is held not to have met his burden of proving that the creditor was undersecured at some time during the preference period.

■ **BLACK LETTER RULE** Payments made to a creditor secured by a floating lien, who is fully secured on the petition date, are not preferential unless it is shown that the amount of indebtedness under the floating lien was greater than the amount of collateral at some point during the preference period.

■ **PROCEDURAL BASIS**

Appeal of a decision by the district court, affirming a decision by the bankruptcy court, which found that the trustee had not proved that specific transfers to a creditor were preferential.

■ **FACTS**

Transamerica Commercial Finance Corporation (TCFC) (D) was one of Smith's Home Furnishings, Inc. (Smith's) primary lenders, who financed Smith's purchase of some merchandise, the "prime inventory," consisting of electronic goods and appliances for the Smith's home furnishing stores. TCFC's (D) loans were secured by a first-priority floating lien on the prime inventory and the proceeds from it. Under the loan agreement, TCFC (D) would grant approval to various manufacturers, who in turn ship merchandise to Smith's after receiving the approval. When Smith's sold a product financed by TCFC (D), it paid TCFC (D) the wholesale price of that product. However, Smith's did not segregate its sales receipts, but instead deposited all its sales proceeds into commingled bank accounts at the end of each day. Smith's bank swept the accounts daily, leaving the accounts with balances of zero. The next day, the bank advanced new funds to Smith's if sufficient collateral was available, which Smith's would use to pay operating expenses and creditors, including TCFC (D). Because of this, the allegedly preferential payments were not made directly from the proceeds of the sales of TCFC's (D) collateral. In 1994, Smith's suffered a substantial loss, causing TCFC (D) to reduce Smith's line of credit from $25 million to $13 million by August of 1995. Simultaneously, TCFC required substantial paydowns of Smith's debt, and Smith's paid TCFC (D) most of its available cash in a series of 36 payments totaling $12 million, between May 24 and August 22, 1995. On August 18, 1995, TCFC (D) declared a final default, accelerating the entire debt due from Smith's and for the first time, required that Smith's segregate the proceeds from its collateral. Smith initiated a chapter 11 bankruptcy proceeding on August 22, 1995, owing $10,728,809.96 to TCFC (D). TCFC (D) took possession of its collateral and liquidated it, receiving $10,823,010.58. On October 11, 1995, the case was converted to a chapter 7 liquidation and Michael Batlan (Batlan) (P) was appointed trustee. Batlan (P) discovered the $12 million in payments Smith's had made to TCFC (D) during the 90 days before the petition date, and believing that they were preferential, asked TCFC (D) to return the money to the bankruptcy estate. When TCFC (D) refused, Batlan (P) initiated an adversary proceeding, seeking to avoid the payments as preferential

In re Smith's Home Furnishings, Inc. (Continued)

transfers under 11 U.S.C. § 547(b), and to recover the money for the benefit of other creditors under 11 U.S.C. § 550(a). The bankruptcy court ruled that Batlan (P) had failed to meet his burden of proof in showing that the payments were preferential transfers, reasoning that because the value of the collateral on the petition date ($10,823.010.58), exceeded the amount of TCFC's (D) claim on the petition date ($10,728,809.96), TFCF was oversecured by $94,200.62. Therefore, since TCFC was a floating-lien creditor, Batlan (P) was required to prove that TCFC (D) was undersecured at some time during the preference period in order to avoid the transfers. Subsequently, after filing a motion for reconsideration that proved unsuccessful, Batlan (P) appealed to the district court, who then affirmed the decision of the bankruptcy court. Batlan (P) appeals to the Ninth Circuit Court of Appeals.

■ ISSUE

Can preference period transfers to a floating-lien creditor be avoided when the creditor was fully secured throughout the relevant period?

■ DECISION AND RATIONALE

(Hall, J.) No. Payments made to a creditor secured by a floating lien, who is fully secured on the petition date, are not preferential unless it is shown that the amount of indebtedness under the floating lien was greater than the amount of collateral at some point during the preference period. 11 U.S.C. § 547(b) permits a trustee to "avoid any transfer of an interest of the debtor in property," if certain conditions are met. One of these conditions as set forth by § 547(b)(5), is that the transfer enable the creditor to receive more than such creditor would receive if: 1) the case were a case under chapter 7 of this title; 2) the transfer had not been made; and 3) such creditor received payment of such debt to the extent provided by the provisions of this title. Section 547(g) places the burden of proof on the trustee to show all of the conditions of § 547(b). Accordingly, in the instant case, Batlan (P) has the burden of proving that the 36 payments made during the preference period, enabled TCFC (D) to receive a greater amount than it would have if the transfer had not been made, and there had been a hypothetical chapter 7 liquidation as of the petition date. Batlan (P) contends that he satisfied his burden because: 1) the 36 payments plus the amount that TCFC (D) received from the post-petition sale of its collateral is greater than the amount received from the post-petition sale of the collateral standing alone; and 2) TCFC (D) has not traced the source of the allegedly preferential payments to sales of its collateral. We disagree. Batlan (P) tried to satisfy his burden by adding the amount of the 36 payments to the amount TCFC (D) received as a result of the post-petition sale of its remaining collateral, and comparing this amount to the obviously smaller amount of the post-petition sale. Although, this "add-back" method has been used by some bankruptcy courts to determine the status of a creditor on the petition date, it does not satisfy Batlan's (P) burden here. Generally, prepetition transfers to a creditor that are fully secured on the petition date are not preferential because the secured creditor is entitled to 100% of its claims. This, however, is not a hard and fast rule. For instance, payments that change the status of a creditor from a partially unsecured to fully secured at the time of petition may be preferential. In addition, a transfer may be avoided when the creditor is fully secured at the time of payment, but undersecured on the petition date. Batlan (P) failed to show, however, that TCFC (D) was undersecured at any time during the preference period. Instead, the evidence submitted showed that as of the petition date, the value of the collateral held by Smith's exceeded its indebtedness to TCFC (D). If TCFC (D) was never undercollateralized, then it could not have received more by virtue of the 36 payments, than it would have in a hypothetical liquidation without the payments. TCFC (D) did not loan a fixed amount, but instead held a "floating lien," which is a financial device where the creditor claims an interest in property acquired after the original extension of the loan and extends its security interest to cover further advances. It is a lien against a constantly changing mass of collateral for a loan value that will change as payments are received and further advances are made. Cases that apply the "add-back" method do not deal with floating liens. Under this type of lien, the 36 payments are used to liquidate part of the debtor's debt. Then, new credit under the floating lien is extended and secured by new collateral. Thus, it is not enough for Batlan (P) to show that the 36 payments plus the amount received upon dissolution exceeded the amount of TCFC's (D) secured claim as of the petition date. Since collateral and indebtedness changed throughout the preference period, these values do not prove that TCFC (D) received more by virtue of the payments. Batlan (P) must show that the amount of indebtedness under the floating lien was greater than the amount of collateral at some point during the 90-day period. Batlan (P) further argues that the existence of the floating lien means that the burden is shifted to TCFC (D) under § 547(c)(5), which provides an affirmative defense for creditors when the trustee has successfully demonstrated that the creditor received more from the payments than under a hypothetical liquidation. It insulates the transfer of a security interest in after acquired property, provided that the creditor does not improve its position during the preference period. In effect, Batlan (P) argues that the existence of a floating lien means that he does not have to prove that the creditor was undersecured. We reject this argument as well. In *In re Castletons,* the creditor held a floating lien on the debtor's inventory, accounts receivable, and proceeds. The trustee sought to avoid the payments given by the debtor to the creditor during the preference period. The Tenth Circuit held that the trustee failed to show that the creditor received more from the challenged payments than it would have in a chapter 7 liquidation, since all payments to the creditor came from assets already subject to its security interest, and that the nature of the security interest in debtor's assets was never altered during the preference period. Most importantly, the court in *Castletons* recognized that the creditor held a floating lien, explaining that while the identity of individual items of collateral changed, the overall nature of the security interest remained the same. It is true that other courts have evaluated floating lien cases by proceeding directly to § 547 (c)(5), but in those cases the § 547(b)(5) burden had already been satisfied. Batlan (P) also contends that the use of the "add-back" method is permissible because TCFC (D) had not shown that the source of the allegedly preferential payments were sales of TCFC's (D) collateral. However, there is no evidence indicating that Smith's did not sell off enough of TCFC's (D) collateral to account for all of the challenged payments. We believe that the trustee has the burden of proving every essential controverted element resulting in the preference by a preponderance of the evidence, and hold that the language of the statute places the burden of demonstrating the source of such preferential payments squarely on the trustee, regardless of who is in a better position to decipher the debtor's financial actions, and regardless of whether the funds are commingled or not. Therefore, it is up to Batlan (P) to show that the payments did not come from TCFC's (D) collateral before he can use the add-back method to satisfy his burden. Affirmed.

Analysis:

This case provides a good illustration of voidable preferences and the underlying policy of § 547. In sum, the court found that TCFC (D) could not have received more by virtue of the thirty-six payments than it would have received in a hypothetical Chapter 7 liquidation without the payments, because at no point within the preference period did the collateral value fall below the outstanding debt. Therefore, Smith's pre-petition transfers to TCFC (D) were not preferential, since TCFC (D) was entitled to 100% of its claims as a secured creditor. The underlying policy behind § 547 is equality of distribution among creditors. In order to ensure that an insolvent debtor does not impermissibly pay one particularly favored creditor to the detriment of others, § 547 allows the trustee to reach back ninety days and reclaim certain transfers.

■ CASE VOCABULARY

FLOATING LIEN: A security interest that can attach to property acquired after the original extension of the loan, and extend to cover further advances.

SECURED CREDITOR: A creditor who possesses some form of payment assurance such as a mortgage, collateral, or lien.

CHAPTER TWENTY-FOUR

Proceeds

Farmers Cooperative Elevator Co. v. Union State Bank

Instant Facts: Co-Op (P) unsuccessfully claimed priority in livestock by arguing that its purchase money security interest in feed continued in hogs as proceeds or part of a mass.

Black Letter Rule: A purchase money security interest in feed for livestock does not continue in the livestock once consumed, either by declaring the livestock as "proceeds" of the feed or by declaring the feed part of a "mass."

HCC Credit Corp. v. Springs Valley Bank & Trust Co.

Instant Facts: HCC (P), a secured creditor, sued Bank (D), the recipient of the debtor's cash proceeds, claiming priority, even though cash proceeds were paid out of checking account.

Black Letter Rule: Where cash proceeds are commingled into a debtor's checking account and paid out in the ordinary course of business, a secured party does not have priority rights to the proceeds.

Farmers Cooperative Elevator Co. v. Union State Bank

(Secured Party In Feed) v. (Secured Party In Hogs)
409 N.W.2d 178, 4 UCC Rep. Serv.2d 1 (Iowa 1987)

SECURITY INTEREST CONTINUES IN *PROCEEDS* OF COLLATERAL

■ **INSTANT FACTS** Co-Op (P) unsuccessfully claimed priority in livestock by arguing that its purchase money security interest in feed continued in hogs as proceeds or part of a mass.

■ **BLACK LETTER RULE** A purchase money security interest in feed for livestock does not continue in the livestock once consumed, either by declaring the livestock as "proceeds" of the feed or by declaring the feed part of a "mass."

■ **PROCEDURAL BASIS**

Appeal from ruling on motion to adjudicate law points in action seeking establishment of priority rights to security liens.

■ **FACTS**

Rodger Cockrum, a farmer, obtained financing over a period of years from Union State Bank (Bank) (D) for his farm and hog confinement operation. In 1981, Bank (D) loaned Cockrum money and took a security agreement covering "all equipment and fixtures . . .; all farm products including but not limited to, livestock, and supplies used or produced in farming operations whether now or hereafter existed or acquired. . . ." In late 1983 and early 1994, Cockrum entered into several purchase money security agreements with Farmers Cooperative Elevator Co. (Co-Op) (P) for livestock feed. Co-Op (P) filed with the Secretary of State, for each transaction, a financing statement, which stated that it covered collateral described as "all feed sold to Debtors . . . and the proceeds of any described Collateral." Cockrum defaulted on his obligations to Bank (D) and Co-Op (P). Co-Op (P) sued Cockrum for possession of collateral. Bank (D) filed a statement of indebtedness and requested that its security interests be established as a first security lien on Cockrum's hog inventory and any sale proceeds therefrom. Co-Op (P) amended its petition to join Bank (D) as a defendant and alleging that its right to the hogs was superior to Bank's (D). [Since the hogs ate the collateral, Co-Op (P) wanted the hogs.] The district court ruled that Bank's (D) security interest in the hogs was prior and superior to Co-Op's (P), and Co-Op (P) appealed.

■ **ISSUE**

Does a purchase money security interest in feed for livestock continue in the livestock once consumed, either by declaring the livestock as "proceeds" of the feed or by declaring the feed part of a "mass"?

■ **DECISION AND RATIONALE**

(Larson) No. We hold that a purchase money security interest in feed for livestock does not continue in the livestock once consumed, either by declaring the livestock as "proceeds" of the feed or by declaring the feed part of a "mass". Co-Op (P) asserts that its interest in the livestock and proceeds therefrom is superior to Bank's (D). UCC § 554.9312(4), now § 9-324(a), provides: "A purchase money security interest in collateral other than inventory has priority over a conflicting security interest in the same collateral or its proceeds if the purchase money security interest is perfected at the time the

Farmers Cooperative Elevator Co. v. Union State Bank (Continued)

debtor receives possession of the collateral or within twenty days thereafter." The issue is whether a security interest in the feed continues in livestock, which consume the feed. Co-Op (P) took the purchase money security interests to secure the price of the feed, not the hogs. Thus, it does not have a purchase money security interest in the hogs. Co-Op (P) argues that the hogs are "proceeds" of the feed, relying upon a UCC section that defines "proceeds" to include "whatever is received upon the sale, exchange, collection or other disposition of collateral or proceeds." A previous court decision has held that cattle consuming the collateral does not equate to proceeds to which the security interest may attach. Thus, ingestion of feed is not a type of "other disposition" within the meaning of the UCC. Co-Op (P) also argues that it should prevail over Bank (D) because the feed became commingled with the hogs. It relies upon another UCC section which provides that if a security interest in goods was perfected and the goods become part of a product or mass, the security interest continues in the product or mass if "the goods are so manufactured, processed, assembled or commingled that their identity is lost in the product or mass...." The previous court decision also held that cattle are neither a "product" nor a "mass," and once the feed is eaten, it does not become part of the mass. Ingestion is a process not contemplated by the UCC section. [Co-Op's (P) argument was rejected on all four hooves.] Affirmed.

Analysis:

0*Proceeds* is defined in UCC § 554.9306, now § 9-102(a)(64), as "whatever is acquired upon the sale, lease, license, exchange, or other disposition of collateral." Co-Op (P) relies upon the "other disposition of collateral" to argue here that the hogs are "proceeds" of the feed. The court did not agree. Co-Op (P) also attempted to assert that the feed commingled with the hogs, became lost in the "mass," and thus the security interest continues in the mass under former UCC § 554.9315(1), now § 9–336. The court noted that feed lost through "ingestion" is not a proper interpretation of § 554.9315.

■ CASE VOCABULARY

FINANCING STATEMENT: A document filed with the Secretary of State or other public body by a secured party giving notice that a security interest exists in goods to secure a debt.

MOTION TO ADJUDICATE: Requesting that the court make a decision on the legal issues and render a judgment.

STATEMENT OF INDEBTEDNESS: A certificate of indebtedness whereby a lien may be created on property that is superior to the rights of general creditors.

HCC Credit Corp. v. Springs Valley Bank & Trust Co.

(Secured Party) v. (Recipient of Funds)
669 N.E.2d 1001, 38 UCC Rep. Serv. 2d 1231 (Ind.App.1999)

AN EXCEPTION EXISTS AS TO A SECURED PARTY'S PRIORITY RIGHTS IN CASH PROCEEDS OF COLLATERAL IN A DEPOSIT ACCOUNT

■ **INSTANT FACTS** HCC (P), a secured creditor, sued Bank (D), the recipient of the debtor's cash proceeds, claiming priority, even though cash proceeds were paid out of checking account.

■ **BLACK LETTER RULE** Where cash proceeds are commingled into a debtor's checking account and paid out in the ordinary course of business, a secured party does not have priority rights to the proceeds.

■ PROCEDURAL BASIS

Appeal from summary judgment in action to establish priority rights of secured creditor and return of paid out proceeds.

■ FACTS

HCC Credit Corporation (HCC) (P) provided financing to Lindsey Tractor Sales, Inc. (Lindsey) in order for it to purchase farm equipment from Hesston Corporation (Hesston) for resale. In the security agreements which governed Hesston's, HCC's (P), and Lindsey's relationship, Lindsey granted HCC a security interest in all the equipment it purchased from Hesston and in the proceeds from their sale. Lindsey also agreed to pay HCC (P) immediately from the sale proceeds, but was not required to deposit or segregate proceeds from the sales in a separate account. In 1991, the Indiana State Department of Transportation agreed to purchase 14 Hesston tractors from Lindsey. Financed by HCC (P), Lindsey acquired the tractors from Hesston and received payment from the State in the amount $199,122 on August 15, 1991. The proceeds were then deposited in Lindsey's checking account at Spring Valley Bank & Trust (Bank) (D), which contained $22,870 at the time of deposit. On August 16, 1991, Lindsey wrote a check on this account payable to the bank (D) for $212,104.75, for debts owed by Lindsey to the bank (D). These debts were evidenced by four promissory bank notes, representing previously refinanced debts, three of which were not yet due. The bank (D) and Lindsey did not discuss paying off these notes prior to this payment, nor did the bank seize the account to pay the notes. More importantly, Lindsey did not tell the bank (D) that $199,122 of the payment was from the sale of Hesston products. During the previous eight years, Lindsey borrowed funds or refinanced debts in excess of 100 times with the bank (D), with an average debt balance between $100,000 and $200,000. After the notes were paid, Lindsey owed the bank (D) between $2,00 and $15,000. In December of 1991, Lindsey filed a bankruptcy liquidation and dissolved. At trial, HCC (P) sought to recover the $199,122 in proceeds from the sale of the tractors that the bank received from Lindsey. Each party moved for summary judgment. The trial court granted summary judgment in favor of the bank, the Court of Appeals affirmed, and HCC (P) appeals.

■ ISSUE

Does the commingling of cash proceeds into a debtor's checking account and paid out in the ordinary course of business prevent a secured party from obtaining priority rights in the proceeds?

■ DECISION AND RATIONALE

(Sullivan) Yes. Under both the security agreement and Article 9 of the Uniform Commercial Code

HCC Credit Corp. v. Springs Valley Bank & Trust Co. (Continued)

(UCC), HCC (P) had a valid and perfected security interest in the $199,122 proceeds from the sale of the tractors. Article 9 gives the secured party, upon a debtor's default, priority over all others except as otherwise stated by the remaining UCC priority rules. However, Official Comment 2 (c) to § 9–306, appended at the time of the 1972 version of Article 9, appears to be an exception to the general priority rules although never adopted as authoritative. It provides: "Where cash proceeds are covered into the debtor's checking account and paid out in the operation of the debtor's business, recipients of the fund of course take free of any claim which the secured party may have in them as proceeds. What has been said relates to payments and transfers in the ordinary course. The law of fraudulent conveyances would no doubt in appropriate cases support recovery of proceeds by a secured party from the transferee out of ordinary course or otherwise in collusion with the debtor to defraud the secured party." Accordingly, the bank (D) argues that the subject payment was paid out of Lindsey's account in the ordinary course of Lindsey's business without any collusion with the bank (D), and is therefore free of any claim which HCC (P) had in it as proceeds. It is clear from prior case law that if a bank were to exercise its contractual right to set-off, a secured party with a perfected security interest in the proceeds would have priority over a bank. In this case, the Bank (D) does not claim set-off rights, but instead a right as ordinary course transferee. We acknowledge that there are strong policy interests in giving *ordinary course* a broad meaning so to prevent ordinary third party transferees from having to return ordinary payments made to them by the debtor. Official Comment 2 tells us that the payment (1) will be in the ordinary course if it was made in the operation of the debtor's business but (2) will not be in the ordinary course if there was collusion with the debtor to defraud the secured party. We hold that a transferee can take free of a secured party's claim unless the payment would constitute a windfall to the transferee. A windfall occurs when the transferee recipient has no reasonable expectation of being paid ahead of a secured creditor because of the extent to which the payment was made outside the routine operation of the debtor's business, because the recipient was aware that it was acting to the prejudice of the secured party, or because of both of these factors in combination. Applying these rules to this case, we hold that Lindsey's payment of $199,122 to the Bank (D) was not in the ordinary course of the operation of its business. The Bank (D) was aware of HCC's (P) perfected security interest, it admitted that the payment of $199,122 was extraordinary and was the largest ever made on any debt Lindsey owed it, and it declared that anytime a significant loan balance is paid off, it is viewed as not a normal trade transaction. Moreover, the payment was for a debt that, for the most part, was not due. Thus, the payment was not in the ordinary course of business. [How could those lower courts have found otherwise?] If the Bank (P) were to prevail, it would result in a windfall because it had no reasonable expectation that Lindsey could or would pay the Bank's (D) debt prior to paying HCC (P). The exception set forth in Official Comment 2 does not apply, and HCC (P) is entitled to the $199,122. Having previously granted transfer thereby vacating the decision of the Court of Appeals, the judgment of the trial court is reversed and remanded with directions that the trial court enter summary judgment for HCC (P).

Analysis:

The revised Article 9 contains § 9–332, which expressly provides that a "transferee of funds from a deposit account takes the funds free of a security interest in the deposit account unless the transferee acts in collusion with the debtor in violating the rights of the secured party." The general rules concerning proceeds and a secured party's rights on disposition of collateral are now set forth in § 9–306. This case contains a well reasoned explanation for its holding, by combining the holdings and policy reasons set forth in other cases and applied to the facts of this case. Note that the appeal was from the granting of summary judgment. The court commented that, "[w]hile the determination of ordinary course is a question of law, sometimes an evaluation of the extent to which the payment was routine or the extent of the recipient's knowledge will require factual analysis. In such a situation, summary judgment would be inappropriate." However, the court, after considering the facts concerning non-routine payment and lack of knowledge by the Bank (D), remanded the matter to the trial court with directions to enter summary judgment for HCC (P).

■ CASE VOCABULARY

MOTION FOR SUMMARY JUDGMENT: A legal motion requesting the judge to enter judgment, before trial, on the grounds that the action has no merit or there is no defense to the action.

SET–OFF: The right of a bank, by self-help, to take priority over others claiming a right to the funds on deposit in the depositor's account.

CHAPTER TWENTY-FIVE

Default

State Bank of Piper City v. A–Way, Inc.

Instant Facts: Secured party, Piper (P), sought to enforce its security interest in proceeds of grain sale against warehouser A–Way (D) after obtaining judgment and partial satisfaction against the debtor.

Black Letter Rule: A secured creditor is not barred under either the doctrine of merger or the doctrine of res judicata from suing on the underlying obligation and then suing to enforce the security agreement.

Klingbiel v. Commercial Credit Corp.

Instant Facts: Vehicle purchase mortgage contract assignee, Commercial (D), repossessed Klingbiel's (P) vehicle without notice or demand, and before installment payment was due.

Black Letter Rule: Purchaser must be given notice or demand of acceleration before default can be declared, and default is required in order to foreclose.

Williamson v. Fowler Toyota, Inc.

Instant Facts: Car dealership, Fowler (D), that repossessed vehicle through its independent contractor, by cutting chain and trespassing, was liable for breach of the peace and trespass.

Black Letter Rule: A secured creditor has a nondelegable duty to refrain from breaching the peace when repossessing secured collateral.

Hilliman v. Cobado

Instant Facts: Cattle were repossessed by seller, Cobado (D), under agreement permitting repossession by peaceable entry onto premises without debtor's interference, but debtor objected and seller breached the peace.

Black Letter Rule: Despite a self-help provision in a security agreement permitting the secured party to enter the debtor's premises peaceably and take possession of the collateral, without resistance or interference by the debtor, breach of the peace may occur if the conduct involved in the repossession is likely to, or does, produce violence, consternation or disorder.

R & J of Tennessee, Inc. v. Blankenship–Melton Real Estate, Inc.

Instant Facts: R & J (P) filed suit to collect a deficiency judgment after a foreclosure sale, and Blankenship–Melton (D) claimed that the foreclosed property was not sold in a commercially reasonable manner.

Black Letter Rule: The determination of whether a sale of collateral was commercially reasonable requires a consideration of the totality of the circumstances surrounding the sale, and looks at whether the sale was conducted according to prevailing trade practices among responsible businesses engaged in the same or similar business.

Coxall v. Clover Commercial Corp.

Instant Facts: Clover (D) repossessed a car purchased by Coxall (P), and Coxall (P) alleged that the subsequent sale of the vehicle was unreasonable.

Black Letter Rule: In a consumer transaction, a secured party may not recover a deficiency judgment from the debtor if the sale of the collateral was commercially unreasonable, but the debtor may recover damages for the creditor's failure to comply with the legal requirements for a sale.

Reeves v. Foutz & Tanner, Inc.

Instant Facts: Secured creditor, Foutz (D), after sending notice to debtors of intent to retain collateral, sold the collateral without accounting to the debtors for the surplus of the sale.

Black Letter Rule: A secured party in possession of collateral who sends notice of intent to retain collateral, does not have the right to sell the collateral in its regular course of business without having to account to the debtor for any surplus.

State Bank of Piper City v. A-Way, Inc.

(*Secured Party*) v. (*Grain Warehouse*)
115 Ill.2d 401, 504 N.E.2d 737, 105 Ill.Dec. 452, 3 UCC Rep. Serv. 2d 379 (1987)

A SECURED CREDITOR'S RIGHTS UNDER UCC ARTICLE 9 ARE CUMULATIVE AND MAY BE EXERCISED CONSECUTIVELY

■ **INSTANT FACTS** Secured party, Piper (P), sought to enforce its security interest in proceeds of grain sale against warehouser A-Way (D) after obtaining judgment and partial satisfaction against the debtor.

■ **BLACK LETTER RULE** A secured creditor is not barred under either the doctrine of merger or the doctrine of res judicata from suing on the underlying obligation and then suing to enforce the security agreement.

■ **PROCEDURAL BASIS**

Appeal to State Supreme Court from court of appeal's reversal of trial court's dismissal of complaint seeking enforcement of security interest.

■ **FACTS**

State Bank of Piper City (Piper) (P) sued A-Way, Inc. (D) to enforce its security interest in grain and the proceeds from the sale thereof stored by A-Way (D) in a warehouse on account for Brenner, a debtor of Piper (P). Piper (P) had previously obtained a judgment against Brenner in the sum of $131,083.01 for default on promissory notes, secured by grain owned by Brenner and stored in A-Way's (D) warehouse. In a proceeding to enforce the judgment, Piper (P) learned that A-Way (D) was storing in its warehouse 5,141.20 bushels of grain on behalf of Brenner. Piper (P) sought and obtained a court order requiring A-Way (D) to pay Piper (P) $5,141.20, as partial satisfaction of the judgment. Piper (P) made a mistake and confused the 5,141.20 as the value of the bushels of grain, when actually it was the number of bushels. A-Way (D), acting upon the court order, sold the grain for $11,310.64, remitted $5,141.20 to Piper (P) and applied the balance to the outstanding charges due A-Way (D) on Brenner's account. Months later, Piper (P) realized its mistake and sued to enforce its security interest in the proceeds of the grain sale over and above the $5,141.20. Acting as a secured creditor, Piper (P) sought to enforce its article 9 security interest in the surplus proceeds from the sale of grain, proceeds that had mistakenly been omitted from the enforcement of judgment proceeds. The court dismissed the complaint on the grounds that the doctrines of merger and res judicata barred the suit. [Put another way, the court was saying, "you had your chance and blew it by making the mistake".] The appellate court [realizing that there was more than one way to collect money due] reversed and A-Way (D) appealed.

■ **ISSUE**

Is a secured creditor barred under either the doctrine of merger or the doctrine of res judicata from suing on the underlying obligation and then suing to enforce the security agreement?

■ **DECISION AND RATIONALE**

(Ward) No. We hold that a secured creditor is not barred under either the doctrine of merger or the doctrine of res judicata from suing on the underlying obligation and then suing to enforce the security agreement. A-Way (D) contends that the doctrine of merger supports the dismissal of the complaint

State Bank of Piper City v. A-Way, Inc. (Continued)

because any rights Piper (P) had under the promissory notes merged into the judgment, extinguishing any interest it had in the grain. The general rule is that the contract or instrument sued upon merges into the judgment, and further legal proceedings under the contract or instrument are barred. We disagree with such contention. Under UCC § 9–501(1), now § 9–601, a secured creditor, upon a debtor's default, "may reduce his claim to judgment, foreclose or otherwise enforce the security interest by any available judicial procedure.... The rights and remedies referred to in this subsection are cumulative." When a secured creditor obtains a judgment lien to enforce his judgment, it shall relate back to the date of the perfection of the security interest in the collateral, and serve as a continuation of the original perfected security interest. Thus, any efforts to collect the debt through the judicial process will not destroy the security interest vis-à-vis the debtor or impair its priority over third parties. We hold that the doctrine of merger does not preclude a secured creditor from enforcing its security interest in property given as collateral. Thus, although the notes merged in the judgment precluding further action on the notes, that merger does not preclude Piper (P) from bringing this action to enforce its security interest in the grain. That security interest was set forth in security agreements separate from the notes. A-Way (D) also contends that Piper (P) is barred from bringing action under the doctrine of res judicata. Such doctrine provides that a final judgment is conclusive as to the rights of the parties, and constitutes an absolute bar to a subsequent action involving the *same* claim, demand or cause of action. Article 9 of the UCC provides for multiple and cumulative remedies upon the debtor's default. Res judicata will not bar a secured creditor from exhausting his remedies under the UCC. To do so would defeat the purpose of Article 9. The order entered in the citation proceedings was done in execution of Piper's (P) judgment against Brenner. In this action, Piper (P) is acting as a secured creditor seeking to enforce its Article 9 interest in the proceeds from the grain sale. [Translated, this means that Piper (P) first tried to collect on its judgment against Brenner for defaulting on the promissory notes and now it's trying to exercise its rights against A-Way (D) based upon the security agreement and the UCC.] Judgment of the appeal court is affirmed.

Analysis:

This case demonstrates the general principle that a secured creditor's rights under UCC Article 9 upon a debtor's default are cumulative and may be exercised consecutively. A secured creditor, under § 9–601, may obtain a judgment against the debtor, which is what Piper (P) initially did when it obtained the judgment against Brenner. It also has the right to foreclose on the collateral, without having to first obtain a judgment against the debtor. Finally, it may enforce the security interest by any available judicial procedure, which is what Piper (P) sought to do by bringing an action against A-Way (D). Under the doctrines of merger and res judicata, Piper (P) could not have sued again under the terms of the promissory notes, because that had already occurred in its initial suit and judgment against Brenner. However, because Piper (P) had rights under Article 9 concerning enforcement of the security agreement and the security interest, it was able to sue A-Way (D) to obtain the supplemental proceeds from the grain sale.

■ **CASE VOCABULARY**
something.

DECREE IN CHANCERY: Equivalent to a judgment in a court of law, but rendered in a court of equity.

INTER ALIA: Latin for among other things.

MERGER: Based upon the doctrine of merger whereby a judgment merges the original claim into the judgment and subsequent suit is brought on the judgment rather than on the original claim.

MOTION TO DISMISS COMPLAINT: Challenging the right of the court to entertain the matter before it on various legal theories.

MOTION TO VACATE: To undo or void some act, record or judgment.

PARTIAL SATISFACTION OF JUDGMENT: Indicating, usually by way of a formal document filed with the court, that a judgment has as been partially paid.

Klingbiel v. Commercial Credit Corp.

(Vehicle Owner) v. (Repossessing Finance Co.)
439 F.2d 1303, 8 UCC Rep. Serv. 1099 (10th Cir.1971)

A RIGHT TO ACCELERATE WITHOUT NOTICE OR DEMAND IS NOT SYNONYMOUS WITH THE RIGHT TO REPOSSESS WITHOUT NOTICE OR DEMAND

■ **INSTANT FACTS** Vehicle purchase mortgage contract assignee, Commercial (D), repossessed Klingbiel's (P) vehicle without notice or demand, and before installment payment was due.

■ **BLACK LETTER RULE** Purchaser must be given notice or demand of acceleration before default can be declared, and default is required in order to foreclose.

■ FACTS

Mr. Klingbiel (P) sued Commercial Credit Corp. (Commercial) (D) for the unlawful conversion of his automobile following its repossession by Commercial (D). He purchased his new vehicle from a Ford dealership, and entered into a purchase mortgage contract that provided for a down payment and a series of monthly installment payments. The contract contained acceleration and enforcement provisions, which allowed the unpaid balance to become due forthwith if the seller or its assignee "should feel itself or Vehicle *insecure" and permitted seller or its assignee* to repossess the vehicle. Shortly thereafter, Commercial (D) became the assignee of the contract. Before Klingbiel's (P) first monthly installment payment was due, Commercial (D) felt *insecure* and directed its repossessing agent to repossess the vehicle. The repossession took place four days before Klingbiel's (P) first monthly payment was due, at a time when he was not in default, and without prior notice, demand or communication with Klingbiel (P). [What made Commercial (D) so insecure to do this?] The trial judge interpreted the contract to mean that acceleration was permissible without notice or demand, but upon acceleration, demand or notice was required. Because Commercial (D) failed to give notice of demand, it was held liable for unlawful conversion. Commercial (D) appealed.

■ ISSUE

Must a purchaser be given notice or demand of acceleration before default can be declared?

■ DECISION AND RATIONALE

(Brown) Yes. We hold that a purchaser must be given notice or demand of acceleration before default can be declared, and default is required in order to foreclosure. If Commercial (D) felt itself insecure, under the acceleration terms of the contract, it, as assignee of Seller, could require Klingbiel (P), as purchaser, to pay off the balance in full *upon demand* or it could require redelivery. However, before Klingbiel (P) was bound to do either, Commercial (D) had to indicate which course of action it required. The language in the contract "*upon demand*" is unavoidable. Commercial (D) also contends that no notice was necessary prior to repossession based upon the enforcement clause in the contract, which provides that the mortgage "may be foreclosed [a] . . . or [b] Seller may, without notice or demand for performance or legal process, . . . lawfully enter any premises where Vehicle may be found, and take possession of it." This clause however follows the previously discussed declared acceleration clause, which requires notice/demand. The "take possession" language regarding no notice or demand for performance or legal process refers only to a *foreclosure*. This means that there must be a default on

HIGH COURT CASE SUMMARIES 345

Klingbiel v. Commercial Credit Corp. (Continued)

the part of the purchaser. Such default can take the form of a failure to perform by failing to pay the installments or failing to perform an acceleration. However, a failure to perform an acceleration requires a notice/demand before a default can exist. [Common courtesies dictate notice and demand as well.] If the proper notice/demand were given and there was a failure to perform an acceleration, then a default would exist and would justify repossession. However, without the proper notice/demand for acceleration, there can be no default that triggers the foreclosure clause. Finally, we hold that there was sufficient evidence presented to sustain the finding of punitive damages, and any error in the instructions was harmless. Affirmed.

Analysis:

This case demonstrates that there must be a default before foreclosure may occur. UCC § 1–208 provides that a party to a contract with an acceleration term may "accelerate payment or performance or require collateral" when the party "deems himself insecure." However, such power exists only if the party in good faith believes that the prospect of payment or performance is impaired. In this case, there were no facts presented to show why Commercial (D) felt *"insecure."* UCC § 9–503 deals with the secured party's right to take possession of the collateral after default. The court of appeals affirmed the trial court's interpretation of the contract and held that notice of payment in full or demand of return of the vehicle was required upon Commercial's (D) electing to accelerate because of feeling insecure. Without the notice/demand, there could not be *default* under the acceleration clause, so as to permit foreclosure.

■ **CASE VOCABULARY**

ACCELERATION CLAUSE: A term contained in an agreement that requires payment of the balance due sooner than the due date because of the happening of some event described in the contract, such as failure to make a payment due under an installment contract.

PURCHASE MORTGAGE CONTRACT: A contract that has the effect of securing performance of an obligation incurred in the purchase of property.

Williamson v. Fowler Toyota, Inc.
(*Victim of Repossession*) v. (*Car Seller*)
1998 Okla. 14, 956 P.2d 858, 36 UCC Rep. Serv. 2d 951 (1998)

IF ACT OF REPOSSESSION RESULTS IN BREACH OF PEACE, CREDITOR WILL BE LIABLE

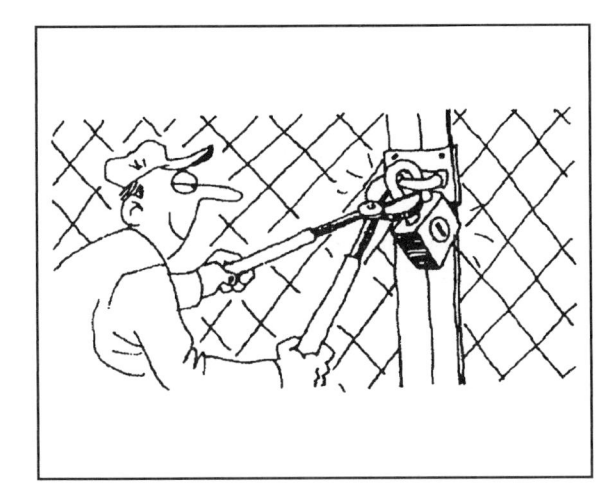

■ **INSTANT FACTS** Car dealership, Fowler (D), that repossessed vehicle through its independent contractor, by cutting chain and trespassing, was liable for breach of the peace and trespass.

■ **BLACK LETTER RULE** A secured creditor has a nondelegable duty to refrain from breaching the peace when repossessing secured collateral.

■ **PROCEDURAL BASIS**

Certiorari to State Supreme Court from appellate court's reversal of judgment following jury verdict awarding actual and punitive damages for trespass and breach of the peace.

■ **FACTS**

Fowler Toyota, Inc. (Fowler) (D) sold a car to Robert Gilmore pursuant to a purchase installment agreement, with Fowler (D) retaining a security interest in the car. Gilmore became ill, donated the car to Camp Hudgens, and stopped making payments. The Camp took the car to Williamson (P) for purposes of determining whether it was safe to sell. Williamson (P) had no knowledge of Fowler's (D) lien, or that Gilmore was in default. Thereafter, Williamson (P) arrived at work to find the car gone, with the gate open and the chain and lock missing. The car had been repossessed by Fowler (D), through an independent contractor, Clint McGregor. When McGregor was hired, he was not told the car's location, but thereafter discovered the location through Gilmore's relatives. He went to Williamson Auto, cut the chain to the gate with bolt cutters, and towed the car away. He [claims, probably so he can keep getting repossession work that he] attempted to call Williamson (P) before repossessing the car but received no answer, and he called the police before he left town to inform them that he had repossessed the car. When he turned the car over to Fowler (D), he told them what he had done, but neither he nor Fowler (D) attempted to contact Williamson (P). Fowler (D) [slapped him on the wrists and] told McGregor to not trespass in the future when he repossessed cars. Williamson (P) sued Fowler (D) for damages caused by its independent contractor, McGregor. The jury awarded Williamson (P) actual damages of $45.00, based upon the value of the lock and chain ($15.00) and lost billable time ($30.00), plus punitive damages in the sum of $15,000.00. The court of appeal reversed and Williamson (P) appealed to the State Supreme Court.

■ **ISSUE**

Can a secured creditor be held liable for damages caused by an independent contractor who breaches the peace when repossessing the creditor's secured collateral?

■ **DECISION AND RATIONALE**

(Wilson) Yes. We hold that a secured creditor has a nondelegable duty to refrain from breaching the peace when repossessing secured collateral. The general rule is that an employer is not liable for the negligence of an independent contractor except where the work is inherently dangerous or unlawful or where the employer owes a contractual or defined legal duty to the injured party in the performance of

Williamson v. Fowler Toyota, Inc. (Continued)

the work. In other words, if the work or service of the independent contractor is illegal, dangerous or harmful, the secured party can be held liable for the tort of its independent contractor. Fowler (D) contends that because Section 9–503, now § 9–609, expressly allows secured creditors to repossess collateral, the work of repossessing cannot be inherently dangerous. However, other jurisdictions have held precisely the opposite of Fowler's (D) contention. One court, in construing section 9–503 observed that under the statute the secured party has a right to repossess if it could be done without breach of the peace. However, the court further noted that the tactic chosen by the repossessor guaranteed generating fright, anger, or both, if discovered, and was therefore fraught with the peril of provoking a breach of the peace of the most serious kind. Another court found that where the law of the State required the secured party to repossess peaceably, the duty to do so is nondelegable. Other courts have also held that the duty to repossess peaceably under UCC § 9–503 was nondelegable. In the case before us, the law of the State provides that a secured creditor may repossess as long as it is accomplished without breach of the peace. Breach of the peace has been described as the use of force, such as breaking or removing a padlock. This is because the potential for breach of the peace as a result of unauthorized intrusions on property escalates in direct proportion to the presence of fences, gates, signs etc. Williamson (P) did not consent to McGregor entering onto his property, and thus McGregor committed trespass. A secured creditor's duty to exercise the right to self-help in a peaceable manner is not delegable. [In other words, you can't avoid liability by passing the buck to your agent.] Fowler (D) is therefore liable for McGregor's trespass and breach of the peace, regardless of whether McGregor was an independent contractor or an employee. With respect to the punitive damages award, we hold that the evidence showed McGregor was acting in complete disregard for the rights of Williamson (P). Because the duty not to breach the peace is nondelegable, Fowler (D) is vicariously liable even for punitive damages for McGregor's actions. The opinion of the Court of Appeals is vacated and the judgment of the trial court is affirmed.

Analysis:

This case involves the issue of whether a breach of the peace occurred. The factors to consider are whether there was an entry onto the debtor's premises, and whether the debtor consented or objected to the entry and repossession. In this case, there was a breaking of the lock and removal of the chain to gain access. The court felt that this conduct, without notifying Williamson (P), was sufficient to constitute breach of the peace. If the car had been on the street, there would not have been liability. However, if Williamson (P) had been on the street and vehemently objected to the repossession, resulting in the risk of altercation, there may have been liability if the car was repossessed. The rationale is that the scene on the streets could have very easily escalated to a breach of the peace. Finally, note that this case demonstrates that a duty to repossess peaceably under UCC § 9–503 is nondelegable.

■ CASE VOCABULARY

CLEAR AND CONVINCING EVIDENCE: Evidence that proves something by more than a preponderance of the evidence but less than proof beyond a reasonable doubt.

EXEMPLARY DAMAGES: Damages awarded to injured party to punish the defendant for acting in a malicious, oppressive or fraudulent manner so as to make an example of the defendant.

INDEPENDENT CONTRACTOR: Employment relationship where one works pursuant to his own rules and control.

TRESPASS: An actual physical invasion of the real estate of another without permission from the one lawfully in possession.

WANTON: Extreme recklessness, maliciousness, or acting in disregard of the rights or safety of others.

Hilliman v. Cobado

(*Purchaser of Cattle*) v. (*Seller & Repossessor*)
131 Misc.2d 206, 499 N.Y.S.2d 610, 1 UCC Rep. Serv. 2d 327 (1986)

AGREEMENTS THAT AUTHORIZE REPOSSESSION ARE NOT ENFORCEABLE IF A BREACH OF THE PEACE OCCURS

■ **INSTANT FACTS** Cattle were repossessed by seller, Cobado (D), under agreement permitting repossession by peaceable entry onto premises without debtor's interference, but debtor objected and seller breached the peace.

■ **BLACK LETTER RULE** Despite a self-help provision in a security agreement permitting the secured party to enter the debtor's premises peaceably and take possession of the collateral, without resistance or interference by the debtor, breach of the peace may occur if the conduct involved in the repossession is likely to, or does, produce violence, consternation or disorder.

■ **PROCEDURAL BASIS**

Order to show cause in trial court for injunctive relief seeking return of livestock following repossession.

■ **FACTS**

Hilliman (P) bought a herd of cattle from Cobado (D). Eventually, the parties entered into three security agreements, denominated as "collateral security mortgage" and "chattel mortgage." Under the terms of the sale, the buyer was to make monthly payments, and Cobado (D) was given a chattel mortgage in a certain number of cows. The latter two agreements provided for seizure of the collateral by permitting the secured party to enter the debtor's premises peaceably and take possession of the collateral, and the debtor agreed not to resist or interfere. Although there was no default in the required payments, Cobado (D) was disturbed by the buyer's practice of culling poorer cattle from the herd. Without warning, Cobado (D), accompanied by two deputy sheriffs, arrived at the premises of Mr. and Mrs. Szata (P2). The deputy sheriffs advised them that Cobado (D) was there to repossess the collateral under the agreement. Mr. Szata (P2) said that he was not in default, and that Cobado (D) was to leave immediately and could not have the cattle. Cobado (D) ran to the barn saying, "to hell with this we're taking the cows." [He must have felt confident with two sheriffs with him.] One deputy told the Szatas (P2) that Cobado (D) had a violent temper and reputation, and that if Mr. Szata (P2) got out of line he would be arrested. The Szatas (P2) again told Cobado (D) to stop rounding up the cattle. He was beating the cattle and trying to herd them through a barn door. Mrs. Szata's (P2) mother arrived and told Cobado (D) to stop. Before Cobado (D) could load the cattle onto the trucks, a Sheriff's Lieutenant [the good guy] arrived and told Cobado (D) that if he left with the cattle he would be arrested. Cobado (D) ignored him, left with the cattle, and was arrested for possession of stolen property. Hilliman (P1) and the Szatas (P2) sought injunctive relief requiring Cobado (D) to return the cattle.

■ **ISSUE**

Can breach of the peace occur even when the security agreement contains a self-help provision permitting the secured party to enter the debtor's premises peaceably and take possession of the collateral, without resistance or interference by the debtor?

Hilliman v. Cobado (Continued)

■ DECISION AND RATIONALE

(Horey) Yes. Despite a self-help provision in a security agreement permitting the secured party to enter the debtor's premises peaceably and take possession of the collateral, without resistance or interference by the debtor, breach of the peace may occur if the conduct involved in the repossession is likely to, or does, produce violence, consternation or disorder. The terms of the agreements giving Cobado (D) the right to enter the debtor's premises peaceably and giving him rights as to repossession accorded under the UCC are not in conflict because the repossession rights granted under the UCC may only be exercised without breach of the peace. The issue is whether there was a *breach of the peace.* The highest court of the State has defined breach of the peace as "a disturbance of public order by an act of violence, or by any act likely to produce violence, or which by causing consternation and alarm, disturbs the peace and quiet of the community." The right of repossession is limited and exercisable only without a breach of the peace. It is not required that there be physical confrontation or the threat thereof to effect a breach of the peace. In this case, Cobado (D) engaged in conduct, which was likely to, and did in fact, produce violence, consternation and disorder. He ignored the order of the Szatas (P2) to desist and leave, ignored the admonition by the Lieutenant to desist, demonstrated contempt for all restraint by saying "to hell with this we're taking the cows," released, beat and herded the cows to the trucks, and ignored the warnings that continuation would result in arrest. This conduct is sufficient for us to find that the retaking of the cattle was a breach of the peace. [This certainly does not constitute orderly conduct.] Cobado (D) is ordered to redeliver the cattle repossessed by him at his cost and expense forthwith.

Analysis:

The case demonstrates that the courts will ignore a clause in a security agreement that authorizes repossession and requires the debtor to agree not to resist or interfere, if a breach of the peace occurs. It also sets forth the type of conduct that will constitute breach of the peace. Although there was no physical altercation, the conduct by Cobado (D) produced violence (by beating the cows), consternation, and disorder. Another significant point in the case is that the right of repossession, even when the agreement expressly provides for entry onto the premises, is limited and exercisable only without a breach of the peace. Note that the repossession here was done in the presence of the debtors, even though there was no default in payment.

■ CASE VOCABULARY

COLLATERAL SECURITY MORTGAGE: An agreement that secures the instrument pledging collateral as security for the debt.

INJUNCTIVE RELIEF: Seeking a court order for an injunction to command an act or to prohibit or restrain an act.

ORDER TO SHOW CAUSE: An order commanding one to appear in court to show why a certain proposed action should not occur.

R & J of Tennessee, Inc. v. Blankenship–Melton Real Estate, Inc.

(Promissory Note Purchaser) v. (Debtor)
166 S.W.3d 195 (Tenn. Ct. App. 2005)

WHAT CONSTITUTES A REASONABLE TIME FOR NOTIFICATION OF DEFECTS DEPENDS ON THE CIRCUMSTANCES OF THE CASE

■ **INSTANT FACTS:** R & J (P) filed suit to collect a deficiency judgment after a foreclosure sale, and Blankenship–Melton (D) claimed that the foreclosed property was not sold in a commercially reasonable manner.

■ **BLACK LETTER RULE:** The determination of whether a sale of collateral was commercially reasonable requires a consideration of the totality of the circumstances surrounding the sale, and looks at whether the sale was conducted according to prevailing trade practices among responsible businesses engaged in the same or similar business.

■ **PROCEDURAL BASIS:**

Appeal from an award of a deficiency judgment for R & J (P).

■ **FACTS:**

Blankenship (D), as the acting president of Blankenship–Melton Real Estate (D), entered into a loan agreement with the Bank of Henderson County. As a part of the loan agreement, Blankenship–Melton (D) executed a security agreement that gave the bank a security interest in a boat, a tractor, a truck, and a mobile home. The bank estimated the value of the collateral to be at least $40,000. Blankenship (D) also executed a personal guaranty in which he agreed to remain personally liable on the loan. The guaranty listed his home address as "2820 Shady Hill Road." Larry Melton and Steve Melton, officers of Blankenship–Melton (D), also executed personal guaranties.

The loan agreement was renewed twice, with the due date extended six months each time. The loan went into default. Blankenship (D) claimed that he communicated with the bank and asked it to foreclose on the collateral, but a representative of the bank did not recall any such communication. Blankenship (D) never personally paid any of the loan.

Larry Melton and Steve Melton approached the president of R & J of Tennessee (P), asking for help with some outstanding loans of Blankenship–Melton (D). R & J (P) purchased the promissory note for the loan from the bank. When the note was purchased, Blankenship–Melton (D) was in default and the bank had started foreclosure proceedings on the collateral. Only the truck, the tractor, and the mobile home remained as collateral. At the time R & J (P) purchased the note, Steve Melton was living (rent-free) in the mobile home, Larry Melton had possession of the truck and was driving it daily, and the tractor was inoperable.

R & J (P) began the foreclosure process in June 2002. Steve Melton continued to live in the mobile home, and Larry Melton continued to drive the truck. On June 11, notice was sent to Blankenship (D) that a public sale of the collateral would be held on June 21. The notice was sent certified mail to the address listed on the promissory note. Similar notices were sent to Larry Melton and Steve Melton, and

R & J of Tennessee, Inc. v. Blankenship–Melton Real Estate, Inc. (Continued)

notice was posted at R & J's (P) office, at the courthouse, and on the collateral. Blankenship (D) had, however, moved without notifying the bank of his new address, and the notice was returned as "not deliverable" on June 28.

The sale was held on June 21. Only Johnny Melton, majority shareholder and president of R & J (P), and Larry Melton were present. R & J (P) was the only bidder on the property, and the mobile home was purchased for $8,000, the truck for $11,000, and the tractor for $1,000. Johnny Melton testified that he used his previous experience in banking and mobile home sales to assess the value of each item of collateral. After the sale, R & J (P) brought an action against Blankenship (D) for a deficiency judgment of $13,388.40, pursuant to the guaranty. The general sessions court found for Blankenship (D), and R & J (P) appealed to the circuit court. After a *de novo* bench trial, a deficiency judgment was entered against Blankenship (D) for $10,847.29.

■ ISSUE:

Was the sale of the foreclosed property commercially reasonable?

■ DECISION AND RATIONALE:

(Highers, J.) No. The determination of whether a sale of collateral was commercially reasonable requires a consideration of the totality of the circumstances surrounding the sale, and looks at whether the sale was conducted according to prevailing trade practices among responsible businesses engaged in the same or similar business. The factors examined include:

- The type of collateral involved;
- The condition of the collateral;
- The number of bids solicited;
- The time and place of the sale;
- The purchase price received or the terms of the sale; and
- Any special circumstances involved.

These factors are viewed as necessary and interrelated parts of the transaction. The secured party seeking the deficiency bears the burden of proving that the sale was not commercially reasonable.

Blankenship (D) claimed that the timing of the sale shows that it was done in a commercially unreasonable manner. The sale was conducted seven and one-half months after R & J (P) purchased the promissory note, and Blankenship–Melton (D) was already in default. Article Nine of the U.C.C. does not set out a period within which the sale must be made; however, if the secured party holds the collateral for a long period of time without disposing of it and if there is no good reason for holding the property, the secured party may be found not to have acted in a commercially reasonable manner. In this case, R & J (P) did not offer a reasonable explanation as to why it waited so long to sell the collateral, during which time Steve and Larry Melton were allowed to use the property. The continued use of these items would cause them to depreciate more quickly. In addition, the continued use increased the amount of the deficiency, because R & J (P) was required to use reasonable care when the property was in its custody. Allowing the continued use of the property constituted bad faith.

In addition, R & J (P) did not advertise the sale in a newspaper, and an experienced auctioneer was not used. R & J (P) was the only bidder at the sale and also valued the collateral, instead of using an independent appraiser. Although an independent appraiser is not required in every case, the lack of one in the case at bar is an additional factor showing that the sale was not commercially reasonable.

Lack of reasonable notice of the sale is another factor in determining the commercial reasonableness of a sale. Blankenship (D) argued that he should have received actual notice of the sale before it could proceed. The U.C.C. requires that notification must be "reasonable." It is left to the court to determine, on a case-by-case basis, whether "reasonable" requires a second try after a secured party sends notice and learns that it was not delivered. Reasonable notice affords a debtor a reasonable opportunity to avoid the sale by discharging the debt, or to see that the collateral brings a fair price. A notice that does not give this opportunity is not reasonable, and a sale under it is not commercially reasonable. Ordinarily, sending notice certified mail, return receipt requested, is reasonable notice, but making only one attempt at contacting the debtor, and proceeding with the sale less than two weeks after sending

R & J of Tennessee, Inc. v. Blankenship–Melton Real Estate, Inc. (Continued)

the notice, is not reasonable notice. Although Blankenship (D) bears some responsibility for moving and not informing the bank of his new address, R & J (P) should have made greater efforts to find him before proceeding. Blankenship (D) did not waive notice of the disposition of the collateral. Such a waiver must be made when the agreement is entered into, and authenticated after default.

R & J's (P) failure to provide adequate notice of the sale may allow Blankenship (D) to recover damages from R & J (P). When a creditor conducts a commercially unreasonable sale of collateral, there is a presumption that the debtor is damaged to the extent of the deficiency claimed. A commercially unreasonable sale does not, however, extinguish the deficiency. The presumption shifts to the creditor the burden of proving the amount that should have been recovered from the sale. If R & J (P) can rebut the presumption, it will be entitled to recover the deficiency. Here, there is insufficient evidence in the record to determine the actual value of the collateral sold. On remand, the trial court must determine whether R & J (P) has presented sufficient evidence to rebut the presumption; if so, the court must determine whether the deficiency should be offset by any damages due Blankenship (D) for the improper sale. Reversed and remanded.

Analysis:

It is clear that the parties involved had a close relationship that preceded the transaction in this case. Steve and Larry Melton were, like Blankenship (D), guarantors of the loan to Blankenship–Melton Real Estate (D), but they were not named in the suit to collect the deficiency; in fact, they were allowed to use the collateral until the sale was made. The close relationship of the parties may have led R & J (P) to believe that it could cut corners without any consequence.

Coxall v. Clover Commercial Corp.

(Car Buyer) v. (Finance Company)
4 Misc.3d 654, 781 N.Y.S.2d 567 (N.Y.City Civ. Ct. 2004)

CREDITORS MAY BE BARRED FROM COLLECTING A DEFICIENCY AFTER A COMMERCIALLY UNREASONABLE SALE

■ **INSTANT FACTS:** Clover (D) repossessed a car purchased by Coxall (P), and Coxall (P) alleged that the subsequent sale of the vehicle was unreasonable.

■ **BLACK LETTER RULE:** In a consumer transaction, a secured party may not recover a deficiency judgment from the debtor if the sale of the collateral was commercially unreasonable, but the debtor may recover damages for the creditor's failure to comply with the legal requirements for a sale.

■ **PROCEDURAL BASIS:**

Judgment after consolidated trials.

■ **FACTS:**

Coxall (P) and Utho Coxall purchased a 1991 Lexus automobile from Jafas Auto Sales. The price of the car was $8,100, and Coxall (P) paid $3,798.25 in cash and financed the balance through a retail installment contract and security agreement. The security agreement was assigned to Clover Commercial (D). The contract provided that, after repossession, the car could be sold after ten days' notice. The contract further provided that notice would be deemed reasonable if sent to Coxall's (P) current address at least ten days before Clover (D) acted on the notice.

Coxall (D) began experiencing mechanical difficulties with the car soon after he purchased it, and so he made no payments on the installment contract. Clover (D) took possession of the car four months after the purchase, on February 19. The next day, Clover (D) sent two letters to Coxall (P). The first stated that Coxall (P) could redeem the car by paying $5,969.28, plus storage charges and a redemption fee. The second notified Coxall (P) that the car would be offered for private sale after noon on March 3. On March 3, the car was sold back to Jafas Auto Sales for $1,500. On April 22, Clover (D) wrote to Coxall (P) demanding payment of a "remaining balance" of $4,998.

Coxall (P) brought an action against Clover (D) for wrongful repossession of the car. He sought damages of $8,000. After Coxall (P) commenced his action, Clover (D) brought an action against Coxall (P) and Utho Coxall, seeking $4,630.62, plus interest from the date of purchase and attorney's fees.

■ **ISSUE:**

Is Clover (D) entitled to collect the deficiency from Coxall (P)?

■ **DECISION AND RATIONALE:**

(Battaglia, J.) No. In a consumer transaction, a secured party may not recover a deficiency judgment from the debtor if the sale of the collateral was commercially unreasonable, but the debtor may recover damages for the creditor's failure to comply with the legal requirements for a sale. The absolute bar to

Coxall v. Clover Commercial Corp. (Continued)

collection of a deficiency is the rule in the Second Appellate Department of the New York court, and applies only to consumer transactions. The plurality rule (which also applies in the Second Department for non-consumer transactions) is that there is a rebuttable presumption that compliance with the legal requirements for the sale of repossessed collateral would have brought in proceeds from the sale sufficient to satisfy the secured debt. In the case at bar, the result would be the same even if the plurality rule applied. Clover (D) presented no evidence regarding the amount of the proceeds that would have been realized if it had complied with the legal requirements for the sale.

The sale of the car was not commercially reasonable. The notice sent out was insufficient. The purpose of notification is to provide the debtor with an opportunity to protect his or her interest in the collateral, to challenge any aspect of the sale, or to interest other potential buyers in purchasing the collateral. The notice must be sent within a reasonable time, and must not be sent so near to the sale that a reasonable person could not be expected to act on the notice. Reasonableness is a question of fact. In non-consumer transactions, ten days' notice is usually deemed reasonable. In this case, Coxall (P) received eleven days' notice, excluding the date the notice was mailed and the date of the sale. Eleven days was not reasonable here. Furthermore, in addition to being untimely, the notice did not contain the required information. Coxall (P) was not told that he was entitled to an accounting of the unpaid debt, and as not told what the charges for such an accounting would be. In addition, there is no evidence that Utho Coxall, the co-debtor, ever received notice of the sale.

The contract provided that notice would be deemed reasonable if sent to Coxall's (P) current address, and if it was sent at least ten days before Clover (D) took action on the notice. The revised Article Nine of the U.C.C. would permit the enforcement of such clauses unless "manifestly unreasonable." It is not necessary to a determination of this case to decide whether the contract notice provision is enforceable. In the absence of evidence of the reasonableness of notice by ten days' prior mailing, the matter will be left "for another day."

In addition, the sale of the car was not commercially reasonable. Commercial reasonableness is a question of fact, and a secured party who seeks a deficiency bears the burden of proving commercial reasonableness. Every aspect of the sale must be reasonable. New York courts have held that the test for commercial reasonableness is whether the secured party acted in good faith and to the mutual best advantage of the parties. Private sales, as opposed to public auctions, are encouraged, based on the assumption that a private sale will often result in a higher sales price, which benefits all of the parties.

Clover (D) did not present any evidence regarding any details of the sale: there was no evidence concerning the procedure for the sale, the identification of prospective buyers, the fair market value of the car, or any other details of the sale except for the price. There was no evidence that the sale was done according to the usual practices for selling repossessed automobiles. The price was the only evidence regarding the sale. Clover (D) received $1,500 for a car that had been purchased four months earlier for $8,100. A low-price sale is not automatically unreasonable, but should be scrutinized carefully by the courts to make sure that every aspect of the sale was commercially reasonable, especially where, as here, there is a potential for self-dealing. A low price may indicate depreciation in the value of the collateral, but in this case, Clover (D) acknowledged that the car had not sustained any physical damage in the time Coxall (P) possessed it. Clover's (D) claim that the low price was due to the mechanical defects noted by Coxall (P) was contradicted by its own testimony that the car ran fine when it was repossessed; in any event, that claim was specious.

Coxall (P) is entitled to recover damages for Clover's noncompliance. Revised Article Nine of the U.C.C. does not allow a debtor in a non-consumer transaction to recover damages in cases in which the deficiency has been cancelled due to the creditor's conduct. The Code does not explicitly bar such damages in consumer transactions, however, and prescribes minimum statutory damages of not less than "the credit service charge plus ten percent of the principal ... or the time-price differential plus ten percent of the cash price." The terms in the damage formulae are not defined, but are left to the construction of the court. According to the contract in this case, the time-price differential is $1,036.24, and ten percent of the cash price is $810, for a total of $1,846.24. Coxall (P) is entitled to recover this amount, even though he has not sustained any actual damages.

Although Clover (D) is not entitled to a deficiency judgment, it is entitled to recover the amounts owed to it prior to the repossession, as well as the repossession charges. Coxall (P) is not discharged from all

Coxall v. Clover Commercial Corp. (Continued)

liability under the contract. When the car was repossessed, there were three monthly payments unpaid, totaling $1,001.04, plus late charges of ten percent, or $100.11. Clover (D) claimed $325 for repossession and other charges, but since no documentation for this amount is provided, Clover (D) will not be allowed to recover that amount. Judgment is entered for Coxall (P) in the amount of $745.09, representing the difference between his statutory damages and the amount recoverable by Clover (D). Utho Coxall did not appear, and made no claim for damages, so judgment is entered against him for $1,101.15, plus interest.

Analysis:

The rebuttable presumption that a commercially unreasonable sale bars a creditor from seeking a deficiency judgment, unless the creditor proves that a reasonable sale would not have resulted in a higher price paid for the collateral, puts a higher premium on substance than on form. The creditor is not assured of any recovery after a commercially unreasonable sale, but is given an opportunity to show that the debtor was not harmed, because a reasonable sale would not have reduced the deficiency any more. In effect, the rebuttable presumption makes the proceeds of the sale the most important factor in judging a sale of collateral. A creditor will be asked to do no more than realize the highest price possible for the collateral.